SAVED FROM SACRIFICE

SAVED FROM SACRIFICE

A Theology of the Cross

S. Mark Heim

WILLIAM B. EERDMANS PUBLISHING COMPANY
GRAND RAPIDS, MICHIGAN / CAMBRIDGE, U.K.

© 2006 S. Mark Heim
All rights reserved

Published 2006 by
Wm. B. Eerdmans Publishing Co.
2140 Oak Industrial Drive N.E., Grand Rapids, Michigan 49505 /
P.O. Box 163, Cambridge CB3 9PU U.K.
www.eerdmans.com

Printed in the United States of America

11 10 09 08 07 06   7 6 5 4 3 2 1

Library of Congress Cataloging-in-Publication Data

Heim, S. Mark.
Saved from sacrifice: a theology of the cross / S. Mark Heim.
p.   cm.
Includes bibliographical references.
ISBN-10: 0-8028-3215-6 / ISBN-13: 978-0-8028-3215-3 (pbk. alk. paper)
1. Jesus Christ — Crucifixion. 2. Sacrifice — Christianity.
3. Atonement. I. Title.

BT453.H45 2006

232'.3 — dc22

2006008546

The poem that appears on pages 271 and 272 is from THE SHIELD OF
ACHILLES by W. H. Auden, copyright © 1955 by W. H. Auden. Used by permission of Random House, Inc.

Unless otherwise indicated, the Scripture quotations contained herein are
from the New Revised Standard Version Bible, copyright © 1989 by the Division of Christian Education of the National Council of the Churches of
Christ in the U.S.A. Used by permission. All rights reserved.

For my daughter,
Sarah Elizabeth Lewis Heim,
Beautiful and Beloved

"The girl has brains and character and honesty . . ."

— Paul Austin Delagardie on Harriet Vane,
in a short biography of Lord Peter Wimsey

Contents

PART THREE

In Remembrance of Me

The Cross That Faith Keeps Empty

Preface

This book has simmered long in my mind, along with the suspicion (or hope) that it would be written by someone else. There are books that do so well what parts of this book does (I think particularly of René Girard's *I See Satan Fall like Lightning* and James Williams's *The Bible, Violence, and the Sacred*) that I have been tempted in places to simply say, "Go read book *X*," or "Let me quote this entire chapter," and then go on. But in the process of writing I have become aware of why the gap I sensed is hard to fill. To flatly endorse or condemn something — a doctrine or idea — is straightforward. To propose one alternative to replace another is likewise pretty clear, though the details can become complicated. But to explain how something of surpassing value with only a subtle twist becomes a twin of almost opposite character and effects, or how a teaching that rightly merits rejection might still contain rare and profound truths we lose at our peril — these things are hard to do. And, at times, very important. This is the task, as I see it, in regard to Christian belief in the saving significance of Jesus' death. It is a question with profound spiritual and cultural implications. Understanding of the cross is a snarled theological knot at the center of a wide web of assumptions and practices, in church and society. Until it is untangled, it tugs everything else askew, a little or a lot.

I should underline at the beginning a point that bears repeating at intervals. There is more that is important about Jesus than his death. And the significance of that death is not exhausted in the treatment given here. My aim is to answer some specific questions. Within the context of the whole "work" of Christ, what is the distinctive saving significance of

ix

the cross? It is important, for instance, that Jesus lives a life of faithfulness to God's will. This is exemplified in all the facets of his life. The cross in this sense is no different from his teaching or his healing as another instance of that truth. The reason it is important is the same in all cases: it was an act of love. But why is this particular kind of death included in that love at all? Even more specifically, if a number of things are special about the cross, which ones ought we to take as primary and which ones as secondary? Where is the right place to start, even if it is assuredly not the only place to stop? This is a book on Christology and salvation, but it is not anything like a complete Christology or a full view of salvation. We look closely at one limited and troubled corner in a much larger landscape. It deserves the attention. But it would compound the problem if we were to mistake a piece for the whole.

Some say Christianity would be better off without the cross. That's a clear message. Some say the teaching that Christ died in our place to bear the punishment for our sins and satisfy the wrath of God's justice, so that God can love and accept us in all eternity, *is* Christianity, and without it there would be nothing left. That's clear too. And some say the cross is a necessary part of the Christian gospel, but that the understanding just described needs to be replaced with an alternative that dispenses completely with the categories of sacrifice and substitution. Plain enough. When I respond to these proposals by saying no, no, and no, the immediate natural impression is confusion. What I mean is not clear. And although the basic idea of this book (I doggedly continue to believe) is quite simple, the treatment of it has a disturbing tendency to go in several directions at once. We need to tell the same story three times before we really succeed in telling it at all. Such a preface may sound suspiciously like an excuse. If I understood my topic better, perhaps I could explain it more quickly. But it's mainly a request for the reader's patience. Our path may circle the summit on our way up, but there's something to be seen from each side. Even a generous reader might request a map as well as a promise. The introduction provides such a map. In anticipation, I'll give a brief summary of my argument here.[1]

---

1. A more extensive brief summary can be found in the following two articles: S. Mark Heim, "Christ Crucified: Why Does Jesus' Death Matter?" *Christian Century* 118, no. 8 (2001); S. Mark Heim, "Visible Victim: Christ's Death to End Sacrifice," *Christian Century* 118, no. 9 (2001).

Double Vision

The event of Jesus' death, his condemnation, suffering, and execution, is a bad thing. The Gospel accounts emphasize this. Christians remember it, retell it, and even celebrate it as a unique and saving action. The day of Jesus' death is *Good* Friday. The New Testament emphasizes that too. This is odd. The main, first thing is not to miss that fact. Everything worth learning has its hard parts, the tricky passages, like math problems where there's one point where it's so easy to go astray. The difference between being right and being wrong is both small and enormous, like performing one last multiplication and remembering whether it should come out *negative* one billion or *positive* one billion (and that's a difference of *two* billion!). We have to add up all the oddities or it won't come out right. Jesus' death is that passage in Christianity. The answer balances on a razor's edge.

Is this God's plan, to become a human being and die, so that God won't have to destroy us instead? Is it God's prescription to have Jesus suffer for sins he did not commit so God can forgive the sins we do commit? That's the wrong side of the razor. Jesus was already preaching the forgiveness of sins and forgiving sins before he died. He did not have to wait until after the resurrection to do that. Blood is not acceptable to God as a means of uniting human community or a price for God's favor. Christ sheds his own blood to end that way of trying to mend our divisions. Jesus' death isn't necessary because God has to have innocent blood to solve the guilt equation. Redemptive violence is our equation. Jesus didn't volunteer to get into God's justice machine. God volunteered to get into ours. God used our own sin to save us.

We humans took a terrible thing — scapegoating violence against the innocent (or against those who are guilty of something, but not the demonic effects we claim) — and made it a good thing. It brings us together, stops escalating conflict among us, unites us against a common enemy. We overcome our differences and make peace by finding a common victim, by hating together. We restrain violence with violence. Satan casts out Satan, and becomes all the stronger for it. This isn't a random, pointless evil. It is woven into the way our communities work, and the problem it solves is real.

Is there any point in Jesus dying this particular, specific kind of death? Is he dying for our sins, in order to save us? Yes, because his death exemplifies a specific kind of sin we are all implicated in and we all need saving from, and acts to overcome it. Only the divine power of resurrection and revelation could do that. God was willing to be a victim of that bad thing we had made apparently good, in order to expose its nature and liberate us from it. In so doing, God made that occasion of scapegoating sacrifice (what those who killed Jesus were doing) an occasion of overcoming scapegoating violence (what God was doing). It is the same event, but what is happening in that event for the people who kill or accept the killing or fail to oppose it (in short, for all involved) is not what's happening in that event for Jesus, for God, and hopefully for the church. God used our sin to save us from that sin. And the result, uneven but real, is that victims of such acts become harder to hide. They look too much like Jesus. The challenge, all too often failed, is to build another basis for peace than unity in violence. That is what the gathering around the communion table attempts to do.

There is a saving act of God in the cross, and there is a sinful human act. The two are so close together that it is easy for them to get mixed up in our understanding, and in our theology. The saving part is so real that it exercises an effect even when distorted almost beyond recognition in our interpretations. The sinful part is so ubiquitous that even the best theology is subject to a kind of gravitational degradation. Without the language of sacrifice, innocence, guilt, punishment, substitution, and blood, we can't tell the truth about our situation and what God does to liberate us, a truth that the cross makes available to us in a new way. With it, we always run the risk of taking the diagnosis for a prescription. Sacrifice is the disease we have. Christ's death is the test result we can't ignore, and at the same time an inoculation that sets loose a healing resistance. The cure is not more of the same.

This is why Christian theology has what sounds like the same language overlaid on this event twice, once for what it means according to our sacrificial usage, once to turn it around. Christians say the cross is a sacrifice . . . but to end sacrifice. They say "blood shed for us," but blood shed once for all. They say, "We are reconciled in his blood," but they mean we have been freed to live without the kind of reconciliation that requires blood, the kind Caiaphas and Pilate and Herod had in mind.

That is what this book tries to explain.

I'm thankful to all those knowing and unknowing who have contributed to this project. Any value it has comes primarily from them. The debts I owe to other writers should be evident in the book and the notes. Certainly some who appear there have also challenged and instructed me in personal, conversational terms as well. I want to express special gratitude to the many who have contributed in unwritten ways to the substance of what appears here and to the spirit that inspired me to pursue the task. Chief among these would be my students at Andover Newton Theological School, who both in the classroom and in their subsequent careers as ministers have helped me to see the shape and the urgency of this question. Three friends made special contributions. Kate Layzer lent her editorial eye and substantive suggestions. Lee Harding offered keen insights that informed my thinking. And Isabel Best supported the project with her prayers, her testimony, and, most of all, her faithful questions.

I thank the trustees and administration of Andover Newton for the sabbatical leave that allowed me to complete this manuscript. Many thanks as well to all my Andover Newton colleagues, and particularly to Gabe Fackre, Ben Valentin, Sharon Thornton, Sze-kar Wan, Greg Mobley, and Mark Burrows. I am particularly grateful to Matthew Boulton, who read and commented on the entire manuscript. Sharon Taylor, the director of the Trask Library at Andover Newton, and the members of her staff, especially Diana Yount and Cynthia Bolshaw, supported all manner of research requests. I have been steadily enriched by the conversations of the Boston Theological Society, and in regard to the material of this book I think particularly of the contributions of Fr. Robert Daly, whose work on the Christian understanding of sacrifice and whose knowledge of the Girardian literature are unsurpassed. I am grateful to the *Christian Century* for permission to use material first published in two articles in that journal, and grateful to David Heim both for the invitation to write the articles and for the conversations on these and other topics that are a steady pleasure over the years. I thank the Calvin College seminars in Christian scholarship program and their foundation supporters for the 2001 summer seminar that allowed me to explore the connection between Girard and evolutionary thought. Peter Schmiechen kindly allowed me to read an advance draft of portions of his book, *Saving Power: Theories of Atonement and Forms of the Church.* Incisive and pastorally minded at the same time, his work provides a rich account of the wider theological landscape in which my study tries to specify a specific location. Chris Leighton and the Institute for Jewish-Christian Studies in Baltimore allowed me to present some of this material in an early form to a program for ministers and rabbis. Thanks are due also to Robert Neville and to Amos Yong and Peter Heltzel, the editors of his Festschrift, for the opportunity to review Neville's stimulating work on the atonement for my contribution to that volume. I also have fond memories of the conversation and information developed in a presentation of some aspects of this topic in the meetings of the Boston Ministers' Club.

There is little in what follows that worked its way into my understanding without being filtered in some part through conversations with Melissa. Academic enlightenment was rarely the motive of such talk, but it was sometimes the result. As a contribution to this work, those conversations should rank first in the list, though in an account of my thanks to her they would be hard put to make the list at all.

Finally, I know that this book touches on what is for a great many the very heart of their faith. The study traced out here has come to my own belief in the cross much as Christ came in a more global sense, not to destroy but to fulfill. May my faults in presentation or understanding not block readers of this book from finding their own measure of light and benefit in its substance.

In Christ,
S. Mark Heim
Newton Centre, MA
June 2005

A Stumble to Start With

[A]s I was walking between the living room and dining room one day I discovered that I had lost the meaning of the crucifixion. I don't mean that I didn't know what Christians said about the cross . . . I knew that. I don't mean that I had lost my faith. It was much stranger than that, something more like what I would imagine a stroke victim experiences when she looks at a familiar object like a book or a dinner plate in an ordinary setting, and can't understand what she is seeing. On that day I looked at the cross and it made no sense.

Roberta Bondi[1]

It is difficult to describe Christianity and leave out the crucifixion. This image of suffering death is seeded through the forms of every Christian tradition. Protestants historically confess that we are justified by faith, reconciled with God in this event: "we preach Christ, and him crucified." Roman Catholics make celebration of Christ's sacrifice the sacramental center of Christian life, with the words from the Gospel of John, "The Lamb of God, who takes away the sins of the world." Eastern Orthodox position the significance of the cross in relation to resurrection, with the words of the Easter liturgy, "Christ has risen from the dead, by death

---

1. Roberta C. Bondi, *Memories of God: Theological Reflections on a Life* (Nashville: Abingdon, 1995), 111-12.

trampling upon death and bringing life to those in the tomb." The Gospels, the heart of Christian scripture, are in large measure passion narratives. The central Christian liturgical act, the celebration of the Lord's Supper, insistently remembers this death: "Every time you eat this bread and drink this cup, you proclaim the Lord's death, until he comes." The peak of the Christian year, at Good Friday and Easter, revolves around it.

Christians believe God's action decisively centers in Jesus of Nazareth. From the earliest period, this conviction itself centered on that person's death by crucifixion and resurrection from the dead. This is expressed in innumerable ways in the language of Christian tradition. Christ died for us. He gave his life as a ransom for humanity. Our lives are fundamentally changed by Christ's death. Atonement and reconciliation — words used to refer to an explanation of what this change is — describe one detail in the Christian story. Yet they often become a short statement of the entire story.

Some might give the impression that nothing was important about Jesus' life except its end. But Christian faith is equally unimaginable without Jesus' actions and teaching. We could hardly form a clear notion of the crucifixion without knowing the person whose death it is, and the life that led to it. From the early time that "Gospel" became the primary Christian scriptural form, Jesus' life, death, and resurrection became a seamless unity. Modern attempts to construct a view of Jesus that drops all emphasis on the death (focusing for instance on only a message Jesus taught without reference to his own person and fate) are historically implausible. They only reverse the parallel distortion that comes from a focus on the cross that ignores everything else.

The hymn "There Is a Green Hill Far Away" contains the familiar lines: "He died that we might be forgiven, / He died to make us good, / That we might go at last to heaven, / Saved by his precious blood." This reminds us that piety and tradition have not merely recorded the fact of Jesus' death. They have often lingered graphically on his bodily suffering and spilled blood. The Book of Common Prayer prescribes statements before reception of each element in communion. The content if not the wording is familiar to most Christians. "The Body of our Lord Jesus Christ, which was given for you. . . . Take and eat this in remembrance that Christ died for you, and feed on him in your heart by faith, with thanksgiving. The Blood of our Lord Jesus Christ, which was shed for you. . . . Drink this in remembrance that Christ's blood was shed for you, and be thankful." The cannibalistic terms of this ceremony and the fixation on the brutal physicality of Jesus' execution expressed in this language of "blood shed for you" may be dulled from long familiarity. Or they may appear as outlandish as the tongue of an unknown people. In either case, they may convey very little meaning.

This book is written because many find it hard to make sense of "Christ died for us." And it is written because others find it perfectly understandable and entirely objectionable, a dark brew of self-abnegation, violence, and abuse. They contend that belief in the redemptive power of Jesus' death amounts to masochistic idealization of suffering. Saved by blood, Christians are charter bound to glorify sacrifice and to encourage the oppressed to embrace their misery "in imitation of Christ." Despots would be thick indeed not to applaud such teaching. The good news of Jesus' resurrection is, on such a view, not nearly good enough to cancel the evils of the violent ideal it presupposes. The cross is a religious symbol soiled with persecution and psychological conflict. It entangles destructive ideas of original sin and overpowering guilt with unhealthy fixation on blood and death. At the least, a complete reconstruction of Christianity is demanded, one that would get the cross out of the center. At the most, Christianity itself needs to go.

Condemnation is not the only flavor of engagement with the topic. You may care about the subject because the message of the cross has come to you as a word of life and liberation. Yet you recognize that others respond quite differently and that atonement theology has been associated with Christianity's complicity in many historical evils. You may care about the cross because you are a Christian long familiar with the language, and vaguely accepting of it. Yet it conveys nothing clear or important to you, and you suspect that the plainer its meaning became, the less you would be inclined to believe it. You may care because you are drawn to the teachings and example of Jesus and the hope of resurrection, the worship of God and the community of the church, but are repelled by a teaching that appears contrary to the nature of the God represented in Jesus' ministry. You may care because you are anything but a Christian. Yet you would like to comprehend what Christians are talking about, and talk of the cross is blank as static.

Different as they are, these cases have something in common. For all, the cross is a question and a problem. That is where we can start. There is at least good precedent for this. "We preach Christ crucified, a stumbling block to Jews and folly to Gentiles" (1 Cor. 1:23 RSV). We start by stumbling.

Variety in Tradition

Through Christian history people have pointed to the cross as a solution. In our time it is unavoidably a question. If we expect something so basic to Christian life as the crucifixion to have a universal, agreed meaning, we will be disappointed. Early creeds and confessions specified belief in the incarnation and in the Trinity. There was an "official" view on who and what Jesus was, and what kind of God God was. There was no similar formulation of exactly what Christ had done that saved us or specifically why Christ's death was important. The church found no compelling need to thin the ranks of explanation, especially when one did not rule out another. That the death *was* important, scripture, creeds, liturgy, and early Christian writings all clearly proclaim. A frightening and brutal execution had become a keystone in the good news these early Christians celebrated, a change as unlikely to the believers as to critics outside the church. It took time for that horrible sign to become familiar, even comforting. Today the reverse has happened. For long centuries the image of Jesus' death stood not only in the center of church life, but at the heart of Western thought and culture as well. A stroll through any great art museum will illustrate that fact. The meaning of that image seemed clear and positive. Now, long commonplace understandings of the crucifixion increasingly perplex or offend.

Criticism mainly targets the view of Jesus' death that became most prominent in Western Christianity, came in fact to seem almost identical with the image of the cross itself. That view is substitutionary atonement, the belief that God's redemptive plan revolves around offering an innocent Jesus for punishment and death in place of a guilty humanity, allowing a just God to practice mercy by saving sinners whose debt had been paid by God's suffering on their behalf. Raw material for this interpretation is already present in the New Testament and doctrinal formulation of it begins in early Christianity, but the fully systematized doctrine familiar to us did not appear until the medieval period, and particularly the work of Anselm. Eastern Christianity never incorporated the doctrine as a major feature of its theology. Some regard a form of substitutionary atonement belief as the essential heart of Christianity itself. But this can hardly be true, for one major stream of Christianity managed without such a teaching for all of its history, and all of Christianity managed without it for a large part of its history.

Though this specific doctrine is not a universal feature in Christianity, many of its constituent elements are in fact shared by all Christian traditions as aspects of the understanding of Jesus' death: ideas of sacrifice, of

Jesus dying "for us." One of the key arguments among different Christian theologies has concerned whether these words and images can receive cogent interpretations other than those of an Anselmian sort. In broad ecumenical perspective, it is clear that Christians have assembled the materials about Jesus' death in several models, with individual ones receiving major emphasis in particular traditions, even as the others are present in less prominent roles. Typically, substitutionary atonement is regarded as one of three or four major models. A second is the moral influence or "exemplarist" theory that suggests the death is meant to save us by making such a moving exhibition of God's love that we are inwardly stirred to gratitude and service in return.[2] Jesus' death is heroic. It demonstrates perseverance in the right to the final limit of a human life. Jesus' death demonstrates God's love to us because it shows the extent to which God is willing to identify with our lot as mortal creatures. It is a kind of shock therapy, appealing to the human conscience in the same way that Gandhi's willingness to suffer sought to awaken his opponents' shame and repentance. The tone is expressed in the line from an Isaac Watts hymn, "Love so amazing, so divine, demands my soul, my life, my all."[3] The exemplary view has a somewhat different flavor depending on whether the emphasis falls on Jesus as an example of human faithfulness toward God or on the appeal of the incarnate God's humble display of identity with us. In either case, the death is not a transaction but an inspiration.

Another major option is the *Christus Victor* theory that sees in the cross a victory of God over third parties that hold humanity in bondage, whether these parties be death, sin, or demonic powers.[4] Related but distinct views portray God as winning humans freedom from their deserved subjection to Satan through the payment of ransom or through some form of trickery. The emphasis on Christ as victor makes Jesus' death a turning point in the battle against evil powers arrayed against the divine aim. This is reflected in the Easter hymn that says "The powers of death have done their worst, / but Christ their legions hath dispersed."[5] These powers are often now understood as economic, social, and political in nature instead of or in addition to spiritual ones. Jesus' death is a moment of active resistance to evil. It is the moment of apparent loss that actually

---

2. It is associated with medieval theologian Peter Abelard.

3. "When I Survey the Wondrous Cross."

4. It points to elements prominent in writings from the early church and was advocated in the last century by Gustaf Aulén. See Gustaf Aulén, *Christus Victor: An Historical Study of the Three Main Types of the Idea of the Atonement* (London: SPCK, 1970).

5. "Alleluia! The Strife Is O'er."

marks the turning point that assures final victory, when the resurrection comes and others take up the struggle for justice on Christ's behalf. This element has a strong affinity for liberation perspectives. As might be the case with a martyred resistance fighter, Christ's execution is the leading edge of a new society in which the powers behind this death will themselves be overthrown. In both of the approaches just mentioned, Jesus' death acquires its significance by connection with other aspects of Jesus' life that are regarded as fundamentally saving. For the exemplarist approach, Jesus' message of God's love is the saving act and the death is simply a supreme illustration of that teaching. For the *Christus Victor* approach, a struggle against the powers is the real work of Christ, and his death is one engagement or stratagem in that struggle.

Yet a fourth approach views the incarnation as a whole as the saving work. It is Bethlehem as much as Calvary that changes us. The divine nature is infused into humanity, and Christ is the vaccination point from which this healing power radiates into the bloodstream of our collective human nature. God retraces the whole pattern of human life — from birth and growth to vocation and death — transforming from within what has gone wrong with sinful humanity. Christ breaks a path through our fallen nature, renewing it and so changing the journey for all others who travel the human road. On this view, Jesus' death has a special character because here the path has been broken through the deepest barrier. It is God's presence in the human condition that saves. Death is notable only as the most unlikely aspect of that condition for God to share, the farthest country to be visited. It is the extreme instance of the general rule of the incarnation, the occasion through which divine immortality can be communicated to our human mortality.

Despite the dominance of substitutionary theologies in the postmedieval West, all the perspectives we noted have intertwined in various proportions in Christian tradition. Christ can be at once a sacrifice, a teacher, a victor, and a healer. The church has preferred to add these together rather than exclude any one of them. Advocates of one of the models can readily accept the others (as supplements, not replacements). Those who seek to purge Christianity of sacrificial and atonement theologies fill the resulting space with some combination of these other models.[6] And yet

6. Thus the argument to replace those elements with "narrative Christus Victor" in J. Denny Weaver, *The Nonviolent Atonement* (Grand Rapids: Eerdmans, 2001), and the argument to replace them with a "ministerial vision" of Jesus' teaching and example in Delores S. Williams, *Sisters in the Wilderness: The Challenge of Womanist God-Talk* (Maryknoll, N.Y.: Orbis, 1993).

there is nothing about exemplarist views or *Christus Victor* or incarnational ones that intrinsically rules out combination with sacrificial elements. For that purpose, they must take on a sharpened new absolutism, purified of any subsidiary sacrificial elements that may have attended them.

Movements to eradicate substitutionary beliefs thus have two challenges: to convince people that a previously prominent view should now be forbidden, and to reinterpret (or justify the dismissal of) those elements of scripture and tradition that point toward sacrifice and atonement. Excluding the substitution model from Christian belief can mute the criticisms that atonement theology attracts. This positions the alternative views as "atonement lite," sanitized of sacrificial images. The drawback is that language of sacrifice remains inextricably lodged in Bible, liturgy, sacrament, and hymnody, even while theology is silent about it. This contrast reinforces the perception that substitutionary views are more biblical and more inclusively Christian, since they do not rule out the other approaches and include positive readings of the central sacrificial texts and image of the tradition that are cast aside by those who reject substitutionary theology.

The central criticisms raised against atonement theology cannot be met by changing the subject. What is needed is an interpretive path *through* the problematic texts and not around them, a theological vision that does not depend on excluding all atonement themes but provides the most convincing account of their true significance. I agree that the theology of the cross has in fact gone astray, though not always for the reasons the critics suppose. The church has not been mistaken to place itself under the sign of the cross, uncomfortable as it is to live in that shadow. There is truth there, profound and saving, but also paradoxical and difficult. The difference between being very right and very wrong can be vanishingly small, and the same words may sometimes carry people to dramatically different destinations.

What This Book Is Not About

Because we are focusing so intently on the death of Christ, it is important to remind ourselves what is being left out. Left out, but not denied. Our topic is not the sum total of Christian faith. It's not the answer to every theological question. But it directly addresses some of the most pointed concerns about Christianity today.

We've talked above about the variety of models in Christian tradition in regard to Jesus' saving work — models that emphasize Jesus' life, message, example, incarnation, and struggle with evil powers as well as his death and resurrection. This diversity in what Christ does is matched by a diversity in the tradition regarding what about us is affected by that work. Christian tradition has always had a multidimensional view of Christ's redemptive activity, and various groups or individuals have stressed different aspects. Human beings are shaped and defined by three dimensions of relation: our relations with God, with others, and with created nature. The biblical story of our creation highlights each one, and describes the way each one has gone astray. Christian theology traditionally then sees three elements of the human condition that are in need of transformation: sin (estrangement from God), evil (estrangement among humans), and death (mortality, and our estrangement from nature).

The story of Eve and Adam expresses this in a powerful narrative form. The first humans mistrust and disobey God, breaking that relation. They introduce shame and recrimination, becoming estranged from each other. And an original peace with creatures and their own bodies is changed into conflict, pain, and death. Christians have argued with each other about which of these comes first or is more basic than the others. Is "pride" — the breaking of faith with God — the sin from which mortality follows as a punishment? Or is evil — our breaking of moral laws and betrayal of love toward our neighbor — the disobedience that leads to estrangement from God? Is it the anxiety and desperate longing for security that comes with the certainty of death that disorders all our other relations?

However we arrange these, the end result is that humans are fallen in all these ways. And Christ addresses all of them. The three "offices" of Christ — priest, prophet, and king — are a shorthand expression of this. Christ's priestly work is to restore our connection with God. Christ's prophetic work is to overcome the evil that breaks relations among humans. Christ's royal work as king is to restore and renew the divine purpose in created nature, defeating death. Jesus' crucifixion is often associated primarily with the priestly work, with Jesus' sacrifice the crucial condition for humanity's reconciliation with God, the way in which the legitimate claim of God's justice against human sin can be satisfied and sinners forgiven. Substitutionary sacrifice doctrine strongly emphasizes this connection. But Jesus' death is also an important feature of the prophetic work of overcoming human evil or the royal work of restoring harmony with nature.

In fact, the various models of atonement that we reviewed above have tended to cluster around these three dimensions of human brokenness. Substitutionary doctrines, obviously, tend to cluster with the priestly work of Christ. The *Christus Victor* theories point toward the royal "office," where for instance death's power to reduce all nature to futility is defeated by Christ's resurrection and gift of eternal life. The exemplarist models often emphasize the prophetic work, where Jesus' teaching and example, including the example of his selfless death, inspire us to live different personal and social lives.[7] One of the great benefits of ecumenical theology is that Christians increasingly appreciate the significance of all these dimensions for a full expression of their faith.

Given this background, we can locate the corner of the landscape treated in this book. We focus on the death of Christ, which is only one aspect of the whole work of Christ. We focus on the significance of this death primarily for one dimension of the human condition, the dimension of interpersonal evil. And finally, even here we are concerned almost entirely with the way the cross might bear on one crucial and specific type of social evil, sacrificial scapegoating. Jesus' death has profound significance for other aspects of our condition (for human relations with God and with nature, for instance). And other aspects of Jesus' work (his teaching, for example) may have important relevance for transforming interhuman evils. These dimensions do not receive equal time in this book not because they do not deserve it, but because we have limited the field. I have chosen this focus because it is a particular sore point, a point that today attracts the most challenges. Of all the dimensions of Christ's work and of human brokenness, it is the pairing of the cross with redemption from human evil that evokes the most perplexity and critique. To many, atonement theology is itself a prime source of evil and no solution to it. So this is the point where the question must be faced.

An Anthropology of the Cross

To outline things in this way already lets us preview part of our argument. We are focusing on how the cross (which is a part of Christ's work) bears on our practice of sacrificial scapegoating (which is a part of our broken human condition). In this connection we find the special thread that

7. The incarnational model seems to find no obvious single partner in the prophet, priest, king typology, which may reflect the fact that the typology is drawn from the experience of Western Christianity and the incarnational model is more prominent in Eastern Christianity. Or it may indicate that the incarnational model necessarily encompasses all these other dimensions.

leads to an understanding of what is decisive and saving about Jesus' death, an understanding of the need, if you will, for it to happen in the specific way the Gospels say it happens. Jesus' death has important meaning in relation to other aspects of Christ's work and our condition. It is obviously necessary to the gospel message about resurrection and the hope of eternal life, for instance. But for most of these purposes another kind of death would have served as well. Many aspects of Jesus' saving work may be represented in his death in a general way, without turning on the specific character of the cross.

To give an important example, Jesus' death may have something to do with our separate, individual sin and our "private" relation with God. One form of atonement theology has specified this. All our disparate individual sins are canceled out by Christ's punishment on the cross. The details of Christ's death are specifically tailored to build up a reservoir of merit that can then be credited to our personal accounts, one by one. In Jesus' death we do see an overpowering image of the truth such theologies assert: that forgiveness is costly, and that God is willing to suffer on behalf of each person in order to redeem us. But, and this is the crucial point, the cross *represents* that truth. It is not the precondition for it (except in the broadest sense that one might say God's entire redemptive plan is the precondition for any part of it). The divine aim to forgive individuals for their many individual evils did not dictate that Jesus must die in pain, falsely accused of crimes both political and religious, through a collusion of all the relevant authorities, with the endorsement of a mob, by crucifixion, abandoned by his disciples, and so on. The elements of violence and punishment are not prescribed and initiated by God. They come from elsewhere and are accepted by God for a saving purpose, entirely consistent with the work of individual forgiveness (for we are each individually involved in the sin of scapegoating too) but also clearly distinct. Regarding a person's purely individual sins that affect no one else (if in fact it were possible to isolate such things), the right doctrine of the cross may well be an exemplarist one. But since our problem is larger than sin so defined, that doctrine is not enough. We need a theology that addresses sacrifice and substitution also. We make a mistake, however, if we frame our understanding of sacrifice entirely and exclusively in terms of individual "private" sin.

A key feature of this book is the contention that the significance of the cross stands out with particular clarity when seen in the light of a particular aspect of evil, a dynamic of scapegoating violence that encompasses both the individual and society. One figure more than any other is responsible for casting that light on the subject: René Girard.[8] This book could not have been conceived apart from his extraordinary cross-disciplinary work. He has described that work as "a search for the anthropology of the Cross."[9] It has left a trail of consternation and fascination across fields from psychology to biblical studies, from literature to anthropology. The many facets of his thought revolve around a simple question: How do victims become visible? To put it another way, where do our antisacrificial sensibilities come from? His answer is straightforward. Those sensibilities are rooted in biblical revelation, particularly in the Gospels, above all in the passion narratives. Girard has a judolike response to condemnations of the cross as divine sadism: we could not accuse the Gospels of victimization in this manner if we had not already been converted by them. Our increasing discomfort with the cross is itself an effect of the cross. Far from being a rationalization of redemptive violence, the passion accounts definitively undermine it.

On the largest scale, Girard's thought offers an account of the origins of human religion and society, indeed a hypothesis about human nature itself. Discussion and debate over its adequacy will continue for a long time. Girard's importance for our topic does not depend on a global acceptance of his approach, on the model of absolutist systems like those of Freud or Marx. For my purposes it is not necessary to assume that the origins of religion and human society took place just as Girard imagines. The main point is not whether he describes what happened at the unseen beginnings, but whether he describes a reality actually functioning in human religion and societies as we find them in the past, and in the world we see around us.[10]

Theology's constant task is to give clear and concrete content to elements of faith that may be at once inherently mysterious and historically distorted in their expression. Doing this always involves illustration and appropriation from other consonant disciplines. Theology frequently

---

8. There is no shortage of books by and about Girard. James Alison, Gil Bailie, Anthony Bartlett, Robert G. Hamerton-Kelly, Raymund Schwager, and James Williams have produced striking works shaped by his insights. My debt to them is only slightly less than that to Girard himself. Representative works are given in my bibliography, but an excellent place to begin is René Girard and James G. Williams, *The Girard Reader* (New York: Crossroad, 1996).

9. Williams, *The Girard Reader*, 288.

10. Girard regards the biblical tradition as a unique and decisive antisacrificial revelation, though he recognizes that other historical sources (like Greek tragedy or early Buddhist critiques of sacrifice) offer major insights into the nature of myth. It lies beyond the scope of this study to evaluate his hypothesis in an interreligious perspective. See Leo D. Lefebure, *Revelation, the Religions, and Violence* (Maryknoll, N.Y.: Orbis, 2000).

fails to make faith either intelligible or important. But there are also dangers in success, when the interpretation of Christian faith reduces it to nothing but an example of the theory (perhaps very important in itself) used to explain it. In this case, that would mean that once we see the things Girard describes, we don't need the Gospels themselves. We would take Christian tradition simply as an adjunct to Girard's theory, rather than Girard's theory as illuminating an aspect of biblical truth. Girard himself contends that the proper relation here is the second. And I hope this book will help to bear out that conclusion. The greatest gift I have received from Girard and from those writers inspired by him, is the experience of reading the Bible with surprise. His writing points insistently to things lying in plain sight in its pages. In the end, this book is about what I found when I looked where he was pointing.

Girard is open to criticism from two sides. On the anthropological side one may contest the truth or the scope of his theory about religion, society, and violence. On the theological side one may contest whether his treatment of the cross is adequate or complete. I believe there are valid criticisms to be made on both scores. But these criticisms are essentially that Girard has in some respects overstated his case or has left out things that are essential to a fully formed Christian theology. They do not change the fact that he has seen something crucially important and offered us a genuinely new perspective to bring to some of our traditional problems. I agree with the conclusion Walter Wink draws at the end of his critical review of Girard's work: "Even if aspects of Girard's overall thesis fail to convince, his understanding of mimetic rivalry and conflict and of the scapegoat are among the most profound intellectual discoveries of our time, and will remain permanent contributions to our understanding of the meaning of the crucifixion."[11] I have chosen to focus in this book on the attempt to make those contributions and their relevance clear.

So, for instance, I do not think that Girard's thought represents the global truth about mythology, early religion, human psychology, and community that its more extreme devotees maintain. Likewise, I agree that if taken as an exclusive account of Christian theology or even as an

---

11. Walter Wink, *Engaging the Powers: Discernment and Resistance in a World of Domination* (Minneapolis: Fortress, 1992), 155. There are many who essentially agree with this valuation. See, for instance, the balanced critiques in the following: John Milbank, *Being Reconciled: Ontology and Pardon,* Radical Orthodoxy Series (London and New York: Routledge, 2003); Kevin J. Vanhoozer, "The Atonement in Postmodernity: Guilt, Goats and Gifts," in *The Glory of the Atonement: Biblical, Historical, and Practical Perspectives,* ed. Charles E. Hill and Frank A. James (Downers Grove, Ill.: InterVarsity, 2004).

exhaustive account of the cross, Girard's writing can be faulted for tending toward the impression that all that is needed in Christ's work is a particularly dramatic demonstration of a truth we need to learn, as opposed to a divine act by whose power we are transformed.[12] Yet on both of these fronts Girard offers us crucial insights precisely relevant to the questions most sharply raised about atonement today.

Girard himself puts it this way: "There is an anthropological dimension to the text of the Gospels. I have never claimed that it constitutes the whole of Christian revelation. But without it, Christianity could scarcely be truly itself, and would be incoherent in areas where it need not be. To lose this dimension is to lose an essential aspect of the very humanity of Christ, of the incarnation. We would not see clearly in Christ a victim of people such as we all are, and we would be in danger of relapsing into the religion of persecution."[13] If the saving effect of Jesus' death refers to only the next life, or to transformations in the inaccessible inner lives of individuals, then the whole question remains a matter of belief. Girard's contention is that there is a distinct, empirical level on which the cross illuminates and affects human history, a level that can be grasped rationally and is not a matter of subjective belief.

Girard's hypothesis explicates a crucial turning point in the formation and maintenance of human society, and a fundamental dynamic that continues to underlie religion and culture. He is convinced that the biblical tradition, and especially the passion narratives, has played a decisive role in revealing and transforming this human condition. He believes, quite unfashionably for a scholar in nontheological disciplines, that there is an objective revelation in the biblical tradition. Yet he is equally clear that Christians have often been groping and blind to the logic of their own tradition.

Historical Christianity, in its sacrificial versions, stands under the judgment of its own gospel.[14] The effects of the cross pass through the

---

12. This is essentially the critique offered by George Hunsinger. He suggests that Girard offers an "essentially 'Pelagian' solution to an inherently 'Augustinian' problem." See George Hunsinger, *Disruptive Grace: Studies in the Theology of Karl Barth* (Grand Rapids: Eerdmans, 2000), 28. I agree with most of Hunsinger's positive proposals, but I think that in his more recent work Girard does not reduce the work of the cross to the conveying of information and does recognize the need for grace to appropriate its meaning.

13. René Girard, *La Route Antique des Hommes Pervers* (Paris: Grasset, 1985), 184, translation mine.

14. For a perspective that appropriates Girard's outlook but regards Girard himself as insufficiently critical in applying it to the Christian tradition itself, see Anthony W. Bartlett, *Cross Purposes: The Violent Grammar of Christian Atonement* (Harrisburg, Pa.: Trinity, 2001).

church but are not limited to the church. To grasp the distinctive nature of the passion story and the biblical setting behind it is to know the failures of the church only more deeply. To Girard's mind this fact is coordinate with the true objectivity of the revelation. The substance is so real that it makes its impact not only by means of perfect teachings and full understanding, but even through partial and obscured forms. His outlook is an interesting mix of the apologetic and the critical. Thus on the one hand his perspective reaffirms traditional convictions on the saving significance of the cross and orthodox views of Jesus' divinity, but on the other hand, it just as strongly condemns much of the church's theology and practice as distorted, and in need of renewal. Christ's work, even the work of Christ's death, includes more than the reversal of sacrificial scapegoating. To grasp this aspect does not tell us the whole story. But that aspect is crucial for understanding the mixed legacy of doctrines of atonement, a trail of destructive as well as transforming effects. It is crucial for our constructive understanding of the cross here and now.

Plan of the Book

The next chapter fills out an introduction to our topic, reviewing the current crisis in atonement theology, particularly the criticisms raised against substitutionary theories of the cross. The rest of the book is divided into three parts. These try to indicate how we may interpret the death of Jesus theologically today, by coordinating three dimensions of meaning. The three "sides" of the cross can be taken in a number of ways: as three layers of meaning in the scriptural texts, as three cumulative stages in a historical development, as three facets of revelation. You cannot see all sides of a three-dimensional object at once, but you have to register the reality of all three dimensions to perceive its full reality. Insofar as we look at a three-dimensional object from only one fixed perspective, the surfaces directly opposite us are effectively invisible. Yet without taking account of that hidden dimension, our perception is inadequate. So with the cross, it is virtually impossible to see all three dimensions at once in any description, but none can be left aside if we want to grasp the whole.

There is one particular dimension of depth that we need as a background to grasp the Gospel treatment of Jesus' death. This is the subject of part 1. We might call this missing dimension the mythical and sacrificial side of the cross. The story of Jesus' death fits into a preexisting pattern, a pattern that existed long before the Bible and continues to exist apart from it. The passion narratives revolve around that plot the way murder mysteries revolve around the formula elements of such stories or a musical composition communicates its message through variant treatments of the same theme. It would make little sense to say a book "breaks all the rules of a murder mystery" if we did not have some idea what those rules were, if we could not see, so to speak, the invisible book in contrast with this one. To take another kind of example, those who observe patriarchal bias in classical texts or a political bias in most elite media or education recognize that what they describe was/is largely invisible to those immersed in it. It is not so much purposefully advocated as unquestioningly assumed. People don't describe their own unexamined actions or perceptions as distorted or biased. They register them under quite different categories. Something has to happen before we see the missing dimension as a dimension at all.

The biblical tradition within which Jesus' death is set, the light thrown on it by his teaching and resurrection, and the life of the community that remembered it — all are keystones in just such a happening. We live in its wake. We take for granted what they brought into view. The irony is that to understand the gospel of the cross we have to remember or imagine a world without it, one where it never appears. The missing side of the cross is the mythical story about sacrifice, the story we once told ourselves (and still do), in which victims stay invisible.

There is no doubt that the key category for the arguments over Jesus' death is sacrifice. The Bible and Christian tradition interpret the meaning of the crucifixion in large measure through parallels to sacrifice, whether Abraham's near sacrifice of Isaac or the ritual animal sacrifices in the temple in Jerusalem. But of course, the practice of sacrifice is much wider than that presented in the biblical tradition, and is rooted in the history of virtually every culture. We are faced with two crucial questions. What is sacrifice doing in human religious history? And is the biblical understanding of sacrifice, rooted in the Hebrew scriptures and then applied to Jesus' death, different in any important way from that more general phenomenon?

Here is where René Girard's work comes into play. He contends that the practice of sacrificial scapegoating is a cornerstone of human society and religion. Communities solve their internal conflicts by uniting against a chosen victim. This violence staves off more generalized factional or retributive violence. The importance of this sacrificial foundation is recognized in the extraordinary aura that surrounds it, the sacred power attributed to it. This aura is also necessary for the effectiveness of the practice, as it induces in the sacrificing community agreement on the nature of the offering and complete confidence in its necessity as a divine command. Where the offering of sacrificial victims proceeds untroubled, "successfully," violence is done but none is perceived. Sacred killing does not register as killing. Sacrifice is seen as natural and as beneficial as the turn of seasons, or the cycle of predator and prey. The falling of leaves presents us with no moral issue, nor does sacred violence in mythical perspective. Sacrifice harnesses a bad thing, collective violence against the marginal, to avert even worse bloodshed and assure the good of social peace. What is evil about this act is entirely swallowed up in sacred awe.

At this basic point of departure, biblical sacrifice is no different from this sacrifice, and God sometimes figures as its patron. In fact, what is different in the Bible requires this identity, for the difference is that in the Bible the violence of sacrifice is unveiled. In the Bible, even where in the first instance sacrifice is affirmed in terms continuous with this wider practice, *what it does* is described in unusually graphic terms. Elsewhere sacrifice is a kind of magician's practice, where violence is the essential act, but in the representation of the event one's eyes are always directed elsewhere at the moment the ax falls. Above all, what is typically hidden is the view and voice of the victim as a victim. But the Bible tells us with staggering bluntness that the violence is the magic. The power is in the blood. Improbably, powerfully, in the Bible we come to hear the objections of the sacrificed.

The Bible brims with violence. I am thinking not only of the space devoted specifically to cultic animal sacrifice, and not only of the descriptions of war, murder, rape, and persecution, but also of the fiery inner passion for revenge that glows in much of the poetry of the Psalms. That uncomfortable material, and its preoccupation with bloodshed, is one major focus of this section. The other key reference point is the sacrificial world outside the Bible, and those religious mythological traditions that appear free of the Bible's brutal character. The Bible is frequently said to express religious patterns just like those found in other religions. It is also frequently said (often by the same people) to express a unique and perversely violent religious vision, different from other religious traditions. It is hard to see how both can be true. Yet these comments make sense if we should suspect that mythical traditions that do not explicitly describe violence are not necessarily free from practicing it. One feature of the Bible may be that it makes plain what is elsewhere clouded, a difference that requires similarity.

Part 2 turns explicitly to the passion narratives themselves and their interpretation of Jesus' death. Its focus is the paradox firmly entrenched in the Gospels: Christ's death saves the world and it ought not to happen. This puzzle is the key to the drama in the passion accounts, and to the interpretation of the subsequent varieties of atonement theories. The narrative of Jesus' death is in fact two stories laid on top of each other. One is the description of Jesus' execution as a kind of sacrificial business as usual, an explicit specification of the invisible pattern we discussed in part 1. The second story is of God's redemptive action and purpose, played out "in, with, and under" the script of the first story, but to a very different effect. The good news of the cross can be heard only in this kind of stereo, a sacrifice to end sacrifice.

We understand the crucifixion through the lens of the treatment of sacrifice in the Hebrew scriptures. As outlined in part 1, that treatment both unveiled violence as the operative element in sacrifice and (in the Psalms, the book of Job, the Prophets, and elsewhere) gave a place to the voice of the victim. The Gospel passion narratives express the Christian conviction that in the death of Jesus this revelatory process reached a dramatic climax. The sacred dynamic of sacrifice is reversed. In pure sacrificial myth scapegoats never appear as scapegoats. They are forgotten and hidden under other signs. The passion narratives tell the old story of redemptive violence, but tell it entirely from the point of view of the sacrificed one. Even more dramatically, they tell the story of redemptive violence as a sinful human construct for peacemaking, not a divine institution. God is not the author of the process, but the one crushed by it. God reverses the violence of the cross and vindicates the victim executed on it. All this is laid out in the New Testament. But from very near the beginning there was a strong tendency to assimilate this new vision to the mythical pattern it was breaking. At the end of this section we discuss two paradigmatic expressions of that tendency, in gnosticism and Christian anti-Semitism.

Part 3 follows this story from the New Testament into the early church and later history. Christ's resurrection undoes the "good" of sacrifice, an undoing that brings not only hope of eternal life but also an apocalyptic challenge: How can human communities live without sacrifice? Much of the discussion in parts 1 and 2 might sound as if the primary impact of Jesus' death was simple revelation. It changes things by showing us the nature of the sacrificial web in which we are enmeshed. We once were blind, but now we see. But seeing alone is hardly a recipe for salvation. Indeed, such revelation does have an objective effect, but insofar as that effect only undermines the effectiveness of sacrifice, the effect is not necessarily a peaceful one. The discussion of apocalyptic literature in this section illustrates that point.

To appropriate this revelation requires an additional transformation. What difference does it make that Christ "died for us"? What does it mean to live without sacrifice? The answers to these questions involve personal conversion and a new form of social reconciliation. The resurrection of the crucified one brought with it not righteous vengeance but the formation of an odd new community that gathered around him. This community deployed a whole range of elements to substitute for scapegoating. Christians celebrated their ritual remembrance of Jesus' death not with copycat killings or new sacrifices, but with a meal of bread and wine. This was the "sacrifice of praise" that they believed powerful enough to do what violent scapegoating had hitherto done in human history. They celebrated not their unanimity against a victim, but their identification with the crucified one, and so with all those placed in a similar position. They remembered that at this death Jesus' disciples had played the roles of betrayer, deserter, and denier. Therefore they faced a reminder that they too were not free of the sin that leads to the cross, and were in need of conversion.

This leads us in the final chapter to a review and assessment of the theology of the cross, an attempt to restate the doctrine of the atonement. The three sides of the cross explored in these three parts do not represent a simple progression, where the first two represent past stages of thought or faith and all one needs is the final step. In that case the first two would be of only historical interest, like surveying old discredited medical theories about bleeding or bodily humors before learning our best current science. The three sides — myth revealed, sacrifice reversed, a new basis of reconciliation substituted — go together. The truth of one coheres with the truth of the others. The history of Christian faith and theology is not the story of slow transition from one stage to the next but rather one of the uneven struggle to maintain the depth of vision that comes with a grasp of all three at once.

We go astray if we remythologize the passion by assimilating it completely and approvingly to the sacrificial pattern outlined in part 1. We go equally astray if we confine our theology to a nonviolent ideal taken from part 3, without any grounding in the true nature of sacrificial realities. And we go astray if we narrow our context for the cross only to the scope of the material in part 2, for then we too readily confuse God's becoming a victim of our violence to overcome it with God prescribing violence to save us. That is, without the surrounding context, and above all the Hebrew scriptures, it is all too easy to abstract the passion from the problem it directly addresses. Such abstraction leads to the need to invent another problem for the cross to solve, which is what certain atonement theologies have done in shifting the emphasis to a concern for divine satisfaction or quantitative human moral debt.

In scriptural and theological context, the three sides of the cross are simply different entry points for telling the same story, a story that always comes round all three points. We can have no clear knowledge of the cross without the context of myth on one hand and the context of the community with the crucified on the other. But the most decisive reference goes in the other direction, for it is from the cross that we have come to know both of the others. With these three elements in hand, we can address the key problems of atonement theology. We have a framework, for instance, for interpreting the various and sometimes contending scriptural passages that bear on our subject. We can address very concretely the question of what saving purpose or need there might have been for Jesus to die the very specific kind of death the Gospels say he did. We can give the most adequate and honest account of both the good and the bad that have flowed from Christian interpretations of the cross. We can see why the elements lumped under the heading of the substitutionary or sacrificial doctrine of the atonement are essential to Christian faith, even as they must be structured anew.

CHAPTER ONE

Atonement on Trial

I don't think we need a theory of atonement at all. . . . I don't
think we need folks hanging on crosses and blood dripping
and weird stuff.

Delores Williams[1]

Why is the death of Christ significant? Much of the church is sure it
knows the answer — it is an atoning sacrifice — and much of the
rest of the church is deeply uncomfortable with the question. There is today a widespread disinclination to dwell on Jesus' death, either in fact or
in theory. As fact, represented in tradition, literature, and art, many find it
a morbid theme. Christian services of communion are acted-out remem-
brances of Jesus' death, but many branches of American Christianity
downplay this aspect. In Australia a state education department recently
banned a passion play. An official said the ruling showed that the state
"will not tolerate violence in the schools."[2] Ironic as it may seem in light
of the content in contemporary movies, TV, and computer games, a crucifix strikes many as primitively graphic. The brutally explicit film *The Passion of the Christ* met with polarizing waves of reverence and outrage, each
with its own complex inner currents. The outrage stemmed in part from

1. Remarks at the Re-Imagining Conference in 1993, quoted in Robert Sherman, *King,
Priest, and Prophet: A Trinitarian Theology of Atonement*, ed. Wallace M. Alston, Robert Jenson,
and Don S. Browning, Theology for the Twenty-first Century (New York: T. & T. Clark,
2004), 8.

2. Associated Press, "Passion Play Is Banned," *Boston Globe*, May 16, 1997.

legitimate concerns that the movie traded in traditional anti-Semitic motifs. But it seemed also that the explicit abuse of a cinematic Jesus somehow registered in viewers a horror we might expect to be the ordinary, authentic reaction to any actual violence . . . a reaction notably uncommon for the steady representations of violence in entertainment and even in world news. In a culture somewhat numbed by simulated gore and reports of actual massacres, the suffering of this one figure struck a dramatically live nerve.

An Impossible Gift

The discomfort and repugnance I note are directed particularly at the doctrine most strongly associated with the cross: penal substitutionary atonement. The cross is a punishment for sin (hence penal). The punishment is applied not to a deserving guilty humanity (us) but to the innocent, divine Jesus (hence substitutionary). And the result is forgiveness, acceptance, and reconciliation between God and humanity (atonement). We might summarize the doctrine this way. We are guilty of sin, against God and our neighbors. The continuing sinful acts themselves, the self-loathing or malicious desires that prompt them, the twisted social patterns that become the environment for human development, the guilt we bear for such ungrateful response to God's good gifts — all of these together separate us from God, poison our relations with each other, and are far beyond any human power to mend.

Someday we might finally become truly righteous. Our wills might finally be remade to trust God with delight. We might live in harmony with our neighbors. Even if all that happened, this perfected love, faith, and hope would not change the past, nor would they make restitution for it. The criminal who becomes a saint can never undo all the losses of his victims. We can conceive a crude recompense that adds something on the other side of the scales, as a burglar might return all she had taken and more besides. A reformed offender could voluntarily treat people much better than simple justice requires, as before he treated them much worse. And if an offender can offer no compensating gift to the injured party, it might still be possible to make some kind of negative restitution. Perhaps she could accept the full appropriate punishment and then some more as a contribution to reconciliation, a sign of true repentance. If my lies have deprived you of some deserved reward, it is right that I should give up anything I unjustly gained as a result. And perhaps I might choose to give up something more as well, even if it provides no direct benefit to you.

This kind of calculus won't work with sin against God. We can't offer extra goods to balance out our prior wrongs, as we owe everything to begin with. And if the appropriate punishment is to pay with our lives, there is no further gift we can make in addition. Not only are we unable to go beyond what justice requires, we cannot even come up to balance, to zero. The theory says we deserve more punishment than we can ever undergo and that to offer every possible positive gift to God would do no more than originally required before our failures. Sin catastrophically unbalances the human-God relation so that it can never be evened again. Not from our side. A gap exists. God steps into this gap directly by becoming a human being, and by accepting the suffering and death of the crucifixion. God provides what is missing in this hopeless equation, a human being who deserves no punishment and who has fulfilled all the created good of human nature. Christ offers something fallen humanity cannot, standing in our place, bearing the punishment we deserve and he does not. In so doing, Christ offers an "over and above" gift to God that restores the broken relation. An innocent, sinless human accepts what is not deserved — punishment and death — and so offers to God something even the most rigorous justice could not expect. Here is the superfluous gift that can cancel out the egregious offense. It is a substitution because one human occupies the place that belongs to others. And it is a substitution because, as there is no existing human able to do that, God substitutes God's self rather than any other candidate. Were the crucified one not human, it would not be human sin that was being punished. Were the crucified one not holy, the punishment would cancel nothing, would have no reconciling or atoning power. This was the job description for incarnation, for a real human being who was truly of a divine, sinless nature.

This only sketches a theology that has various forms and a surprisingly complex history. It has nourished much authentic Christian piety. But I would not be writing this book and you would probably not be reading it if this theology were not under fierce attack, indicted for many offenses. Indictments presuppose that enough evidence has been presented to demand a trial. And it appears that there are more than enough reasons to be uncomfortable with the doctrine of substitutionary atonement.

Multiple Indictments

First, such doctrine always trades in the language of sacrifice. Increasing numbers of people find this language empty, literally unintelligible, or actively offensive. The first time I visited the Kali temple in Calcutta, I literally stepped in pools of blood from a sacrificed goat. I felt revulsion, and yet I saw the irony in that reaction. I have attended worship services all my life in which people talked and sang about blood shed for me. I never walked away with any on my shoes before. If I was comfortable with the abstract idea, why did I shrink from the reality?

The New Testament writers approach Jesus' death in a world where ritual sacrifice is a commonplace event and the details of temple sacrifice in Jerusalem are vivid in their minds. It is no more natural for people in our society to regard Christ as a sin offering who removes our guilt than for them to consider sacrificing oxen on an altar in the neighborhood playground to keep their children safe.[3] A familiar practice of sacrifice was once taken as a known quantity, used to explain the strange and wondrous meaning Christians had discovered in the cross. But in our cultural world, it is this explanation that needs explaining. To speak of Jesus' death as saving and a sacrifice is strange at both ends.

Sacrificial practices are found in nearly all the historical strands of human religious development. But there is no agreement on why they originated or what they mean. Few care about the answers to such questions, for we feel certain that sacrifice is a primitive artifact of an earlier stage of human development, an irrelevant form of magic long since retired by science. A good part of atonement theory today for Christians consists in conjuring up some idea of sacrifice from this dim prior history, one that we can half-believe in long enough to attribute meaning to Christ's death. Sacrificial images flow past us like the archaic language in a mortgage or a will. We may trust specialized experts to make sense of it, if need be, but it conveys little more than musty solemnity. This indictment charges that atonement theology is empty and outmoded.

Second, few can be unaware that the cross has been the keystone of Christian anti-Semitism and anti-Judaism. The "deicide" charge that Jews are responsible for Jesus' death draws its virulent strength from the assumption that this death was somehow uniquely horrible and uniquely important. Social animosity becomes something even darker

---

3. We should note that this "tone deafness" to sacrifice is not a universal cultural fact even today outside most of the West.

with the added theological claim that Jews are collectively responsible for killing God. If atonement theology requires a divine victim, it may endow the supposed villains of the piece with an almost supernatural evil, a guilt beyond redemption.[4] The crucifixion has been directly entangled with anti-Semitism. Lent and Good Friday have historically been particular occasions for Christian pogroms against Jews. The eucharistic memorial of Christ's death has sometimes figured in legends in which Jews are supposed to profane the host for magical purposes and repeat their supposed violence to Christ's body and blood. The sign of the cross has become an image of fear for many Jews who remember how often it has been associated with their persecution and suffering. There are Jewish and Christian thinkers who maintain that the only real solution to this problem is a root-and-branch excision of atonement theology from Christianity itself. James Carroll puts it in typically unequivocal terms: "[T]he cross must be reimagined, and deemphasized, as a Christian symbol."[5] Belief in the atonement stands indicted for linking Christian salvation with demonization of Jews.

A third charge stems from the fact that our knowledge of world religions and mythology puts Jesus' death in an unavoidably comparative context. The Gospels attribute unique significance to the cross. Yet since the rise of modern anthropology, we know that tales of dying and rising gods are a common feature across human cultures. How could there be something special about this tale alone, when we know of Osiris, the myths of the corn kings, and so many other stories? Only Christian near-sightedness can stare fixedly at just one cross while standing in a forest of others. Some who are best acquainted with this vast literature tell us that these dying and rising gods express symbolic truths about the cycles of nature, the quest for psychic wholeness, the healing of inner wounds. The Christian gospel of death and resurrection is but a variant of these common themes, historically successful perhaps but also rather degenerate in form. The charge is that non-Christian myths convey these symbolic truths much more elegantly and peacefully, neither marred by the crude moralism of the Christian passion stories nor troubled by their fixation on literal historical events. The theology of the cross is indicted for ignorant parochialism and spiritual immaturity.

4. The "infinite" extent of human sin addressed in the atonement and the unrestricted guilt attributed to Jews in Christian anti-Semitism look rather similar. This question is considered at greater length in chapter 7.

5. James Carroll, *Constantine's Sword: The Church and the Jews; A History* (Boston: Houghton Mifflin, 2001), 587.

Fourth, traditional interpretations of the crucifixion are criticized for moral failings, especially in the picture they paint of God. The specific ways Christians have understood the cross often involve transactional analogies of substitution, ransom, or satisfaction. Christ is sent to die so that a merciful God can fulfill the demands of a just God's law. Legal or economic analogies frame human guilt in terms of a debt that must be paid, and Christ's sacrifice as the payment of that debt. The language of ransom frames Jesus' death as an offering given to evil powers that hold humans hostage. Feudal language frames sin in terms of an offense against God's honor that must be satisfied. Such categories explain Jesus' death, but in such a way as to pose further troubling questions. If a debt is owed to God, why can't God simply forgive it, as Jesus apparently counsels others to do? If God is ransoming us from other powers, why does God have to submit to their terms? If this is God's wise and compassionate plan for salvation, why does it require such violence? The idea that God sent his Son to be sacrificed for us is indicted here for impugning the moral character of God. We can hardly imagine God demanding the suffering and death of one innocent as the condition of mercy toward guilty others. This tension between wrath and mercy can twist God into a cipher, a dualistic deity who understandably evokes ambiguous responses of both gratitude and fear.[6]

Fifth, a rising chorus charges that Christian ideas of atonement foster toxic psychological and social effects. Feminist and womanist theologians have perhaps made this case in the most powerful terms, but they are not alone.[7] In exalting Christ's death, do we not glorify innocent suffering and encourage people to passively accept roles as surrogate sufferers for others, "in imitation of Christ"? What earthly despot would not be glad to have the weak and oppressed adopt this as their spiritual ideal? By making the cross God's recipe for salvation, do we validate violence as a divine way of doing business? A theology that has the heavenly Father punish his

6. Defenders of the doctrine rightly point out that many of these objections do not take seriously Christian belief in the Trinity. The death of Jesus does not involve God sending someone *else* to suffer. God is the one on the cross and the innocent suffering is God's, shared between the Word and the Father as grief is shared between two spouses, one who must die and one who must remain. This is powerfully set forth in Jürgen Moltmann, *The Crucified God: The Cross of Christ as the Foundation and Criticism of Christian Theology*, 1st U.S. ed. (New York: Harper and Row, 1974).

7. See, for instance, Joanne Carlson Brown and Carole R. Bohn, eds., *Christianity, Patriarchy, and Abuse: A Feminist Critique* (New York: Pilgrim, 1989); Carter Heyward, *Saving Jesus from Those Who Are Right: Rethinking What It Means to Be Christian* (Minneapolis: Fortress, 1999); Delores S. Williams, *Sisters in the Wilderness: The Challenge of Womanist God-Talk* (Maryknoll, N.Y.: Orbis, 1993).

innocent Son to redeem the world looks uncomfortably to some like a charter for child abuse, with an innocent son sent to bear the wrath of a "heavenly father" to make things right for the entire extended family.[8] Who ultimately administers the torments of crucifixion, "for everyone's good," if not the God whose redemptive plan requires it? Critics find the cross-centered atonement faith of Christianity a toxic nexus of guilt, retribution, and violence, twisting everything it touches, from gender relations to legal systems.

The spirituality of identification with Jesus' sacrifice can sour in an individual psyche into a questionable brew of morbid fantasies and masochistic eroticism. Ascetic forms of self-mortification are threaded through Christian history, and some truly great figures, like Francis of Assisi, combine sublime virtues with forms of self-abuse for which we would almost certainly seek clinical attention today. Recently I had the opportunity to view an impressionistic film on the life of Edith Stein, the famous Jewish convert to Catholicism who became a nun, perished in Auschwitz, and was canonized as a saint. The movie was shown at a conference of Jewish and Christian scholars, and for obvious reasons sparked some raw exchanges. The movie portrays Stein, whose monastic name was Sister Teresa Benedicta of the Cross, as prone to fits of agony in which she sprawls on the floor, arms outstretched in a cruciform manner, or squeezes a crucifix in her hand until she bleeds, stigmata-like. She accepts her immolation by the Nazis as an act of atonement for her own failings (represented by a friend whose disappointed love for her helps lead him into the Nazi party) and, by implication, those of her people.

The movie concentrates many of the elements we have been listing in a single, highly charged story. A Jewish woman shared her puzzlement at the faith depicted in the movie. "Suffering doesn't impress me. I don't see what's holy about it. This all seems sick." At the extreme represented, perhaps caricatured, in the film, there are many Christians who would agree. Christlike humility, self-sacrifice, and submission are an unbalanced prescription for women or others who may be exploited, powerless, or struggling for identity. Victims of domestic abuse don't need advice to persevere in their suffering as a way of sharing in Christ's redemptive work. Whether we are thinking of society as a whole or as individuals, this indictment states that the cross should carry a label: this religious image may be harmful to your health.

8. Rita Nakashima Brock, "And a Little Child Will Lead Us: Christology and Child Abuse," in *Christianity, Patriarchy, and Abuse.*

Any one of these indictments would be significant. Though persons may differ about which charge is most telling, there is an implicit sense that they are linked and mutually reinforcing. They assert no minor flaw in Christianity, but a consistent fault line in the whole foundation that runs from distorted views of God to spiritual guilt fixation to sacrificial bloodshed to anti-Semitic persecution to arrogant ignorance of world mythology. All this adds up to a fatally skewed faith, revolving around a central narrative based on sacred violence and the glorification of innocent suffering. This book will not spend more time amplifying these criticisms, which can be pursued at length in a number of works.[9] There is substance to these concerns, and real-life experience that verifies the dangers they name. Contemporary treatments of the atonement, no matter their theological orientation, feel compelled to address these issues.[10]

The critiques of atonement theology are like magnets run over the biblical texts. They attract and lift out a whole range of problematic portions about which the church generally practices discreet avoidance. This would include the vast tracts of Hebrew scripture that deal with detailed purification rules and taboos, with sacrifice and its proper exercise or abuse. It would include the apocalyptic texts with all their martial imagery and catastrophic destruction. It includes the fact that biblical narratives and visions are laced with violence on every side, from Cain and Abel to Moses, David to Job, Tamar to the unnamed concubine of Judges 19, John the Baptist to John of Patmos. Children are massacred at the start of the Jesus story and he is executed at the end of it. Problematic passages include the long portions of the Psalms that harp harshly on the punishment of the wicked, portions regularly edited out of our responsive readings. In other words, the concerns about the cross readily connect with unease about elements in the Bible and Christian tradition more generally.

These are not academic matters. Rebecca Parker and Rita Nakashima Brock quote Lucia, an abused woman: "Mostly [my husband] is a good man. But sometimes he becomes very angry and he hits me. He knocks me

---

9. See, for instance, Rita Nakashima Brock and Rebecca Ann Parker, *Proverbs of Ashes: Violence, Redemptive Suffering, and the Search for What Saves Us* (Boston: Beacon Press, 2001); J. Denny Weaver, *The Nonviolent Atonement* (Grand Rapids: Eerdmans, 2001).

10. This is true for instance in the collective defense of a traditional theology of the atonement in Charles E. Hill and Frank A. James III, eds., *The Glory of the Atonement: Biblical, Historical, and Practical Perspectives; Essays in Honor of Roger Nicole* (Downers Grove, Ill.: InterVarsity, 2004). See Robert Sherman's argument to maintain a balance between a full range of atonement theories in Sherman, *King, Priest, and Prophet*. And it is true in Williams, *Sisters in the Wilderness*.

down. One time he broke my arm and I had to go to the hospital. . . . I went to my priest twenty years ago. I've been trying to follow his advice. The priest said I should rejoice in my sufferings because they bring me closer to Jesus. . . . He said, 'If you love Jesus, accept the beatings and bear them gladly, as Jesus bore the cross.'"[11] They sum up the short circuits and dead ends they see in any attempt to make saving sense of atonement theology:

> To say that Jesus' executioners did what was historically necessary for salvation is to say that state terrorism is a good thing, that torture and murder are the will of God. It is to say that those who loved and missed Jesus, those who did not want him to die, were wrong, that enemies who cared nothing for him were right. We believe there is no ethical way to hold that the Romans did the right thing. We will not say we are grateful or glad that someone was tortured and murdered on our behalf. The dominant traditions of Western Christianity have turned away from the suffering of Jesus and his community, abandoning the man on the cross.[12]

At an even more elemental level, Roberta Bondi tells of her own terrifying dream:

> I dreamed I was with Richard [her husband] in my great-aunt Blacky's farmhouse. . . . It was the middle of a good-smelling early summer day, with the insects humming and the hassock fan whirring on the front porch. Sunlight poured through the kitchen into the back hall where I was in darkness. I was sobbing and wringing my hands outside her green-tiled bathroom. In the bathroom Richard was kneeling in the bathtub, his neck held over the drain by a powerful looking, dark-haired man with a huge knife I knew had come to kill me. "Don't hurt her," Richard was saying. "Take me; just don't hurt her; take me."
>
> In my dream I was dying with grief. I wanted to shout "No, no; I'm here, leave Richard alone," but I couldn't make any sound. As I watched in horror, the killer slit Richard's throat and red blood flowed all over the green tiles.
>
> Then the dream was over, and I began to rise out of sleep, shiver-

---

11. Brock and Parker, *Proverbs of Ashes,* frontispiece.
12. Brock and Parker, *Proverbs of Ashes,* 49.

ing, sobbing, and covered with sweat. . . . In the very same instant the words formed in my mind, "this is what you've always thought the crucifixion is about, but this is not it," and I knew that both were true.[13]

But if this is not it, what is? That is our question.

Amazing Grace

To answer it, we have to take account of another sort of evidence as well. If we think globally, for every Christian who rejects or critiques sacrificial atonement (or in some cases, whose tradition simply has not emphasized it) there may well be several who affirm it. Countless lives have been liberated and transformed by that message. Take the example of a homeless gang member and terrorist in an African country who was about to lead the firebombing of a Christian evangelistic meeting. As he sat in the crowd for a few moments, waiting to signal for the killing to begin, he listened to what the preacher was saying about Jesus being executed by those he came to save, and making peace with God for us by his death.

> I could identify with this Jesus. He had suffered in all the ways that I knew so well. Poverty, oppression, hunger, thirst, loneliness. I had known all of these, and so had he. But the amazing thing was, he had not needed to know such suffering — but he had accepted it for my sake, to pay the price for my sins. My wages were death, but Jesus paid the price for me. On the cross he had become a nobody that I could become a somebody. . . . The transaction that Jesus was offering me suddenly became clear. . . . Tears for all the pain, loneliness, self-hatred and fear I had known coursed down my cheeks.[14]

The effect was profound and immediate. The man who had come for violence left in peace. Faith in the crucified one would lead him not only out of illiteracy and grinding poverty, but into a completely new life focused on reconciliation and service.

---

13. Roberta C. Bondi, *Memories of God: Theological Reflections on a Life* (Nashville: Abingdon, 1995), 112-13.

14. Stephen Lungu, with Anne Coomes, *Out of the Black Shadows: The Amazing Transformation of Stephen Lungu* (London: Monarch, 2001), 80-81.

One of my students, who had emerged from a grim history of abuse and addiction, shared her experience.

> Becoming a Christian did not make life easy. In fact, it was hard to deal with so many issues from my past that I had blocked out for so long. The change that saved me was feeling worthy to go on. I had been abused, and then misused my body so many times, that it felt like there was no way back. I don't need to do that anymore. To know that I was precious to God, so precious that Christ would bear that suffering for me, meant I was worth something, even if I couldn't feel it at first. I didn't even have to explain what it was like. God's been there. It's like being cleansed from the inside out.

An African American pastor in Brooklyn, famous for leadership in rebuilding his neighborhood, put special emphasis on reaching out to black men who were underrepresented in the church and socially endangered in so many dimensions. He focused that message of empowerment and renewal in an Easter sermon. "I've got news for you this mornin'. Brothers, I don't care who you are. I don't care what you done. I don't care what you ain't done. Jesus loves you. Jesus loves you, man. Paul said, 'But God commendeth His love toward us in that while we were yet sinners Christ died for us.' Do you know the gospel well enough to know that when Jesus died, He died for sinners? . . . When Jesus said, 'Come unto me, all ye that labor and are heavy laden,' He was talking to black men, too."[15]

André Trocmé, the legendary pastor of the French village of Le Chambon, led its people in the rescue of thousands of Jews during World War II, and went on to lead the Fellowship of Reconciliation. He stated concisely the conviction that animated his work: "Basic truth has been taught to us by Jesus Christ. What is it? The person of any one [hu]man is so important in the eyes of God, so central to the whole of His creation, that the unique, perfect being, Jesus, (a) sacrificed his earthly life for that one [hu]man in the street, and (b) sacrificed his perfection [by taking the blame for his sins] in order to save that single [hu]man."[16] The strangers who fled to Trocmé's door were people whose worth had already been es-

---

15. Samuel G. Freedman, *Upon This Rock: The Miracles of a Black Church*, 1st ed. (New York: HarperCollins, 1993), 189.

16. Quoted in Philip Paul Hallie, *Lest Innocent Blood Be Shed: The Story of the Village of Le Chambon, and How Goodness Happened There*, 1st ed. (New York: Harper and Row, 1979), 160.

tablished by the cross. He and his neighbors would risk going to the cross themselves to save them.

A prison reform advocate tells of traveling to visit a notorious prison in Latin America whose administration had been handed over to a Christian organization. The visitor reviewed improvements in health care and nutrition for inmates, and the partnerships established between each inmate and a family on the outside in preparation for release. He heard from the prisoners themselves who now did most of the work in running the institution and testified about the development of skills and a new sense of worth. His report contained the following portion:

> My guide escorted me to the notorious punishment cell once used for torture. Today, he told me, that block houses only a single inmate. As we reached the end of a long concrete corridor and he put the key into the lock, he paused and asked, "Are you sure you want to go in?"
>
> "Of course," I replied impatiently. . . . Slowly he swung open the massive door, and I saw the prisoner in that punishment cell: a crucifix, beautifully carved by the . . . inmates — the prisoner Jesus, hanging on the cross.
>
> "He's doing time for all the rest of us," my guide said softly.[17]

If the indictments we reviewed in the first part of the chapter are correct, then wherever you find people who actively embrace the theology of the cross, you should find destructive self-loathing, authorization for oppression, ready violence, and a religion of wrath. The cross holds back the weak and holds up the strong. Is that the case? There seems to be abundant evidence, to the contrary, that the cross can bring a power of release to the captive and a spirit of renunciation to the powerful.

As a supposed charter for oppression, the theology of the cross has a peculiar history among the poor and the marginalized. The testimony of numberless such persons indicates that they do not see in the cross a mandate for passive suffering of evil. Instead, in the midst of a world that regards them as nobodies, they see an unexpected and extraordinary affirmation of their individual worth. That Christ, that God, was willing to suffer and die specifically for them is a message of hope and self-respect that can hardly be measured, one that transforms their lives. That God

---

17. Rick Ezell, *Defining Moments: How God Shapes Our Character through Crisis* (Downers Grove, Ill.: InterVarsity, 2001), 43.

has become one of the broken and despised ones of history is an unshakable reference point from which to resist the mental colonization that insists that God belongs to the side of the powerful.

The liveliness of substitutionary atonement theology in storefronts and barrios and in the emerging centers of world Christianity in Africa and Latin America and Asia could stem from false consciousness, internalization of an oppressive ideology. Or it may arise because the social as well as the spiritual effects of the cross are more complicated than some assume. It may be that those powerless ones find the crucified Jesus in their place a source of self-respect that the rulers of this world cannot take away. Some protest that this affirmation comes at a cost. You cannot receive it unless you first abase yourself as a lost and helpless sinner in need of redemption. It is insult added to injury to ask those who are weakest to focus on their own shortcomings in this way. Of course, the oppressed are rarely unaware of their weakness. If anything, they have fewer means than the advantaged to deceive themselves about their need or their sins. They may be less offended that atonement theology presumes a human situation of bondage and moral need that they know all too well than they are grateful that the cross meets them precisely at this place, with the extraordinary insistence that nevertheless they are loved, worthy, and precious.[18]

Joy in God's love and grace, power for resistance, release from the burden of guilt and reproach, unstinting service to one's neighbors, heightened sensitivity to the suffering of the least — all these things have blossomed in the message of Christ's saving death. Such transforming and positive power appears regularly in the conversion stories of individuals and the substructure of movements.

The more closely we look, the more confused the situation seems. People are apparently considering the very same doctrine and concluding it is either the very best or the very worst, the most precious or the most pernicious. Even more perplexing, thoughtful people of either view recognize in some measure the reality represented by the other. Focus on Christ's sacrificial death has produced wildly divergent social effects. The cross has been carried at the head of crusades and pogroms. It has also hung in countless hospitals and inspired numberless acts of love and charity. It has challenged people to have compassion for the suffering, a compassion so far from condescension that it has gone to the point of identification.

18. See, for instance, Sharon G. Thornton, *Broken yet Beloved: A Pastoral Theology of the Cross* (St. Louis: Chalice, 2002).

It has inspired social reform. It has been a motive for ruthless persecution. It has drawn people into ascetic abnegation, sometimes to self-mutilation. It has stimulated extraordinary gratitude and confidence.

If nothing else, the atonement is a puzzle. The existing views seem to require a very large ad hoc component. That is, atonement theology is a profoundly destructive ideology that becomes for many the vehicle of life-changing grace and health. Or it is a precious revealed truth that frequently and inexplicably sows violence and dysfunction in its wake. No wonder those not passionately committed to either approach despair of sorting it all out. A solution to this mystery will have to do justice to these apparently conflicting realities. And that is the task we turn to now.

PART ONE

Things Hidden from the Foundation of the World

The Cross No One Sees

This was to fulfil what was spoken by the prophet: "I will open my mouth in parables, I will utter what has been hidden since the foundation of the world."

Matthew 13:35 RSV[1]

---

1. This text provides the title for René Girard, Jean-Michel Oughourlian, and Guy Lefort, *Things Hidden since the Foundation of the World* (Stanford, Calif.: Stanford University Press, 1987). Part 1, and especially chapter 3, draws on the substance of that book, and of René Girard, *The Scapegoat*, Johns Hopkins paperback ed. (Baltimore: Johns Hopkins University Press, 1989); René Girard, *Violence and the Sacred* (Baltimore: Johns Hopkins University Press, 1977).

CHAPTER TWO

The Cross No One Sees

Invisible Scapegoats

[M]ay we hate with a single soul: for this is man's great remedy.

Aeschylus, Eumenides[2]

Myth is the guilt of Oedipus; Truth is the innocence of Christ.

René Girard[3]

The New Testament and Christian tradition mold their understanding of Jesus' death around the story already begun in the Old Testament: the history of Israel stretching back to Genesis, and including the practice of sacrifice and the language of the Psalms and the prophets. Critical scholars add that this understanding was also influenced by the religions and culture of the Greek-speaking Mediterranean world of early Christianity. A favorite detail in paintings of the crucifixion shows a skull (variously understood as Adam's or Abel's) buried under the cross, a link between the way the good beginnings of the human story went astray and the way God has responded to set it right.

---

2. Quoted in René Girard, *Job, the Victim of His People* (Stanford, Calif.: Stanford University Press, 1987), 148.

3. René Girard and Michel Treguer, *Quand Ces Choses Commenceront* (Paris: Arlea, 1994), 154. This and subsequent translations from this book are my own.

We miss something crucial unless we start with this long view as well, setting the cross in the frame of all of human history as the early Christians did. They were convinced that the crucifixion directly addressed a universal human condition, a profound conflict between God and evil, and not merely the peculiar religious needs of a special tradition. But they were also quite aware that this was an odd claim to make for an execution, an event in which the world clearly saw no such thing. The cross and the resurrection changed these believers, by lighting up a problem they had never grasped so fully until they saw it so decisively challenged.

If the work of the cross is a universal saving act, there must be something universally wrong in human life that is directly involved in Jesus' death. But it must not be universally apparent, otherwise the crucifixion would be obvious good news rather than foolishness and a stumbling block. This is an odd prescription. We're looking for something invisible, a background so standard we can't see it, as a necessary context for the cross. As it turns out, in its use of the Old Testament to interpret Jesus' death, the early Christian community recognized that this context was already provided. But that is the focus of the next chapter. In this chapter I present one way that the death Jesus died is actually related to the very fabric of our wider human life, to the way we ward off uncontrollable violence and deal with crises of conflict in our communities.

The path of that presentation takes us directly into two of the problems that we briefly outlined in the last chapter. The first is the meaning of sacrifice. The treatment of Jesus' death in the New Testament and in later tradition is permeated with the language and images of sacrifice. To make sense of this we would seem to need some idea of what is going on in sacrifice generally. If educated people today don't think sacrifices actually work, why should we think Jesus' sacrifice changed anything? The second issue is related. Christians make extravagant claims about the significance of the cross, but study of world religions and mythology finds dying and rising gods on every side. If in fact there is value in such stories, Christianity makes a comparatively poor showing alongside traditions where the death and resurrection of deities is a regular occasion. Rather than having the unique dying and rising god, perhaps Christianity is unique for having *only* one, and in wanting to dispense with all others. If there is supposed to be spiritual value in the story of Jesus' passion, shouldn't there be as much value — or a lot more — in other myths? Religious history is full of sacrifices. Why should Jesus' sacrifice be more important than any other?

Our Problem with Sacrifice

Ritual sacrifice has been a feature of virtually every human civilization. It would seem that the purpose and function of anything so widespread, so evidently central in our developmental past, ought to be clear to us. The short and fascinating answer is that they are not. Several centuries of anthropology and the history of religions have made this a highly detailed mystery, but no less a mystery. We do not lack for theories, theories that link sacrifice to the hunt and to human dependence upon animals as prey; theories that link it to the maintenance of fertility in humans, animals, and crops; theories that see it as a bargaining exchange with divine powers; theories that see it as an artificial patriarchal construction of kinship to supplant the natural one in which women are preeminent as the birth-givers.[4]

Few besides specialized scholars show any interest in the contest among these theories, because we are confident it has no great importance. Our ancestors made a mistake. It doesn't much matter which one. We may not know what sacrifice meant in the past, but we are sure it means nothing now. Regardless of the details, sacrifice was simply a kind of protoscience, an illusory means to manipulate gods or nature when the two were not clearly distinguished. Sacrifice was a deluded technology. Its language lingers in our culture in the form of metaphor, as when we speak of someone making "the ultimate sacrifice." But the language does not refer to anything real.

Sacrifice was a practice found virtually everywhere in ancient religion. But those religions were also a bewildering tangle of mythic stories and elaborate codes of taboo and obligation. Our modern script on early human religion has two parts. The first part expresses our certainty that any belief in ritual or sacrificial causality recedes where science advances with knowledge of real causes. Sacrifice is extinct. We do not kill persons or goats to avert plagues; we get immunizations. The second part deals with what we might call the paraphernalia of ancient religion — the stories, images, and

---

4. A representative sampling is given in Jeffrey Carter, ed., *Understanding Religious Sacrifice: A Reader,* Controversies in the Study of Religion (London and New York: Continuum, 2003). For an interpretative summary of many of these theories, see John Milbank, "Stories of Sacrifice," *Contagion* 2 (1995). For an intense conversation among representatives of several major perspectives, see Walter Burkert et al., *Violent Origins* (Stanford, Calif.: Stanford University Press, 1987). To stress one theory does not necessarily imply that the elements described by others play no role, or deny that there may in fact have been different kinds of sacrifice.

myths that loosely belonged to the same cultural complex as the blood rituals. These materials we can treat in one of two ways. On the one hand, we are free to see in them the naive projections of earlier historical contexts, to see in the literature of early Israel, for instance, nothing but a cosmic projection of the landscape of a nomadic, herding community. The moral of this story is the same as the verdict on sacrifice as bad technology: these materials have nothing to do with us. On the other hand, we may find value in these texts, and even in their sacrificial imagery, as windows into deep structures of human imagination. Myth might speak in a language of symbolic archetypes that psychologists or anthropologists could plumb to discover something about enduring psychic dynamics. Taken literally and historically, myth is absurd. Its moral implications (if it had any) are likely obsolete. But treated as literature, it may illuminate human experience.

We believe real sacrifice — actually cutting a goat's throat, let alone entombing a man in the footings of a bridge — is foreign to us. It belongs to the past. When we find extensive instructions and regulations for the practice of blood rituals in traditional religious materials, we dismiss them as irrelevant to our religious understanding. When we encounter elaborate cultic traditions in which there is minute attention to the details of ritual practice, we pay little attention to the sacrificial models on which they may be patterned. When we encounter sacrificial themes in great texts of world religions (when we read in the Hindu Vedas, for instance, of the creation of the universe out of the sacrifice of a cosmic man, or of the royal horse sacrifice), we often find them in a mythic setting that readily allows us to treat them as symbolic parables. Such texts often (to our minds at least) show very little investment or interest in a literal reading of their own sacrificial scenarios. The biblical texts, by contrast, are increasingly perplexing to us precisely because of their literal attention to sacrificial practices and their serious engagement with issues of sacrificial causality. To some observers, this is an indication that Christianity is fatally entangled in prescientific notions of ritual effect, notions that are morally and mentally primitive. The death of Christ is the prime example.

Man's Great Remedy

More than any other individual, René Girard has challenged the assumptions we have just described. He has offered a dramatically different reading of sacrifice, religion, and society. For him sacrifice is not just a passing aspect of traditional religion, a dead end of prescientific ideas of cause and effect. It is much more central than that. Its origins date from a crucial transitional moment when life in the earliest social groups was just in the process, literally, of making us human. Sacrifice is the discovery that stands at the structural origin of both human society and human religion, explaining why the two emerge hand in hand. Girard's theory is that sacrifice is not a mistake. It is based on an actual cause and effect relation, one as real today as it ever was. Humans develop awe for a mysterious power of the "sacred" and society overcomes its first "political" problems because sacrifice works.

We can quickly paint this original situation as Girard imagines it. What distinguished emergent humans from other primates was an increased mental plasticity coupled with susceptibility to cultural formation, a combination that spurred an explosion beyond simple genetic selection.[5] In practical terms this meant that humans developed a radical mimetic capacity, a capacity not only to imitate others' behavior but also to shape our own inner life and consciousness on models we infer from others, through the empathetic "reading" of other minds. The result is a dramatic new level of novelty and creative advance, even though the process operates largely beyond conscious human control.

Our repertoire of behaviors is no longer fixed by a simple genetic plan. We are genetically programmed to be programmable through interaction with our environment, and above all through interaction with our human environment. We are face-readers, emotion-detectors, who from the beginning of our dependent infancies grow our own desires and patterns of behavior on the basis of models taken from others. No biological drive could be more basic than self-preservation, and yet human infants supplied with all the necessities of life but deprived of emotive interaction with adults sicken and die at catastrophic rates. It appears that we cannot even learn to love ourselves without a subjective model, without another whose affection directed at us we can imitate and make our own. We love because others first love us. Beyond a rudimentary set of intrinsic drives like hunger, thirst, and sex, we learn to desire what we infer other notable individuals in our circle find desirable.[6]

---

5. This seems to cohere well with much current scientific work on cognitive development. See S. Mark Heim, "A Cross-Section of Sin: The Mimetic Character of Human Nature in Biological and Theological Perspective," in *Evolution and Ethics: Human Morality in Biological and Religious Perspective,* ed. Philip Clayton and Jeffrey Schloss (Grand Rapids: Eerdmans, 2004).

6. This is a shorthand statement of Girard's "mimetic theory," which is the subject of books in its own right. Girard has most notably traced this dynamic in literature. See, for instance, René Girard, *Deceit, Desire, and the Novel: Self and Other in Literary Structure,* Johns

This dynamic obviously draws humans together into communities of a particularly intense sort. Mimetic openness brings a supercharged capacity for learning and a radical acceleration in transmission of new behaviors or information through a population. Culture becomes as important as biology. An individual's fortunate accident or discovery can quickly become the shared habit of a group and be passed on to subsequent generations. In fact, our facility at inferring others' motives and goals is itself a powerful engine for innovation. Humans frequently project onto their models programs of behavior or intentions *not* actually intended by those models, and such variations sometimes prove to be effective, drawing imitation in their turn. This is a rough analogy to gene mutation, though what has been altered in transmission in this case is not a molecular structure but a mental one.

This breakthrough comes with a dramatic drawback. This mutual responsiveness communicates destructive dynamics as quickly as constructive ones, with none of the innate limitations of purely biological inheritance. Anger, suspicion, and fear ricochet quickly from one mind to another like light bouncing from mirror to mirror, and their power multiplies. Accordingly, Girard believes that the primeval problem of early human groups was the contagion of retributive violence. Particularly in its infancy, social life is a fragile shoot, fatally subject to plagues of rivalry and vendettas. A purposeful or accidental injury to one person calls forth a response in kind from the injured party or the party's clan or tribe, which then calls forth the same in turn, until such feuding threatens to consume society. The exchange of tit for tat, once started, can engulf any community. "Lower" animals rarely fight to the death with their own kind, and there seem to be biological circuit breakers that curb the violence in tests of dominance, for instance, before it gets out of hand in a way that may destroy all participants. In gaining new powers, humans lost this protection. In rising above our animal neighbors, we fall below them as well, with distinctive new capacities for destruction that deserve their own name: sin.

One of the notable features of mimetic sensitivity is that we respond not only to others' concrete actions but also to perceived intentions. The person harmed may read an inadvertent injury as one inflicted on purpose. He or she responds with an intentional attack, aiming to do similar

---

Hopkins paperback ed. (Baltimore: Johns Hopkins University Press, 1976); René Girard, *A Theater of Envy: William Shakespeare, Odeon* (New York: Oxford University Press, 1991); René Girard, *"To Double Business Bound": Essays on Literature, Mimesis, and Anthropology* (Baltimore: Johns Hopkins University Press, 1978).

damage. This in turn is read as an assault driven by murderous hatred, and so elicits an all-out onslaught in terrified self-defense. Girard proposes that in a situation with no legal power and no mediating institutions, the contagious escalation of violence is the archetypal social disease. Without a cure, human community cannot get off the ground. As quickly as people are drawn together by these emergent sensibilities, they are driven apart by a parallel new class of interpersonal conflicts.[7]

As human communities struggle with this crisis, the means to break this vicious cycle appear as if miraculously. No one thought out this prescription. The antidote comes about without planning, and (a key point for Girard) its continued effectiveness depends upon a certain obscurity about how it works. At some point, escalating feud threatens to dissolve the community — a moment of "sacrificial crisis" in Girard's terms. Spontaneous and irrational collective violence rains down upon some distinctive person or minority in the group. The conflict rending the community is said to be all their fault, because of their "evil eye" perhaps, or because of some offense that has brought pollution and punishment to the group on their account. They are accused of the worst crimes the group can imagine, crimes whose very enormity would be sufficient to cause the terrible plight the community now experiences. They are lynched.

Thus far we have a picture of only an arbitrary act, a desperate lashing out against an illusory enemy. The reason such events did not remain sporadic, emotive footnotes in history is simple. The sad good in this bad thing is that it actually works. In the train of the murder the community finds that this sudden war of all against one delivers it from the war of each against all. The sacrifice of one person as a scapegoat discharges the pending acts of retribution between members of the group. It "clears the air." The contagion of reciprocal violence is suspended, a circuit breaker has been thrown. The collective violence is reconciling because it reestablishes peace. This benefit seems a startling, even magical result, an outcome much greater than could be expected from a simple mob execution.

---

7. This view assumes that violence was a common problem in early human groups and that normal life was marked by the reality and the anticipation of this threat. If violent conflict among humans arose only much later, then Girard's theory of origins has the wrong time line, though it could still be quite accurate as an empirical description of a later "fall" into mimetic conflict. Despite a tendency among many anthropologists during a certain period to assume the peacefulness of early societies, evidence seems to point strongly in the opposite direction. See Lawrence H. Keeley, *War before Civilization* (New York: Oxford University Press, 1996); Steven A. LeBlanc and Katherine E. Register, *Constant Battles: The Myth of the Peaceful, Noble Savage,* 1st ed. (New York: St. Martin's Press, 2003).

Such dramatic results confirm the desperate charges made against the victim to begin with. If the scapegoat's death is the solution, the scapegoat must have been the cause.

On the other hand, the restored peace sheds an aura of gratitude over the same scapegoat. The death has such reconciling effect that it seems the victim must possess supernatural power. The one mobbed as the most reprehensible criminal now is revered as the bringer of peace, one with a divine vocation to die and restore order for the people. So the victim becomes a god, memorialized in myth, and the killing becomes a feature of a foreordained plan, a pattern and a model. In the face of future threats, a similar response will be required. Rituals of sacrifice originated in this way, tools to fend off social crisis. And in varied forms they are with us still. This, in a nutshell, is Girard's account of the origin of religion, which is twinned with the beginning of human society proper.

The ritual cure is a homeopathic one. It uses violence to drive out violence. But a very specific dose and type are required. It is crucial that it be collective violence (in which all, at least implicitly, participate) and that it not itself set off any further cycle of vengeance. The divisions in the community must be reduced to but one division, the most unbalanced one possible, many against a few or one. The victims must also meet certain criteria. They must be persons who are least likely to enlist kin or allies, or call forth any retaliation on their behalf. It is eminently reasonable then to fix particularly upon the marginal and the weak. To forestall any motive for revenge and to maintain the unanimity of the persecutors there must be unassailable justification for the sacrifice of the individuals in question. Therefore it is predictable, Girard maintains, that these individuals will be charged with violating the community's most extreme taboos. It would be well if the victims themselves affirmed their guilt, or could be claimed to have done so.

Perhaps an example that helps Western readers grasp that we are not talking about something in only a hypothetical prehistory is that of classical Greece. Athens in the fifth century B.C. was the city of Pericles, of an early (if very limited) democracy and of an artistic flowering that had just built the Parthenon. It was also, Girard reminds us, a city that continued an ancient practice of maintaining a stable of captives and criminals as sacrificial victims for times of special crisis.[8] On those occasions one of these

8. It is interesting to note that the famous band of sculptures that ringed the Parthenon itself depicts a procession that includes sacrificial animals and vessels, long thought to be a procession for a celebration of a festival of Athena, the patron goddess of Athens. It has

would be led around the city to be abused by all the citizens and then executed or violently driven out. The word for such persons was *pharmakos,* derived from *pharmakon,* a word that can mean both poison and remedy (from which we get "pharmacy"). The person sacrificed served at once to absorb and represent all that was wrong — the infection in the body — and also (by his death) to provide the antidote or remedy for the problem. Violence is the disease that needs curing, and violence is the cure.

One of the most profound features of Greek tragedy is that in it extraordinary flashes of awareness of the reality behind this practice occasionally surface. Girard notes, for instance, a passage from Aeschylus's *Eumenides* in which a plaintive hope is expressed:

> This I pray: May faction, insatiate of ill,
>   never raise her loud voice in this city.
> May not the dust that drinks the black blood of citizens
>   in its passion for vengeance,
>   demand a bloody ransom to still the city's frenzy.
> May joy be exchanged for joy
>   in a common love
>   and may we hate with a single soul:
>   for this is man's great remedy.[9]

What is wished *never* to be so is, by implication, precisely what is regularly the case. Faction arises in the city and the violent conflict among citizens rouses a passion for vengeance that can be satisfied only with a "bloody ransom" of the *pharmakos* type. Uniting in hatred toward the sacrificial victim is the only way to still the city's frenzy. And even in wishing for a world in which no divisions ever arise, and so no violence ensues, and then no sacrifices are required, the writer still wholeheartedly endorses the underlying principle of unanimity that depends on "hate with a single soul."[10]

---

recently been proposed that instead the central scene of the procession depicts a mythical founding event for the city, when to save it from defeat the king offered his three daughters as sacrifices. See Joan B. Connelly, "Parthenon and Parthenoi: A Mythological Interpretation of the Parthenon Frieze," *American Journal of Archaeology* 100, no. 1 (1996).

9. Aeschylus, *Eumenides,* quoted in Girard, *Job,* 148.

10. The prospect of a world without sacrifice is a deeply unsettling one for the writers who achieve this level of insight, and Aeschylus here raises what he sees as the danger of such a world. The city cannot survive without the power of collective hatred to maintain unity, and this prayer expresses the reassuring hope that the power of such hate — the great remedy — would not be lost even if there were no internal divisions in the community.

The few unsettling glimpses of the "back stage" of sacrifice in Greek tragedies end with a drawing back, a fatalism and even fear. In another play by Aeschylus, *Agamemnon,* after the failure of animal offerings the king proceeds to sacrifice his own daughter. He commands a gag to be brought, lest her pleas be heard and weaken the community's resolve. At the climactic moment of killing, there is no description given. The chorus in one voice says,

> The rest I did not see,
> Nor do I speak of it.[11]

The glimpse behind myth has its limits. Any reservations about sacrifice could weaken its effectiveness and deliver the community over to complete disintegration. It is better not to have inquired into these things. And if one has already learned too much, it is better to forget. So the chorus concludes in Euripides' *The Bacchae:*

> No mortal ought
> To challenge Time — to overbear
> Custom in act, or age in thought.
> All men, at little cost, may share
> The blessing of a pious creed;
> Truths more than mortal, which began
> In the beginning, and belong
> To very nature — these indeed
> Reign in our world, are fixed and strong.[12]

Sacred Violence

Obviously, Girard has no direct evidence for his prehistorical scenario any more than others do who offer their own versions of the origin of society (like Rousseau or Hobbes or Freud). A "founding murder" is not an event we can verify. It is a hypothesis whose value depends on its capacity to account for a wide range of evidence that otherwise seems contradictory or

---

11. See the discussion of this text in Gil Bailie, *Violence Unveiled: Humanity at the Crossroads* (New York: Crossroad, 1995), 32.

12. Euripides, *"The Bacchae" and Other Plays,* trans. Philip Vellacott (Baltimore: Penguin Books, 1972), 223.

unintelligible. There are no smoking guns for founding murder, only arguments that attempt to integrate many odd pieces of religion and culture into a single puzzle. Among other things, it helps us understand why in so many cultures the observance of sacrificial rites is attended with such seriousness, with such concern for unanimity and detail, and with profound dread of catastrophic results if the event goes wrong. To defuse social conflict, the sacrificial process plays out the disease it is to cure, stirring up an epidemic of animosity or fear in order to focus it on the ritual act. If this epidemic gets out of hand, no one is safe.[13] The elaborate cautions and awe that mark these rituals in traditional societies testify that this process is always fraught with danger. Ritual sacrifice is like a backfire started to consume the dry fuel in the path of a raging forest fire, and so to protect a town. The element of defense is the same as the element of destruction. Everything depends on using it in a carefully controlled and limited way. Failed sacrifice only inflames the problem it was to solve.

This is a crucial aspect of the reconciliation that flows from sacrifice. If it is to succeed in "burying the hatchet," there must be no raw edges left that can set off recrimination or conflict. This is the same logic that even in modern societies prescribes masks for public executioners. Individual identity is hidden to foreclose impulses toward revenge, for the point of legal capital punishment is to stop the exchange of private violence with a measured act carried out impersonally by the entire community. In unsuccessful sacrifice, that unity and certainty are lacking. Extraordinary steps are taken in the ritual process to try to separate off this violence from the kind it is meant to stop (to make it not even "count" as violence), to distinguish the reconciling blood of the scapegoat from the incendiary blood of ordinary conflict. But all these steps can fail. And then the attempt at unifying murder does not produce peace and a unanimous "cover story" but instead becomes itself an occasion of division and escalating conflict, violence that begets violence. The execution of a rebel or the leader of a faction, a martyrdom, is almost necessarily ineffective as a sacrifice for these reasons. It entrenches conflict and whets the appetite for revenge.

Anthropologists have long remarked on a duality in traditional religion. On the one hand, any violation of religious taboos brings a heavy

---

13. This is illustrated in Euripides' *The Bacchae*. A sacrificial festival is disrupted and the result is an orgy of indiscriminate violence in which people are so maddened that they cannot distinguish each other from animals.

burden of impurity and sanction on the offender, and yet the most sacred religious rituals practiced in the community often expressly require violations of those same taboos. The one offered as a sacrifice is reverenced as holy, but at the same time is held guilty of or made to formally act out some horrific crime. The being ritually sacrificed is typically to be "without blot or blemish" according to the purity standards of the culture. But the sacrificial process often involves a violation of those same standards — for instance, a specific mutilation of the offering. The sacrificed subject is the object of both condemnation and honor.

This contradictory situation makes sense in Girard's view. The sacrificial mechanism produces this polarity, since the victim is viewed as powerful and holy, because capable of producing such benevolent results, but also eminently deserving of death for having transgressed the most profound commandments. One will search in vain for a consistent list of features inherent to the entities classified in the category of "the sacred," even though the category itself exists in all cultures. Girard claims to see the explanation for both the differences and the commonality. Persons are not chosen to be killed because they are sacred, because they belong to some special if elusive class. They are "sacred" because they are chosen to be killed. It is designation for sacrifice, by whatever formula, that constitutes something as sacred. Designated victims are holy because their death has a supernatural, reconciling power.

The great anthropologists catalogued innumerable variations on this process. In some cases it is a king or a priest who ritually transgresses the most awful taboos as a preliminary to being sacrificed (literally or figuratively) to renew the people. In other cases it is a prisoner of war, an outcast, or a common criminal who is elevated to a place of honor and rendered all manner of service prior to sacrifice. This model is well known from the Aztec example. What prisoners of war from outside a society and kings who rule in it have in common is that they can easily be isolated, the one by their strangeness and the other by their eminence (kings belong to a class that by definition has only one member). Ideal sacrificial victims must be without ties or supporters that would stand in the way of their execution, but their identification with the community must be sufficient so as to embody the evil, the polluting crime to be purged with their destruction. The cause of the sacrificial crisis is to be found somewhere within the community itself, but in someone whose supposed offense removes any possible ties or sympathy. The contrary treatments of the criminal and the king thus point in the same ultimate direction, meeting the requirements of the sacred. The king, who is a consummate insider, must be dramatically separated and condemned, while the prisoner of war, who already bears the onus of a criminal or enemy, must be adopted in such a manner as to have a veneer of identity with his captors.

The disorienting inconsistency in the condemnation and honor extended to the victim is understandable in light of those two essential if paradoxical qualities of the sacred: the transgressions that rightly merit sacrifice and the honor due one whose death saves society. Girard suggests that only such an insight can make sense of data like an African investiture hymn for a king that contains the following formula.

You are a turd,
You are a heap of refuse,
You have come to kill us,
You have come to save us.[14]

Incest is one of the classic prohibitions that figure in this ritual process. In an example from another African tribe, there is at intervals a sacrificial rite in which the king and his mother are brought before the people, bound like captives condemned to death. Beside them, a bull and a cow are clubbed to death and slaughtered, and some of the blood poured over the king. Then, to great acclaim and reverence, he resumes his royal role.[15] Thus, Girard suggests, an original scenario in which the sacrificial victims were charged with incest is played out and the benefits of social cohesion harvested.

The same contradictory tensions are imparted also to the deities that preside over sacrifice. The most ancient tradition of the god Dionysus presents him as a deity who inspires his worshipers to violent mob frenzies. It is striking that this figure, who instigates such terrible outbreaks of bloodshed, is regarded not only with fear but also with profound gratitude and reverence. Dionysus represents both the consuming violence that threatens to destroy society and the decisive sacrificial violence that preserves it. Since the cure is a special dose of the disease itself, it makes sense that the master of one is the master of the other.

The gods of sacrifice are often also worshiped and praised as the sources of culture and the arts, patrons of all the blessings of civilized life.

---

14. Girard, *Violence and the Sacred,* 107.

15. Girard, *Violence and the Sacred,* 106. Girard quotes from an account by Luc de Heusch, "Aspects de la sacralité du pouvoir en Afrique," in Luc de Heusch, *Le Pouvoir Et Le Sacré* (Brussels: Université libre de Bruxelles Institut de sociologie, 1962).

This is not far from the actual truth, for it is the reconciling effects of uniting around the victim that make that life possible. Buried in the complicated complex of ritual and myth is the knowledge that our life together is bought with a price, and that the price must be paid regularly.

These "primitive" practices perplex us, who feel ourselves insulated from the dangers they address. We see the extravagant accusations of crimes, and wonder why these people have such an irrational approach to justice. We see the honor and awe directed at the sacrificed one, and wonder why the admirers are so fickle. But if we see nothing but superstition, Girard argues, we are the primitives. Sacrifice meets a desperately real problem, a problem for which we have not yet entirely substituted a different solution.

Myths of Sacrifice

However, we still have only part of the picture. So far we have focused on explicit accounts of sacrificial rituals. But we noted that the scapegoating process itself is mysterious to those who participate in it. Its effectiveness has a miraculous quality. Its actual components are hidden on several levels. First of all, the only problem that sacrifice truly has the power to solve is social division. Yet the community usually names the crisis it is experiencing in other, more proximate terms: the prospect of defeat in war, an infestation of plague, a curse from the gods or attacks from demonic forces. Real, or believed to be real, all such situations have the same effect. They threaten to immerse the community in what Girard calls nondifferentiation, a crisis in which all the distinctions and roles that block mimetic contagions of envy, suspicion, and retaliation fall away and conflict threatens to run wild. The ordinary curbs on our extreme mutual susceptibility are erased. A plague or a siege may bring a community to the extreme point where parents compete with children for food, and neighbors fear and suspect each other of treason or infection. Everyone becomes a model for everyone else, and everyone models the same thing: defensive fear, preemptive attack. Sacrificial rituals or mob persecution won't stop germs or invading armies, but they can address the quite real effects of both on the internal life of a community.

Second, the cause of the crisis is misattributed in a consistent manner. As to *what* wrong brings on the crisis, it is assumed to be a violation of the most sacred obligations that the society knows, offenses so dramatic that they seem to draw collective disaster upon the group. A community's taboos are largely constructed precisely to limit the negative propagation of imitative competition and conflict, by erecting differentiation among groups and individuals, specifying kinship locations and roles. Being too much the same leads too easily to rivalry and social conflict. The worst violations then are crimes that blur these distinctions. Incest blurs the family differentiation. Bestiality blurs the species distinction. Blasphemy blurs the line between gods and humans. For some tribal groups, even using the face painting or clothing that is the signature of another clan can be a cataclysmic offense.

As to *who* is guilty of the crisis-causing act, the accusation will name someone who has committed incest, or witchcraft, or blasphemy, or some other crime that upsets order and offends the divine. The one named will likely prove to have qualities quite unrelated to the accusation, qualities that make her or him liable to marginalization or isolation. Whether one person or a few, they will start with few natural defenders and end with none. If becoming too much the same is a cause of crisis, being too different makes you a prime candidate to become the scapegoat blamed for the crisis. The choice of a victim is in truth an arbitrary act. It does not have to do with the guilt of the accused but with the need of the community. This arbitrariness is sometimes given implicit expression in sacrificial rituals by the use of games of chance or casting lots to fix on the final victim from among several options. This is associated with the belief that chance reflects the divine will. The god identifies the chosen one in this impersonal manner, one that further insulates sacred murder from the nexus of interpersonal revenge. No specific accuser can be held responsible for the choice, and the collective nature of the violence is enhanced.

In other words, in perfectly good faith both the nature of the crisis and the kind of behavior responsible for it are described in mistaken terms. This misunderstanding serves to increase the effectiveness of the sacrificial process. It works more smoothly when "we know not what we do." If it were obvious to all that sacrifice was a ploy in the ordinary round of rivalry and violence, a bone thrown to satisfy everyone's lust for revenge, it would be much less effective. The questions would turn inevitably back upon the act itself. Without a canopy of sacred awe and the conviction of unspeakable crimes, suspicions might arise about whether the victim was chosen arbitrarily, about the interests of those who picked the victim, about the possibility that we too could become victims. In virtually all traditions it is not considered safe or auspicious to pry too much into the sacrificial mysteries, for fear that this will derail their success.

Participants in sacrifice believe they are (a) revenging an appalling offense against the entire community, (b) expelling a contaminating evil from their midst, and (c) obeying a divine mandate. In fact, the entire process is viewed as an organized supernatural plan for human benefit, with even sacrificed victims retrospectively endorsing the event when they become a patron deity for the community or are identified with that deity. After the fact of a scapegoating episode, and, even more emphatically, after the ritual enactment of such a scapegoating event, the participants perceive nothing questionable about what has happened. The category of murder, or even of killing, does not enter their minds at all, any more than some of us may spontaneously deploy those terms in reference to spiders in our housecleaning or fish as we shop at the grocery store. What is perceived and remembered is a mythical image of what the event does and what it means.

Ritual sacrifice is only one feature of traditional religion, which includes much more. Notably, it includes myth, a wide range of stories and imagery, some dealing with questions as apparently straightforward as how the leopard got his spots, some obscure and puzzling in the extreme. Myths are another example of odd pieces of evidence, many of which fall into meaningful order around the scapegoat hypothesis. Girard's contention is that much of the mythic tradition, and especially those myths associated with the origins and identity of a community, is in fact sacrificial in content. Often such myths are explicitly featured in the rituals themselves. But on the surface these myths describe something quite different from the sacrificial event. Scapegoating is the event. Myth is the memory and the image of the event as perceived by those who carry it out. The first is real, bloody and effective. The second is oblique and much less explicit about the violence and its nature.

Myth is on the one hand a record of this sacrificial practice and a prescription for its future repetition. It is a literary account that remembers the pharmacy of antidotes to be applied when the community faces crisis. But as a record it is also, necessarily, a lie. Myth is an account of a murder that routinely obscures the fact that it was murder at all. It describes a collective killing that was completely justified, entirely necessary, divinely approved and powerfully beneficent. It is a record that stems, after all, from killers who are untroubled by any doubt about what they have done. The myth understands the sacrifice it embodies as something like a force of nature or an action of the gods. The one sacrificed may be clearly present in the myth, but there is no actual victim apparent there. The one sacrificed has been dehumanized or divinized beyond recognition. The unbroken continuity of consciousness between producers and consumers of the myth from generation to generation is precisely the invisibility of the victim as a victim. Like the chorus in the Greek tragedy, they can say, "The rest I did not see, nor do I speak of it."

Girard relates an Ojibwa myth that says the five constitutive clans of the Ojibwa people originated when six supernatural beings emerged from the ocean to mingle with humans.[16] One kept his eyes covered constantly and dared not look at the people. But overcome with curiosity, he finally lifted the veil slightly, and his glance fell on a person who was struck dead instantly. The five other beings therefore immediately "caused him to return to the bosom of the great water." From these remaining five, the five clans of the people descended. This tale describes no explicit sacrifice, but Girard maintains it reflects the founding, scapegoat dynamic. One in the group has an "evil eye" that deals death. There is no wider context or explanation given. The six divine beings are the same, except that one is set off by this destructive power and the guilt (even accidental) of killing by this uncanny means. As a result, the other five unite against him and throw him in the ocean. And from that collective violence of the five originates the entire lineage of the people. The expulsion of the sixth is the founding of culture and community.

One of Girard's favorite examples is the myth of Oedipus. This is the familiar Greek story of a stranger, ignorant of his own parentage, who comes to Thebes, marries its widowed queen and becomes its king. Plague and crisis descend on the city. Oedipus embarks on an unrelenting quest to discover the great criminal in the community whose offenses have brought this punishment from the gods, only to realize that he is the offender. All unknowing, he has killed his father and married his mother. For these violations of the most fundamental order, he mandates and accepts his own violent expulsion. The story underwent many transmutations in the Western tradition, from a mythic tradition, to the great tragic play cycle of Sophocles, to Freud's famous psychological theory that boys subconsciously desire to displace their fathers and marry their mothers. In all these variations of the story, Girard notes, one key point remains fixed: Oedipus is guilty as charged. This is the premise of the myth itself, and even those like Freud whose whole interpretation prides itself on seeing beneath the literal face value of the story never question it. The assumption seems to be a necessary part of the story, even if the story itself never happened.

But Girard sees the story as a classic myth of sacrificial crisis, oriented

---

16. The myth is recounted in Lévi-Strauss, *Totemism,* and quoted by Girard in Girard, Oughourlian, and Lefort, *Things Hidden,* 105-6.

in this case to unanimous focus on the king as the scapegoat. The setting is clearly just the sort of crisis for which Athens kept its *pharmakos* captives. Thebes is wracked by plague and the city is disintegrating in mutual suspicion over who is to blame. The charges against Oedipus have exactly the extreme character that would account for the turmoil and unite citizens in horror against him. The story's report that Oedipus committed his crimes by mistake, that he is as horrified as anyone else, and that he in fact joins the unanimous judgment in favor of his punishment reflects the perception of the community regarding the sacrificial act. That is, these elements deflect any possible doubt about the course of action and affirm a restored, universal agreement. There is no trace of any contestation of the charges. Oedipus is the chief witness for the prosecution. It was all an implacable mystery of fate, and Oedipus's punishment is in accord with a divine wisdom before which humans can only bow in a kind of shocked awe.

Sacrifice and myth are thus two sides of Girard's theory. His view of founding murder as the basis of sacrifice has not replaced all the other contending theories.[17] But even many who think sacrifice originated in some other way or serves additional purposes accept that it may also have the scapegoating dimension he highlights. A larger number object to his treatment of myth, particularly his insistence on seeing violence behind texts that outwardly have no such explicit theme. Doesn't Girard's approach become as arbitrary as Freudian psychology, imposing its preferred interpretation on obscure images with no real empirical test? What makes us think we can look "behind" these myths with such confidence?

Suspecting Myth

To this objection he has a very specific response, drawn not from the prehistorical past but from relatively recent history. In his book *The Scapegoat*

---

17. Girard's view need not be seen as a totalistic account of traditional religion. That is, sacrifice can be more than Girard says it is, and traditional religion can be more than sacrifice. So there may be certain practices of sacrifice that are about exchange with the divine, even in private, individual terms. And there are features of religion that deal with other issues important in their own right, such as life after death, moral codes, coming-of-age events, and so on. My argument is not that traditional religion was nothing but the practice of sacrifice or that there are no other factors in ritual sacrifice but the scapegoating ones. For the purposes of this book it is fully sufficient that the dynamic Girard describes has been a real factor in sacrifice and religion. It is this factor that is of special interest for understanding the cross.

Girard begins with an examination of a fourteenth-century poem by Guillaume de Machaut that recounts the devastation of the Black Death in a northern French city. The poem is replete with tales of extraordinary events. It describes Jews in the city killing large numbers of its citizens by poisoning the rivers, and enumerates various grotesque practices by Jews. It recounts massacres carried out against the Jewish community in the city. It details miraculous heavenly signs. Girard notes that modern readers decode this text with confident unanimity. We discriminate between what is historically true and what is historically false in the chronicle. There really was an epidemic of disease. Masses of people really died. Jews really were massacred and were really blamed for the plague. But stars did not fall to earth. Jewish women did not practice bestiality and give birth to piglets. The rivers were not actually poisoned. There was no conspiracy to kidnap and torture Christian children. The poem reports all these things as facts. But we conclude that the true story was actually this: frightened citizens persecuted a religious minority, projecting blame for the plague on them and seeking by violence to stop the dissolution of their community.

Girard asks a simple question. With an author who reports so many things we regard as fantastic, why do we credit anything he says as true — let alone suppose we can pick out fact and illusion in such a detailed way? The answer of course has something to do with general knowledge. Interspecies breeding of pigs and humans is not possible. But the primary kind of knowledge involved is a rather different type, a knowledge of what he calls "texts of persecution." We don't take this story at face value. We see through it precisely when it takes up certain anti-Semitic themes. The moment Jews are mentioned in connection with plague, the moment they are accused of poisoning the water supply, of bearing physical deformities, of practicing sexual perversions, bells go off. These are stereotypes, trotted out again and again as preludes to pogroms. They are characteristic "marks of the victim" brought forward as justification for the violence. We do not credit them as reports of facts. We have learned to read such a text quite against the grain of the writer who composed it, for whom these matters were as real as the death of neighbors on the one hand and celestial omens on the other. We practice a hermeneutic of suspicion against persecution. We have become actually quite obsessive about reading texts this way, always alert to a possible hidden story of domination that runs against the surface meaning.

We may well ask where this way of reading came from. And we will return to that question in coming chapters. But for the moment Girard has another question. Why don't we read myths this way? The criticism was

that Girard insists on applying an arbitrary and idiosyncratic interpretation to mythology. Girard turns this around: Why do we fail to ask the
same questions of myth that we ask of all other texts? When the same dynamics, the same stereotypes of persecution, appear in myths, why do we
fail to apply any of the principles just noted? Because, we will be told,
myths are not historical at all. There is no need to draw a line between
truth and falsehood in them because they do not belong to a category
where such labels apply. Only an uneducated literalist would look for historical truth in mythic stories. They belong to an entirely different plane,
where we ask entirely different questions. We are sophisticated people,
who have passed beyond naive notions that myths deal with facts. They
are all about images and symbols. And so they are exempted from our historical suspicions.

Girard views this attitude as anything but rational. In fact, he views it
as the height of superstition. Many myths have a very concrete historical
and social content. They are quite literally about sacred murder, the collective violence whose aim is to contain the spread of interpersonal conflict. When we read the story of Oedipus, we should be suspicious of exactly the same elements we are suspicious of in de Machaut's poem.
Oedipus has many of the marks of the victim. He is a foreigner and
stranger who has become surprisingly powerful and prosperous. He is
both a minority and an object of envy and resentment. He has a physical
deformity (a lame leg). He is charged with some classic scapegoat offenses:
incest, killing his father. Oedipus is presented to us as both a king and a
criminal, a prime profile for sacrifice. We can infer a victim behind the
Oedipus text as well as we can infer one behind de Machaut's poem.

People in the past, who took myth literally, were at the same time con-
firming the society's sacrificial practice and misconceiving it. They remained blind to what the myth itself suppresses, the scapegoating of an
innocent victim. Such myths are in fact themselves texts of persecution, in
which we find regularly all the same elements as may be found in
Guillaume de Machaut's fourteenth-century anti-Semitic chronicle.
Myths record and replicate the collective violence of sacrifice, but in such
a way as to cover up the murder at the same time. The collective persecution of an arbitrary, innocent victim does not appear as such, but only in a
guise that obscures the innocence of the victim, or the arbitrariness of the
victim's selection, or the reality of the collective violence, or all three. To
repeat, the myth that does this is accurately reflecting the sincere view-
point of the whole community that practiced the sacrifice, but not telling
the truth.

Girard argues that our dominant modern interpretations of myth — "demythologizing" and avant-garde though they fancy themselves — are in large measure similar to traditional literal readings. They perform the same function as the literal reading, which is to draw attention away from the collective violence that occasioned the myth. Such interpretations shield myths from the hermeneutic of suspicion that has been otherwise extended to all historical texts. The sacrificial mechanism is alive and well among us, and for this reason myths have profound relevance to us today. But Girard suggests that those who are the greatest enthusiasts for myth systematically miss the true nature of that relevance. In determinedly steering all who would approach myth into any avenue but serious consideration of their collective sacrificial function, in convincing us that myths must be read differently than other human texts (and so immunized to the hermeneutic of suspicion), such intellectuals play a role identical to that of ancient priests who warned people against looking too closely into the sacred mysteries.

We can take a simple example of what Girard means. It comes from one of the major interpreters of myth in our time, Joseph Campbell, and his dialogues with Bill Moyers. Campbell explains that the death and resurrection of a savior figure is a common motif in the legends of agricultural societies, since it represents the reality of the cycle of the growth of vegetation: seeds are sown in the earth, grow up into plants that then die and decompose into the earth from which new life arises.

> **Campbell**: The death and resurrection of a savior figure is a common motif in all these legends. . . . Somebody has had to die in order for life to emerge. I begin to see this incredible pattern of death giving rise to birth, and birth giving rise to death. Every generation has to die in order that the next generation can come.
>
> **Moyers**: You write, "Out of the rocks of fallen wood and leaves, fresh sprouts arise, from which the lesson appears to have been that from death springs life, and out of death new birth. And the grim conclusion drawn was that the way to increase life is to increase death. Accordingly, the entire equatorial belt of this globe has been characterized by a frenzy of sacrifice — vegetable, animal and human sacrifice."
>
> **Campbell**: There is a ritual associated with the men's societies in New Guinea that actually enacts the planting-society myth of death, resurrection and cannibalistic consumption. . . .

Campbell goes on to describe a long religious festival and sexual orgy, where all kinds of taboos are broken and some young boys undergo sexual initiation. The boys come one by one into a specially constructed log hut to have their first sexual experience with a young woman dressed up as a deity.

> **Campbell**: . . . And when the last boy is with her in full embrace, the supports are withdrawn, the logs drop, and the couple is killed. There is the union of male and female again, as they were in the beginning, before the separation took place. There is the union of begetting and death. They are both the same thing.
>
> Then the little couple is pulled out and roasted and eaten that very evening. The ritual is the repetition of the original act of the killing of a god followed by the coming of the food from the dead savior. In the sacrifice of the Mass, you are taught that this is the body and blood of the Savior. You take it to you, and you turn inward, and there he works within you.
>
> **Moyers**: What is the truth to which the rituals point?
>
> **Campbell**: The nature of life itself has to be realized in the acts of life. In the hunting cultures, when a sacrifice is made, it is, as it were, a gift or a bribe to the deity that is being invited to do something for us or to give us something. But when a figure is sacrificed in the planting cultures, that figure itself is the god. The person who dies is buried and becomes the food. Christ is crucified, and from his body the food of the spirit comes.
>
> The Christ story involves a sublimation of what originally was a very solid vegetal image. . . .[18]

This is a quite extraordinary passage. Campbell is certain that the myths in question represent the natural agricultural cycle of life, under the image of a dying and rising god whose body is the food. He notes that there are even sometimes rituals in which people literally act out the mythical image. What is amazing is that though actual killing is at the very center of the event Campbell narrates, it seems virtually invisible to him. What are we to make of Campbell describing how in reality the sacrificed "little couple" are pulled out, cooked, and eaten, only to have Moyers ask, apparently with a straight face, "What is the truth to which the rituals point?" In other words, the truth is not that two people have been killed. That is only a ritual detail that points to the real meaning of the

---

18. Joseph Campbell and Bill D. Moyers, *The Power of Myth,* 1st ed. (New York: Double-day, 1988), 106-7.

myth, its representation of nature's process of birth and rebirth, the unity of male and female, death and life.

The killing happens before their very eyes, so to speak, and it does not register at all, except as a symbolic sign. Myth is the true reality; sacrificial violence is only a simpleminded pantomime of it. For some reason these tribal people felt compelled to literally act out what was only a metaphor to begin with: the story of a dying god, whose actual meaning merely refers to the natural cycles of plant life. Campbell has the highest regard for the wisdom reflected in this violent ritual practice. But, not to put too fine a point on it, his admiration presumes that these people are much stupider than Girard believes them to be. They are murderers for no real reason. They kill to reinforce the natural cycle by feeding it human blood.

Girard's view is quite the reverse. Campbell believes that first there was myth, using the metaphor of dying and rising to describe nature, and then people started to actually act out the metaphor in ritual. But Girard contends that first there was actual violent scapegoating, and then comes the mythologizing of this practice, using themes like the agricultural cycle to make human violence as natural and unexceptionable as the seasons. Even leaving aside the question of which came first, Girard's argument is that sacrifice endured because it had real social effects, not just because people couldn't catch on that it had no causal control over the natural world.

He maintains that behind the mythic stories there are real victims whose reality and voice have been ignored in the telling, just as Moyers and Campbell ignore them in this telling. The violence of ritual sacrifice is not an odd quirk of playacting, but a serious repetition of the active reconciling ingredient in original religion. It is not an accident that the festival Campbell describes was marked by riotous violation of the community's rules, or that the selected victims were engaged in a sexual relation between a human and a figurative god, a blurring of boundaries likely to bring calamity and worthy of being punished. All the social functions of sacrifice are seen by Campbell as somehow analogies from nature. But to Girard, the overlay of analogies to nature is secondary to the primary social origins and function of sacrifice.

Campbell is explicit about the reality of sacrifice in a way traditional myth is not, even as he glosses over it. This testifies implicitly to a sea change we will begin to take up in the next chapter. Yet so enamored is Campbell of the mythic account, that even when it is clearly enacted in history with real victims in the roles, those victims virtually disappear. Spellbound by myth, we don't register the violence in front of us. The symbols are real. The "little couple" isn't. Girard says founding myths are not imaginary things presented in the misleading guise of historical or literal narrative. They reflect a very literal history, veiled in the misleading guise of symbolic imagery. The central plot of much myth is a very real and recurrent historical event. Myth itself is a lie humanity has been telling itself about that event. And much modern self-congratulatory critical study swallows the lie as much as any ancient tribe did. "Our lack of belief serves the same function in our society that religion serves in societies more directly exposed to essential violence."[19]

Sacrifice Now

What distinguishes Girard's view is the conviction that sacrifice is a real solution to a real problem. Even more controversially, he suggests that the problem remains real for us as well. We have many features in our society that separate us from early human communities. We have police forces and legal systems, meant to preserve a monopoly of force for the government and to prevent outbreaks of the private justice and escalating conflict that so threatened traditional societies. We have the more recent religious arrivals, the great world religions, each of which cultivates its own prescription for how people can combat the mimetic temptations created by our emotional and cognitive sensitivity to each other. These are very significant changes indeed. But important as they are, Girard suggests that we are subject to the same dangers and liable to practice the same solutions.

To take some examples (not all of similar scope and scale), we may consider the Stalinist terror in the Soviet Union; the National Socialist terror in Germany; and in the United States, the red scare after World War I, the practice of racial segregation, and the day-care child abuse hysteria of the 1990s. One feature of interest in all these cases is that the legal and political systems themselves, in principle curbs against sacrificial crisis, were in various measures consumed by it. In the face of real or perceived threats of social dissolution and destruction, the cause of the crisis was attributed to systematic violation of the most sacred rules of the community, isolated minorities were identified as the offenders, and ostracism and destruction of those scapegoats became a unifying passion. In Communist Russia the charge might be treason against the new egalitarian humanity; in Nazi Germany or the Jim Crow South it might be violation of racial pu-

---

19. Girard, *Violence and the Sacred*, 262.

rity; in 1920s America it might be undermining democracy and free enterprise; in the day-care cases it might be sexually defiling the sanctity of childhood. In all such cases the magnitude of the crime seemed commensurate to the magnitude of the threat to society. The charges took on a highly ritualized character, as did the descriptions of the accused. And enormous energy was expended not only in pursuing those charged, but in compelling all who might side with them, or withhold judgment on their guilt, to join in right-minded unanimity. Stalin's famous show trials make little sense as judicial processes or even in terms of expeditious execution of opponents, but eminent sense as acts of collective cleansing in which a fractured community unified against a scapegoat (it was a notable feature of such trials that the accused typically made it literally unanimous by confessing and condemning himself).

If sacrifice was simply failed science, and accomplished nothing, it would have no importance for us now. But it does work, and continues to work, whether the community in question is a clique of middle school girls or a country in the grip of economic collapse. Despite the added safeguards in modern societies mentioned above, our communication and media have also exponentially expanded the capacity for mimetic contagion. Opinions and fashions spread with dizzying speed. In less time than it takes to recount, a rumor becomes assured fact to thousands and the basis for their interaction with millions more whose subsequent actions then are the basis for untold others to react. And so on. Traditional communities regarded situations of intrinsic rivalry with superstitious fear, whether the situation was courtship or the selection of political leadership or the birth of twins. This was because all these carried the seeds of conflict, and conflict threatens runaway escalation. We rightly feel some of the same apprehension when looking at our exquisitely sensitive networks of exchange, whether they are global economic systems or powerful communications media.

The same scapegoating dynamic is alive in our setting. Yet our conventional perception that ritual sacrifice has faded from our culture, and that we do not live by traditional myth any longer, is also in large measure correct. This is not entirely reassuring. The problem sacrifice addresses is very real. Yet the traditional ways of applying a sacrificial solution are in fact in bad repair. To suppose that we have completely replaced them, or that their enfeeblement poses no threat to us, is naive.[20] Our ancestors

---

20. We will return to this question, the apocalyptic possibilities of the demise of sacrifice, in chapter 9.

saw sacrifice as the pillar that literally supported the world. If it was not actually supporting anything, then it need not concern us that it has become rotten. But if it actually was holding up our social world, it is no small matter to ask how we will do that job without it.

Let me be clear. Scapegoating sacrifice is a shape-shifting dynamic. There is no permanent class of victims, no permanent members of the unanimous mob. This by no means denies that, for instance, racism, economic exploitation, and gender discrimination are realities. These are forms of oppression with their own logic, and ones easily co-opted to sacrificial ends. In a crisis, scapegoats are likely to be chosen from those already marginal and isolated according to one of those factors. But it is also true that the mimetic dynamic is distinct and independent from these other forces. That is part of its disturbing power. Humans have always been divided by interest, race, language, gender, class, and so on. For that reason there is always a special premium on a process that can unite a community precisely across those internal divisions in the face of external threat or internal disintegration, a process that can sweep all those divisions (or all save one) before it. So, for instance, in the face of war and social dissolution, the Marxist-Leninist rulers of Russia did not hesitate to turn to old categories of nationalism and Orthodox Christianity to rally the population into a unified effort, one that cut across the class structures and recycled traditional scapegoat charges.

We began this chapter by asking what sacrifice is about, in hopes this would help us understand the cross. The two topics of sacrifice and myth do not at first glance seem to provide that help. We can see the actual practice of ritual sacrifice in ancient religion — the killing of animals or persons in religious settings. But the death of Jesus doesn't look anything like that. It is a public execution, not an offering on an altar. So the comparison with sacrifice doesn't seem to tell us much. On the other hand, we can consider myths, like the Ojibwa myth Girard describes. This story has no apparent relevance to Jesus' death. So we gain no illumination here either. Sacrifice and crucifixion are both about killing, but the killing seems to have nothing in common. Myth and the passion narratives are both stories, but myth doesn't appear to be about scapegoating, while the passion definitely is.

Girard's insight, however, links sacrifice and myth in a way directly relevant to the cross. He contends that the enduring significance of sacrifice is based on a real connection between collective violence and social reconciliation, and its effectiveness depends on the fact that people who practiced scapegoating sacrifice systematically misrepresented that connection in mythic constructions. This suggests that ritual sacrifice has an original setting (the founding murder) and prescribes an ongoing practice (scapegoating) that is not limited to ritual, and that myth reflects a reality different from what it directly describes. If this is so, then the truth behind both ritual sacrifice and certain founding myths is a fact that looks uncannily like Jesus' death — the exclusion and execution of a scapegoat to reconcile a community in crisis. There is a profound relation between Jesus' death and mythical sacrifice, but it is the reverse of what is usually supposed. The issue is not to interpret Jesus' death in terms drawn from the practice of cultic, ritual sacrifice, or to interpret it in terms drawn from myth. Rather the point is to interpret both of those things from the perspective of the reality of Jesus' death. To understand the cross the Gospels insistently present to us in Jerusalem, we have to look by its light at the landscape beyond. The connection to the world of sacrifice and myth is the invisible victim behind both, the cross nobody sees. What lies behind both the practice of sacrifice and the formulation of founding myths is in fact a cross just like that of Jesus. To know this, let alone to change it, required something special to happen in history.

Girard's most famous book, *Violence and the Sacred*, was an anthropological analysis of ancient religion and myth that seemed to presage a similar treatment in the future for Christianity as well. It won him admiration from thinkers who saw his work as a general deconstruction of religion, a welcome contribution to a general critical analysis of all human institutions in terms of underlying relations of power, violence, and domination. However, one such thinker, Michel Foucault, reproached Girard for his insistent concern with violence and sacrifice: "It is not necessary to build an entire philosophy on the victim." To which Girard replied, "No, not a philosophy — rather a religion. . . . But one already exists!"[21] It was in the Bible.

---

21. Girard and Treguer, *Quand Ces Choses Commenceront*, 112.

CHAPTER THREE

The Voice of Job

Sacrifice Revealed and Contested

More in number than the hairs of my head
are those who hate me without cause.

Psalm 69:4

These are obviously troubled texts, but what troubles them
is the truth.

Gil Bailie[1]

S capegoating sacrifice is the prototypical "good bad thing" in human culture, a calibrated dose of unjust violence that wards off wider, unrestrained violence. Scapegoating is one of the deepest structures of human sin, built into our religion and our politics. It is demonic because it is endlessly flexible in its choice of prey and because it can truly deliver the good that it advertises. The sacrificial dynamic is most effective where it is most invisible. Victims are *called* criminals, gods, or both. So long as we are in the grip of the practice, we do not see our victims as victims.

If this is a fact of human history and community, then some important conclusions follow. Texts that hide scapegoating foster it. Texts that show it for what it is undermine it. Nonmythical description, even if given in support of sacrifice, starts to drain much of the power and mystery

---

1. Gil Bailie, *Violence Unveiled: Humanity at the Crossroads* (New York: Crossroad, 1995), 135.

from the process. And most disruptive of all is any recognition of the authentic voice of the sacrificed.

Sacrifice is successful when no one takes the side of the suffering one, no one thinks that person is innocent, no one withholds participation in the collective violence against the person, no one considers his or her death a murder, no one remembers the victim as such after the victim is gone. In fact, the collective memory of what is done puts it in a completely different category from the cycle of violence it was meant to cure, treating it as a divine transaction. Myth is the medium for such memories.

So, classically, when religion or politics has been all about the practice of scapegoating, it has been entirely silent about any direct account of it. So long as we are immersed in it, we can conceive what we are doing only in other terms. "It cannot appear as such, therefore; most religions are too completely dominated by their scapegoat *mechanism* to accede to a scapegoat *theme* in any form."[2] James Frazer, the author of *The Golden Bough*, catalogued what he called "scapegoat rituals" in various religions and cultures, but none of those who practiced the rituals would have regarded them as involving a scapegoat in the terms Frazer and we mean by it (an arbitrary victim punished for purposes other than the ostensible ones).[3] It is a major accomplishment to see anyone's scapegoats. Our own are always invisible to us, for as soon as we recognize them as scapegoats, they lose most of their sacrificial power.

It is telling that Frazer drew the term "scapegoat," the term that signifies a more critical awareness, from a ritual described in the Old Testament. In the light of the background we have surveyed, it is time to turn to the Bible. For Girard makes a startling claim: "In the Jewish and Christian Bible, we can see the gradual emergence of scapegoating in the modern and critical sense. It is there and there only that a genuine *theme* or *motif* of the scapegoat can make its appearance and, simultaneously with it, a growing realization that we will not become fully human unless we confront and restrain this unconscious activity of ours by all possible means."[4]

The Bible is riddled with a dangerous honesty about sacrifice. At times it describes and frankly endorses it. At such times it is unusually concrete and blunt in its description. Simultaneously, it seems obsessed with the

2. René Girard, foreword to *The Bible, Violence, and the Sacred: Liberation from the Myth of Sanctioned Violence*, by James G. Williams, 1st ed. (San Francisco: HarperSanFrancisco, 1991), v.

3. James George Frazer, *The Golden Bough: A Study in Magic and Religion*, 3rd ed. (New York: Macmillan, 1935).

4. Girard, foreword to *The Bible*, vi-vii.

voice of victims. It comes to look through the eyes of scapegoats. This is what Girard means when he says the Bible is remarkable for containing an explicit theme of the scapegoat. And this is part of what it means to say that it contains revelation.

In turning to the question of sacrifice in the Bible, our path takes us through another of the problem areas we listed at the beginning: the violent content of the Bible. That content is undeniable. But we have already seen good reason not to assume that where violence is not described, it is not practiced. The question is, what is the description of violence doing in the Bible?

Violence Unveiled

Leaving aside the crucifixion itself, when people talk of the violence in the Bible they usually have the Hebrew scriptures in mind. Christians often respond to criticism of a blood-soaked Bible by contrasting the two Testaments. But this attempt to shift the blame is misguided in several ways. It too easily becomes an attack on Judaism itself. These texts are scripture for Christians as well as Jews, and they have played an essential role in shaping Christian tradition. Old Testament texts have been used to justify much more Christian than Jewish violence. And most particularly, we can have no adequate understanding of the cross apart from these scriptures. It is the continuity between the two Testaments, and not their contrast, that is most important for our question.[5]

The first thing to be said about the Bible generally, and the Hebrew scriptures specifically, is that it is very bad myth. In the modern period the historical plausibility of many biblical accounts has long been questioned. But the overwhelming body of the scriptures is undeniably "history-like." That is, it speaks descriptively and concretely. The figures in the Bible are clearly human, and not very ideally human at that. Even the poetry and plainly nonhistorical materials have a down-to-earth quality. These texts are relatively distant from classic myth, which is populated with fantastic cosmic creatures and marked by events that take

---

5. I do not mean to suggest that all instances or types of violence in the Bible can be understood through the categories of this discussion. To give only one example, war and the violence attendant on Israel's conquest of the land pose questions that are not adequately addressed simply by considerations around sacrifice, although some of the practices associated with Israel's war making, such as the killing of captives, may fall at least partly into the sphere of sacrifice.

place in an indeterminate time and place. In many eyes this is a prime failing of the Bible. Rather than the universal abstraction of myth, it gives us the tales of a tangled tribal family, an ancient petty state and its jealous deity.

Violence and sacrifice are constant and explicit themes in the Bible. Does this show us that the biblical God is specially brutal and that God's followers are uniquely bloody?[6] Or does it offer a diagnostic glimpse into exactly the process we described in the last chapter, active everywhere, but invisible? A sensational movie with shoot-outs in which villains fall but no blood is ever seen may be rated much less violent than a graphic medical training film of trauma care in an emergency room where the wounded are treated. This tells us about the appearances but little about the effect. As Gil Bailie puts it, "There is plenty of violence in biblical literature. These are obviously troubled texts, but what troubles them is the truth. Myths exist to spare us the trouble."[7]

He reminds us that the God depicted in the Bible need not always be identified with the God of the Bible, a point recognized as much by conservative interpreters as by liberal ones. When we take the Old Testament and the New Testament together, we can say God at one time clearly sanctioned polygamy and as clearly forbade it at another. Ritual sacrifices were regarded as obligatory at one point, but were later rejected as unnecessary. Dispensationalists have said that God directly commanded first one standard and then another to supersede it, to apply to different ages of revelation history. Liberals have said the earlier norm was the best understanding of God that humans could grasp at that stage of their development and gave way to a more adequate appropriation of God's true intentions. Both in fact agree that though the God described at one point in the text has the same "biographical" identity as the God described in another, we interpret some texts in terms of others we believe are the clearest and deepest focus of the biblical message. The God who commanded Abraham to sacrifice his son is the same God who stays his hand. The God depicted in the first half of that event is narratively the same as the God in the second half. But the God of the first half cannot

---

6. Some maintain this of monotheism generally. See Regina M. Schwartz, *The Curse of Cain: The Violent Legacy of Monotheism* (Chicago: University of Chicago Press, 1997). For a more nuanced treatment see Rodney Stark, *For the Glory of God: How Monotheism Led to Reformations, Science, Witch-Hunts, and the End of Slavery* (Princeton: Princeton University Press, 2003); Rodney Stark, *One True God: Historical Consequences of Monotheism* (Princeton: Princeton University Press, 2001).

7. Bailie, *Violence Unveiled*, 135.

be taken in isolation as the God Jews or Christians worship. And yet that part of the story of God is necessary to the full picture.

One (conventionally liberal) approach to biblical authority may find in scripture pearls of truth and revelation set amid errors and misapprehensions that never should have had a place there to begin with. Another (more conventionally conservative) approach may find the truth binding on us set amid inspired commandments that were God's providential truth to their time but obsolete in ours. It falls somewhere between the two to suppose that there are portions of scripture that may have continuing revelatory content, though what they present is not something to be emulated or endorsed. The Bible, the faith that it expresses, and the God that it describes are all entangled in the dynamics of mythical sacrifice. To assume otherwise would suppose an absolute discontinuity to revelation, a truth dropped with no key to its context. If our human religious history has the qualities we have suggested, an alternative to the violent sacred could only be posed as an argument about God. And it must make reference to the only kind of god sacred violence knows, a sacrificial one. The Bible is engaged in a struggle over the sacred. It is a struggle waged in the substance of the texts themselves.

According to one survey, more than six hundred passages in the Bible speak of nations or individuals attacking and killing others. And by the same estimation, "The theme of God's bloody vengeance occurs in the Old Testament even more frequently than the problem of human violence. Approximately *one thousand passages* speak of Yahweh's blazing anger, of his punishments by death and destruction, and how like a consuming fire he passes judgment, takes revenge and threatens annihilation."[8] This fact is not news to any who have sat down with the intention to read through the Bible cover to cover, seeking comfort and inspiration, only to find themselves slogging through just this kind of material.

There is nothing remarkable about Yahweh in this respect. We know well enough that it was the common job description of gods to destroy other nations and defend their own. Such warrior attributes are not unique, although the biblical God is notable for lacking the wider divine life exhibited in other mythologies that deal with everything from the amatory intrigues of the gods to all kinds of timeless tales of cosmic battles and origins. Girard's argument asked us to consider that such mythology is populated by gods of violence, even when — particularly when — they

8. Raymund Schwager, *Must There Be Scapegoats? Violence and Redemption in the Bible,* 1st ed. (San Francisco: Harper and Row, 1987), 55.

are not described so. The near constant wars of tribes and later of nations, and the coordinate internal crises and conflicts, fostered the even more constant practice of sacrifice.

The emerging monotheism of the biblical tradition concentrates and heightens all these elements. The God of the early Old Testament is notable for at least two prominent characteristics. This is a God like blazing fire, like high-voltage electricity, who is a raw, impersonal threat to any who get too close. The people of Israel are warned back from Mount Sinai for this reason when God meets there with Moses. This is also a God of fierce judgment and jealousy, laying down commandments and enforcing them with violence. These qualities encapsulate quite well the primary features of the sacred, of foundational religion, as Girard understands it. The sacred revolves around the restraint of the conflagration of social conflict through the limited violence of sacrifice. The divine is precisely the embodiment of this raw, volatile, and violent power, a power threatening and destructive on the one hand but beneficent and protective on the other . . . forest fire and backfire, electrical storm and electric light. The other key aspect of the sacred is the table of prohibitions set up to keep mimetic fires from starting, to keep conflict from breaking out. And when crisis comes, the same prohibitions are the basis for the scapegoating charges to be brought against the sacrificial victims. In the Old Testament, these qualities are all subsumed and consolidated in a single personal God.

The biblical God manifests these qualities. A historian would say the Israelites borrowed much of their idea of divinity from the prior traditions around them. And that is certainly true. This observation is often counted against the idea that the Bible contains revealed truth about God. The element our last chapter should have added to this picture is that if in fact there was in religion generally the very real and powerful dynamic Girard suggests, then the attendant qualities very much need to be present in the biography of the biblical God if their true nature is to be unveiled, addressed, and transformed.

One other word needs to be said before we discuss a few Old Testament texts. Those texts have complex compositional histories, which cannot be engaged in this limited space. But the lack of attention to such questions is not merely a circumstantial constraint. It is a conscious choice. In this book the primary interest in these texts is the framework they provided, and provide, for Christian understanding of the cross. They provided that framework as they stood in a scriptural tradition. However they came to be in the form they were in, it was the ways that they were and could be read together that had the theological effect we are most interested in. To put it another way, all the valid historical-critical questions of origin are for this purpose secondary to the one historical-critical question of effect. Early Christians saw a plot in their Hebrew scriptures that implicated the death of Christ. In stringing together some of the texts Christians most readily referenced for this purpose, we are trying to draw out a dimension of them that is rarely grasped. To put it otherwise, I am suggesting that the logic connecting them with each other and with Jesus' death is by no means as arbitrary and fanciful as is sometimes supposed. The complex histories behind these texts and the ambivalent features in them testify to an ongoing struggle. My contention is that the struggle has a consistent theme, and it is that theme that requires our attention.

Creation and Murder

The Genesis creation accounts are a striking exception to the prevalence of violence in the Bible. In comparison with the founding and creation myths of most traditions, no acts of expulsion, battle, or bloodshed are essential for creating the world. The text reflects clear awareness of myths of this type — of Marduk's slaying of the great water goddess Tiamat in the Babylonian creation story, for instance. But instead God moves over the face of the watery chaos and speaks through it to bring the universe into being. The world is not founded on violence or the expulsion of a cosmic scapegoat.[9] Girard suggested that our social world is historically founded on human forms of sacrifice, and that myths of origin often misrepresent that fact by veiling it in symbols or transposing it into mythic space. At this crucial point the Bible insists that the true origin is a nonviolent one. An ontology of peace is more fundamental than the reality of conflict.

In almost the next breath, however, Adam and Eve fall away from the preconditions of peace and Genesis presents another story, the story of Cain and Abel. Here we do have a story of violent origins. But it is plainly a secondary story. The ultimate, divine origin was a peaceful one.[10] In

---

9. See Williams, *The Bible*, 28-29.

10. Cain and Abel may be the story of the original social sin, the "fall" of the founding murder. But in Genesis it is clear that this is not the first or original sin, which has already occurred in Eden and is a more basic problem of which scapegoating is only one manifestation — i.e., the corruption of our mimetic natures to rivalry and envy (Eve and Adam's mimetic construal of God's inner life as intending to deprive them of something or to prevent them from attaining what God has).

Cain and Abel we meet not the original sin, but the first murder: the original social sin.[11] This is a story of the human origins of violence, and one told in concrete antimythical terms. One man kills another, in a field, for motives of rivalry and jealousy that are in some obscure way connected to their sacrificial practices (God "had regard" for Abel's offering from his flock, but "had no regard" for Cain's offering from his fields).

Cain is angry at what he sees as God's preference for Abel, and commits murder. There is, famously, no explicit explanation for the success of Abel's offering and the failure of Cain's, but interpreters have supplied them without end. God prefers herders with their animal offerings to farmers with their vegetable offerings. Blood sacrifice is the only effective kind. In any event, Cain is cautioned by God that in his anger sin is lying close at hand, but he must overcome it. Instead, he kills Abel. One simple way to read this story is that a successful sacrifice does not lead you to kill your brother, and an unsuccessful one does.

The "fall" of Adam and Eve addresses why we humans need sacrifice. Our capacities for deep empathy with each other are twisted to construct intentions and instigate conflict of a sort that did not exist before. The story of Cain and Abel reflects the fact that sacrifice is not the source of creation (as in some myths of origin) but is a strategy to deal with a fallen creation. And the story encapsulates the true nature of sacrifice, in which violence fends off violence. Abel's bloody sacrifice does so. Cain's nonbloody offering (despite God's caution) does not. God is an enigmatic figure in this story. God says to Cain, who perceives that his sacrifice is unsatisfactory, "If you do well, will you not be accepted? And if you do not do well, sin is lurking at the door; its desire is for you, but you must master it." Does God mean that Cain should sacrifice animals like Abel and then things would be all right, but in the meantime he should take care not to fall into murder? Or does God mean that if Cain resists falling into violence his offering will be acceptable, but if he continues to view the situation as one of rivalry with Abel for God's favor, then he risks falling into murder?

The story of Abraham and Isaac suggests that animal sacrifice arises as a way of backing off from human sacrifice. This text suggests something strikingly different. It pictures a time after sin had entered but when there was a kind of testing whether it might be restrained effectively with animal sacrifice or even with the more limited offering from the field, before it led to any murder at all. And it is in the train of this failed

---

11. For a more extensive discussion, see James Alison, *Raising Abel: The Recovery of Eschatological Imagination* (New York: Crossroad, 1996).

experiment that the full weight of sacred violence descends. Abel's blood cries out from the ground. Confronted by God, and sentenced to be a fugitive and wanderer on the earth, Cain raises the specter of reciprocal violence ("whoever finds me will slay me"). God places a mark of protection on Cain, promising that if anyone kills him God will take vengeance against that person sevenfold — deterring killing with the threat of more killing. Abel's murder becomes the occasion for a law against murder, whose prescribed punishment is multiple murder in return.

Cain goes on to build a city and to found civilization. The rest of the story is told only in the genealogy of his children and the occupations they invented, except for a brief song from his descendant Lamech: "I have slain a man for wounding me, a young man for striking me. If Cain is avenged sevenfold, truly Lamech seventy-sevenfold" (Gen. 4:23-24 RSV).[12] There could hardly be a clearer expression of progression from one murder to unlimited blood revenge. Death now is returned not for death but for a blow. With this hair trigger of escalating retaliation, society spirals quickly into such unbridled violence that God regrets the creation of humanity and contemplates the destruction of the entire world. We go quickly from Cain and Abel to Noah and the flood.

No one would suggest that Cain is a hero of the Bible and a model to believers. His story launches an acute diagnosis of the particular human evil we are concerned with. It unveils what myth hides. Rival brothers appear frequently in mythology. A well-known example would be the story of the brothers Romulus and Remus and the origins of the city of Rome. Romulus kills Remus for not respecting the boundaries he has set out for the new city. This is the founding event, looked back on in later Roman tradition not as a crime but as a sacred beginning. Romulus's action is approved, and the account lacks entirely the supervening framework of condemnation and horror provided by God's confrontation with Cain. The Bible looks back to Cain and Abel as a point at which things all went dramatically wrong, following on the original fall in the garden. The Romulus example demonstrates that we should not take it for granted that stories of a "first murder" would naturally have such a flavor. They were more likely to be seen as part of how things went right.

12. Interestingly there is no mention of worship of God among Cain's descendants, but in Gen. 4:25 the story switches back to Eve and Adam, who have another son, Seth, whom God has appointed to replace Abel. Seth has a son, Enosh, and the text says, "At that time men began to call upon the name of the LORD." Then the text follows the genealogy of Seth down to Noah, with several of the names being almost identical to names in Cain's descendants. In a certain sense, Seth is an alternative history to that of Cain.

There is no foundational violence in God or God's creation of the world. But the biblical God is quickly implicated in killing. In fact, the story of Cain and Abel begins a short, vivid portion of scripture in which God is caught up in the intensive spiral of violence at the end of which God destroys the entire world (save Noah and his ark) by flood. The explanation given for this is, "Now the earth was corrupt in God's sight, and the earth was filled with violence" (Gen. 6:11). Just as Cain's descendants escalate their levels of retribution, God is recruited into this dynamic. God breaks out in violence . . . against violence. From Cain and Abel the world has spiraled into a relentless reciprocal destruction. The response is a massive attempt to drive out violence by violence, an attempt God then declares will never be repeated. The rainbow marks this unilateral covenant promise. To put it baldly, God too became subject to this disease, or was forced to violent judgment by it. By the end of the tenth chapter of Genesis, one response to the problem of human violence — greater and greater violence — has been tried both by humans and by God, and found wanting.

God is prompted to the rainbow promise when Noah sacrifices some animals as a burnt offering. "And when the LORD smelled the pleasing odor, the LORD said in his heart, 'I will never again curse the ground because of humankind . . .'" (Gen. 8:21). Human life is restored, and ritual blood sacrifice is at the center. It is the occasion for God to forswear manifold retribution against humanity. And in fact, God gives a new law: "Whoever sheds the blood of a human, / by a human shall that person's blood be shed" (Gen. 9:6). This is a dramatic de-escalation of the sevenfold vengeance promised before. The act of sacrifice is associated with the restriction of runaway divine and human violence, with its limitation to a strict equal exchange.

What is striking about this is how sharply the opening verses of the Bible outline the fundamental human problem of violence. In the train of the first murder, the remedy of escalating revenge is tried (by humans and by God). This leads to total destruction. Then God and humanity begin again, with new limitations on the extent of both human and divine retaliation, a dispensation marked by Noah's blood offerings. In some way these are substitutions for the now-forbidden violence. Humanity is given clear permission to sacrifice and eat animals (though not their blood). Perhaps this too is some kind of compensation. From a world of wholesale violence we have entered the realm of proportioned violence, the realm of sacrifice. Though the problem of violence originates with humans, the response to it implicates both God and humanity. Caught up in a mimetic rivalry they attribute to God, humans then conceive God as the mirror image of their own escalating conflict. This chapter of the story ends with God destroying a world given over to violence. Then God appears as an enforcer of prohibitions to avoid the escalation of violence and a power who underwrites sacrifice to defuse it. If we are to judge from the Bible's own plot, none of these representations gives a full or adequate characterization of God's true nature. But they do tell fundamental truths about the human condition and our relation with God. Without such pictures, it is hard to see how we could grasp our situation, even if the full biblical story makes clear that we cannot stop with them.

A few chapters later we move from God's destruction of an entire violence-ridden world, with only a tiny remnant saved, to Abraham's intercessory argument with God about the cities of Sodom and Gomorrah (Gen. 18:22-33). Now God agrees that if only ten righteous ones can be found in the city, all its guilty inhabitants will be spared. In contrast with the idea that the guilt of a few can contaminate and pollute an entire community and bring divine destruction on it (a classic scapegoating assumption), an alternative idea is introduced suggesting a positive contagion, a good pollution, in which the virtues of a minority can save a corrupt community.

Practicing Sacrifice

The new arrangement, the new covenant with Noah, will not hold. The first few chapters of Genesis lay the groundwork on which scapegoating sacrifice appears, but do not explicitly address it yet. In the vast stretch of the Bible that remains, that will happen with striking regularity. To begin with, there are some cases of matter-of-fact scapegoating practice. Consider this brief story from Leviticus, which comes in the midst of long sections in which God prescribes in detail the festivals, sacrifices, and laws the people are to observe: "A man whose mother was an Israelite and whose father was an Egyptian came out among the people of Israel; and the Israelite woman's son and a certain Israelite began fighting in the camp. The Israelite woman's son blasphemed the Name in a curse. And they brought him to Moses. . . . The LORD said to Moses, saying: Take the blasphemer outside the camp; and let all who were within hearing lay their hands on his head, and let the whole congregation stone him" (Lev. 24:10-14). Given the mythic model, this is a very familiar pattern. Mixed birth is already a marker that may make this person suspect. The accusation is a predictably maximal one of blaspheming the sacred name of Israel's God. The blame or pollution of those who so much as heard this enormity is to be placed on his head, and the execution is to be by a unanimous act of collective violence. The text endorses this procedure, and it figures as an occasion for God to draw the moral of the story and promulgate a number of laws in the verses that follow. "He who blasphemes the name of the Lord shall be put to death; all the congregation shall stone him. . . ." Interestingly, the string of laws includes the injunction that whoever kills a man will be put to death, anyone who kills a beast will make it good, "life for life." And "When a man causes a disfigurement in his neighbor, as he has done it shall be done to him, fracture for fracture, eye for eye, tooth for tooth. . . ."

Even in this passage, which straightforwardly endorses scapegoating, we can note several things. First, the behavior is the same that recurs constantly in human religion and culture, but the description is not. It is presented in a flat and quite nonmythical setting. Instead of an elaborate story that seems to be about something else, we get a direct account. The account even tells us about the fight the victim was involved in, which is likely what set off conflict in the community and was the occasion to focus accusation on the victim. Second, behavioral rules and specifications for ritual practice (including descriptions of rituals being carried out) are the whole substance of Leviticus. Chapters typically begin "The Lord spoke to Moses, saying . . ." and continue with detailed commandments. The scapegoating event we just noted is one of only two brief narratives that appear in the entire book.[13] Third, the sacrificial killing is linked explicitly to the prohibitions whose purpose is to prevent the escalation of retribution, the problem that sacrifice has to solve. "An eye for an eye" is a standard to limit violence by balancing it with an imitated violence of exactly the same dimension and so ending its exchange. But where such laws fail, the community will have to resort to communal unity against a scapegoat to restore peace. For that case a more majestic charge than "not obeying the eye for an eye rule" is needed, and blasphemy against the Name will serve. Fourth, God has become the focus of the act. In myth it may be a matter of ancestral spirits, or a kind of natural process or a pantheon of rival deities. Here it is a direct command of the only God Israel acknowledges. So the question of sacrifice has become a question of the

---

13. The other is the story of how two of Aaron's sons offered "unholy fire before the LORD, such as he had not commanded them. And fire came out from the presence of the LORD and consumed them, and they died before the LORD" (Lev. 10:1-2). Thus in the midst of interminable verses about ritual sacrifices and regulations, the only two things that actually happen are this killing by divine power and the collective killing we just described. If we assume these incidents are not here by accident, they strongly reinforce the connection of ritual to human victims.

character of God, in a way that can happen only with monotheism. In short, most of the mythical smoke around such events has been blown away, and what we get is a very bare description.

Israel has its own extensive ritual sacrificial practice, in many ways similar to the ritual practice ubiquitous in human history. After Israel received the law at Mount Sinai, there was a ceremony to ratify the covenant between God and the people (Exod. 24:3-8). Moses constructed an altar upon which animals were sacrificed. Blood from them was gathered in bowls and thrown against the altar and thrown over the people. It is a gory scene, and one well suited to express the various aspects of the sacrificial complex: the laws were to protect against conflict in the community, and violating them could result in the shedding of each other's blood; the blood of victims can unite the community; and the blood of the victim must be "on" (the responsibility of) all without exception.

In the period immediately preceding the time of Jesus, a particularly explicit ceremony became a keystone event in the yearly cultic cycle in the temple at Jerusalem. This sacrificial event, the Day of Atonement, was based on traditions found in the book of Leviticus.[14] Its celebration survived the destruction of the temple to become one of the great holy days of rabbinic Judaism, Yom Kippur. In the rite described in Leviticus, the high priest sacrifices a bull and takes the blood into the inner sanctuary — an offering that is to purge the pollution and sin from the priests and the temple itself. Then a further sacrifice is made of two goats. By lots one of these is chosen to be killed on behalf of the people, its blood also offered in the sanctuary. The other goat is made the vehicle for the transferal and expulsion of the sins of the people. The high priest lays hands on it and makes a confession of communal sins. Then the goat is led away and driven out of the city by all the people, who gather and strike it, curse it, and spit on it. It is driven out along a designated path into the wilderness, and eventually over a cliff. Legend had it that a scarlet thread on the door of the temple turned white at the time of the goat's death, indicating the removal of sins.[15] This is the scapegoat, from which we derive the word and concept so central to this discussion. The goat driven out in this way was said to belong to "Azazel." The word is an odd one, taken vari-

14. See Lev. 16. Some of the elements of this observance described in the following paragraphs are not found in Leviticus but stem from later sources, most notably a tractate in the Mishnah devoted entirely to this ritual, which may include some details of temple practice from the Second Temple period.

15. Some believe that this legend is referred to in Isa. 1:18: "though your sins are like scarlet, / they will be like snow."

ously to refer to a "goat that departs," or to the place to which it is expelled (a rugged cliff), or to a demon inhabiting the desert (sometimes identified with the ringleader of rebel angels who tempts humanity, similar to Satan).

So at the center of Israel's ritual life we find an event bearing all the marks we outlined in the last chapter. The community centers its collective violence on a representative sacrifice, which is charged with all the guilt and sins that pollute and threaten the people, and driven out and off a cliff — the very image of mob violence against a human scapegoat.[16] What is striking about the ritual is not that it differs from that model, but that it is so extraordinarily explicit in expressing the underlying dynamic. This is the very reason that we take its language, "scapegoat," as the name for the behavior we are identifying. The classic sacrificial victim was seen as the cause of the crisis in the city, the sole source of contamination, the single guilty party. It is notable then that this biblical ritual has become so open about a transference, in which it is actually the guilt and offenses of all the people that are placed on the victim, and thus expelled. *They* are the ones who are guilty, but the substitute sacrificed will remove that guilt. This is a thoroughly sacrificial act that at the same time expresses a great measure of insight into the nature of sacrifice. The larger context of the ritual draws out that insight.

The Day of Atonement required not simply that people associate themselves with the collective violence against the scapegoat, but that they all participate by fasting and repentance for their own sins. The blood of the sacrifice may purge the temple from pollution, but only true inward repentance will do the same for persons. And even this is effective by itself only for sins between humans and God. Sins committed against others are included only if one has made restitution and peace with them as well. This emphasis is not found in the Leviticus text, but it is characteristic of later rabbinic Judaism's treatment of the Day of Atonement. With the temple itself destroyed, the actual practice of sacrifice and of the scapegoat ritual is ended, though the imagery (and perhaps the theoretical obligation) re-

16. Indeed, some scholars believe that this vivid feature of the celebration was added to the slaughter of the two other animals by popular demand, that "The incorporation of the rite of the scapegoat into the Day of Atonement ritual may represent a concession to popular taste" (J. C. Rylaarsdam, "Atonement, Day Of," in *The Interpreter's Dictionary of the Bible*, ed. George Arthur Buttrick [Nashville: Abingdon, 1962]). From Girard's point of view, this would mean that there was collective pressure toward a more explicit expression of what stands originally behind the sacrifices themselves, toward something closer to the real thing.

mains. The Day of Atonement turns entirely toward this inward reconciliation with God and neighbor, and becomes explicitly antisacrificial.

The ritual and the title "scapegoat" are emblematic for our study. Both represent the sacrificial dynamic. As we first encounter them in the Bible, they embody its logic with unusual honesty and appear to have divine support. Scapegoating sacrifice is upheld, in the literal stoning in Leviticus or in the explicit ritual of the Day of Atonement. But both eventually have come to represent a process we discover in many aspects of our social life, something we reject and condemn. The word "scapegoat" now means to us the *recognized* prey of an unjust and blinded crowd. And this recognition happens in the Bible itself.

Listening to Scapegoats

In addition to its violence, the story of Cain and Abel marks other elements common in scripture: envy, rivalry, family conflict. The Bible dwells on these with the conviction that they are of religious importance, though the reader of the more sordid passages in the accounts of Abraham and David may wonder why. This emphasis makes sense in that these dynamics represent one particular dimension of sin that religion, at its historical root, addresses. In other words, in its series of dramas the Bible breaks down the dynamics that lead to scapegoating in clear, small-scale terms we can readily grasp, rather than clouding them in mystical misapprehension.

A good example is the long and famous story of Joseph. Joseph's brothers are consumed with envy and rivalry because their father Jacob makes this youngest child his favorite. They conspire together first to kill Joseph and then instead to sell him into slavery in Egypt. There is no simple unanimity among the brothers. One proposed slavery as a way of at least saving Joseph's life. Another advocated leaving him in a pit in the wilderness, with the possibility of later rescue. But they all consent together to his victimization. And once the act is done, they all agree together on their common story. They dip a piece of Joseph's cloak in the blood of a slaughtered goat, and present it to Jacob as all they could find, implying that Joseph was killed and carried off by a wild beast.

After Joseph rises to great power under the pharaoh, and through interpretation of the ruler's dreams persuades him to prepare for a coming famine, he encounters his brothers when they come to Egypt desperately seeking food. He is reunited with his father, like one returned from the dead. At the climax of the story and the close of the book of Genesis, Joseph addresses the brothers' fear that he will take retribution against them: "Fear not, for am I in the place of God? As for you, you meant evil against me; but God meant it for good, to bring it about that many people should be kept alive, as they are today" (Gen. 50:19-20 RSV).

In this very human story we see the way persecution arises. Jacob's preference for the younger brother Joseph (and especially the fact that this preference upsets the settled differentiation of children by age) awakens rivalry among the brothers, who overcome this dissension by collectively turning against him. We see the reality that unanimity has to be manufactured. We see the agreement on a cover story that removes all responsibility for the act of violence (it was a natural event, an "act of God"). Joseph is the cause of the problem (in the brothers' eyes), but the scriptural account makes it clear that his primary crime was to be an occasion for resentment. With Abel and Joseph, Genesis begins a long trail of biblical texts we might call the true lives of scapegoats.

In this connection we can hardly overlook the Genesis account of Abraham and Isaac, a central text for both Judaism and Christianity. Abraham is commanded by God to sacrifice his heir Isaac, and at the last moment God stays his hand and provides a ram as a substitute. This presents the two sides of the question starkly. The same God requires sacrifice and then prevents it, or scales it back. Like the story of Cain and Abel, this strips the act of ritual sacrifice down to its most brutal and isolated simplicity, as well as framing it as the violation of the most basic bond of parent and child. Juxtaposed with the more classic, collective violence described in the example from Leviticus we noted above, this text poses the question in an inescapably individual way. "But if it were up to you, acting alone, not in a crowd, and the victim were someone you loved . . . ?"

The sacrifice is also clearly framed as relating exactly to the founding or originating social scenario that Girard suggests. Abraham has been promised that he and Sarah will be the parents of a great nation, and Isaac is the providentially supplied son who will be the means by which that nation is generated. Abraham and Isaac are, after all, the source of the community of Israel itself. Yet the biblical tradition does not look to the killing of Isaac as its origin (analogous to the killing of Remus, say). It looks instead to the calling of Abraham, the exodus from Egypt, and the giving of the law at Sinai as the key originating events. The image of Abraham and Isaac has distinctive power. It expresses compactly rejection of human sacrifice and recognition of the innocence of the victim, along with the clear moral that Abraham's faith in God is no less radical than that required by such sacrifice. And there could hardly be a more straightforward expression of the actual meaning of animal sacrifice: it is a replacement for human sacrifice.[17] The Jewish tradition refers to this text as the *akedah,* or "binding," of Isaac, while Christians typically call it the sacrifice of Isaac.[18] The term "binding" emphasizes what actually happens in the Genesis text (Isaac was tied but not killed), and the Christian usage emphasizes what was averted. These can be sharply contrasted, to play one tradition against another. On this line, Jews might say the Christian exaltation of Jesus' sacrifice and insistence on reading the Isaac story in its light represent a regression toward a priority on human sacrifice that the Genesis text is already leaving behind. And Christians might regard the story of Abraham and Isaac as important only for its prefiguration of the real thing, a truly effective sacrifice. As I will try to make clear in the next section, there is a profound way the two emphases can be understood as consistent, mutually reinforcing aspects of the same truth.

Abel, Isaac, and Joseph are just three examples where we can see the Bible's violent content providing revelatory glimpses into a dynamic all too common elsewhere but rarely directly displayed. Another prominent case in point is the Psalms. We are all familiar with some of their lyrical lines of worship and comfort, with Psalm 23 or Psalm 8. But anyone who has read the whole book, or even allowed his or her eyes to wander further down the page during a responsive reading in church, knows that we are rarely far from a very different spirit. The poetry in many of these songs is a white-hot fire of revenge.

Psalm 137 is a lament of the people of Israel in exile, beginning with the famous lines "By the waters of Babylon, / there we sat down and wept,

17. The sacrifice of children was a very real phenomenon, outside and even inside Israel. Jon Levenson makes this case and indicates that the Genesis text of the *akedah* does not necessarily represent a prohibition on sacrifice of the firstborn so much as an example of God's special permission to meet that obligation on occasion with an animal substitute. See Jon Douglas Levenson, *The Death and Resurrection of the Beloved Son: The Transformation of Child Sacrifice in Judaism and Christianity* (New Haven: Yale University Press, 1993). See particularly chapter 11. The connection of the *akedah* with a definitive replacement of human sacrifice by animal sacrifice can be more concretely located in later interpretations that associated the site of the temple (and thus the entire sacrificial system) with the site of Isaac's binding. See chapter 14.

18. Rabbinic interpretation, what Levenson calls the "rewritten *akedah* of Jewish tradition," has many fascinating aspects. Some sources suggest Isaac was actually killed, or at least shed blood. And there is a good deal of emphasis in the later tradition on Isaac's active and voluntary participation in the proposed sacrifice. He offers himself as the victim. The *akedah* comes to be seen as a prototype for Passover. It is the "blood" of Isaac that God sees represented in the blood of the lamb smeared on the doorposts that causes the plague of death to pass over Israel's male children in Egypt. Isaac's offering is the power that averts later bloodshed and destruction. See Levenson, *Death and Resurrection,* 180.

/ when we remembered Zion" (RSV). In a few verses it reaches its climax in a curse on the conquerors:

> O daughter of Babylon, you devastator!
>   Happy shall he be who requites you
>   with what you have done to us!
> Happy shall he be who takes your little ones
>   and dashes them against the rock! (vv. 8-9 RSV)

Nor is this attitude reserved for only foreign enemies. Psalm 109 is clearly directed at others within the same community. It is almost a litany of curses, apparently countering and escalating the curses the author believes have been directed at him:

> May his days be few;
>   may another seize his goods! . . .
> May his children wander about and beg;
>   may they be driven out of the ruins they inhabit! . . .
> Let there be none to extend kindness to him,
>   nor any to pity his fatherless children! (vv. 8, 10, 12 RSV)

This note of anger comes again and again. By some estimates, as many as 100 of the 150 psalms deal in some way with enemies.[19] Even if these psalms are formulated as righteous anger against evil, what we see is the unbridled and unmistakable desire to return injury for injury, the unrestricted horizon of escalating hatred. The intensity of this venom and the free play given to it are extraordinary. Such texts have been enlisted to give religious authorization to war and hatred. From the very beginning Christians have been troubled by these texts, revering them and yet recognizing that like many strong medicines they are a poison if taken improperly. Interpreters have taken two main tacks in treating these passages. They have allegorized them on the one hand, for instance taking them as calls to destroy our sins rather than other persons. And they have treated them "diagnostically," as uncomfortable mirrors that force us to confront our own reflected emotions and desires. The value of such texts is to bring us to face our own condition, a condition that calls out for transformation. Just as the story of Cain and Abel starkly depicts the violent retributive act, the Psalms exhibit the motive, the imitative retaliation against another's attack or perceived ill will.

---

19. Schwager, *Must There Be Scapegoats?* 97.

But the most striking thing about the Psalms goes a dramatic step further than this. A great many of them give this general theme of revenge a specific and unusual twist. Alongside the fierce expressions of anger there is a regular refrain we might regard as a kind of paranoia. It runs to the following effect. I am surrounded by a crowd of people who plot against me. I am accused unjustly. I am alone with no one to support me. Those who oppress me think they are serving God. I am persecuted and about to die. Don't let me be wiped out without a trace. Don't let the persecutors' version of the truth, their slander, be all that is remembered of me. Punish them and vindicate me.

This plea for deliverance seeks relief from an oddly specific kind of evil: conspiracy of a whole community or crowd against a weak and abandoned one, the crushing of an arbitrarily chosen person on a false pretext, leaving no record. In other words, this is what the sacrificial scapegoating practice looks like from the side of the victim. We can take Psalm 142 as an example:

> In the path where I walk
>> they have hidden a trap for me.
> Look on my right hand and see —
>> there is no one who takes notice of me;
>> no refuge remains to me;
>>> no one cares for me.
> I cry to you, O Lord;
>> I say, "You are my refuge,
>> my portion in the land of the living."
> Give heed to my cry,
>> for I am brought very low.
> Save me from my persecutors,
>> for they are too strong for me. (vv. 3b-6)[20]

Or we can look at Psalm 140:

> Deliver me, O Lord, from evildoers;
>> protect me from those who are violent,
> who plan evil things in their minds
>> and stir up wars continually.

20. For more examples see Pss. 31, 38, 55, 69, 109, 118, and the discussion in Schwager, *Must There Be Scapegoats?* 91-108.

They make their tongue sharp as a snake's,
>and under their lips is the venom of vipers.
Guard me, O LORD, from the hands of the wicked;
>protect me from the violent
>who have planned my downfall.
The arrogant have hidden a trap for me,
>and with cords they have spread a net,
>along the road they have set snares for me. . . .
Do not grant, O LORD, the desires of the wicked;
>do not further their evil plot. . . .
Let burning coals fall on them!
>Let them be flung into pits, no more to rise!
Do not let the slanderer be established in the land;
>let evil speedily hunt down the violent!
I know that the LORD maintains the cause of the needy,
>and executes justice for the poor.
Surely the righteous shall give thanks to your name;
>the upright shall live in your presence. (vv. 1-5, 8, 10-13)

The voice that speaks in these psalms is insistently the voice of one un-justly persecuted, threatened with death, set upon by a unanimous multi-tude, a reviled person whose very memory will be blotted out unless God vindicates her or him. Is this just exaggeration and paranoia?

In light of the scapegoating process we described earlier, these partic-ular characteristics in the Psalms leap out with striking clarity and co-herence. These elements seem far less arbitrary, and the repetition that hammers home this situation again and again quite appropriate. What these psalms address is not just a peevish individual psychology but a fundamental social-religious dynamic. With incessant monotony they give us the voice of the scapegoated victim, a voice silenced in myth. Ac-cused falsely of monstrous crimes, isolated on the basis of some defect or minority status, universally condemned, held guilty for the entire com-munity's crisis, the subject of all this can see it only as an inexplicable plot.

Three features that appear again and again in various combinations are the vast number of the adversaries, the deceitful nature of their con-spiracy, and the intensity of animosity toward the persecuted one (who has given no reason for it).[21] Psalm 69 presents all three in short order:

---

21. Schwager, *Must There Be Scapegoats?* 99.

More in number than the hairs of my head
    are those who hate me without cause;
many are those who would destroy me,
    my enemies who accuse me falsely. (Ps. 69:4)

Psalm 109 has two in two verses.

For wicked and deceitful mouths are opened against me,
    speaking against me with lying tongues.
They beset me with words of hate,
    and attack me without cause. (Ps. 109:2-3)

The unanimity of the condemnation brings abandonment even from those closest to the speaker.

My friends and companions stand aloof from my affliction,
    and my neighbors stand far off. (Ps. 38:11)

In these texts we hear a protest, an antisacrificial cry, expressed in the most direct and even violent terms. At its harshest level, we hear the cry of someone who lusts after escalating vengeance, the seventyfold vengeance of Lamech, but lacks the means to execute it and appeals to God to be the avenger. This alerts us to the fact that righteous retribution is itself no necessary solution, but a source of yet further destruction. Like the more general laments found in the Psalms, these protests can turn in one of two ways. Frequently, as in Psalm 137, the lament turns implacably toward revenge. On other occasions the dominant note is not the desire for retribution but the hope of ultimate vindication and restoration for the victim. This is the case, for instance, in Psalm 22, to which we will return in the next section, as it is the scapegoat psalm Jesus quotes from the cross.

The Failed Scapegoat

The book of Job has come to rest next to the Psalms in our Bible. Many fail to see the logic by which Job was included in canonical scripture at all. It makes no explicit reference to Israel. It is probably the Old Testament book in which Satan gets the highest billing. It is famous for posing the problem of theodicy, of God's responsibility for evil. It certainly does that.

But the book does not deal with evil in a general sense. Rather the evil it has in view is precisely the type we have been discussing. The book is a major contribution to the advancement of the primary scriptural plot of sacrifice. I said earlier that in the Old Testament the issue of sacrifice became an issue of God's character. Nowhere is that case put more dramatically than in this text.

Job is a rich, powerful, and righteous man. God points him out to Satan as particularly praiseworthy. But Satan asks, "Does Job fear God for nothing?" and argues that if he is subject to distress he will curse God. God authorizes Satan to bring on Job a series of disasters. Raiding parties attack, slaying Job's servants and destroying his farms and livestock. A storm collapses a house, killing all his children. Finally Job himself is afflicted with loathsome diseases. Under these blows, even his wife tells him to curse God and die. But Job maintains his piety: "The LORD gave, and the LORD has taken away; blessed be the name of the LORD" (Job 1:21). The text says, "In all this Job did not sin or charge God with wrongdoing" (1:22). Here God is presented as the ultimate author of violence (for Satan acts only with God's permission).

These developments fill only the first two chapters, and an account of the rewards with which God recompenses Job for his fidelity takes up part of the last chapter. The remaining thirty-nine chapters are devoted to extended dialogues between Job and several "friends."[22] Throughout, Job maintains that he is being unjustly afflicted by God, and his friends insist that he should acknowledge he is in the wrong. They are agreed that such calamity could come in response only to extreme transgressions. Job has committed some great crime, and his suffering is the punishment of a righteous God.

What we have in the book of Job is an interview with a scapegoat. It presents yet another biblical instance of a mythical scenario interrupted, examined, and to some extent reversed. We see our familiar scenario, but now presented from a very critical angle. In many cases the Bible shows us clearly the entirely human and sinful origin of the scapegoating impulse (as with Cain and Abel, the Joseph story, or the mirror to our own hatreds held up in the Psalms). In others it explicitly links human sacrifice with

---

22. The book of Job is "textually the most vexed in the Old Testament" (see Marvin H. Pope, *Job*, 3rd ed. [Garden City, N.Y.: Doubleday, 1973], xliii). Many interpreters see a clear contrast between the terse tale of testing and reward framed in the brief prologue and epilogue and the long poetic exploration of suffering and theodicy in the bulk of the book in between. Our interest is in neither the book's authorship nor the history of its composition, but in its canonical form and influence.

ritual animal sacrifice (as with Abraham and Isaac). But in this case it focuses directly on the religious rationale for the process. That rationale hides the reality of the violence by attributing it to divine agency and justice. The text takes as its starting point the premise that Job's suffering — the destruction of his loved ones, the loss of all his goods, his physical diseases, his ostracism and condemnation, the unanimous accusation from all around him that he has committed a grave sin — *does* in fact come from God. The little mob around Job is only defending that premise. They deploy all the variations on the sacrificial themes.

The way Job describes his situation also fits the scapegoating model:

> On my right hand the rabble rise,
>   they drive me forth,
>   they cast up against me their ways of destruction.
> They break up my path,
>   they promote my calamity;
>   no one restrains them.
> As through a wide breach they come;
>   amid the crash they roll on.
> Terrors are turned upon me;
>   my honor is pursued as by the wind,
>   and my prosperity has passed away like a cloud.
> And now my soul is poured out within me;
>   days of affliction have taken hold of me.
> The night racks my bones,
>   and the pain that gnaws me takes no rest.
> With violence it seizes my garment. (30:12-18 RSV)

We hear here the same voice we heard in the Psalms. Though I vanish without a trace and all agree that I was a wrongdoer and deserved whatever happened to me, yet I call out to be vindicated.

The Psalms generally express confidence or at least plaintive hope that God will answer the cry of these victims. Yet Job makes no such assumption. God figures among the ranks of Job's enemies. The book of Job confronts directly — through its prologue (where Satan is a divine associate of some kind) and the extended arguments of Job's friends — the presumption that the sacrificial dynamic is itself God's work. If the victim stoned to death in the passage from Leviticus were allowed to speak, he would say what Job says. If "god" is in fact the divinity that requires the sacrifice of the innocent, then Job will appeal for justice against this god of the violent sacred. The book of Job can be read as a kind of struggle for the soul of the biblical God, a trial as to whether this is a divinity of the classic, mythical, sacrificial sort, or something different.

In Job's speeches we hear the voice of the scapegoat psalms, but with a more radical twist. In those psalms it is the crowd and their persecution that stand out as the objects of the victim's despair and anger. Only occasionally and obliquely does the speaker's reproach turn against God. But Job raises his complaint directly to God. This is God's work and God is the chief persecutor.

> He has torn me in his wrath, and hated me;
>> he has gnashed his teeth at me;
>> my adversary sharpens his eyes against me.
> Men have gaped at me with their mouth,
>> they have struck me insolently upon the cheek,
>> they mass themselves together against me.
> God gives me up to the ungodly,
>> and casts me into the hands of the wicked.
> I was at ease, and he broke me asunder;
>> he seized me by the neck and dashed me to pieces;
>> he set me up as his target,
>> his archers surround me. (16:9-13 RSV)

It is the entire community and God together who are condemning and crushing Job. And still he cries out:

> O earth, cover not my blood,
>> and let my cry find no resting place.
> Even now, behold, my witness is in heaven,
>> and he that vouches for me is on high.
> My friends scorn me;
>> my eye pours out tears to God,
> that he would maintain the right of a man with God,
>> like that of a man with his neighbor. (16:18-21 RSV)[23]

23. The French biblical text Girard quotes from has a variation for verse 20 that is even more striking: "Ma clameur est mon avocat auprès de Dieu, tandis que devant lui coulent mes larmes" [My outcry is my lawyer before God, while my tears run down before him]. Girard, *La Route Antique des Hommes Pervers* (Paris: Grasset, 1985), 158.

In the Psalms the scapegoat cries out to God for vengeance against or deliverance from the persecutors. But Job is all too aware that God is their assumed ally and organizer. In his book on Job, Girard notes that the psalmist's impulse seems unremarkable to us. We are hardly surprised that the afflicted should cry out to God for help. "Deprived of all human support, the victim turns to God; he embraces the concept of a God of victims. He does not permit his persecutors to monopolize the idea of God. We live in a world where nothing is easier or more natural than this appropriation of God by the victim."[24] We take this so much for granted that we cannot grasp what a new departure it represented. The very oddness of the book of Job alerts us to this. There is nothing "naturally religious" in assuming God would side with scapegoats — just the opposite. Sacrifice was always about the crushing of scapegoats with unquestioned divine approval.

Job realizes that he must appeal for help *against* God. Hence the ambiguity in the passage we just quoted. Job claims that he has a witness and a defender in heaven to represent him (apparently before God). But at the same time, he says his tears are an appeal for God to support a person's right to justice against God, like that of the right to justice between two human neighbors, an appeal to God's better nature, we might say.

Job's indictment of God could hardly be clearer:

Know then that God has put me in the wrong,
    and closed his net about me.
Behold, I cry out, "Violence!" but I am not answered;
    I cry aloud, but there is no justice.
He has walled up my way, so that I cannot pass,
    and he has set darkness upon my paths. (19:6-8 RSV)

Job hopes that even if he dies, somehow his testimony might not be lost.

Oh that my words were written!
    Oh that they were inscribed in a book!
Oh that with an iron pen and lead
    they were graven in the rock for ever!
For I know that my Redeemer lives,
    and at last he will stand upon the earth. (19:23-25 RSV)

24. Girard, *Job, the Victim of His People* (Stanford, Calif.: Stanford University Press, 1987), 139.

The redeemer or vindicator is a next of kin or heir who will avenge murder. Job challenges God to a direct confrontation, a kind of cosmic courtroom argument, where he will make his case. He cries out that he needs and believes there must be a vindicator who will defend him against God. Just as the story began with Satan as a kind of prosecutor figure instigating the targeting of Job, Job imagines some parallel divine figure who would defend him and be an accuser of God. At times Job clearly calls out for an advocate over against God. At others he contends that the true God must not be his persecutor.

On this point he contends that it is the tradition, the crowd, the friends who claim God's endorsement for his affliction, who are truly blaspheming and deserve judgment. In response to their arguments Job says, "Will you speak falsely for God, / and speak deceitfully for him?" (13:7 RSV). He refuses to worship their God or to accept that he has sinned in defying that God. The friends argue that Job must be guilty of wickedness to receive God's punishment and that, guilty of wickedness or not, Job is surely guilty of not accepting this suffering (whatever its mysterious divine purpose) in the right manner, with submission and resignation.

Job insists throughout the book on his innocence, and many interpreters see this as a failing. Is Job really *perfectly* righteous? Who can claim that? Perhaps the friends are right in suggesting that it is Job's pride that merits his treatment by God. The centrality of the issue of innocence makes little sense in terms of our views of psychology, where self-righteousness may be a defect. But it makes critical sense if we are addressing the scapegoating process, where the accusation is crucial. Sacrificial charges always involve enormous crimes, but one will hardly deflect them by pleading guilty to lesser sins, since these will be used as confirmation of the charges. Job's friends demonstrate this, since they are convinced his offense may even be some inner, secret attitude. To truly challenge this dynamic, you need the test case of a truly righteous person.

Transgression and punishment are two key features. When Job's wife tells him to "curse God and die," she brutally summarizes this recipe. The vocation of the scapegoat is to commit or be believed to commit a horrific, threatening crime ("curse God") and then to be collectively killed ("and die"). The book of Job is a failed sacrificial event where the victim inexplicably has the stage and is interrogating his persecutors, including the divine power appealed to as the foundation for sacrifice.

Where the scapegoating dimension of this text is ignored, Job is simply praised as a hero because through all his testing he maintains his faith, he refuses to curse God. But from the point of view of his friends, and the point of view of myth, this is Job's great failing. If only he would curse God, provide the crime of blasphemy that the whole attack against him presumes, then all would be right again in the world of sacrifice. Job would play into the hands of Satan and confirm the original accusation. This is part of the demonic catch-22 in scapegoating. Those selected as victims are charged with blasphemy against the gods and their punishment is presented as a divine prescription. If they object to their persecution, they are defying God and so provide proof that the accusation is true. It is not at all a question of a punishment that fits the crime, but simply a requirement to associate the violence and the crime. Job refuses to provide this missing link. He insists on the disjunction between the ills visited upon him and any justification for them.

It is striking that Job's defiance should appeal to some kind of legal process. Job wants an adjudication of the specific accusations against him. But this is precisely what is not at issue in the ritual sacred. His opponents see the very idea as irreligious, impious, and incomprehensible. The God of sacrifice has no interest in justice, only in reconciliation. The community's certainty of the guilt of the scapegoat needs no proof and wants no inquiry, as those questions could only undermine the unifying effects of the sacrifice.

At the conclusion of the book, God appears directly to speak to Job out of a whirlwind. This speech is a long affirmation of God's transcendence and a reproach to Job for his limited understanding of God's mysteries. God catalogues the many wonders of nature and asks Job whether he is able to make or understand such things. Job acknowledges he cannot. He is not the creator. He does not know how the universe works. Yet, as any ordinary reader of Job feels, the speech changes the subject. It ignores the question of Job's innocence and suffering. Taken alone, it could very well function as precisely the misdirection and cloudy theology that the friends deploy to justify Job's suffering.

God's speech to Job does not directly address the substance of his complaint. It neither accepts nor rejects it. But alongside this poetic speech, God has a very concise and unequivocal comment for Job's friends: "My wrath is kindled against you . . . ; for you have not spoken of me what is right, as my servant Job has" (42:7 RSV). Various points of view, as well as different historical sources, jostle against each other in this text, without smooth unity. One of the most striking of these tensions is that after so much space has been given to the speeches of the friends, who have defended God at every turn and justified the violence against Job as divinely mandated, we find this flat conclusion that they have not spoken the truth. Job, who has called God his persecutor and denounced God's injustice and indifference, has spoken what is right. There is hardly a more amazing line in the Bible. Job has seemed to talk of two different Gods — an adversary God for whom he is only a sacrificial target, and a divine vindicator, the God who sides with victims. And we may say that Job has spoken what is right about both of them. Some may see this as an incoherence in Job's position or as a conflict in the book's sources. In either case, it may reflect not merely a literary but a historical struggle between two religious realities, a sacrificial divinity and the God of victims.

A Test for God

Sacrificial religion assimilates the divine into the dynamics of human rivalry and revenge. The problem it addresses begins with the escalation of mimetic conflict in human social life and ends with the reconciliation granted to the community when it enlists divine powers in unanimous violence against the outcast. In the Bible this dynamic is already evident in Eden. The serpent in the garden suggests to Eve and Adam that God is not motivated by love toward them but by jealousy: "God knows that when you eat of it [the tree] your eyes will be opened, and you will be like God, knowing good and evil" (Gen. 3:5). The serpent suggests that God is threatened by the idea that humans might become like God. Once they adopt the idea that God is out to thwart them, Eve and Adam determine to become just like God — that is, to act against God's will as they believe God has acted against theirs. This distrust rapidly spreads into the relationship between Eve and Adam and throws the entire creation into disorder. They are expelled from paradise — the realm constituted by positive mimetic relations, imitation of each other's good. God's act of expelling them could itself be viewed as sacrificial — a way to remove conflict and restore peace — except that Eve and Adam are not erased. Instead they remain the center of humanity, and the entire history of creation proceeds through the expelled ones.

In the book of Job, Satan plays the role of the serpent, this time tempting God rather than humans. In Eden the serpent suggested humans should suspect God's inner motives, intimating that God was animated by competition and jealousy rather than love. In the book of Job, Satan suggests to God that Job's secret inner motive is greed. He wants what God can give him. God yields to this fear of deception, to resentment. He authorizes Satan's violence. Earlier I said that in the Bible the question of sacrifice becomes a question of the character of God. Here we see it clearly. The personal God has a mind, an inner spirit. The question is whether God's spirit is a mirror of the rivalry and violence embodied both in the social crisis and the sacrificial solution, or whether God transcends and opposes them.

Job's address to God puts this in inescapable terms: Are you on their side or mine? In this struggle over the identity of God, God finally sides with Job. Or perhaps we could say the Bible sides with Job's God. There would be no place for this book in the Bible if the God revealed in the Bible were not the God Job sought. But a true God who sides with victims cannot be known until we see the victims and recognize the false gods of sacred violence. And that is impossible without the display of violence itself.

The presentation of violence to the end of overcoming violence is always a dangerous undertaking. The presentation of the trials inflicted on Job is no different. I have indicated the quite extraordinary way in which this book raises the complaint of victims against God. But interpretation of the book can become virtually a replay of the struggle described in the book. One traditional way of reading this text closes its eyes to Job's critique of God and emphasizes his steadfastness under suffering and his enduring faith. And a traditional nontraditional way of reading the text is to see it as a rejection of belief in God in the first place, the atheist's favorite book in the Bible. But like God's long speech at the end of the book, both are simply ways of avoiding the sacrificial issue.

As readers we can see Satan and Job as the book's two opposing advocates, with God as the audience. Satan provides God a temptation, a logic by which God can conform to the violent sacred. It is important to note that this logic would not be needed were the standard mythical framework for sacrifice not in some measure already undermined by this biblical God.[25] What from the human side can be seen as the necessary offering up of a sinful (but in fact arbitrarily chosen) victim for the good of the people, can from God's side be rationalized as a test of the faithfulness of that same victim. Human community can have its reconciling sacrifice, go about its scapegoating business, and continue to treat the accused as

25. In the intertestamental book of *Jubilees,* a new prologue is provided to the story of Abraham and Isaac, in explicit parallel with the book of Job. Just as Job's trial was instigated by a prosecutor, the Satan, in God's court, so the test of Abraham is initiated by a similar figure who suggests to God that Abraham loves Isaac more than he loves God. This explicit contrast highlights the fact that in the *akedah* God does not allow the actual killing and violence that take place in Job. This test of Abraham's faith draws a line short of actual sacrifice. See Levenson, *Death and Resurrection,* 176-78.

guilty. God could rationalize the community's persecution as a test for true righteousness. In that case, the will of God and the wills of the human scapegoaters have a convenient practical convergence in supporting the violence, if for slightly different reasons.

This is the final gambit of those who wish to side with Job's friends. A mysterious "testing" by God becomes essentially indistinguishable from retributive punishment for enormous offenses. This is a recipe for keeping the monotheistic God firmly within the logic of sacrifice. Job pleads with God for another path, offers another job description. God should become the vindicator Job hopes for, who sides with the isolated and outcast. God should become antireligious insofar as religion is constituted by this collective sacrifice. Instead of providing the ultimate authorization for this process, God should oppose it and become the champion of those it destroys. The fact that in the Psalms we so readily hear the voices of people scapegoated by their own community, calling out to God with anger and hope, shows that Job's plea was not in vain.

Steadfast Love and Not Sacrifice

Arguably, the two topics that receive the most space in the Hebrew scriptures are (1) violence and (2) ritual and cultic practice (the center of which is ritual sacrifice). I have suggested that these are actually one connected topic. Animal sacrifices and related rituals are most powerfully derived from human sacrifice, and in many cases such animal sacrifice retained an explicit awareness of its substitutionary character. Such substitution is a positive development, a way of curbing the violence that curbs violence, an attempt to stop human violence in a way that sheds no human blood. On the other hand, such practice is also a reinforcement and validation of the sacrificial mechanism it exhibited. When such sacrifice failed, it pointed inexorably toward escalation to human subjects. And when it flourished, the pattern of scapegoating was intensified elsewhere in the community.

It is no accident, then, that many of Israel's greatest prophets linked their outspoken rebuke of violence and exploitation in society with a critique of sacrifice. At the simplest level, they attacked those who held that fulfillment of cultic obligations was more important than meeting God's covenant commandments for justice and mercy to one's neighbors. Only at a few points did they go to the extreme of rejecting the validity of sacrifice completely. But the primary point of disagreement is about what we might call the trajectory of sacrifice. From one perspective, existing forms of sacrifice could be seen as an extension and affirmation of the logic of founding, scapegoating sacrifice, simply expressed by different means. What was valuable about sacrifice was that it used victims to get benefits.[26] From another perspective, existing rituals could be seen as an important if incomplete weakening of that logic. What was valuable about them was that they had stopped explicitly using human victims. Insofar as they supported sacrifice, the prophets were more in line with this second trajectory, and wished to see it extended further. Thus most of the prophets do not clamor for a complete end to the rituals, but they insist more and more that their true value should be found in the spirit of the worshipers. The value should be found not in the number and type of animal victims substituted for human ones, but in the empathy and justice shared with human victims.

In chastising Israel for falling away from its covenant with God, and in particular in criticizing its cultic preoccupations, the prophets charge that the people have misunderstood and misremembered their own beginnings. Israel itself was the persecuted outcast, the collective victim, when it was enslaved in Egypt. The prophet Amos sees an inverse relation between spiritual purity and the practice of sacrifice. "Did you bring to me sacrifices and offerings the forty years in the wilderness, O house of Israel?" (Amos 5:25). When deliverance from bondage was fresh in mind and their own experience as victims remembered, Israel did not have temple sacrifice. By contrast, in his own time he sees its well-oiled practice supported by the same ones who "push aside the needy in the gate" (5:12). For that reason God says,

> I hate, I despise your festivals. . . .
> Even though you offer me your burnt offerings and grain offerings,
>   I will not accept them;
> and the offerings of well-being of your fatted animals
>   I will not look upon. . . .
> But let justice roll down like waters,
>   and righteousness like an ever-flowing stream. (5:21-24)

26. This relates to the point whose discussion I have already noted in Levenson, *The Death and Resurrection of the Beloved Son.* In Exodus we find both a commandment that the firstborn (including human firstborn) belong to God for sacrifice and a commandment that the firstborn can be ransomed, i.e., that some other sacrifice can be substituted for them. This is antisacrificial in rescuing infants, but pro-sacrificial in affirming that in principle their lives are owed to God and are spared, so to speak, only by exception.

Hosea delivers a similar word:

> For I desire steadfast love and not sacrifice,
>   the knowledge of God rather than burnt offerings. (Hos. 6:6)

Both Ezekiel and Jeremiah single out the sacrifice of children with particular horror. Ezekiel is especially notable. He generally presents this practice as stemming from other gods and religions. Israelites who practice it have essentially forsaken their own faith. But in one passage the prophet reviews the various ways God considered punishing Israel for the people's failures when they were in the wilderness. Ezekiel relays this extraordinary admission from God: "Moreover I gave them statutes that were not good and ordinances by which they could not live. I defiled them through their very gifts, in their offering up all their firstborn, in order that I might horrify them, so that they might know that I am the LORD" (Ezek. 20:25-26). This sounds like an apology for God's requiring Israel to carry out its own practice of child sacrifice, saying this commandment was given to them either as a kind of punishment for their sin or as a kind of reverse object lesson. Some interpreters argue that it refers to God allowing the Israelites to go aside into the practices of other religions. That God "gave" them those statutes means God gave way and let them have them. At any rate, we can see this explicit disavowal of divine support as another step disentangling the biblical God from mythical, sacrificial prototypes, moving in the same direction as the book of Job.

The varied messages of the prophets about justice and God's concern for the widowed and poor and alien amount to this: "To know God is to know the cause of the victim."[27] Implicitly and explicitly, they saw a direct connection between the social victim and the ritual victim. The crowds that gathered in complete unity to kill the animal offerings looked strangely like the collective activity of the powerful in relation to the weak. Prophets see the scapegoat *theme* behind sacrificial practice and apply it to the social world around them. If Girard is right that ritual sacrifice largely comes from our social conflicts to begin with, then the prophets are only following it back to its roots. The prophets warned that people who believed that the practice of sacrifice would maintain peace and security were wrong. The prophetic warnings sowed dissent and provoked conflict in the heart of the community, witnessing that there would be no silent unanimity around the mistreatment of the innocent.

27. Williams, *The Bible*, 155.

This prophetic call is clearly connected with the voices we heard in the scapegoat psalms. In fact, the two flow together in Psalm 51 to point a path away from sacrifice.

> Then I will teach transgressors your ways,
>   and sinners will return to you.
> Deliver me from bloodshed, O God,
>   O God of my salvation. . . .
> For you have no delight in sacrifice;
>   if I were to give a burnt offering, you would not be pleased.
> The sacrifice acceptable to God is a broken spirit;
>   a broken and contrite heart, O God, you will not despise.
>
> (Ps. 51:13-17)

Who Could Have Imagined His Future?

For later Christians the revelation of persecuting sacrifice that is so deep in the Old Testament reaches a special climax in the "songs of the servant" in the book of Isaiah.[28] Here in the figure of the suffering servant we find perhaps the single most prominent scriptural text for early Christian interpretation of the cross. It is worth considering the fourth servant song at length:

> See, my servant shall prosper;
>   he shall be exalted and lifted up,
>   and shall be very high.
> Just as there were many who were astonished at him
>   — so marred was his appearance, beyond human semblance,
>   and his form beyond that of mortals —
> so he shall startle many nations;
>   kings shall shut their mouths because of him;
> for that which had not been told them they shall see,
>   and that which they had not heard they shall contemplate.

---

28. The stylistic integrity of these passages, which sets them off from earlier portions of the book, was a key element in the identification of a text identified as the work of "Second Isaiah." Interpreters have disagreed strongly over whether the figure of the servant is an individual person or a collective reference (to all of Israel, for instance) or a combination of both. This point is not crucial for our purposes.

Who has believed what we have heard?
    And to whom has the arm of the LORD been revealed?
For he grew up before him like a young plant,
    and like a root out of dry ground;
he had no form or majesty that we should look at him. . . .

He was despised and rejected by others;
    a man of suffering and acquainted with infirmity. . . .
Surely he has borne our infirmities
    and carried our diseases;
yet we accounted him stricken,
    struck down by God, and afflicted.
But he was wounded for our transgressions,
    crushed for our iniquities;
upon him was the punishment that made us whole,
    and by his bruises we are healed.
All we like sheep have gone astray;
    we have all turned to our own way,
and the LORD has laid on him the iniquity of us all.

He was oppressed, and he was afflicted,
    yet he did not open his mouth;
like a lamb that is led to the slaughter,
    and like a sheep that before its shearers is silent,
        so did he not open his mouth.
By a perversion of justice he was taken away.
    Who could have imagined his future?
For he was cut off from the land of the living,
    stricken for the transgression of my people.
They made his grave with the wicked
    and his tomb with the rich,
although he had done no violence,
    and there was no deceit in his mouth.

Yet it was the will of the LORD to crush him with pain.
When you make his life an offering for sin,
    he shall see his offspring, and shall prolong his days;
through him the will of the LORD shall prosper.
    Out of his anguish he shall see light;
he shall find satisfaction through his knowledge.

The righteous one, my servant, shall make many righteous,
    and he shall bear their iniquities.
Therefore I will allot him a portion with the great,
    and he shall divide the spoil with the strong;
because he poured out himself to death,
    and was numbered with the transgressors;
yet he bore the sin of many,
    and made intercession for the transgressors. (Isa. 52:13–53:12)

These words are so familiar, and so freighted with tradition, that it is hard to hear them say anything new. But compare them with the description of the sacrificial scapegoat presented in our last chapter. This passage says concisely in a few sentences all that was contained there. Consider it first not as a mystical job description for a unique messiah, but as an anthropological account of a repeated reality. As Gil Bailie says, "The Suffering Servant Songs combine two insights: first, that the victim was innocent and his persecutors wrong, and second, that his victimization was socially beneficial and that his punishment brought the community peace."[29]

This is presented in great detail. "He had no form or majesty that we should look at him." The persecuted one is likely chosen from the marginal or those whose appearance is marred, and so is more easily rejected. "He was despised." The person chosen is without supporters, isolated and abandoned. "Surely he has borne our infirmities and carried our diseases." The victim has been chosen and will suffer because of *our* problem, our collective disease of rivalry and conflict. The impetus comes not from some offense in the victim but from a need in us. "Yet we *accounted* him stricken, struck down by God." We thought this, but we were wrong. Though the problem is ours, we believed it was this one who was the cause, this one who was hated by God, this one who deserved the Job and the Joseph and the Abel treatment.

"But he was wounded for our transgressions." In fact, it is because we could not maintain peaceful relations that we require a sacrifice. We wound because of our iniquities. And wounding *is* another iniquity. "Upon him was the punishment that made us whole." We are actually reconciled and freed by this violence, even though the victim is wrongly charged and we are the actual guilty ones. Hating together unites us, stops our divisions. What hurts him helps us. "All we like sheep have gone

29. Bailie, *Violence Unveiled*, 44.

astray." We are all involved. We do this together; we have all turned to scapegoating. "By a perversion of justice he was taken away." The entire procedure by which we carry out this killing may claim to have some moral basis, but there is no justice in it.

This is about as clear as it can be about religious scapegoating violence. It is an unequivocally bad thing, with undeniably good results. To perceive this sacrificial mechanism in others is unusual, a breakthrough. To face it explicitly in our own behavior may be, literally, miraculous.

Of course, there is another element in the text, expressed most powerfully in two lines: "And the LORD has laid on him the iniquity of us all" and "Yet it was the will of the LORD to crush him with pain." Otherwise the passage is giving an uncannily clear description of violent sacrifice as the unjust if fruitful persecution of an innocent victim, wrongly attributed to God rather than to our own evil. But these lines appear to turn around and say it is all God's idea after all.

The different biblical voices we have been examining in various ways exposed and criticized this foundational religious dynamic, and set God against it. The trail of attention to scapegoats in the Bible leads to this moment of blinding clarity about what is going on. And at this point, it seems, the writer blinks, and in a few words draws the whole thing back under divine authorization. That long struggle to hear the voice of victims backslides into a passive acceptance, the surrender of a crushed Job who mumbles that it must be right after all.

Is that what's going on? No. But let's suppose for a moment that it were. If we stop there, we still have something completely new. In the past the participants in persecuting sacrifice, including the divine participants, endorsed it as something other than what it actually was. They accepted a mythical account, the validity of the accusations, the guilt of the victim. They did it because they thought it was right. What is proposed in this text would be a *knowing* acceptance of sacrifice for what it actually is. God knows and we know that it is the evil killing of an innocent, for our own benefit.[30] This is the way the world works. We go ahead anyway. It's wrong, but useful. This is a God who has read Nietzsche, and agrees.

But this isn't what the text is saying. The writer is not talking about divine approval for sacrificial business as usual, and the sign is in the way God's will is distinguished from the will of the persecutors. Isaiah says

---

30. It is highly questionable how well this can actually work. Can we find harmony and peace with each other by persecuting a scapegoat, when we are aware that is what we are doing? That is an issue we will return to in chapter 9.

that we, the sacrificers, esteemed the victim stricken by God. But the whole tenor of the text is that it was wrong to think that. We are the ones who wounded and crushed the scapegoat with our iniquities. If what is being done is so clearly wrong, why would God support it? If it was wrong to think that God inflicted the punishment, what does it mean to turn around and say that God laid on him the iniquities of us all? It can mean only that there are two different things going on. When we inflict our iniquities on the victim, it is not the same event as when God lays those same iniquities on him. The writer of the servant song brings these two together with the suggestion that "the victim was allowed to be struck down by a God who counted his sufferings as an atonement for the faults of the very mob that inflicted them on him."[31]

God is doing something different from what the persecutors are doing. The Isaiah text gives us many plain indications of this shift. It ends with exaltation of the servant. And it begins with verses that already presume the vindication of the sacrificed one. "See, my servant shall prosper; / he shall be exalted and lifted up. . . ." The victim's cause will be upheld, in a way that will startle the nations, "for that which had not been told them they shall see, / and that which they had not heard they shall contemplate." Though what is happening is old and common (even if the blunt description of it is new), *this instance* of it is going to be dramatically different. It has a purpose counter to, but superimposed on, the standard purpose of sacrifice. This is powerfully reflected in the lines "By a perversion of justice he was taken away. / Who could have imagined his future?" Clearly, those doing the sacrifice do not imagine it, a sign that God is not playing the same game they are.

The text says, "When you make his life an offering for sin, / he shall see his offspring, and shall prolong his days; / through him the will of the LORD shall prosper." In other words, when you sacrifice him as a sin offering, it won't work. Instead of falling into death and oblivion, the servant will live long and see descendants. Through him the will of the Lord — and not the will of his killers — will prosper. The servant will be blessed ("Out of his anguish he shall see light") and will bless many others ("the righteous one, my servant, shall make many righteous"). Traditional sacrifice may accomplish something very real. It may still our strife for a time. One thing it cannot do is make its practitioners righteous, since they must sin to carry it out. Somehow the servant's death is to save them from what led to the killing.

31. Bailie, *Violence Unveiled*, 45.

We can understand this better by comparing the servant in this passage with Job. Job is a full-scale resister to his scapegoating, but the servant is patient, like a sheep that before its shearers is dumb. Job protests his personal innocence while the friends enlist God to argue his guilt, and the outcome is up in the air. The servant songs are crystal clear that the servant is suffering unjustly for other people's sins, and it is a mistake to think the servant guilty. Job demands some kind of vindication from God. He does have his earthly prosperity restored, but gets no unequivocal verdict in his favor, no reply to his plea for an accounting from God. The entire episode of his suffering is still posed as a test proposed to God by Satan, an episode that turns out to be a test of God too. By contrast the servant song is framed by an affirmation of the victory of the victim. The servant does not protest, because the protest has been heard and validated by God. The song directly proclaims the innocence of the servant and the injustice of the persecution. The servant is in league with God to change this dynamic. This sacrifice is not meant to be one in a long line. The servant is a singular figure, and the effect of his life will be something new: "for that which had not been told them they shall see." For a beginning, in this picture of the servant, the nations see what they had not been told about their own scapegoating practice.

The servant song tells a story like that of Job, from a different perspective. This time there is no doubt about the scapegoat's innocence, no doubt about the evil of the suffering inflicted, no doubt whose side God is on. The focus has shifted. Now it rests on the sins of the persecutors. Us. Job poses a question: How can God be justified in face of the arbitrary suffering of a righteous person ganged against by everyone, including God? The servant poses a different question. Assuming that God decides to side with the scapegoat, how can those who do the violence ever be justified? If the first was about how the one can be rescued, the second is about how the many can be saved.

Starting with This Scripture

What is violence doing in the Bible? It is telling us the truth, the truth about our human condition, about the fundamental dynamics that lead to human bloodshed, and most particularly, the truth about the integral connection between religion and violence. There is no way to be truthful without exhibiting these things. If we complain that the tales of Genesis and the bloody sacrifices of Leviticus, and the fire for revenge in the

Psalms, are too sordidly, familiarly human to have any place in religious revelation, we make an interesting admission that they reveal our humanity all too well. We always knew this was the way things were, we claim. We don't need a religious text to tell us so. We need cures, not diagnosis. But is that true? What if our cures need diagnosing?

Chapter 2 suggested that there are at least some crucial kinds of violence whose nature has not been evident to us at all, those kinds of violence whose very role is to stem our conflicts. A simple way to put it would be to say that our reconciling violence is not evident to us, but always goes under another name: revenge, purification, divine sacrifice. If that is a basic fact of human life, then where violence is not being faced it is being justified. Where it is not being explicitly described, it is not absent, but invisible. To exhibit violence is to run the risk of enflaming people's appetite for it. But to veil it under euphemism and mythology, to be piously silent before its sacred power, is to make its rule absolute.

In places (such as the passage from Leviticus that we quoted above) the only real revelatory dimension we can see in the text is that it begins to show us what was usually hidden (not what should be our ideal). Yet even that small step is harder than we understand. Critics of Christianity attack the "violent God of the Old Testament" as the sociopathic cousin in an extended family of much better adjusted deities. But the offense of the Bible might be put the other way around. It suggests that the better-adjusted deities are (literally) a myth. Take the crudest form in which the biblical God appears — a vengeful divine warrior crushing enemies, a deity who delights in blood as the cost and sign of commitment and reconciliation. This is the place to start because this is what the gods of the traditional sacred are. And they are no less powerful where people have stopped going to the religious temple or altar.

The God described in the Bible appears in a variety of characterizations. The God represented in the passage about collective stoning in Leviticus looks different from the God presented in Amos or Isaiah, for instance. Such diversity is a cue for valuable critical-historical investigation. That investigation can lead to a strategy of interpretation in which some textual traditions are preferred over others or earlier, more "primitive" ideas of God may be disregarded in favor of what are taken to be later, more sophisticated ones. If applied narrowly, this approach would suggest that there is no truth revealed in the earlier or the contrasting pictures of God that would be lost when we pass on to later, preferred ones. And this leads us to wonder why the historically or theologically less valued elements should have a place in scripture at all. But at least in some cases this variety embodied in the biblical narrative may be a crucial part of the truth that it has to impart. According to the picture we have been building, certain characterizations of sacrificial violence and God's relation are a crucial part of the whole narrative. They reveal something very important, something not duplicated elsewhere, and something of continuing relevance. They are a necessary part of our understanding, even while they are not themselves a sufficient model for our behavior.

Why, then, doesn't the Bible just describe these things as the nature of *other* gods and religions, and make it clear that this does not apply to the true God, the biblical God, our God, who is always untouched by them? Then we could have the benefit of the analysis of such practices without any suggestion that they belong to our own faith. But such externalization would dramatically amplify the dangers of triumphalism that have been real enough as it is. Instead, the Bible's presentation makes it uncomfortably clear that this description does apply to our God and our religion, since they can easily be entangled in just the same sacrificial dynamic and have been. The scapegoat critique in the biblical tradition emerges as a critique *of* that tradition. This is the weight of the prophetic voices, who reminded Israel that despite the calling of the new and true God they steadily fell away into the old ways, doing so even in the name of God. The way the story is told to us who belong to it forbids that we should suppose we are exempt from the danger it discovers.

What is violence doing in the Bible? It is showing us the nature of the mimetic conflict that threatens to destroy human community. It is showing us the religious dynamic of scapegoating sacrifice that arises to allay such crisis. It is letting us hear the voices of the persecuted victims and their pleas for revenge and vindication. It is showing God's judgment (even violent judgment) against violence, and most particularly, God's siding with the outcast victims of scapegoating persecution. The Old Testament is an antimyth. It is thick with bodies, the voices of victims and threatened victims. This landscape is either the product of an idiosyncratic, bloodthirsty imagination or the actual landscape of history and religion. If the latter, then what is remarkable is not that the scriptures describe it, but that we should think it normal not to.

We have explored some of the elements in the Hebrew scriptures that bear on our topic. I have emphasized several that were picked up in later Christian tradition, and will consider a few more in the next section. This is not mere background material. It unveils a truth without which Christians would be incapable of formulating their own faith, even as they saw their faith extending and realizing that truth.

The book of Acts reports that an angel sent the disciple Philip out onto the road to Gaza from Jerusalem, where he met an Ethiopian eunuch riding in a chariot and reading aloud from the prophet Isaiah. "Do you understand what you are reading?" Philip asked. "How can I, unless someone guides me?" the eunuch responded. The passage he was reading was this one:

> Like a lamb that is led to the slaughter,
>   and like a sheep that before its shearers is silent,
>   so he did not open his mouth.
> By a perversion of justice he was taken away.
>   Who could have imagined his future?
> For he was cut off from the land of the living.

Acts goes on, "Then Philip began to speak, and starting with this scripture, he proclaimed to him the good news about Jesus" (Acts 8:35). Good news about a cross.

PART TWO

Visible Victim

The Cross We Can't Forget

He asked, "Who are you, Lord?" The reply came, "I am Jesus, whom you are persecuting."

Acts 9:5

CHAPTER FOUR

The Paradox of the Passion

Saved by What Shouldn't Happen

Like the light, it is at once the thing that we need to see, and
the thing that permits us to see it.

René Girard[1]

Every spring, Sunday after Sunday, the church reads its way along the
path to Jesus' death on Good Friday and the celebration of Easter.
The first few years I was a pastor, I experienced what it was like to preach
your way through that journey. I became aware as I never had before of an
incredible tension built into the story. The problem was so obvious I
sometimes wondered whether someone was going to stand up in church
to interrupt in pure frustration.

Jesus sets his face to go to Jerusalem. He teaches his disciples that the
Messiah must be delivered over and die. He goes "as it is written" in
prophecy. Despite his own reluctance, he does nothing to avoid the end —
"not my will, but thy will be done," he says. He is supposed to die. Yet the
Gospels are equally emphatic that Jesus is innocent, falsely accused, that
his killing is unjust, that it is shameful for his friends to abandon him,
that those who try and execute him are indifferent to truth, captive to
evil, motivated by expediency and power. It is wrong for him to die.

Which is it? Are Pilate and Judas criminals or saints? Do the Gospels
even have their story straight? It makes you seasick when Jesus himself

1. René Girard and Michel Treguer, *Quand Ces Choses Commenceront* (Paris: Arlea, 1994),
138.

boils it down in a couple of sentences about Judas: "The Son of man goes as it is written of him, but woe to that man by whom the Son of man is betrayed! It would have been better for that man if he had not been born" (Mark 14:21 RSV). In short, Jesus' death saves the world, and it ought not happen. It's God's plan and an evil act. It is a good bad thing.

If the story is so familiar that we don't see this problem, we have lost the key. Until we have this problem, nothing else is going to make sense. The paradox is not there by mistake. The strange shape of the Christian gospel has a family resemblance to the other good bad thing we have discussed: sacrifice. This is the clue we need. It is at the heart of an understanding of the cross.

Leaving Out the Cross

For a moment, let's think about the objections raised to atonement theology the other way around. What would Christianity need to be to avoid all the criticisms about this shocking sight at the center of its faith, the charges of unseemly brutality? What if, in place of the passion narratives of the Gospels, Christians had instead the following text:

> Christ — the living wisdom of God — came down to earth. He visited a great city in the form of a stranger, a swarthy carpenter with a withered leg, whose father no one knew. He came to call back those who had fallen into ignorance. He taught many things to those who had the inner ears to hear. But those who saw only his outward form did not understand the grace he brought. He did many miracles, and the people worshiped him for this reason and made him their king. But still their ignorance was not dispelled. One day the heavens opened in wrath against that land. Each house in the city was set against another, and great fires burned there day and night. So Christ prepared his final miracle. One day he called to him Mary, his mother, and his dearest disciple. He went into the temple and ate the bread in the Holy of Holies, which no person is to touch. They lay together there near the altar throughout the night. While they lay there the earth shook, and many in the city were stricken with a deadly disease and the people were afraid. He sent Mary away, telling her she must return without fail at the first hour and that whatever she found at that time must be cast outside the gates. In the morning, when the people came to the temple, seeking to know what evil had been done

to bring these troubles upon them, they found nothing but the smallest mustard seed lying near the altar. He had taken the form of a mustard seed, carrying the entirety of divinity within him. All the people were greatly distressed at this. Priests and soldiers, foreigners and natives, members of every tribe — all were seized with awe in a kind of trance. Heeding Mary, they rushed together with one spirit to form a procession and carried the seed to a stony hill where they threw it in a great hole that opened there. And each person, without exception, threw in stones to cover it. Miraculously the seed immediately grew up into a great tree, and Christ himself was in the fruit of that tree. Everyone who ate of this fruit awakened as if from sleep, purged from every anger and distress. The people returned to the city rejoicing, and health and peace ruled in those walls.[2]

This is a rich symbolic story, full of allegorical possibilities. There is no offensive violence, no punishment or glorified suffering. How different things might have been if Christians had made such a parable of spiritual self-discovery their text, a tree of life and not a cross of blood. We would not be embarrassed by charges of victimization in our scriptures. As an added bonus, the meaning of this story is not tied down to messy questions about what actually happened. Its spiritual value is the same if we regard it as entirely imaginative rather than historical.

Let us add just one additional clarification, namely, that this text in fact refers to the event of Jesus' execution, which took place as described in the Gospels. The drawback to the text, in other words, is that it is a lie about a lynching. This is an example of what an account of Jesus' death would look like if it were a true myth in Girard's sense. If we suspect that there is an execution behind this story, we can see many telltale signs. There are typical marginalizing marks of the victim (a physical deformity, alien status, uncertain birth), indications of social conflict coming to a crisis point (conflict of one house against another, "fire" sweeping the city), traces of the accusations (incest, profaning holy things), the unanimity of the mob violence (stoning and burying the "seed"), the unifying benefits of the killing.

We can easily see how a ritual could evolve from this story, perhaps the annual offering of a sacrificial victim at the foot of the sacred tree. Above all, what is mythical is that the killing has disappeared from view completely, and no issues of persecution, guilt, or violence are present in the

---

2. This is an imaginary text — an amalgamation I made up, drawing on elements quite common in various myths.

text at all. There is nothing to trouble anyone's conscience from one offering to the next. If we would be happy to substitute this text for the account of the Gospels, knowing that Jesus' death is perhaps the one thing in his life about which we are historically most certain, it says something interesting about us. We like to avert our eyes from victims.

Our text is imaginary, but versions much like it competed to become Christianity. It shows what the cross would normally look like when it cannot be seen. Part 1 showed us the first side of the cross, the glimpse through the veil to real victims and their real suffering. Isaiah pointed us to a second side of the cross, a thought that it might have a use different from and counter to its ancient one. It might be an occasion to overthrow sacrifice. That is our concern now.

Just Another Myth

Christianity claims that Christ's life and work are decisively significant, and that this extends to his death as well. Yet plainly there are many instances of dying and rising gods to be found in mythology and religious traditions. The important thing to grasp is that the kind of uniqueness Christians believe in depends upon a sameness. The whole point of our first section was that what happened to Jesus has happened innumerable times to others. It has been going on not from the very beginning, from the creation of the world, but since the post-Eden human foundation of the world. In a very real way it lies at the root of our existing social world. In this sense Jesus' death is not special at all. To know this, however, we need something like revelation to pierce the veil of myth and to realize that there are real crosses behind it. To know that the outline of Jesus' death fits a pattern common to countless others, we first need to recognize that pattern and realize that other real sacrificial victims exist behind the symbols of myth. Jesus' death, along with the biblical traditions we have reviewed that provide the framework for its interpretation, is the instrument of that realization. It is therefore at the same time an act to reverse the domination of sacrifice.

Between myth and the passion there is an odd mix of profound continuity and radical difference. Girard recounted his shock of recognition in coming to the New Testament passion narratives after his work on violence and sacrifice in anthropology and the history of religion.[3] He found

3. See especially René Girard, Jean-Michel Oughourlian, and Guy Lefort, *Things Hidden since the Foundation of the World* (Stanford, Calif.: Stanford University Press, 1987).

there all the classic elements that characterize sacrificial myths: the crowd coalescing against an individual, the charges of the greatest crimes and impurities, the scapegoating violence, the desire for social peace. But he was startled to recognize that the reality of what was happening was fully explicit, not hidden. It was the same standard story. But this time it was laid out in actual historical narrative. This time it was told from the point of view of the victim, who was unmistakably visible as unjustly accused and wrongly killed. This time God's vindication is unmistakable and universal. As Philip told the Ethiopian counselor, it is the story of Isaiah's servant, but told of a real person, in a specific place, at a certain time.

When anthropologists began to catalogue the various myths of dying and rising gods to be found across cultures, and lumped the Jesus story in with them, some Christians reacted in outrage. They insisted that this disparaged Jesus' importance and contended that he did not belong in that company. One notable exception was the apologist C. S. Lewis. Lewis knew the world's mythological heritage far better than most. He maintained that the match was a good one, that in fact the myths and the Gospels were telling the same story. The only difference was that this story became fact only once, in Jesus. As he put it, "The old myth of the Dying God, *without ceasing to be myth,* comes down from the heaven of legend and imagination to the earth of history. It *happens* — at a particular date, in a particular place, followed by definable historical consequences. We pass from a Baldur or an Osiris, dying nobody knows when or where, to an historical Person crucified . . . *under Pontius Pilate.*"[4]

There was more to Lewis's point than he realized. He saw that the redeemer myths were about an unreal demigod "dying" in some indeterminate time and place. It was only a story, while Jesus was flesh and blood. But we are suggesting that behind the mythical stories there were actually also flesh and blood victims. Jesus' cross wasn't the one time it happened. It was the time we knew it happened, and became able to see others. Lewis is quite right. Against the background of the myths of the dying and rising gods, the special thing about Jesus is that he is real. The concrete reality of this cross allows us to uncover the reality of others. From the per-

---

4. C. S. Lewis, *God in the Dock: Essays on Theology and Ethics* (Grand Rapids: Eerdmans, 1970), 66-67. In fact, this was a key point in Lewis's own journey to conversion. As he recounted, "[T]he hardest boiled of all the atheists I ever knew sat in my room on the other side of the fire and remarked that the evidence for the historicity of the Gospels was really surprisingly good. 'Rum thing,' he went on. 'All that stuff of Frazer's about the Dying God. Rum thing. It almost looks as if it had really happened once.'" C. S. Lewis, *Surprised by Joy: The Shape of My Early Life,* 1st American ed. (New York: Harcourt Brace, 1956), 223-24.

spective of myth, we can look right at it and be blind. From the foot of the cross, we see it for what it is.

The paradox we have noted in the passion narratives is reflected back in much criticism of Christianity. We commonly hear in the same breath that the Christian gospel is "just another myth" and also somehow worse than all others. It is nothing special and uniquely bad. Illogical though this may seem, it manifests an awareness of the same continuity and discontinuity we are describing.

We are familiar, for instance, with the argument that Christians took some original historical story — of a troublesomely charismatic rabbi, say — and gradually projected onto it the mythical superstructure of a savior deity, in order to conform to the religious influences around them. Thus, over a period of centuries Jesus became God. Though still advanced confidently in many places, this well-traveled theory has had to backtrack to a much more tentative and ambiguous form than what was advanced in earlier generations of scholarship. The segregation of low Christologies to earlier periods and high Christologies to later ones has proven impossible to maintain convincingly as a historical conclusion. The elements of each are present in all chronological periods.

From Girard's perspective the truth is almost exactly the opposite of what is supposed in that argument. Its critique of Christianity is entirely understandable. This is what Christianity *should* be, as a religion, since this is the direction traditional religion generally moves. Actual human victims are sacrificed and then their reality and the reality of their persecution are erased by projecting divine figures into their place in memory and myth. Christians confess just the opposite: Jesus was fully God, as well as human, *before* the cross, and remains unmistakably the real, crucified victim after it. The Christian account, nowhere more evidently than in the passion, says it took a divine intervention, a revelatory act, for us to translate supernatural myths into the actual historical realities behind them. For once, God actually was the victim, with the reverse effect of unveiling the humans beneath the symbols.

The fact, if not its significance, is often plainly recognized by those who think it marks a great deficiency in Christianity. A notable study of mythology traces the clashes and amalgamation of a patriarchal, battle-gods mythology with a local, earthbound goddess mythology. It was out of one arena for this collision, the fertile crescent in west Asia, that "the late classical, Hellenistic, and Roman mystery cults developed, of which the Christian sect was a popular, non-esoteric, politically manageable, state-supported variant, wherein symbols that in others were read in a mystic, anagogical way, proper to symbols, were reduced to a literal sense and referred to supposed or actual historical events."[5] In other words, rather than building supernatural structures over history, rather than reading symbols properly, the way they ought to be read (in this writer's perspective), Christians were reducing the symbols back into the history behind them. The Christian account of Jesus' death forced people to look behind myth at the realities of literal violence.

So Christianity is like all the others. And it's not. Along these same lines, some deride "Judeo-Christian religion" for its low symbolic quality and its crude moral literalism. They deplore the Bible's brutal representations of violence, its fixation on persecution and murder. The biblical tradition lacks the beauty and imaginative sophistication of great myth. The story of Jesus' death is a cut-rate version of the sacrifice of the corn king with all the poetry missing, flattened into something that belongs on a police blotter and not in high spiritual culture. Let us suppose that they are descriptively correct about Christianity's unusual focus on this kind of material. Then if it should turn out that in fact there is a transformative and liberating value to such representations, to the unveiling of a violent dynamic that is otherwise largely unrecognized and unchallenged, it would seem such critics have themselves already testified to the Bible's special positive revelation. In that case the criticism is backward. Many major myths are rooted in sacrificial violence, prescribe it and shield us from awareness of our complicity in it. That is why they do not show it directly. The Bible makes violence visible, and therefore makes its victims uncomfortably visible too.

The sensitivity to victims so often now turned against the Bible is itself rooted there. We would not accuse the Gospels of victimization if we had not already been converted by them. Critics would not so insistently contend that the gospel is just another myth and at the same time a uniquely bad one, unless they saw the contrast. As Girard puts it, "From the moment we truly understand myths, we can no longer accept the Gospel as yet another myth, since it is responsible for our understanding."[6] We would not look for scapegoated victims in every corner if the magnifying glass of the cross had not become second nature for us. Enthusiasts for myth think that only spiritual philistines would worry about whether an actual person was literally crucified. The Gospels are of the opinion that this is a religious concern of the first order.

---

5. Joseph Campbell, *The Masks of God,* vol. 4, *Creative Mythology* (New York: Viking Press, 1970), 406.

6. René Girard, *The Scapegoat* (Baltimore: Johns Hopkins University Press, 1986), 205.

This is the meaning of Jesus' passion in the four Gospels. What God demands is not a sacrifice of his Son, not a perfect scapegoat, but the unconditional refusal of scapegoating, even if the price must be death. . . .

Instead of covering up once again the collective ignorance of unanimous victimage, the four texts of the passion disclose it so thoroughly that, in the long run, the hiddenness of scapegoating is everywhere uncovered and its power to persuade gradually undermined.[7]

The scapegoating process is stripped of its sacred mystery, and the collective persecution and abandonment are painfully illustrated for what they are, so that no one, including the disciples, the proto-Christians, can honestly say afterward that they resisted the sacrificial tide. In myth no victims are visible as victims, and therefore neither are any persecutors. But in the New Testament the victim is unmistakably visible and the collective persecutors (including in the end virtually everyone) and their procedures are illustrated in sharp clarity.

One value of our new angle of vision is that it helps us to see that the tension in the passion narratives over whether Jesus' death is a good thing or a bad thing is not an embarrassment to be smoothed over somehow. This "contradiction" indelibly marks the whole story. Its prominence as the driving narrative theme of the Gospels in fact perfectly mirrors their message. The sacrificial necessity that claims Jesus is a sinful mechanism for victimization, whose rationale maintains it is necessary that one innocent person die for the good of the people. The free, loving "necessity" that leads God to be willing to stand in the place of the scapegoat is that this is the way to unmask the sacrificial mechanism, to break its cycles of mythic reproduction, and to found human community on a nonsacrificial principle: solidarity with the victim, not unanimity against the victim.

In the balance of this chapter we will go over the account of Jesus' death in more detail, to draw out its relation with the sacrificial prototype.

---

7. René Girard, foreword to *The Bible, Violence, and the Sacred: Liberation from the Myth of Sanctioned Violence,* by James G. Williams, 1st ed. (San Francisco: HarperSanFrancisco, 1991), vi.

The Old, Old Story

The basic setting for scapegoating is a crisis of conflict or the threatened escalation of conflict within a community. The Jerusalem of Holy Week certainly qualifies. Here we have a subject people ruled by imperial conquerors of different race and religion. Over this simmering political, cultural, and religious tension we lay the various divisions between factions within the Jewish community and between the Roman governor and the local client-king Herod. Then we add the heightened passions that come with the yearly holiday of Passover, which brings crowds of Jews from many lands into the city to the temple to recall their origins as a people and to take part in hallowed sacrificial rites. It is a week that has seen riot and massacre in the past. Finally, we mix in the uncertainty and excitement focused around a charismatic preacher and his following. The police and the military are on full alert. It is the type of situation in which even a purely personal incident in the market or temple can quickly become a brawl between factions and just as quickly escalate to engulf the entire community of poised opponents in strike and counterstrike.

This is the scene that Jesus enters, offering many classic marks of a candidate for sacrifice. He is of humble (perhaps illegitimate) birth. He, like many of his followers, is an outsider, from Galilee, a region of mixed religious practices without close ties to the temple cult. His preaching and healing have isolated him into a precarious prominence and attracted whispers that he is in league with demonic powers. Crowds follow and acclaim him. But during his ministry crowds have also on occasion just as quickly formed to threaten him with death. He is readily perceived as a possible threat and rival by both political and religious leaders.

The charges brought against him are commensurate with the level of crisis in the situation. He is accused of the most extreme offense possible to Roman political authorities, sedition. "We found this man perverting our nation, forbidding us to pay taxes to the emperor, and saying that he himself is the Messiah, a king" (Luke 23:2). And he is accused of the most extreme offense possible to the religious authorities, blasphemy. "Then the high priest tore his clothes and said, 'He has blasphemed! Why do we still need witnesses? You have now heard his blasphemy. What is your verdict?' They answered, 'He deserves death'" (Matt. 26:65-66). Before he is killed, he is mocked in the garb of royalty, as a kind of criminal king. He is condemned in the midst of a mob, led through the streets of the city and executed publicly.

A crucial aspect of scapegoating sacrifice is its unanimity. And a striking feature in the Gospel narratives is the way we see the collective violence form. A follower betrays him, another denies him, the rest drop away into silence in the face of a crowd that finally calls for crucifixion with one voice. By the end of Friday afternoon Jesus is dead and there is peace in the city. The quiet includes his closest friends and followers. They are thoroughly dejected, with no courage or inclination to publicly dissent from the official epitaph that declares Jesus a condemned heretic and traitor. They have no alternative meaning to propose.

Surely This Man Was Innocent

So all the pieces are in place. It is the standard pattern. But the enormous difference is that the pieces are *visibly* in place. Successful sacrifice is like a magic trick. What actually happens and what everyone believes is happening are two different things. The passion narratives break the spell. They describe the trick with all its moving parts. They highlight what is always in shadow: the innocence of the scapegoat, the arbitrary and unjust way the victim has been selected, the ulterior purposes sacrifice exists to serve. This reversal can be described very simply. In traditional sacrifice the community is unquestioningly in the right and the scapegoat is universally condemned. But when we think of the cast of characters in the passion — Judas, Peter, Caiaphas, Pilate, Herod, the crowd — what do they conjure in our minds? What reputations do they carry for their part in this event, from the beginning, in the text itself? They stand for cowardly, immoral complicity at best and active evil at worst. To be likened to any of them is not a compliment. The sacrificial model may be a war of all against one. But this telling condemns the many, not the one.

The Gospel accounts are written in stereo, we might say. On one side is the underlying pattern with all its mythic components in place. On the other side is a constant counterpoint of elements that reveal the hidden realities, the true structure of scapegoating. Judas, the betrayer, brings back his thirty pieces of silver, saying, "I have sinned in betraying innocent blood" (Matt. 27:3-4 RSV). A thief crucified with Jesus says, "We are receiving the due reward of our deeds; but this man has done nothing wrong" (Luke 23:41 RSV). In the Gospel of Luke, at the moment of Jesus' death the centurion at the cross exclaims, "Surely this man was innocent." This is not the voice of myth. It is a profound counterconfession, a voice of dissent raised at the very moment all dissent should be ended.

What we see before us is the climax of the same old ritual, but we do see it. The unanimity of the act is still irresistible, but the passion accounts are seeded with these moments when participants are made to speak the truth. There is no invisible violence, no veiled reference to Jesus "being returned to the bosom of the waters." The assumption that Jesus is a terrible criminal who has brought disaster on the whole people does not go unquestioned. We see what is actually going on — the execution of an innocent victim — and we see the real reasons, not the stated ones.

We see the explicit social crisis. We see the motives that lead various factions to choose Jesus as the most useful object of persecution. In myth, collective violence is a kind of divine madness that sweeps up everyone. But in truth, unanimity has to be assembled through a combination of fear, hatred, and contagion. We see the power of this process at work, even when Jesus has alerted the disciples in advance. We see the fear that leads to Peter's denial. We hear that at Jesus' appearance before the high priests, "many bore false witness against him, and their witness did not agree" (Mark 14:56 RSV). We see Pilate's hesitation, his attempt to barter victims and his self-serving agreement with the crowd. And we are allowed to see the small ineffectual cracks in the unanimity as well. The cock crows for Peter. The two Marys and a disciple of Jesus stay by him at the cross. Joseph of Arimathea stands forward to ask for the body.

Consider the two key charges against Jesus: sedition and blasphemy. These are classic scapegoat charges, threatening disaster for all. But the Gospel accounts strip things to the bone, the better to make them clear. Everyone, including the persecutors, speaks with greater clarity and awareness than is natural to those actually taking part in the sacrificial process, let alone to the story produced after the fact to rationalize it. The mystery of that process is ruthlessly punctured. The charges against Jesus are given in a clear and "demythologized" form in the Gospels' account, so that they carry us to the root of the matter: the unity of the community in the midst of escalating division and conflict. The waters are not muddied with accusations of incest or bestiality or magically spreading disease. Things are very much in the open, including the persecutors' accounts of their motives. Pilate, for instance, says outright that he finds no guilt in Jesus, and yet is perfectly willing to execute him for the sake of peace. It is finally a matter of indifference to him whether the victim is Jesus or Barabbas. The focus is clearly on the arbitrary need for a victim as a political sacrifice.

We see how Jesus is pressed into the mold of a maximal criminal, whose death will be a service. The "marks of the victim" are present. Jesus is a Galilean outsider, isolated by his charismatic prominence. But the Gospels keep the focus on the process that molds Jesus into the victim's role, even while they note those features that may provide an excuse for people to turn against him. When Roman soldiers drape Jesus in royal robes, this is presented as a straightforward, sadistic persecution and not some sacred ritual. In rites of sacrifice a king might be subjected to abuse and taunts before the killing, or an outcast criminal might be accorded all the trappings of power and paraded in royal style prior to execution. These mythical signposts appear in the passion, but are firmly tied to the actual conflictual dynamics from which they arise.

The collective nature of sacrificial violence is a key element, and the passion narratives give particular attention to the role of the crowd. This is reflected in the dramatic contrast between the throngs that acclaim Jesus on his entry into the city on Palm Sunday and the mob that cries for his death on Friday. Pilate, rather than dominating this mob, seeks to manipulate it, and yet seems to be influenced and recruited by it instead. The texts emphasize the participation of virtually all the possible players in the condemnation of Jesus.

The crowd gathering against Jesus is augmented by the steady dropping away of the disciples gathered around him. Peter will not even acknowledge that he knows Jesus, for fear he may be caught on the wrong side of the overwhelming polarity that is rapidly developing — everyone against Jesus. It is a crucial point in the passion narratives that no one can claim to have not been at least a tacit participant in Jesus' death. This is an emphasis the Gospel writers press even though it does not reflect well on the apostles themselves, nor on communities identified with them. In the self-perception of those who practice scapegoating sacrifice, there is no awareness that any injustice or sin is being committed by the community. The writers of the Gospels not only make it clear that evil is being done. They make it clear that the community that does it includes them.

Whitewashed Tombs

In the passion narratives we see the scapegoating process unfold from the side of the scapegoat. And there is not only description. There is also commentary. Some of the most notable commentary comes in Jesus' words anticipating his death. Interestingly, in light of our discussion above about the uniqueness of this death, Jesus himself stresses that the path he follows is a well-traveled one. A significant passage on this score is Jesus' so-called Woes on the Pharisees. This is a text from which Christians rightly shrink because its words resound now with their later employment in centuries of Christian anti-Semitic bloodshed and slander.[8] That terrible fact needs to be addressed in its own right, and is in chapter 7. It is all the more important to see that there is an understanding even within this passage itself to block such effects.

In the Gospel of Matthew the text goes this way. Jesus says:

> Woe to you, scribes and Pharisees, hypocrites! For you are like whitewashed tombs, which on the outside look beautiful, but inside they are full of the bones of the dead and of all kinds of filth. So you also on the outside look righteous to others, but inside you are full of hypocrisy and lawlessness. Woe to you, scribes and Pharisees, hypocrites! For you build the tombs of the prophets and decorate the graves of the righteous, and you say, "If we had lived in the days of our ancestors, we would not have taken part with them in shedding the blood of the prophets." Thus you testify against yourselves that you are descendants of those who murdered the prophets. Fill up, then, the measure of your ancestors. You snakes, you brood of vipers! How can you escape being sentenced to hell? Therefore I send you prophets, sages, and scribes, some of whom you will kill and crucify, and some you will flog in your synagogues and pursue from town to town, so that upon you may come all the righteous blood shed on earth, from the blood of righteous Abel to the blood of Zechariah son of Barachiah, whom you murdered between the sanctuary and the altar. Truly I tell you, all this will come upon this generation. Jerusalem, Jerusalem, the city that kills the prophets and stones those who are sent to it! How often have I desired to gather your children together as a hen gathers her brood under her wings, and you were not willing! See, your house is left to you desolate. For I tell you, you will not see me again until you say, "Blessed is the one who comes in the name of the Lord." (Matt. 23:27-39)

In this passage there is no claim of christological uniqueness. Jesus figures here as one in a succession of prophets. What is emphasized is not that

---

8. Girard's stress on passages like the "Woes on the Pharisees" has in some quarters earned him condemnation as anti-Semitic, even though his entire thesis is that the logic of the Gospels requires such passages to be read against any such conclusion. To use them otherwise is to practice the very scapegoating the passages condemn. See René Girard, "Is There Anti-Semitism in the Gospels?" *Biblical Interpretation* 1, no. 3 (1993). See also the fall 1983 issue of *Dialog*, which contains a colloquium on a Girardian reading of Paul and Luther, and addresses this topic at some length.

he is something entirely new and unparalleled, but that he is being treated just as a long line of others has been treated. Most startlingly, Jesus identifies what he sees ahead for him not only with what happened to some prophets, but with "all the righteous blood shed on earth," from Abel, the first person murdered, to Zechariah, the last recorded killing in the scriptures as they were organized in Jesus' time (see 2 Chron. 24:20-22). Jesus' death is likened to that of every murder from the beginning of the Bible to the end. Zechariah was a prophet who reproached the people, and in response "they conspired against him, and by command of the king they stoned him to death in the court of the house of the LORD." As he lay dying, Zechariah said, "May the LORD see and avenge!" (24:21-22).[9] Thus Jesus' own words set his death firmly in the sacrificial context we have been describing.

The general theme of the woes on the Pharisees is hypocrisy. They are charged with obeying in small things and neglecting the most important ones, with making a good appearance but being inwardly corrupt. Yet the description Jesus gives is a striking reference to the act of scapegoating sacrifice itself. You are like whitewashed tombs, Jesus says, which outwardly appear beautiful but within are full of dead men's bones and all uncleanliness. Is this arresting image just a vivid metaphor for general hypocrisy, being different on the inside from the outside? It fits the bill, but seems a very odd choice unless it intends something more specific as well. Few pictures could more aptly summarize the mythical practice of sacrifice as Girard describes it than Jesus' picture of whitewashed tombs, beautiful on the outside (because of the mythical cover stories and the social benefits that result from the death) and full of bones and filth within (the bodies of real victims, along with the unacknowledged lies and the arbitrary violence — the uncleanliness — of their persecution). The parallel passage in the Gospel of Luke has the striking variation "You are like graves which are not seen, and men walk over them without knowing it" (Luke 11:44 RSV). A better image for the foundational role of sacrifice and our systematic blindness to it would be hard to imagine.

Alongside other examples of hypocrisy, the woes focus on the deception, particularly the self-deception, involved in sacrifice. And while the other examples may be taken in individual terms, the focus in this case is clearly communal. As heirs of the biblical tradition, the Pharisees already bear the revelatory insights we reviewed in the last section. And this is reflected in their claim, "If we had lived in the days of our fathers, we would

---

9. And through the agency of the Syrian army, Zechariah is avenged when the wounded and defeated king is conspired against and killed by his own servants. See 2 Chron. 24:23-26.

not have taken part with them in shedding the blood of the prophets." There is recognition of the killing, and denial that one would participate in that persecution. But Jesus harshly says they re-create exactly the same dynamic, and thus become part of the pattern that has been there almost from the beginning. That these words are addressed to the authentically pious and virtuous Pharisees makes it clear that it is not a lack of individual morality that is primarily in view. Jesus is not talking about something that bad people do and good people don't. It is the mechanism by which the community of people, good and bad, maintains itself.

There are many other forms of commentary. Two of the most direct are spoken by Christ from the cross itself. "Father, forgive them; for they know not what they do" (Luke 23:34 RSV). This famous prayer is not a generic regret that Jesus' killers were not better informed. Its diagnosis is more precise than that. We have seen that the collective dynamic of sacrifice generates misapprehension, an active collective blindness where what would otherwise be seen as bad is viewed as necessary and good. Sacrifice would not be effective if we explicitly knew what we were doing; its benefits depend on our conviction that we are doing something else.

The second instance brings us back to the discussion in the last section about the Psalms and the book of Job. We stressed the distinctive clarity with which these texts expressed the voice of the victim. That is the voice we hear lifted up in Jesus' cry from the cross: "My God, my God, why have you forsaken me?" These are the opening words of Psalm 22, one of the scapegoat psalms. These few words piercingly express Jesus' anguish. At the same time, they give a shorthand characterization of his entire situation. Any listener or reader who knows the psalm knows it is the cry of a persecuted person or minority, hemmed in, slandered, and about to be obliterated. His misery is the more profound because all who surround him mock him in the unanimous conviction that his plight is proof of God's condemnation and punishment.

> I am a worm, and not human;
>> scorned by others, and despised by the people.
> All who see me mock at me;
>> they make mouths at me, they shake their heads;
> "Commit your cause to the LORD; let him deliver —
>> let him rescue the one in whom he delights!" . . .
>
> Many bulls encircle me,
>> strong bulls of Bashan surround me;

they open wide their mouths at me,
  like a ravening and roaring lion. . . .

For dogs are all around me;
  a company of evildoers encircles me.
My hands and feet have shriveled;
I can count all my bones.
They stare and gloat over me;
they divide my clothes among themselves,
  and for my clothing they cast lots.

Before the words of Psalm 22 ever reached Jesus' lips, they were an appeal to God not to agree with those who said persecution was God's mandate. And Jesus speaks the one line from the psalm that brings it closest to Job's voice — not only a plea but an accusation. Why have you forsaken me?

We saw that psalms like this turn in one of two directions, toward a fierce cry for vengeance or toward hope against hope for deliverance. Psalm 22 does not end with a cry to God to kill the wicked. It takes the other fork.

But you, O LORD, do not be far away!
  O my help, come quickly to my aid!
Deliver my soul from the sword,
  my life from the power of the dog!

The writer goes on to anticipate deliverance and to praise God for it:

All you offspring of Jacob, glorify him;
  stand in awe of him, all you offspring of Israel!
For he did not despise or abhor
  the affliction of the afflicted;
he did not hide his face from me,
  but heard when I cried to him.

The psalmist's voice is central in understanding the death of Jesus, not just because Jesus evokes these words on the cross, but because they fit so consistently with the passion narratives as a whole. In the Gospel of John, Jesus says of the resistance and hatred that are leading to his death, "It was to fulfill the word that is written in their law, 'They hated me without a cause'" (John 15:25). The quotation is from Psalm 35:19 and appears in slightly different form in Psalm 69:4, two scapegoat psalms. We do not usually think of the Psalms as prophecy, but they are treated that way here by Jesus and in subsequent Christian tradition. Prophecy frequently is equated with prediction, and these texts are treated as so many markers that Jesus goes about matching to prove his identity. But prophecy is as much about telling the truth as about telling the future, though the two of course converge. Jesus is not pointing out the hatred against him to tick off one more item on the divine game plan, but to say that this behavior verifies the analysis of our situation already given in those past texts. This is the reason Jesus will die, and to understand that death you have to understand the insight that anticipates it.

In all three Synoptic Gospels Jesus quotes Psalm 118:22-23: "The stone that the builders rejected has become the cornerstone; this was the LORD's doing, and it is amazing in our eyes." Here is another of those incandescent moments in which the two sides of the gospel are expressed, one on top of the other. The first clause is a succinct statement of the sacrificial mechanism. It is the one who is excluded and condemned who structurally is actually the foundation of human social harmony. This is an empirical but unrecognized truth in human life, of which Jesus' fate is only one example . . . but it is marvelous that it has become a *known* example, one instance that illuminates the others.

This was the Lord's doing? Traditionally, unconscious scapegoating, when we "know not what we do," is ascribed to divine mysteries. So to say the rejected stone becomes the foundation and this is God's doing is to give again a pithy and exact descriptive statement of the social reality of scapegoating and of the perspective held by the community involved in it — a much clearer description than those who practice sacrifice could give. Yet overlaid on this description is another perspective. Jesus has become one of those rejected ones in whom this age-old pattern is played out, showing it up. And a new plot is superimposed on the old one. Jesus becomes another kind of cornerstone, the foundation of a new nonsacrificial community.[10] *This* — this unveiling and its alternative way to reconciliation — is the Lord's doing that is marvelous in our eyes.

---

10. In all three Gospels the psalm is quoted at the climax of the parable of the vineyard or the wicked tenants. An owner of a vineyard sends servants and slaves to collect rent from the tenants, only to have them seized and killed or beaten. Finally the owner's beloved son is sent, only in turn to be seized, thrown out of the vineyard, and killed. As a result, the vineyard will be given to others to manage. Jesus sums up this pattern of collective violence by quoting Ps. 118. The practice of such violence will not lead to inheritance of the kingdom. It must be replaced with an entirely different order. See further discussion of the parable below in chapter 10.

The writer of 1 Peter quotes this passage about the stone that was rejected and provides a commentary on it: "Come to him, a living stone, though rejected by mortals yet chosen and precious in God's sight, and like living stones, let yourselves be built into a spiritual house, to be a holy priesthood, to offer spiritual sacrifices acceptable to God through Jesus Christ" (1 Pet. 2:4-5). Instead of building unity through the succession of dead victims, those who believe in Jesus are to keep his living example of vindication against sacrifice before them, and become themselves living stones, offering spiritual sacrifices without violence to build up a new kind of community.

The Christian tradition recognized this identification of Jesus with the voice of victims by a christological interpretation of the Psalms. The Psalms have been identified with Jesus, and Christians have been advised that they should be prayed spiritually "through Christ," and the words figuratively placed on his lips. We might say that as Jesus used the Psalms to characterize his situation, Christians now do the reverse. They use Christ's situation, his story, as the guide to interpreting the Psalms. Christians have maintained that the curses, the cries for vengeance, the harsh condemnations found there — critical though they may be for recognition of our true condition — cannot be safely appropriated by us except through our identification with one who was in the victim's place and who insisted on another option than retribution. The desire for retribution and for sacrifice to stop the cycles of retribution is a decisive aspect of our sinful reality. We must see it clearly in ourselves. Therefore we must be able to put these words on our own lips, to acknowledge that they are our words. But the dynamic they express is powerful and overwhelming. Once unleashed, it is hard to restrain. Therefore we can appropriate these words only in communion with one who was in the place to take vengeance but who exercised mercy, who not only resisted evil but instituted a way of peace.

Who Believes in Redemptive Sacrifice?

We began this chapter noting the tension in the accounts of Jesus' death: it saves the world and it ought not happen. A review of the passion narratives reveals another, related oddity. In these descriptions of Jesus' last days there are only a few clear positive references to the reconciling effect of Jesus' death as a sacrifice for others, to an explicit atonement theology. The peculiarity is that this view of the crucifixion is endorsed by the wrong people.

The Gospels make clear that it is Jesus' antagonists who view his death as a redemptive sacrifice, one life given for many. There is a curious passage in Luke 23:12, after Jesus has been passed back and forth between Pilate and Herod, interrogated and abused by both. "That same day Herod and Pilate became friends with each other; before this they had been enemies." Jesus' killers intend for his death to be reconciling, and at least for Herod and Pilate it is. It is intended to unite the community, to prevent the outbreak of escalating violence between occupier and occupied, to keep the peace. The verse in Luke points out a very important point: sacrificial violence is not an illusion. It really works. This is part of the extraordinary clarity with which the Gospels paint the sacrificial mechanism.

The Gospel of John presents a fascinating conversation between the "chief priests and the Pharisees" (John 11:45-53). Some raise the fear that many people will follow Jesus, thus alarming the Roman occupiers and leading them to destroy "our holy places and our nation." The high priest Caiaphas responds: "'You know nothing at all! You do not understand that it is better for you to have one man die for the people than to have the whole nation destroyed.' He did not say this on his own, but being high priest that year he prophesied that Jesus was about to die for the nation, and not for the nation only, but to gather into one the dispersed children of God. So from that day on they planned to put him to death."

In this passage the stereo character of the Gospels stands out clearly. The rationale for scapegoating, which in myth is never explicit, and which does not consciously guide the acts of the scapegoaters themselves, is baldly set out by one of the protagonists. But the high priest is not making a Christian confession. The Gospel writer gives a commentary, indicating that the speaker expected a man to die for the people in one way (according to the sacrificial pattern), but that in fact it would turn out to be true in another way. Jesus would die to save the people from the logic of scapegoating, even as he was persecuted according to it. This stereoscopic perspective is quite common in the Bible. We noted that the book of Genesis ends with Joseph's statement to his brothers: "As for you, you meant evil against me; but God meant it for good" (Gen. 50:20 RSV). The servant songs in Isaiah show a similar outlook.

There is a theory about the redemptive value of violence, the saving power of Jesus' death, already present in the Gospel story. It is believed and propagated by the persecutors. Atonement is precisely the good they have in mind. According to the Gospel writers, it is this drive for sacrificial atonement that kills Jesus. Here is a caution for Christian theology. We must beware that in our reception and interpretation of the Gospel we do not end up entering the passion story on the side of Jesus' murderers. The passage we just mentioned in the Gospel of John, with its comment on the words of the high priest, demonstrates the awareness of this tension. Jesus prophesies his death, and so does the high priest. Both see it as sacrificial in some sense. But not the same sense. When Christians affirm the reconciling value of Christ's death, they must mean something different than Pilate and Herod did.

Coming Out of the Tombs

So far we have not touched on the most remarkable feature of the passion narratives, which is the resurrection at their conclusion. The pattern in mythic treatments of sacrifice is clear. The sacrificed one is not perceived as a subject of persecution by those who take part in the collective scapegoating. For that reason the victim, as a victim, completely disappears in memory and subsequent accounts. The kind of information we have just been describing in the passion narrative would not have registered, and the evidence for it would be "written out." In peace and good conscience the community that unified in sacrifice shares the same story about it, a story that erases any trace of the arbitrary and unjust character of the event. We noted that one version of Jesus' woes on the Pharisees includes the line "Woe to you! For you are like unmarked graves, and people walk over them without realizing it" (Luke 11:44). This is a peculiar insult. But it is an extraordinarily apt formulation of the mythically erased sacrificial victims.

With Jesus the situation is reversed. One telling indication of this is the signs that are said to attend Jesus' death in the Gospel of Matthew. "At that moment the curtain of the temple was torn in two, from top to bottom. The earth shook, and the rocks were split. The tombs also were opened, and many bodies of the saints who had fallen asleep were raised. After his resurrection they came out of the tombs and entered the holy city and appeared to many" (Matt. 27:51-53). These elements may seem as gratuitously legendary as anything in the passion story. But they are suggestive on several levels. The text may well be making the point that Jesus' resurrection is connected with a general resurrection. In which case, however, why did these events not come in association with Jesus' resurrection? It is Jesus' death that is connected to the sudden appearance of those long dead. Just as the woes on the Pharisees connect Jesus' death with all past murders, this text connects Jesus' death and resurrection with that of others who have died. And the setting puts special emphasis on certain ones among the dead. The rending of the curtain in the temple, the screen behind which the most sacred ritual sacrifice is offered, clearly means to imply some unveiling of the sacrificial practice, some interruption of it. This is connected with bodies getting up out of their tombs and walking into the city to be seen. The sacrificial victims apparently no longer stay in their tombs. Instead of unmarked graves upon which we walk without realizing it, now there are raised bodies marching where they cannot be avoided. Things are not going at all according to the usual script.

As the story of the crucifixion maintains clarity about the forces that lead to Jesus' death, so the resurrection of Jesus decisively explodes any possibility of mythologizing it. This victim does not stay sacrificed. The story of his death will not be given over to mythical memory, for the persecuted one will return to give his own witness. By resurrection God justifies Jesus against the false accusations that led to his death. If the cry of the scapegoat that resounds in the Psalms and in the voice of Job becomes the cry of Jesus on the cross, then the resurrection is that vindication that Job had so desperately demanded from God.

The ending of the Gospel of Mark is famously uncertain. There are a longer version and a shorter version. In the short version the two Marys and Salome come to the tomb. They find the stone rolled back and they find a young man in a white robe sitting on one side in the tomb. The man tells them Jesus has been raised and will meet the disciples in Galilee. The final verse of the short ending says, "So they went out and fled from the tomb, for terror and amazement had seized them; and they said nothing to anyone, for they were afraid" (Mark 16:8). Why wouldn't they celebrate this news about their beloved friend and teacher? Why the terror? Because, if true, one thing this news would quite naturally imply was that conflict was on the way. It meant that the peace Jesus' persecutors hoped to achieve was not going to hold. And if Jesus really was coming back, with divine support, no one could comfortably look forward to that meeting, knowing what their own roles had been in relation to the crucifixion. There was good reason to be afraid.

If the death of Jesus were a successful sacrifice in the normal mode, it would have succeeded in doing what such sacrifice does: uniting the community, creating calm and (at least for a time) dispelling conflict. As the New Testament makes evident, in these terms the cross is a failed sacrifice, despite the near unanimity with which Jesus is executed. Rather than the entire community assenting to the violence and seamlessly closing ranks over the grave of the scapegoat, on whose behalf no one speaks, the crucified one himself appears, vindicated by divine power. A new countercommunity gathers around the risen Christ, taking the victim's part, identifying with him, maintaining his innocence. Society is divided, not united by this death. Yet it is not divided by retribution on the part of the victim's "kin," by the desire to avenge a martyr, that would ordinarily signal a failed sacrifice. Instead, this new community explicitly rejects both the sacrificial violence that killed Christ and the contagion of revenge that the sacrificial system existed to contain.

Nor is resurrection the same as the deification of the victim that Girard notes takes place in many myths. There the one who is sacrificed because she or he was held guilty of terrible crimes is transmuted into a god because of the wonderful benefits of the sacrifice. But what this actually means is that a god appears in the story by which the community represents the scapegoating event, in place of the actual people killed. To say the victim becomes a god is really the same thing as saying the victim disappears. The "god" is a replacement, a figure to go in the story *instead* of the victim, a way of forgetting.[11] In contrast, the New Testament insistently confesses that the risen Christ is the crucified one, exactly the same one who was persecuted. The resurrected Lord carries the wounds of the cross. There is no mistaking this connection. Collective amnesia is not an option.

The Miracle of the First Stone

The points we have covered in our review of the passion narratives may seem less than earthshaking. The elements we have emphasized may seem like the least supernatural or improbable ones. People wanted Jesus out of the way. The charges weren't valid. Even his disciples fell away from him.

---

11. See as a good example the Tikopia myth Girard reports in Girard, Oughourlian, and Lefort, *Things Hidden*, 106. A foreign god visits the tribes and is given a feast. In the games played as part of the festival, he falls and claims to be injured. But at a certain point he dashes in to steal elements from the feast and then runs off with all in pursuit. He slips and drops four foodstuffs: a coconut, a taro, a breadfruit, and a yam, which the clan gods were able to retrieve. Coming to a high cliff, with the crowd in close pursuit, the god launches himself off into the sky with his stolen gains. Girard thinks it is clear that the original figure behind this myth really did "take a fall." But being presented as a god, this figure never appears to us as a sacrificial victim, but as one who "flew away." However, the record of the crimes of which the scapegoat was ostensibly guilty remains, in the act of theft of the most important food sources of the people.

Surely we know this is the way things work in the world without need for the Bible to tell us so. In fact, the visible violence and suffering of the cross, the evident wrongness of what is done to Jesus, is the premise for most of the criticism of Christianity's doctrine of the cross. The objection is that Christian faith has made its central image an act that is evil. According to this criticism, Christians make all manner of problematic supernatural claims about Jesus' divinity, about Jesus dying for our sins and about resurrection and eternal life. Those are debatable questions of belief. But the plain, unmistakable reality is the obvious wrong of the crucifixion, a bad thing that Christians have lifted up with unhealthy intensity.

What I have been suggesting is that the first truly "supernatural" thing about the passion was the ability to see what we now take for granted. An evil act of sacred violence was already at the center of human religion and community, but unremarked and unresisted. The wrongness of scapegoating violence was anything but evident. It required God's incarnate presence and the power of resurrection to make it so. The thing that now seems most obvious, requiring no religious conviction to recognize, was what was revealed. Our current outlook on things like scapegoating has in fact been largely constituted precisely by the influence of the biblical tradition. With our review of sacrifice, we made an attempt to sketch the prior background against which the biblical developments could be seen by contrast. But it is helpful to draw the contrast after the fact as well, to show that this truth is not such a common commodity as we may assume.

An excellent example comes from the career of a historical figure often compared with Jesus by historians of religion, Apollonius of Tyana.[12] He was a very famous wandering teacher and wonder-worker from the following century. Since he lived after Jesus, and his biographer had explicit knowledge of Christianity (perhaps even framing his book as a pagan competitor to the Gospels), we can be pretty sure that contrasts we find here are not the product of our retrospective projection but are quite real.

Following is the account of one of Apollonius's most spectacular deeds, a solution to an epidemic of plague in the city of Ephesus. After many efforts to stem the epidemic, the Ephesians sought his help.

"Take courage, for I will today put a stop to the course of the disease." And with these words he led the population entire to the thea-

---

12. I take this example from chapter 4 in René Girard, *I See Satan Fall like Lightning* (New York: Orbis, 2001).

tre, where the image of the Averting god [Hercules] has been set up. And there he saw what seemed an old mendicant artfully blinking his eyes as if blind, and he carried a wallet and a crust of bread in it; and he was clad in rags and was very squalid of countenance. Apollonius therefore ranged the Ephesians around him and said: "Pick up as many stones as you can and hurl them at this enemy of the gods." Now the Ephesians wondered what he meant, and were shocked at the idea of murdering a stranger so manifestly miserable; for he was begging and praying them to take mercy upon him. Nevertheless Apollonius insisted and egged on the Ephesians to launch themselves on him and not let him go. And as soon as some of them began to take shots and hit him with their first stones, the beggar who had seemed to blink and be blind, gave them all a sudden glance and showed that his eyes were full of fire. Then the Ephesians recognized that he was a demon, and they stoned him so thoroughly that their stones were heaped into a great cairn around him. After a little pause, Apollonius bade them remove the stones and acquaint themselves with the wild animal which they had slain. When therefore they had exposed the object which they thought they had thrown their missiles at, they found that he had disappeared and instead of him there was a hound who resembled in form and look a Molossian dog, but was in size the equal of the largest lion; there he lay before their eyes, pounded to a pulp by their stones and vomiting foam as mad dogs do. Accordingly the statue of the Averting god, namely Hercules, has been set up over the spot where the ghost was slain.[13]

Apollonius is the hero of this story, and it is presented as one of his crowning achievements. This suggests that the perspective we have been describing in the passion narratives was in fact anything but usual in its time. The pattern we see is hardly strange to us at this point. Ephesus is in turmoil because of an epidemic. In such a time of social disintegration its people turn to Apollonius for help. His solution is to gather the entire population in the theater and to incite them to stone to death a strange beggar, holding him responsible for the crisis as an "enemy of the gods." Once they can be convinced to start the violence, the beggar becomes less and less human in their eyes, so that all are fully caught up in the frenzy

13. The text is quoted by Girard, from Philostratus and Eusebius, *The Life of Apollonius of Tyana, the Epistles of Apollonius and the Treatise of Eusebius,* trans. F. C. Conybeare, Loeb Classical Library (New York: Macmillan, 1912), 1:363-67.

of the act. As a result, once their victim is sacrificed, he does not even appear any longer as a human being, but as an animal. And over his grave the statue of the god is raised.

Girard calls this story a "horrible miracle," and so it is. Apollonius heals with violence, and his magic is able to turn a person into a demon or an animal and then to make the person disappear. The author and consumers of the biography were well aware of the Gospel accounts, and thought the contrast between Apollonius and Christ was much to Apollonius's advantage. Apollonius was the son of a god (Jupiter), like Jesus. He did miracles. He too was subjected to a trial, but unlike Jesus he was miraculously delivered and ascended into heaven. Crucifixion and death were two points at which his biographer had no desire to find parallels, points where Apollonius's superiority seemed clear.

The extraordinary difference between the two is that Apollonius orchestrates scapegoating while Jesus suffers it. The biography makes the case for persecutors, the passion narratives vindicate the victim. In the biblical tradition and the passion narratives we frequently see scapegoats who are treated as demons or criminals revealed to be persecuted persons. In Apollonius's story we see the lynching of a marginal and helpless person transformed into the glorious defeat of a demon. I suspect that in the contrast I have just described, we tend to see Jesus' side as the nobler one. And if a reader suspects that I am throwing too negative a light on Apollonius, the reader will search for evidence that Apollonius was actually more like Jesus in this regard, rather than less. And this is itself a key piece of evidence. The writer and readers of the biography thought this *was* the positive evidence. They saw the contrast, but they read it in exactly the opposite way from the one I'm assuming the reader does. They did not see in the event what we almost automatically are ready to see in the event. I have been trying to explain why that might be so, and why Jesus' death has something to do with the change.

Even apart from the crucifixion, there is a direct parallel to this event in the Gospel of John in the story of the woman accused of adultery (John 7:53–8:11).[14] Jesus comes to the temple to teach, and scribes and the Pharisees bring before him a woman caught in adultery. The law of Moses commanded us to stone such women, they tell Jesus. What do you say? The

---

14. See Girard's discussion of this in Girard and Treguer, *Quand Ces Choses Commenceront*, 179-86. Girard emphasizes that by focusing on the first stone, Jesus highlights the imitative dynamic in collective violence. Casting the first stone is harder than joining in, because one must act without a model.

Gospel tells us that "they said this to test him, so that they might have some charge to bring against him." It appears to be a forced choice. Either join the crowd around the victim or provide grounds for a charge (opposing the divine law) that will make you a victim yourself.

Jesus threads a way through this double bind with a command. "Let anyone among you who is without sin be the first to throw a stone at her."[15] Those who have experienced collective frenzies typically report that they could not imagine having behaved in the same way by themselves. The implicit question in Jesus' word is a differentiating one, turning the focus from a solitary victim to ask which person is willing to stand out alone as responsible for the violence. This short-circuits the current of unanimity driving the sacrificial process and reverses the momentum toward a single mob mind. The logic of sacrifice pulls everyone together against the subject. Jesus' word runs the tape backward. "When they heard it, they went away, one by one, beginning with the elders; and Jesus was left alone with the woman standing before him."

It is important that the woman may in fact be guilty of adultery (Jesus tells her, "do not sin again"). Even a valid accusation can be the stuff of scapegoating if it is driven beyond proportion by a lust for blood and enlisted in other agendas, as here it is enlisted in the crowd's designs against Jesus. The charges against her and her death are all being deployed in the service of an agenda that really has nothing to do with her. And in this, it is exactly like sacrificial practice. Jesus' opposition to the stoning refers not to the woman's perfect righteousness (as if there could be no other objection to this collective violence) but to the impurity and motives of her accusers. In the Sermon on the Mount, Jesus does not reject the moral commandments of the Mosaic law, but intensifies their application. This complicates punishment and commends mercy, not because lawbreaking does not deserve and often directly result in punishment, but because all of us are legitimately in line for it.

In all this, Jesus plays a role opposite to that of Apollonius. Apollonius's

---

15. Immediately before and after his command, Jesus bends down and writes with his finger on the ground. What did he write? Some manuscripts of the Gospel included a phrase to specify that he wrote "the sins of each of them." Girard suggests that it may have been no more than doodling: the point was not to disturb the individualized reflection the statement required, and particularly to avoid direct eye contact with the crowd and any posture that could be read by projection as defiance. In such supercharged contexts of sacrificial conflict, insult and insolence are readily read into others' subjectivity, as is indicated by gang violence sparked by supposed disrespect or lynchings of African American men in segregated America based on supposed lascivious glances at white women.

achievement is to incite the throwing of the first stone, and thus the unanimous violence. Jesus' achievement is to prevent it. Apollonius points the crowd's attention to the unappealing appearance of the scapegoat, but Jesus directs attention back toward the crowd itself. In Apollonius's case we see a beggar who has committed no crime charged with cosmic evil and slaughtered. In Jesus' case we see a person who may in fact have committed a real offense saved from being swept up in a scapegoating program that has escalated far beyond her personal case. The miracle Jesus produces is not a crowd at peace over a grave, but a woman left alive.

It is unlikely that we would have heard the story of the woman taken in adultery if not for the story of the man taken to the cross. Different though they are, the miracles of the first stone and the third day point in the same direction. The miracle Jesus does at the temple prevents a sacrifice. The miracle Jesus lives from Good Friday to Easter reverses his own.

CHAPTER FIVE

Sacrifice to End Sacrifice

Satan's House Divided

> If Satan has risen up against himself and is divided, he can-
> not stand, but his end has come.
>
> Mark 3:26

> The crucifixion of Jesus is a victim mechanism like the oth-
> ers; it is set in motion and develops like the others. Yet its
> outcome is different from all the others.
>
> René Girard[1]

The Christian faith is *not only* a critique of sacrifice and its social dynamic. Human sin and redemption have other dimensions. Jesus'
death is one aspect of his saving work, and liberation from scapegoating
sacrifice is one aspect of the new life it intends. Our particular task is to
lift up this one dimension. So far we have looked at only the passion accounts in the Gospels. Despite all we have found there, some would object
that our approach is at odds with the explicit interpretation of the cross
in much of the rest of the New Testament. Is our reading just a creative
construct invented at this late date, or have Christians through history actually perceived this same dimension of Jesus' death? Aren't the wrongness of Jesus' death and the critique of scapegoating forgotten, with
Christ portrayed simply as a glorious sacrifice who reconciles the world

---

1. René Girard, *I See Satan Fall like Lightning* (New York: Orbis, 2001), 148.

through his death? Doesn't early Christianity finally side with the old sacrificial scheme and recycle it in a new and more absolute form? It is God's saving plan and has God's highest seal of approval. All the precious insights we traced are washed away, in an idealization of death and sacrifice. To put it another way, perhaps there truly is a critique of surrogate social violence and its religious rationale coded in the passion. But did early Christians and later ones actually read that code? Did it belong to the core of the faith they received and proclaimed? In this chapter we will take up these questions with a brief look at some key portions of the New Testament bearing on the early church.

I will readily agree that there are many places in the New Testament where sacrificial language is used positively to describe Jesus' death, and sacrificial categories permeate its reflection on that death. Yet in our brief examination of portions of Hebrew scripture, we have seen how such language can be the medium for revelation and critique of sacrificial practice. Similarly, the New Testament writers communicate through the sacrificial language and images that were so familiar to them. This continuity is also the means by which scapegoating is revealed, opposed, and (in faith) replaced. The fact that this language is used should not blind us to the direction in which it points. Putting such new wine in old bottles is a tricky business, and we need not suppose that every New Testament text approaches the issues in quite the same way. But the substance is there. The nonsacrificial, antiscapegoating dimension is not the whole sum of the gospel. But there is ample evidence that the good news we have been talking about was at the heart of the good news the first Christians saw in Jesus' death and resurrection.

I Am Jesus, Whom You Are Persecuting

Let us look at the concrete way the book of Acts presents the new church and its witness. One striking example is the sermon of Stephen (Acts 7:1-60). This is a passage of great interest for the themes we have been reviewing. First of all, we note that this is part of the story of Stephen's own martyrdom, a death that comes from a spontaneous stoning at the hands of a crowd. As was the case with Jesus, we are told that Stephen is accused by false witness, and is brought before a council. The charge against him is that he has said blasphemous words against Moses and God, and that he never stops saying things against the temple and the law. In defense, he gives a very long speech. Clearly, the occasion calls for a confession of faith, a proclamation of the gospel. I think it is safe to say that many would find Stephen's speech a somewhat odd confession of Christian faith. For one thing, in a speech that goes on for more than fifty verses, Stephen never mentions Jesus by name and refers to him only once, in verse 52. He rehearses the history of Israel, beginning with Abraham, in an interestingly selective way, ending with a passage very reminiscent of Jesus' woes on the Pharisees we discussed above.

What are the key points of Stephen's synopsis of the history of Israel? It has four main phases. The first phase is a general summary of the story of Abraham, putting special stress on the fact that Abraham and his descendants would be "resident aliens" in a country belonging to others, enslaved and mistreated by other rulers but eventually delivered. The second phase is the story of Joseph, who is jealously expelled by his brothers but who, when he has attained great power in Egypt and has his brothers at his mercy, delivers them from famine. The third and longest discussion is given over to Moses. Sinai receives little attention, but nearly a fourth of the account of Moses is devoted to the episode in which the young Moses finds an Egyptian oppressing an Israelite and intervenes by killing the Egyptian. Moses as yet has no call from God to free his people, but the passage continues, "He supposed that his kinsfolk would understand that God through him was rescuing them, but they did not understand. The next day he came to some of them as they were quarreling and tried to reconcile them, saying, 'Men, you are brothers; why do you wrong each other?' But the man who was wronging his neighbor pushed Moses aside, saying, 'Who made you a ruler and a judge over us? Do you want to kill me as you killed the Egyptian yesterday?' When he heard this, Moses fled and became a resident alien in the land of Midian" (7:25-29). One way of ending conflict has been tried and found wanting.

In the verses that follow, Moses receives his call from God out of the burning bush, leads Israel out of Egypt, and receives the Torah, "living oracles." Then we learn how Moses was "pushed aside" again by the people in the wilderness, when they set up an idol and offered sacrifice to it. Here Stephen quotes from the book of Amos:

Did you offer to me slain victims and sacrifices
    forty years in the wilderness, O house of Israel?
No; you took along the tent of Moloch,
    and the star of your god Rephan,

the images that you made to worship;
so I will remove you beyond Babylon. (Acts 7:42b-43; see Amos 5:25)[2]

In Amos this reference back to the time in the wilderness appears to remember it as a time when Israel's relation to God was direct and required no sacrifice. The offering of such sacrifices, including human ones, is condemned as a function of other gods and other faiths. The verses just preceding these are well known:

I hate, I despise your festivals,
     and I take no delight in your solemn assemblies.
Even though you offer me your burnt offerings and grain offerings,
     I will not accept them;
and the offerings of well-being of your fatted animals
     I will not look upon.
Take away from me the noise of your songs;
     I will not listen to the melody of your harps.
But let justice roll down like waters,
     and righteousness like an ever-flowing stream. (Amos 5:21-24)

Stephen's reference to Amos, and to "slain victims," leads to the fourth phase, as short as the original one regarding Abraham. Here Stephen recalls that in the wilderness "our ancestors had the tent of testimony," the tabernacle, as the focus of God's presence. But later, under Solomon, a house was made for God to dwell in, the temple of Jerusalem. Up until here Stephen appears to be on common ground with his judges, even if what he has chosen to recount about this common history may be a bit idiosyncratic in some respects (the time given to Moses' killing of the Egyptian, for instance).

But then Stephen asserts that "the Most High does not dwell in houses made with human hands" and goes on to speak directly to his hearers: "You stiff-necked people, uncircumcised in heart and ears, you are forever opposing the Holy Spirit, just as your ancestors used to do. Which of the prophets did your ancestors not persecute? They killed those who foretold the coming of the Righteous One, and now you have become his betrayers and murderers. You are the ones that received the

---

2. In quoting Amos's reference to sacrifices, to "slain victims," Acts uses the Greek word *sphagia*. The word means "victims to be sacrificed," and it appears in only these two verses in all of scripture (though variants on the root verb, to slaughter, appear elsewhere).

law as ordained by angels, and yet you have not kept it" (Acts 7:51-53). Finally we are told that, full of the Holy Spirit, Stephen looks to heaven and tells the crowd that he sees the Son of Man standing at the right hand of God. At this "they covered their ears, and with a loud shout all rushed together against him." Before dying, Stephen cries with a loud voice, "Lord, do not hold this sin against them."

Stephen has said precious little directly about Jesus. But he has drawn a very long line that is meant to point to him. The usual way to say this is that Stephen presents this history as types of Jesus: Abraham, Joseph, and Moses all prefigure him. This is true. But the interesting thing is *what* about them Stephen takes as "typical." The line that connects them all is the line of the sacrificial victim. Of Israel generally, we are reminded that it has collectively been enslaved and oppressed, that it is the resident alien who is victimized. This note is struck even with Abraham, who himself was not thus subjugated. It is continued in the story of Joseph — who we know was to be killed, but then was sold into slavery. The story becomes much more detailed with Moses. For here we see first his attempts to intervene in reciprocal violence with violence, and then how his attempts to reconcile quarrels are undone by reference to Moses' own violence. Next, after Moses has undertaken his call from God and Israel has gone out from Egypt, we see how people turn aside to offer "slain victims." Moses is particularly interesting because in this telling he figures both as exercising violence and then later as being pushed aside in favor of it. Stephen directly downgrades the temple, the current central, ritual sacrificial site, as the dwelling place of God. And last of all, he says these earlier acts of violence have been continued in the death of Jesus.

This entire episode is one of the key presentations of the faith of the young church in the New Testament. If it is at all representative, Christians saw sacrificial violence as a primary focus of Jesus' saving work. Stephen's story makes it clear that a witness who testifies in favor of victims can well end up becoming one.

This story also dovetails with another one, the most famous conversion story in the early church, that of Paul. Saul (prior to his conversion and the taking of his new name) belongs to the crowd around Stephen, and is part of this collective execution. The crowd placed their coats at his feet. The story of Stephen's death ends with the observation, "And Saul approved of their killing him." The text of Acts goes on immediately to describe the fierce persecution of the church that Paul then led.

It is in the midst of this that something extraordinary happens to Paul. On the road to Damascus, "breathing threats and murder against the disciples of the Lord," he suddenly sees a great light and is thrown to the ground. He hears a voice saying, "Saul, Saul, why do you persecute me?" The text continues: "He asked, 'Who are you, Lord?' The reply came, 'I am Jesus, whom you are persecuting'" (Acts 9:4-5). Paul meets Jesus, and the means by which Jesus is revealed to him are through Jesus' identity with the persecuted victim. This is the answer to *who* Jesus is. The divine voice raises only one issue with Paul: violence. Paul will go on to confess that Jesus is the Son of God, and his own letters will develop many dimensions of theology. But the simple, original substance of Saul's conversion is his change from orchestrating violent animosity against a minority to joining in community with those who were his victims. This is hardly a minor point. For Paul, to accept Jesus is to be converted from scapegoating persecution to identify with those against whom he had practiced it. There could hardly be more powerful continuity with the themes we have been exploring.

After his vision Paul returns to Jerusalem, and while praying in the temple he has a vision of Jesus, who warns him to flee the city to avoid his own murder. At that point Paul makes a confession of his own complicity in violence: "While the blood of your witness Stephen was shed, I myself was standing by, approving and keeping the coats of those who killed him" (22:20). Paul was part of the crowd that stoned Stephen, but he has been called out of that crowd. Direct encounter with the crucified and risen Christ immediately has its impact in converting Paul from the very sin that had claimed Jesus.

This pivot point is so important to the writer of Acts that it appears three times, once as a narrative and twice as part of Paul's testimony offered when he himself is on trial for his life (see 9:5; 22:8; and 26:15). On all three occasions the divine words to Paul, "I am Jesus, whom you are persecuting," are the centerpiece. On the second occasion Paul speaks before the Roman tribune and a crowd in Jerusalem, a scene clearly parallel to Jesus' own path. He confesses and repents his own earlier work of persecution and reports Jesus' words and his conversion. At this point the crowd shouts, "Away with such a fellow from the earth! For he should not be allowed to live" (22:22). And they begin throwing off their cloaks, just like the crowd stoning Stephen, of which Paul had been a part. But this time violence is averted. The Roman tribune protects him from the crowd. When he is brought before the council and the high priest, he is defended by the Pharisees, who say, "We find nothing wrong with this man" (23:9). Whereas in the case of Jesus all, in their way, converge on the killing, in this case some in each group question the surge to unanimity, preventing a sacrifice.

139

Nor is it accidental that Paul's great mission becomes the transmission of the gospel to Gentiles. He is a Jew converted from persecution of Jewish Christians. Christians represent a threat of dissolution in the community, a crisis, and Paul's reaction is to isolate and destroy them in order to purify the people and to maintain unity. Once he becomes a Christian, Paul's hallmark project is to build a community with non-Jews, across all the differing practices that the same Paul would have regarded before as impurities that destroy unity and identity. In his world Gentiles and Jews are prime scapegoats for each other. A community that includes them both is a miraculous reversal of this reality, a reversal he associates directly with the resurrection of Jesus.

It is hard to see how this whole presentation makes sense unless the writer of Acts sees the scapegoating dynamic we have been discussing as a crucial object of Christ's work. Without doubt these passages reflect an early church mounting a defense against its own persecution. The texts have since been used by Christians to demonize Jews, a topic we will take up in the next chapter. But that the means and the determination to address the persecuting process in these terms are present, tells us much about how the elements we considered in the passion narratives were already appropriated in this time. The writer of Acts clearly understands the history of Israel in light of the nonsacrificial character of Jesus' death. Stephen's witness for the victim, Jesus, goes to the extent of sharing his fate. The fruit of that witness is not to multiply martyrs but to convert persecutors.

Acquittal by Resurrection

Paul is a figure of crucial importance, partly because of the extent and influence of his writings, and partly because his letters contain some of the chronologically earliest material in the New Testament. But he is important even more because most would say Paul is the New Testament fountainhead of the church's theology of a sacrificial and atoning death.[3] In turning to his writing, we must keep in mind the framework set by his own conversion.

We will take one passage as an example. Romans 3:21-26 is a key passage in most discussions of the atonement:

---

3. For an extensive Girardian reading of Paul, see Robert Hamerton-Kelly, *Sacred Violence: The Hermeneutic of the Cross in the Theology of Paul* (Minneapolis: Fortress, 1991).

But now, apart from law, the righteousness of God has been disclosed, and is attested by the law and the prophets, the righteousness of God through faith in Jesus Christ for all who believe. For there is no distinction, since all have sinned and fall short of the glory of God; they are now justified by his grace as a gift, through the redemption that is in Christ Jesus, whom God put forward as a sacrifice of atonement by his blood, effective through faith. He did this to show his righteousness, because in his divine forbearance he had passed over the sins previously committed; it was to prove at the present time that he himself is righteous and that he justifies the one who has faith in Jesus.

The premise of this conclusion is that all people, Gentiles and Jews, are under the power of sin. The immediately preceding verses spell this out:

As it is written:
"There is no one who is righteous, not even one;
there is no one who has understanding,
there is no one who seeks God.
All have turned aside, together they have become worthless;
there is no one who shows kindness,
there is not even one."
"Their throats are opened graves;
they use their tongues to deceive."
"The venom of vipers is under their lips."
"Their mouths are full of cursing and bitterness."
"Their feet are swift to shed blood;
ruin and misery are in their paths,
and the way of peace they have not known."
"There is no fear of God before their eyes."
Now we know that whatever the law says, it speaks to those who are under the law, so that every mouth may be silenced, and the whole world may be held accountable to God. For "no human being will be justified in his sight" by deeds prescribed by the law, for through the law comes the knowledge of sin. (Rom. 3:10-20)

These verses are in fact a mélange of snippets (set off in quotation marks) from six psalms and a passage in Isaiah.[4] Three of the psalms are

---

4. In order, Pss. 14:1-3; 53:1-2; 5:9; 140:3; 10:7; Isa. 59:7-8 and Ps. 36:1.

scapegoat psalms, of the type discussed in part 1. The three others are condemnations of the universal evil in humanity. Psalm 14:3 is representative:

> They have all gone astray, they are all alike perverse;
>> there is no one who does good,
>> no, not one.

The Isaiah passage is explicit about the nature of this perversity.

> Their feet run to evil,
>> and they rush to shed innocent blood;
> their thoughts are thoughts of iniquity,
>> desolation and destruction are in their highways.
> The way of peace they do not know,
>> and there is no justice in their paths. (Isa. 59:7-8)

Paul has chosen some passages that speak of universal sin in general (everyone does something wrong) and some that refer to a particular kind of universal sin (a specific thing everyone does). That particular thing is the scapegoating persecution by crowds whose feet are "swift to shed innocent blood." It is a particularly apt example for his theme. We may all alike be sinners, even though each of us sins in his or her particular ways. But the sacrificial dynamic is marked precisely because in our groups we all do the same thing together, at the same time, and none of us is exempt. This is a specific and powerful example that "all have sinned and fall short of the glory of God."

Paul asserts again and again that the law is truly given by God and that it truly expresses God's will for human behavior. It is a positive guide for covenantal faithfulness to God. But it can fall captive to a sacrificial use. "Through the law comes the knowledge of sin." This has been interpreted in a number of ways. Knowing the law makes us aware of our failure to obey it. Knowing the law stimulates our negative and rebellious desires, as with Eve and Adam in the garden when God gives them only one prohibition. As any parent can testify, designating the one thing we are not to do can elicit a powerful attraction. Alongside such truths we can see another. Many of the commandments in the law are the kinds of prohibitions that specifically aim to block the subjective, reciprocal escalations of desire that lead to social crisis, and so to sacrificial violence. Of course, killing or stealing tends to set off direct cycles of retaliation, and is forbidden. But on the same level are commandments not to *covet* anything that is your neighbor's, or to bear false witness. These are behaviors that enflame social contagion and often bring conflict. There are very good reasons for these laws, not only in making us better people, but in avoiding destructive results for the whole community. However, we saw in our examination of sacrifice that when a community looks for victims, these rules that are meant to protect against violence become the basis for accusations that demand it. It is the law that will be used to justify the scapegoating.

In such a case, failure to keep the law becomes a mark that brands people for exclusion. The law becomes the basis for sacrificial accusations. In Paul's view this is the case with the wholesale exclusion of the Gentiles. It was more specifically the case when those like himself who were zealous for the law united against lawbreakers (such as the followers of Jesus) to persecute them because of unrighteousness. Paul makes the connection that the sin that killed Jesus is his (Paul's) own sin, and in fact is one that all people participate in, not as private murderers but as members of their human communities. The fact that the law appealed to in the process is an authentic divine commandment does not mean that the process itself is valid.

Now, says Paul, the righteousness of God has been manifest apart from law. The cornerstone now is not righteousness according to the law, which, though good, can readily be enlisted in sacrificial evil, but faith in the crucified one. This justification comes "through the redemption [the ransoming or buying back] that is in Christ Jesus, whom God put forward as a sacrifice of atonement by his blood, effective through faith." How are we to take the phrase "as a sacrifice of atonement"? Is this a specification of the heart of God's purpose, or is it a description of a position, a place taken up by Christ in the service of God's purpose to redeem and ransom humanity? I incline to the latter. God enters into the position of the victim of sacrificial atonement (a position already defined by human practice) and occupies it so as to be able to act from that place to reverse sacrifice and redeem us from it. God steps forward in Jesus to be one subject to the human practice of atonement in blood, not because that is God's preferred logic or because this itself is God's aim, but because this is the very site where human bondage and sin are enacted. God "puts forward" the divine Word into this location as part of the larger purpose of ransom, of transforming the situation from within. The text immediately points out that the effectiveness of this act lies not in the blood or the violence; it relates to faith.[5]

---

5. There is of course an enormous amount of literature on this difficult passage and specifically on the word *hilastērion* ("sacrifice of atonement," "propitiation," "expiation," "mercy seat," or even an adjective and not a noun, so "with reconciling power"). A key point

The next verse says God did this to show God's righteousness, because God has passed over sins previously committed. Are we talking about only the flock of disparate sins (theft, adultery, etc.) that have accumulated unpunished and are somehow being dealt with now in a summary violence? Or are we talking especially still about the sin outlined by Paul in the previous verses, the collective victimization of the innocent? If God has passed over such sins in the past, then there is a case against God's righteousness. We have already heard that case made vividly in Job and the Psalms. These victims called out to God, with no clear or decisive result. But, Paul says, God has acted "to prove at the present time that he himself is righteous and that he justifies the one who has faith in Jesus."[6] That is, in this instance God is to prove definitively that Jesus (who as a victim has faith that God will vindicate and save him) and those who have faith in Jesus (who stand by the victim and not the crowd) are in fact justified in their hope. God has vindicated God's righteousness by not abandoning the victim. The righteousness of God is manifest in the vindication of Jesus, the scapegoat. And this passage suggests that God will likewise save and vindicate other victims as well. The resurrection of Jesus is a sign that God will not fail on this count. God has made good on the challenge posed by Job.

Paul has yet another concern, however. If the rescue of Jesus from un-

---

from my perspective is the phrase "through faith" that some translations put with "blood" (i.e., through faith in his blood), but that stands just after *hilastērion* and seems to me to belong with it — a *hilastērion* through faith, by means of his blood. The point being that it is not the blood that is the true power. I would put it this way: God has set him forth publicly at the site from which mercy can be appropriated through faith, because he was willing to shed his own blood. On my reading, there is tremendous continuity between Paul here and Heb. 2:14-18: "Since, therefore, the children share flesh and blood, he himself likewise shared the same things, so that through death he might destroy the one who has the power of death, that is, the devil, and free those who all their lives were held in slavery by the fear of death. For it is clear that he did not come to help angels, but the descendants of Abraham. Therefore he had to become like his brothers and sisters in every respect, so that he might be a merciful and faithful high priest in the service of God, to make a sacrifice of atonement for the sins of the people. Because he himself was tested by what he suffered, he is able to help those who are being tested." This last sentence also fits very well with Rom. 3:25b-26.

6. The NRSV lists "who has the faith of Jesus" as an alternative reading, not from a variant text but simply in interpreting the genitive. This alternative reading would only strengthen my suggestion. God justifies, that is, proves correct, those like Jesus who have faith in the vindication of scapegoats. To believe *in* Jesus is to share that faith. This justification then extends also to those — all of us — who have been guilty of gathering against the sacrificial victim, as we discuss in the next few paragraphs.

just accusation and death expresses God's righteousness, how can that righteousness be equally manifest in the justification of sinners, of the very ones who committed the evil Jesus is delivered from? This is the even greater perplexity.

Markus Barth addresses this question helpfully in an underappreciated little book, *Acquittal by Resurrection.*[7] By resurrection Jesus is acquitted of the charges against him. God proves that Jesus was not guilty by siding with him. Barth's theme is the acquittal of Jesus' enemies, of those who brought the charges and carried out the sacrificial violence. For them (and by extension for all of us) it would seem that this same resurrection would have devastating results. "It spells inescapable revenge and disaster. The murderers fail to succeed beyond the murder. God answers them in a way that renders their situation and future hopeless."[8] Jesus will return to crush those who opposed him. This is the natural and apparently just expectation. The blood of Jesus will be the supreme charter for righteous retribution.

For Paul, as for other New Testament writers, the final wonder of the resurrection is the reversal of this expectation. The pointed greeting of the risen Jesus to the disciples who abandoned and failed him at his death is "Peace." He does not return as an avenger, though it is crucial not to lose touch with the logic according to which he could. Paul keeps this before us with his emphasis on the universality of sin and the fact that we all stand under judgment. Ordinarily, to be judged by the very one we have injured would be to face the most prejudicial and severe punishment. And the New Testament makes clear that Jesus is the one whom God has exalted and appointed for that very task. Yet the message is quite unexpected. "He commanded us to preach to the people and to testify that he is the one ordained by God as judge of the living and the dead. All the prophets testify about him that everyone who believes in him receives forgiveness of sins through his name" (Acts 10:42-43). Jesus' resurrection is good news not only to other scapegoat victims but, counterintuitively, to those who sinned against him. It is an assurance of forgiveness.

Barth puts it this way: "When by the resurrection, the function of the *corpus delicti* has been reversed, because the victim's blood stops crying for revenge and calls for mercy by pleading in favor of the trespassers, then

---

7. Markus Barth and Verne H. Fletcher, *Acquittal by Resurrection,* 1st ed. (New York: Holt, Rinehart and Winston, 1964). Barth and Fletcher each wrote sections of this cooperative work. I draw on Barth's portion.

8. Barth and Fletcher, *Acquittal by Resurrection,* 69.

the judge does the right thing, reveals his righteousness, and deserves ac-
clamation in acquitting and releasing the culprits."[9] By resurrection Jesus
is cleared of the scapegoat charges against him. But the resurrection also
acquits those who scapegoated him. While they certainly committed the
crime and are certainly guilty, it is also incontestable that the one they are
charged with killing is alive. They can be declared not guilty of Jesus'
death by the fact that Jesus is not dead. The prosecution cannot proceed
in this capital case without a dead body, and the tomb is empty. What the
resurrection presents in court is a living person, what Barth calls "the evidence of the raised victim."[10] It is thus righteous of God to account the
accused not guilty, or justified by resurrection.

Of course, the risen Christ could justly press for retribution against
those who had wronged him, even if they did not succeed in silencing him
permanently. But this, which is his right, is also his right to decline. And
Christ does so, becoming instead an advocate for sinners. In the first murder, Genesis tells us that the blood of Abel cried out from the ground,
cried out for justice. And God says to Cain, "Now you are cursed from the
ground, which has opened its mouth to receive your brother's blood from
your hand." The letter to the Hebrews picks up this reference directly
when it says Jesus is the mediator of a new covenant in "the sprinkled
blood that speaks a better word than the blood of Abel" (Heb. 12:24).
Christ's blood "speaks better" than the blood of Abel, which cried out
from the ground for vengeance. Christ's blood is that of the crucified and
risen one, one who can speak for himself, in mercy and peace.

Everyone who believes in the risen Christ receives forgiveness in his
name, says Peter in Acts (10:43). Though it means a great deal more, this
sentence has a very simple, basic meaning. If we sinned against Jesus and
do not believe in his resurrection, we do not believe in the basis of our
own acquittal; we have rejected the ground on which we might be delivered. If we are party to scapegoating violence against those in Jesus' place,
the resurrection is the message of salvation, because it definitively brings
to light the evil that must be overcome, brings hope for the redemption of
the victim and at the same time stands against retribution on behalf of
the victim.

Paul is taken as the source of the so-called forensic theory of the
atonement, an understanding of Jesus' death in formal, legal terms. We
are in the dock, God is the judge, and Jesus is the one who has already

9. Barth and Fletcher, *Acquittal by Resurrection*, 94.
10. Barth and Fletcher, *Acquittal by Resurrection*, 72.

paid our debt, taken our punishment. In light of this fact, we who are objectively guilty are declared innocent by the judge, who transfers onto us the merit of Jesus' undeserved suffering to cancel our deserved punishment. Barth agrees that Paul has drawn before us an extraordinary legal drama, but he sees its fundamental elements differently. He paints a picture of people, all of us, on trial for murder. Into the courtroom comes our supposed victim, obviously alive, and obviously bearing the wounds of our lethal attack. Our victim comes to testify on our behalf, to counsel mercy. Of course, the most compelling and overwhelming evidence is the living presence of this person, which by itself makes a verdict of "guilty of murder" appear immediately, if improbably, untenable. To deny the resurrection, Paul implies, is like objecting to this witness, insisting that it must be an imposture, an illusion, and trying to get the testimony and the person thrown out of court. At one level the response is understandable. This living person offers us the possibility of deliverance and yet at the same time confirms our crime beyond any doubt. The only way to acquittal is by admission of guilt. We can be legitimately justified, but only as sinners. For our evil intent and actions we can be forgiven, but not if we insist on rejecting the redemption and witness of the victim. If we do not recognize the right of victims to testify against us, we cannot be acquitted. Thus Paul can say that Jesus was "handed over to death for our trespasses and was raised for our justification" (Rom. 4:25). And he can proclaim that "if Christ has not been raised, your faith is futile and you are still in your sins" (1 Cor. 15:17).

Believing in Christ and in his resurrection thus includes a particular complex of elements that we have tried to highlight. It means the following: recognizing that Christ was a sacrificial victim, like others; believing in Christ in the sense of believing his innocence; accepting his vindication by God and believing in its significance as the "first fruit" of vindication of all scapegoats; believing in his resurrection, his living reality now, as evidence that can reverse the retribution due his persecutors; and believing in the grace of the risen Christ, his advocacy on our behalf instead of his desire for our punishment. Faith unites all these in solidarity with Christ and necessarily implies a new way of life, as we will discuss in part 3.

Satan's House Divided

We can now look in a somewhat different direction, to see how our reading of the passion narratives illuminates some wider themes in the New

Testament. In particular I am thinking of the figures of Satan and the Holy Spirit (the *paraclete*).

Satan, or the devil, is a fascinating figure — to many people notoriously more interesting if not more attractive than God. Part of the fascination is that Satan makes only brief, episodic appearances in scripture. Part of it stems from Satan's perplexing ambiguity not only in scripture, but also in Christian tradition. Satan is an instigator and seducer, planting the germ of suspicion and jealousy in the Garden of Eden and tempting Jesus to choose earthly or spiritual domination. Satan is an accuser, charging Job with hypocrisy and faithlessness and demanding that God try him. Satan is a ruler, the prince of darkness, the reigning power of this world. Our popular images of Satan range from a repulsive and horrifying beast to a sophisticated and highly attractive enticer. The devil is the figure in Christian tradition where mythic features have been given greatest sway.

The paradox of most interest to us is that Satan is a sower of discord and also a bringer of order. The devil delights in nothing so much as in instigating conflict among humans, but also reigns over a very effective kingdom, the powers and principalities of the world. There is a recurrent conviction that if one wants to get really effective results, one is better off enlisting the devil (at whatever cost) than petitioning God. The legends of selling one's soul to the devil (from *Faust* to *The Devil and Daniel Webster*) make little sense except on the assumption that Satan can deliver.

Our hypothesis about the foundational role of scapegoating illuminates this picture of Satan as powerfully as it does the tension in the gospel perspective on the cross. These odd and conflicting characterizations of evil leap into a coherent profile. The devil has us coming and going, we might say, instigating the rivalry and conflict that tear human community apart and then orchestrating the violent sacrifice that restrains that conflagration for a time. The tempter spreads the disease and the prince of this world sells us the cure. The devil has many faces, which is why we can well understand artistic representations that show him in varied and contradictory guises.[11] Satan is the mimetic dynamic that fans envy and rivalry into interpersonal conflict. And Satan is the dynamic of sacrificial scapegoating that tamps down this violence, a dynamic humans seemingly cannot live without and yet ought not live with. Satan is lord of disorder and of order. The depth of our bondage to sin is expressed in the

---

11. Dante, in the *Divine Comedy*, aptly depicts Satan with three faces, a kind of inverse of the Trinity.

fact that the only tools we can use to dig ourselves out are the same ones that dig us in deeper. Turn how we will, it seems we must give the devil his due: either escalating conflict or routinely restraining sin with sin, violence with violence.

A truthful understanding of the situation must acknowledge sacrifice's real power, even the real power for partial good. It is in this connection that Satan appears in a necessarily ambivalent light. In the book of Job, Satan is an instigator of scapegoating, who brings a false accusation against Job, and at the same time a seducer who tempts God to suspicion and anticipatory vengeance. The evil of sacrifice is a supernatural, transpersonal power, in the sense that no one who takes part in it fully understands or intends all that it involves. It is greater than the sum of its parts. But on the other hand it is an intensely personal reality, for it can subsist only within the subjectivity of interpersonal relationships as the host for its parasitic activity. Between a New Testament vision of the power of Satan and the demons and a thoroughly depersonalized and secular view of evil as nothing but ignorance or selfishness, we would be advised to prefer the first as an empirical description.

All three of the Synoptic Gospels begin Jesus' ministry with his temptation by the devil in the wilderness. These are ultimately tests of Jesus' resistance to the subjective contagion of rivalry. Satan challenges a hungry Jesus to prove he is the Son of God by turning a stone to bread, and goads Jesus to test God's love by throwing himself off the pinnacle of the temple to prove that he will be saved. Satan offers Jesus Satan's own authority over all the kingdoms of the world, if only Jesus will worship him, take him as model. In every case the instigation is like that of the serpent in the garden, an attempt to plant competitive or suspicious responses in Christ's spirit. "I don't believe you — prove me wrong." "God promised you . . . but I bet you wouldn't risk it." "Wouldn't you like what I've got?" The setting may be cosmic, but the dynamic is the humble nub of human sin. Jesus is able to resist being drawn into that contagion, the germ of the disease for which sacrifice is the antidote.

Jesus then faces the sacrificial side of Satan, in the run-up to the passion. If Jesus can't be recruited to expand the disease of human conflict, evil will be just as happy to eliminate him as part of the cure. Lies, persecution, and murder are elements the New Testament particularly associates with Satan, echoing the preoccupations of the suffering voices in the Psalms we examined. Indeed, Satan could be well defined by the negative profile outlined in those psalms, as the one who brings about this kind of lament. The qualities of deceit and cleverness attributed to the devil reflect the extraordinarily fluid nature of this destructive dynamic. It cannot be overcome or resisted with static and substantial characterizations. For instance, we cannot avoid this sin by noticing the nationality or the race or the class or the manners of the persecutors (or even the specific individuals involved) in one case and vowing never to side with such people in the future. In so doing, we are well on our way to scapegoating of our own. Satan is delighted to fight one lie with another, for either will serve equally well as a sacrificial rationale. If people from our group are sacrificial victims in the next city, and people from their group are such victims in ours, we are all citizens of Satan's kingdom.

Jesus brings these threads together in a discourse in the Gospel of John:

> Jesus said to them, "If you were Abraham's children, you would be doing what Abraham did, but now you are trying to kill me, a man who has told you the truth that I heard from God. This is not what Abraham did. You are indeed doing what your father does." . . . "You are from your father the devil, and you choose to do your father's desires. He was a murderer from the beginning and does not stand in the truth, because there is no truth in him. When he lies, he speaks according to his own nature, for he is a liar and the father of lies." (John 8:39-41a, 44)

Satan is a murderer, "from the beginning." Those who yield to instigation and imitate Satan's desires become murderers themselves, instead of true children of Abraham, who was the one God turned away from the sacrifice of Isaac. The path toward the collective execution of Jesus is following this age-old pattern. This is an interesting passage, because the Christian church virtually from the beginning used the story of Abraham and Isaac to interpret the cross. Here Jesus himself is doing so, and drawing the conclusion that the point of that story is that his death is the work of the devil, not a desire of God.

But perhaps the most notable passage is this one from the Gospel of Mark.

> And the scribes who came down from Jerusalem said, "He has Beelzebul, and by the ruler of the demons he casts out demons." And he called them to him, and spoke to them in parables, "How can Satan cast out Satan? If a kingdom is divided against itself, that kingdom cannot stand. And if a house is divided against itself, that

house will not be able to stand. And if Satan has risen up against himself and is divided, he cannot stand, but his end has come. But no one can enter a strong man's house and plunder his property without first tying up the strong man; then indeed the house can be plundered." (Mark 3:22-27)

We have just suggested that the ruler of demons does indeed cast out demons. The charge against Jesus is that he opposes evil, but does so through an evil power. We can note that this is exactly the job description for sacrificial violence: Satan driving out Satan. And we can note that Satan tempted Jesus by offering exactly this bargain — if Jesus would worship and serve Satan, he could have dominion over the world Satan ruled, including the demons Satan ruled.

Jesus responds by focusing directly on the premise of his accusers. How can this be? Rather than arguing that it is impossible — Satan can't cast out demons, only God can do that — Jesus actually accepts the premise. If this is the way evil works, it will not be able to stand. If Satan has played both sides of this fence from the beginning, it cannot go on any longer: "his end has come." Jesus concludes the parable with the observation that you cannot plunder a strong man's property without first tying him up. The demons are Satan's property, and Jesus can "plunder" them only because he is exerting power over Satan directly. When the strong man was free, he had power over his property, the demons, including the power to cast them out. That would ordinarily be Satan's business. But Jesus is interrupting that business, in which the demons sow conflict and violence for Satan and then Satan casts them out with more violence.

In Matthew's and Luke's telling of this story, the moral about the strong man is preceded by Jesus saying, "But if it is by the Spirit of God that I cast out demons, then the kingdom of God has come to you" (Matt. 12:28; cf. Luke 11:20). This is not part of the cycle Satan and the demons run to renew their power. The kingdom of God represents an entirely new order, not the one maintained by the ruler of this world. Indeed, in the Gospel of John, as Jesus firmly sets himself on the way to the cross, he says, "Now is the judgment of this world; now the ruler of this world will be driven out" (John 12:31). The fact that demons are being cast out does not by itself tell us everything unless we know by whom and to what end.

Another passage found in the three Synoptic Gospels follows upon Peter's confession that Jesus is the Christ, the Messiah. Jesus immediately teaches the disciples that he is going to suffer and be executed and rise again. At this, Peter takes him aside and rebukes him, saying, "'God forbid it, Lord! This must never happen to you.' But he turned and said to Peter, 'Get behind me, Satan! You are a stumbling block to me; for you are setting your mind not on divine things but on human things'" (Matt. 16:22-23). This is a key text for our interpretation of Jesus' death. Did not the discourse from the Gospel of John discussed above make clear that this death is the work of Satan? How then can Jesus turn on Peter for passionately objecting that this must never happen, and identify Peter with Satan? The rebuke comes because Jesus is not going to the cross to confirm the scapegoat ritual, but to repeal it. Here is the same doubleness we have seen threaded through all the Gospel accounts. Peter's picture of God forbids the Messiah's identification with a victim. Peter rejects the idea of Christ's suffering because of his natural human attachment to Christ, the attachment that leads us always to prefer victims who are not part of our closest circle. And he rejects it because he is hoping for a violently victorious God who will crush the enemies of Israel.

Jesus says Peter is a "stumbling block" to him, offering a real temptation to deflect him from his path. If Peter were flatly wrong, this would not be a live temptation. But Jesus' reaction makes it clear that it is. The objection affects Jesus for different reasons than it appeals to Peter. It appeals to Jesus because of its fundamental truth. This should never happen to Jesus, or to anyone. The wrongness in the cross is precisely what Jesus aims to oppose and overcome in bearing it. If Jesus' death can oppose that evil, then that is why he will do it. But that injustice is also the strongest possible argument why he should not accept it. For all the wrong reasons, Peter has hit on the weakest point of Jesus' resolve, and played Satan's strongest card: to go through with this trip to Jerusalem is to implicitly cooperate in the most unjust in the long line of unjust sacrifices. Why would Jesus want to do Satan's business for him?[12] Precisely because Jesus

12. This is a moment eerily parallel with that faced by Abraham, as viewed by Kierkegaard in *Fear and Trembling*. See Søren Kierkegaard, *"Fear and Trembling," and "The Sickness unto Death"* (Garden City, N.Y.: Doubleday, 1954). Abraham knows, according to Kierkegaard, that killing his son is undoubtedly wrong, according to God's law, and that if it is a genuine call from God to do this horrible thing, it can come only as a unique, individual event for some unfathomable purpose, as an act not to be imitated and one that conforms to no principle. Jesus' "calling" to accept the cross is the same, a calling to accept what is unjust and what — if it were made a rule — would be directly opposite to God's will. We might say that Jesus' acceptance of the cross, Jesus' refusal to agree with Peter, is the closest Jesus comes to sin. "He was made sin for our sake." We think of this as meaning he was treated as if he were sinful, for our sake. But in "setting his face to go to Jerusalem," and in seeing his crucifixion as the necessary path for salvation (despite the firm way he rejects the rationale of his persecutors at each step along the way), Jesus has become, however cir-

is innocent, the strongest temptation to deflect him from his path is the simple truth. This injustice ought not happen. It "ought" to happen only if it can be unlike all the others from the foundation of the world, if it can reverse the practice. We can hardly blame Peter for not seeing how that might be. It requires resurrection, and a new spirit.

Holy Spirit, *Paraclete*

The character of Satan has a parallel in the New Testament in the figure of the Holy Spirit. The risen Christ, the vindicated victim, is a dramatic wrench in the gears of sacrifice. The one who has been killed and silenced appears alive, with power. In this act, the hidden reality of scapegoating is unavoidably presented and God's definitive opposition to it is manifest in identification with the crucified one. But the appearances of the risen Jesus continue for only a brief time, and after that the truth of the resurrection is transmitted in the faith and community of those who witness to it. This is not quite the whole story, however. For Jesus promises something more.

In the Gospel of John Jesus gives a long farewell message to his disciples. In it he cautions them that they will be persecuted as he was. The world will do this because of its ignorance of God and God's true nature. Jesus says his own suffering will fulfill the word written in the Psalms, "They hated me without a cause." Thus he directly links his own fate with that described in the scapegoat psalms. He goes on: "When the *paraclete* comes, whom I will send to you from the Father, the Spirit of truth who comes from the Father, he will testify on my behalf. You also are to testify because you have been with me from the beginning" (John 15:26-27).[13] An hour is coming, Jesus says, when those who kill you will think that by doing so they are offering worship to God. This is just what participants in sacred violence believe they are doing. Jesus acknowledges that such a prospect can only sadden the disciples and make his departure even more discouraging. "Nevertheless I tell you the truth: it is to your advantage that I go away, for if I do not go away, the *paraclete* will not come to you;

---

cumstantially, an accomplice of Satan in something that is unqualifiedly evil. Even though ultimately this may be seen as a deep wisdom that ensnares and defeats Satan, it requires that God is not only willing to suffer in body and spirit, but also willing to suffer the moral ambiguity reflected in this exchange with Peter.

13. In this passage and the following one, I have substituted the transliterated Greek word *paraclete* for the translation "Advocate."

but if I go, I will send him to you. And when he comes, he will prove the world wrong about sin and righteousness and judgment: about sin, because they do not believe in me; about righteousness, because I am going to the Father and you will see me no longer; about judgment, because the ruler of this world has been condemned" (John 16:7-11). *Paraclete* is a Greek word that is variously translated "advocate," or "helper," or "intercessor." These words give a rather vague impression, while the original has a more specific flavor: one who appears on behalf of another, an "advocate" in the sense of representative for the accused, a defense attorney.

In the context of Jesus' speech, which is focused on persecution past and future, the meaning is clear. The work of the *paraclete* is to testify by the side of victims, to be their advocate and to "prove the world wrong." In the sacrificial ganging of all against a few, the few will not be left alone. There will always be at least one divine voice to speak for them. The "world's" view of sin, righteousness, and judgment is summed up in the sacrificial dynamic. Sin becomes an excuse for persecution, righteousness becomes defined as submission to scapegoating, and judgment uses violence against violence. The historical task of the Holy Spirit, which is another name for the *paraclete,* is to prove this wrong, by testimony to Christ. Christ is the counterexample. The world that crucified Jesus is wrong about sin and righteousness because it wrongly accused him of sin and refused to see the righteousness confirmed by God's raising of Jesus, and wrong about judgment because the verdict against Jesus has been reversed. The last point is perhaps most striking. The *paraclete* is directly opposed to Satan. The *paraclete* will prove the world wrong about judgment, because the prince of this world, Satan, has been condemned. It is the sacrificial process that is on trial, the accuser who is accused.

Paraclete is a title that specifies one particular aspect of the identity of the Holy Spirit. The Holy Spirit is and does more than the task we are stressing. But if the interpretation I have just suggested seems improbable to those used to thinking of the Spirit in other terms, we will give a few examples. We earlier discussed Stephen's martyrdom at the hands of a mob. At the climax of that story Stephen testifies against the injustice of Jesus' execution: "You stiff-necked people, uncircumcised in heart and ears, you are forever opposing the Holy Spirit, just as your ancestors used to do" (Acts 7:51). The crowd becomes enraged and begins to gather about him. At this point the text says, "But filled with the Holy Spirit, he gazed into heaven and saw the glory of God and Jesus standing at the right hand of God. 'Look,' he said, 'I see the heavens opened and the Son of Man standing at the right hand of God!'" (7:55-56).

Under the direction of the Holy Spirit, Stephen's witness agrees with the description of the *paraclete*'s work given in Jesus' farewell message. His sermon "proves the world wrong" about sin by testifying that it was the persecution that was the sin and not the supposed crimes of Jesus. He "proves the world wrong" about righteousness by maintaining that scapegoating was not an authentic religious act, not in accord with God's law. Instead it was a murder of Jesus, whom he refers to only as "the Righteous One." The victim was the righteous one, and not the crowd that condemned him. He "proves the world wrong" about judgment, because he rejects the verdict against Jesus as the work of the ruler of this world. And yet Stephen renders this judgment in the spirit of Jesus: "While they were stoning Stephen, he prayed, 'Lord Jesus, receive my spirit.' Then he knelt down and cried out in a loud voice, 'Lord, do not hold this sin against them'" (7:59-60).

This role of the Spirit shows up in a number of places. Peter and John are arrested after healing a lame man and preaching of Christ's unjust death and his resurrection by God. The book of Acts records what happens when they are brought to trial:

> Then Peter, filled with the Holy Spirit, said to them, "Rulers of the people and elders, if we are questioned today because of a good deed done to someone who was sick and are asked how this man has been healed, let it be known to all of you, and to all the people of Israel, that this man is standing before you in good health by the name of Jesus Christ of Nazareth, whom you crucified, whom God raised from the dead. This Jesus is 'the stone that was rejected by you, the builders; / it has become the cornerstone.'" (4:8-11)

The Holy Spirit stands with those who are accused and threatened, witnessing with them and witnessing for Christ, the risen victim. As Paul is returning to Jerusalem prior to his final arrest, he says, "And now, as a captive to the Spirit, I am on my way to Jerusalem, not knowing what will happen to me there, except that the Holy Spirit testifies to me in every city that imprisonment and persecutions are waiting for me" (20:22-23).

Above we reviewed the incident where Jesus was accused of casting out demons by the power of "the ruler of the demons," and Jesus asserted that his own work was actually a replacement of the practice of Satan casting out Satan. If we followed that story in the Gospel of Mark to the next verse, we would find Jesus' statement, "'Truly I tell you, people will be forgiven for their sins and whatever blasphemies they utter; but whoever blasphemes against the Holy Spirit can never have forgiveness, but is guilty of an eternal sin' — for they had said, 'He has an unclean spirit'" (Mark 3:28-30). Those who are actually guilty of the sins charged by scapegoating can be forgiven. But to directly oppose God's witness for the victims is to step beyond the reach of forgiveness, in the same way that Paul argued that a refusal to recognize the resurrection of Christ (because it reveals us as sinners against the victim) cuts us off from the hope and deliverance it offers.

In the Gospel of Luke, Jesus' saying appears in a slightly different context. "And everyone who speaks a word against the Son of Man will be forgiven; but whoever blasphemes against the Holy Spirit will not be forgiven. When they bring you before the synagogues, the rulers, and the authorities, do not worry about how you are to defend yourselves or what you are to say; for the Holy Spirit will teach you at that very hour what you ought to say" (Luke 12:10-12). The Holy Spirit's work is to be with people in precisely this situation. We might say the *paraclete* is sent as the response to Job's demand for a vindicator, an advocate to stand beside everyone who cries out with the voice we heard in the Psalms. As in the case of Stephen, the Holy Spirit brings the presence and truth of the crucified Jesus to the side of every victim.

Satan sows discord, flames the mimetic rivalries and animosities among persons that can blow up into social crisis, and then encourages the persecutory sacrifices by which communities beat down and manage these conflicts. The *paraclete* is an anti-Satan. Jesus says Satan was a murderer from the beginning. But the Holy Spirit is an advocate with the abandoned victims when all turn against them in sacred fury. Jesus says the devil is a liar and the father of lies, but the Holy Spirit is the Spirit of truth, truth that pierces the veil of mythic rationales for redemptive violence. Satan incites violence, the better to justify violence to restrain it. The Holy Spirit nurtures peace and unity to resist the conflicts that lead to sacrifice.

Sacrifice to End Sacrifice

We will take one more example. If there is one book in the New Testament that appears to prove our approach wrong, it is the Letter to the Hebrews. The book's single overpowering theme is the importance of Jesus' death as a sacrificial offering. The writer understands that death through detailed parallels with the practice of temple sacrifice in Jerusalem. The benefits of Christ's death are exalted. His blood establishes a new covenant and is the foundation of our salvation. The whole history of sacrifice is reinforced in the cross, and the importance of the cross is that it is a supersacrifice.

> But when Christ came as a high priest of the good things that have come, then through the greater and perfect tent (not made with hands, that is, not of this creation), he entered once for all into the Holy Place, not with the blood of goats and calves, but with his own blood, thus obtaining eternal redemption. For if the blood of goats and bulls, with the sprinkling of the ashes of a heifer, sanctifies those who have been defiled so that their flesh is purified, how much more will the blood of Christ, who through the eternal Spirit offered himself without blemish to God, purify our conscience from dead works to worship the living God! (Heb. 9:11-14)

This seems clear enough. Killing birds and goats and bulls may get you some benefits. Killing the Son of God will get you infinitely greater benefits. There is nothing antisacrificial about this. Rather than attacking the history of such rituals in Israel, the writer accepts it. "Indeed, under the law almost everything is purified with blood, and without the shedding of blood there is no forgiveness of sins" (9:22).

Stephen and Paul look back through Israel's history and draw a line to Jesus through the voices of scapegoats and victims, through the persecuted prophets and their words against sacrifice. The writer of Hebrews draws a line to Jesus through all of Israel's prior sacrificial practices. These are quite different approaches. It is striking, then, that they reach the same conclusion: Christ has ended sacrifice. The one approach emphasizes that the cross has revealed what was always wrong with sacred violence. The other emphasizes that Christ's sacrifice is better than all the others. It is the one truly effective offering and accomplishes what all the others never could. But these are not really opposed to each other. They are more like two sides of the same thing.

This is reflected in the ways the writer in Hebrews puts a finger on the particular things that were imperfect in prior sacrifice. "For Christ did not enter a sanctuary made by human hands, a mere copy of the true one, but he entered into heaven itself, now to appear in the presence of God on our behalf. Nor was it to offer himself again and again, as the high priest enters the Holy Place *year after year with blood that is not his own; for then he would have had to suffer again and again since the foundation of the world.* But as it is, he has appeared once for all at the end of the age to remove sin by the sacrifice of himself" (9:24-26, emphasis mine).

These verses make a very explicit contrast between Christ's death and a pattern that is *not* being followed. That pattern is illustrated in the action of the high priest who offers victims again and again. This offering, the text underlines, is made with blood that is not his own. If Jesus' sacrifice were to be like that, he would have had to suffer again and again, since the foundation of the world. And, presumably, Jesus and other victims would have to go on suffering. What we have here is a capsule summary of the nature of sacrificial violence, presented as exactly what Jesus' death is not about. Christ's sacrifice is presented as the opposite and in fact the end of that dynamic. His sacrifice is meant to stop it. Christ, our high priest, has offered the one needful sacrifice and makes intercession in heaven for us. No further earthly sacrifice is expected, accepted, or even possible.[14] Jesus, on the cross, speaks the one word that otherwise can never be said of sacrifice: "It is finished." What sacrifice is always being repeated to achieve has actually been accomplished.

The writer accepts the past history of sacrifice in a highly qualified way. It was an imperfect response to an insoluble problem. "Thus it was necessary for the sketches of the heavenly things to be purified with these rites, but the heavenly things themselves need better sacrifices than these" (9:23). They could never succeed; "otherwise, would they not have ceased being offered, since the worshipers, cleansed once for all, would no longer have any consciousness of sin? But in these sacrifices there is a reminder of sin year after year" (10:2-3).

So the writer of Hebrews, this advocate of a sacrificial understanding of the cross, adopts some of the strongest antisacrificial language from the tradition.

> For it is impossible for the blood of bulls and goats to take away sins. Consequently, when Christ came into the world, he said, "Sacrifices and offerings you have not desired, / but a body you have prepared for me; / in burnt offerings and sin offerings / you have taken no pleasure. / Then I said, 'See, God, I have come to do your will, O God' / (in the scroll of the book it is written of me)." When he said above, "You have neither desired nor taken pleasure in sacrifices and offerings and burnt offerings and sin offerings" (these are offered according to the law), then he added, "See, I have come to do your will." He abolishes the first in order to establish the second. And it is by God's

---

14. For some discussion of this, see Raymund Schwager, "Christ's Death and the Prophetic Critique of Sacrifice," *Semeia*, no. 33 (1985): 111.

will that we have been sanctified through the offering of the body of Jesus Christ once for all. (10:4-10, quoting Ps. 40)

These quotations from the Psalms and Isaiah are placed in Christ's mouth. Christ has come to do God's will, a will that does not take pleasure in sacrifices and offerings and burnt offerings and sin offerings. He has come to establish God's will by abolishing such sacrifices, through the offering of his body, once for all.

Christ's death is completely unique. Strictly speaking, it cannot be imitated, and any purposeful repetition of it would go directly counter to the entire logic of the book of Hebrews. To think of doing it again would be certain proof you had no idea what you were talking about. The mythic pattern is an implicit formula that programs us to repeat the sacrifice, with each new act of sacrifice generating the effective power. The New Testament, even in its most sacrificial terminology, reverses this relation by calling believers to constant recollection of Jesus as the one unjustly sacrificed, the one vindicated by God, the one who takes no retribution. The victim is remembered, and the explicit representation of his suffering is a caution against any repetition.

The writer of Hebrews declares that Jesus is the mediator of a new covenant, based in "the sprinkled blood that speaks a better word than the blood of Abel" (Heb. 12:24). Abel's blood called for vengeance, and sparked the cycles of retaliation that we have contained only with more blood, the blood of sacrifice. Christ's death speaks a different, better word than this. In the final chapter we are given one last extended image from the practice of sacrifice.

> For the bodies of those animals whose blood is brought into the sanctuary by the high priest as a sacrifice for sin are burned outside the camp. Therefore Jesus also suffered outside the city gate in order to sanctify the people by his own blood. Let us then go to him outside the camp and bear the abuse he endured. For here we have no lasting city, but we are looking for the city that is to come. Through him, then, let us continually offer a sacrifice of praise to God, that is, the fruit of lips that confess his name. Do not neglect to do good and to share what you have, for such sacrifices are pleasing to God. (13:11-16)

If there is abuse to be suffered for standing with Jesus, it should be borne. But there is to be no more sacrifice . . . or only sacrifice of a different type, the sacrifice of praise, of doing good, and sharing what you have.

The book of Hebrews turns sacrifice inside out. Rather than deny ritual sacrifice any effect (for it has a very real effect) or reject all its practice in the past, this writer presses a koan-like conclusion. If you believe in sacrifice, then you can't practice it anymore, because it has been done completely, perfectly, once for all. This was the sacrifice to end sacrifice. Hebrews is rife with the language of liturgy and ritual, but its premise is the very opposite of what ritual presumes: not repetition but finality.

Both Paul and the writer of Hebrews use sacrificial language as their primary medium to interpret Jesus' death. In Hebrews this death is seen as a "perfect" sacrifice. While some validity is implicitly presumed for the sacrificial models that provide this analogy to apply to the cross, those models are rendered inoperative by the finality and completeness of this event. Sacrifice is ended by a culmination, we might say. For Paul the death of Christ is cast also in sacrificial language but not so much as a culmination of past models. Instead Paul stresses the different mechanism operative in this event — the appropriation of God's mercy through faith in the one unjustly sacrificed. That is, Paul casts the event against similarities in Jewish tradition, emphasizing that this takes place "apart from the law." Although these two texts have contrasting tenors, they point to the same reality.[15]

Deceiving the Devil

The outline we have given of the cross in Christian faith may seem both strange and familiar: familiar because we have covered very well known portions of scripture, strange because these pieces are assembled in ways that may seem unusual. Most notably, we have been saying that the gospel of the crucified one is directly opposed to a practice and understanding of sacrifice that is sometimes advanced precisely as the very meaning of that gospel. There is a sacrificial transaction taking place at the cross, but it is one that humans have organized, not God. And yet God has made this evil transaction the occasion for a better one, one in which scapegoating itself can be overthrown.

Interestingly, we can point to a way in which the theology of the early church assembled these same materials in what may seem like an odd

---

15. See Robert Hamerton-Kelly, *Sacred Violence: Paul's Hermeneutic of the Cross* (Minneapolis: Fortress, 1992). In a footnote on page 80, Hamerton-Kelly says that while the writer of Hebrews is content to argue that "Christ's death is the perfect sacrifice that renders the system passé, he [Paul] argues that Christ's death shows the system always to have been a grotesque error that in fact caused the death of Christ."

shape to us, but one that closely fits our outline. When writers in the first Christian centuries treated Jesus' death, they put primary emphasis on the cross as a great victory over death and sin. Christ defeated the powers that held humanity in bondage and succeeded in restoring the intimacy with God and participation in eternal life that had been lost. "God became as we are, in order that we might become as God is," was an idea frequently expressed in these texts.[16] This is an interesting turn on the serpent's charge, in Eden, that God feared having Eve and Adam become "like God." Quite the contrary. God acts to restore that possibility for humans when it has been lost.

When we move from this general conviction to a more specific level, early Christian writers are famous for their fondness for two images that have perplexed and often embarrassed later theologians. According to one, Jesus' death is viewed as a kind of ransom, paid to Satan for the release of captive humanity. In another, Jesus' death is viewed as a trick, a clever ruse by which evil powers themselves are led to lose their dominion over humanity. Modern theologians generally reject the idea that God would barter with the devil or resort to deceit, seeing these as rather childish, if not morally questionable, characterizations. Further, given modern uncertainty about the whole idea of a personalized power of evil, it seemed wiser to leave the devil out of it entirely.[17] Thus, in discussions of atonement these views (prominent as they were in the early centuries) are usually passed over lightly.

But from our perspective the ancient writers seem to have chosen unusually apt images, and to have demonstrated that they were sensitive to exactly the dynamic we have described. Reference to Satan is the most effective way they could make clear the stereoscopic perspective of the cross, the fact that Jesus' death is not the work of God but the product of an evil process, even as God turns it against itself to a saving purpose. "Ransom" is expressive of just this idea. Victims are kidnapped, and yet other victims (their loved ones) are forced to pay for their release. Both things are done

---

16. "For the Son of God became man so that we might become God" (Athanasius, *De incarnatione* 54.3, in *Patrologia Graeca* 192B). Some attribute the first statement of this idea to Irenaeus.

17. In recent years major theologians have begun to reverse this lack of interest in Satan and principalities and powers. See Walter Wink, *Engaging the Powers: Discernment and Resistance in a World of Domination* (Minneapolis: Fortress, 1992); Walter Wink, *Naming the Powers: The Language of Power in the New Testament* (Philadelphia: Fortress, 1984); Walter Wink, *Unmasking the Powers: The Invisible Forces That Determine Human Existence* (Philadelphia: Fortress, 1986).

under threat of violence. Those who offer ransom are also victims, and their willingness to do so does not legitimate the criminal's control over the captive, since that control is itself the result of a crime. Those who pay hardly see the transaction as their ideal or design. Ransom presupposes that the party who receives it is the persecutor.[18]

The notion that Jesus is given over to death as a ransom to the devil may be troubling to those who fear it compromises notions of absolute divine omnipotence. But it states with unmistakable power that the realm of scapegoating sacrifice is the sphere of Satan. God has stepped into it in the place of the victim under duress, as a hostage. Ransom gives up something to get something in return. This is the normal business of sacrifice. Victims are given in order to achieve peace. So the evil powers view Jesus as more of the same, another ransom or protection payment. But God means the ransom in a radically different way. What happens here is in effect a substitution of hostages. God takes the place of human sinners, ransoms them by exchange on the devil's terms, we might say. Interestingly, this seems to go along with a conviction that it would not be right for God to simply defeat the devil by counterviolence. Irenaeus wrote that God redeemed humanity "not by violent means, as the [apostasy] had obtained dominion over us at the beginning, when it insatiably snatched away what was not its own, but by means of persuasion, as became a God of counsel, who does not use violent means to obtain what he desires; so that neither should justice be infringed upon, nor the ancient handiwork of God go to destruction."[19] God pays the ransom to avoid shedding the blood of others (including the perpetrators), but also in the interest of ending the crime and preventing future ones. God offers a ransom not only to get the captives out of the place of the scapegoat, but to act from that place, the place of utter abandonment, the place from which no cry of complaint or injustice rises, the place from which vengeance could most legitimately be exacted, if the victim had the power to do so. When God, who cannot be silenced and who will not take vengeance, stands in that place, the web of sacrifice collapses.

18. Admittedly, some of these same writers talk at times of Satan having a "rightful" claim on humanity, in the sense that humans have been willing accomplices in their own abduction and bondage, however much they may dislike the result. But they stress equally that Satan succeeded by deceit and violence, taking what was not properly his. Whatever "rights" Satan has might be likened to an appeal to the rules of war (an exchange of prisoners) by an unjust aggressor.

19. Irenaeus, *Adversus haereses* I:527 (5.1.1), quoted in Hans Boersma, *Violence, Hospitality, and the Cross: Reappropriating the Atonement Tradition* (Grand Rapids: Baker Academic, 2004), 129.

And that leads us to the idea of a trick. Gregory of Nyssa expresses it in a striking image, likening the cross to a fishing lure in which the hook of deity is hidden under the "bait" of an apparently merely human Jesus.[20] Gregory uses another striking image when he notes that two persons can mix poison with food, the one in order to kill and the other to administer an antidote and cure.[21] In swallowing his prey, Satan is caught and dispossessed. Not only has Satan grasped a victim who can by resurrection reverse the sacrifice. The patristic writers also explain that by exacting death from one who is truly innocent, Satan has lost his monopoly, the unquestioned ability to enforce death on those who are sinners and have for that reason been under his power. A scapegoat can be innocent of the outsized sacrificial accusations made against him or her, but since we are all guilty of some sins and liable to more, we all can be plausibly tailored to fit the victim's role. In Jesus, however, the accusation process has met its match. The usual demonization of the sacrificed breaks down, and instead casts doubt on the persecutory process.

If Satan represents the sacrificial dynamic itself, the "trick" the early Christian writers marveled at is genuinely worthy of wonder. That dynamic posed a dilemma. Violent resistance against the mechanism only fuels its power, as in the many myths that feature monsters that grow three heads for each one cut off. Yet to simply accept the role of the victim, however nobly, is likewise to reinforce the working of the sacrificial process. Even God was caught in this dilemma. To overcome violence by the fiat of divine power and judgment could only reinforce the image of a wrathful God and justify models of retribution. To put aside all divine power and submit to the same suffering that befalls all sacrificial victims would itself do nothing to stem the violence. To the patristic writers, the wonder of the cross was God's solving of this puzzle. In the temptation in the wilderness, Satan attempted to taunt Christ into the aggressive use of divine power for worldly purposes, which would in effect be to serve him. Jesus resists these temptations toward rivalry, conflict, and retribution, and goes instead to the cross. This option is also fine with Satan. It looks like a sure thing, either way. In Christ's crucifixion the Satan of sacrifice saw nothing but business as usual and "took the bait."

---

20. See Gregory of Nyssa, "The Great Catechism" XXIV, in Philip Schaff and Henry Wace, eds., *A Select Library of Nicene and Post-Nicene Fathers of the Christian Church*, 2nd ser. (New York: Christian Literature Company, 1890), vol. 5.

21. Gregory of Nyssa, "The Great Catechism" XXVI.

The trick, the startling reversal, is that this time simply by doing what it always does, the sacrificial process brings about its own demise. The divine power is neither deployed in violence against Jesus' persecutors nor shelved in empathetic helplessness. Through the resurrection the voice of the victim overcomes the silence of death, but without violence or retribution. The resurrection means that those who abandoned Jesus or turned against him need neither be punished as enemies nor confirmed in their sin. Instead they have the retroactive opportunity to cling to Jesus again. The normal rules of sacrifice break down. In this environment all the ordinary behavior of Satan surrounding the crucifixion becomes suddenly a part of his unmasking and undoing. In carrying out what seemed like a foolproof plan to feed on yet another victim, the sacrificial process has bitten down upon the living God. It is thus caught and exposed. As the Letter to the Colossians says, "Unmasking the principalities and powers, God publicly shamed them, exposing them in Christ's triumphal procession by means of the cross."[22] By taking up the place of the scapegoat, God has entered this human dynamic at one point where divine power may reveal and save simply by becoming the object of human sin. The double bind has been reversed. The only way Satan could have avoided this revelation would have been to refrain from victimizing Jesus.

These writers are struck by the symmetry of the processes of human sin and of redemption: as a tree was the site of the fall, so a "tree" is the site of our liberation; as Satan captured humanity by deceit, so Satan is overthrown by a trick. This fits the pattern we are describing. Mythic sacrifice succeeds because everyone accepts deceptive representations of the victim, and the process itself is defeated through its inability to recognize the true nature of the victim before it on the cross. Our analysis illuminates the paradox in the Gospels and Christian tradition about the crucifixion: it is saving and it ought not to happen. Likewise it illuminates the tension in these classic Christian representations of the atonement, where God is seen in some way to acquiesce in Satan's program and at the same time to destroy it, to be playing Satan's game and yet deceiving him. We can add that our analysis makes sense of the parallel treatment in Christian tradition of a paradox in the devil's attitude toward the cross. In theology and popular piety the devil is portrayed as the supreme enthusiast for the crucifixion and often in the same breath as terrified and dismayed by it. It is evil's great triumph and its great mistake.

---

22. Col. 2:15, as translated by Wink in *Engaging the Powers,* 140.

CHAPTER SIX

The Sign of Jonah and Susanna

Innocent Blood and False Accusers

See, something greater than Jonah is here!

Matthew 12:41

The primary aim of this book is to trace a constructive theological view of the cross. To this point we have pursued that task mainly by examination of scripture. The scope of this study hardly allows us to follow the question through history. But it is important to at least glimpse in that direction. Even if the elements we have described in the New Testament and the earliest church are real, some may object that they have had very little to do in fact with the church's later theology or tradition. Are the interpretations I have emphasized novel and recent ones, entirely absent from earlier ages? Most particularly, are there any indications that the church picked up the same elements we have been stressing, that it saw the connection between Christ's passion and resistance to scapegoating sacrifice?

To put the same point negatively, there are certainly episodes in Christian history that would seem to be definitive counterexamples, times when the church was immersed in that practice itself. There can be no glossing over such facts. Rather, our constructive concern is to ask what kinds of theologies of the cross have been at play in different situations, and especially, what kind of theology of the cross has exercised the most liberating power in contexts of evil and oppression. So we want particularly to look in the shadows of some of the darker moments of Christian history to see if the theology we are describing is present at all, and if so, what kind of influence it exerts.

In this chapter we will look first at some representative evidence that the antiscapegoating interpretation of the cross was in fact part of the broad Christian tradition. Then we will briefly consider the role of the theology of the cross in some of the most violent facets of Christian history.

Images of the Cross

One fact may seem to dramatically counter our thesis that the reversal of scapegoating sacrifice is a major strand, implicit and explicit, of Christian faith. A key part of this thesis is the stark presentation of Jesus' death. But for four centuries and more, Christianity went without explicit pictures of the crucifixion, and veiled the image of the cross in the ambiguous shape of anchors and monograms.[1] To be sure, we have seen how Christ's death was unsparingly described in the Gospels. That passion story was ceaselessly remembered in the church's liturgy, teaching, and preaching from the beginning. Yet no literal depictions of the crucifixion in art survive from this formative period. Representations of Jesus in early Christian art display a healer, a wonder-worker, or a teacher. In fact, the early centuries offer an odd inversion in creed and image. Early creeds focus on Jesus' beginnings and endings, "skipping right from 'born of the Virgin Mary' to 'suffered under Pontius Pilate,' with no mention of Jesus' life and work, while the art appears to take an opposite tack."[2]

The cross and crucifix, such common sights in the rest of the church's history, are images missing at the beginning. This prompts some to conclude that any atonement theology or emphasis on Jesus' saving death must have been missing also, and arose only as a later distortion. This is hardly likely, given the overwhelming evidence on every other front for central focus on the cross.[3] It was, for one thing, an obvious point of controversy between Christians and their critics. The artistic gap cannot be a testimony of indifference, for there was no similar silence in other media.

Perhaps the reality the scriptures described was too gruesome to easily depict, or too readily ridiculed by outsiders and too awesome and mysterious to present directly. Perhaps, in a persecuted and at times martyred church, such an image would be realistically terrifying to most and dan-

---

1. See for instance chapter 4 in Robin Margaret Jensen, *Understanding Early Christian Art* (London and New York: Routledge, 2000).

2. Jensen, *Understanding Early Christian Art*, 131-32.

3. The early history of the Eucharist and of baptism (in which one clearly was participating in Christ's death and resurrection) is one example.

gerously seductive to some. In the Roman world this sight was all too familiar. When Paul spoke of "death, even death on a cross," no one really needed to spell out the details.

There is no single satisfactory explanation for why the cross would figure so centrally in Christian faith and worship but be visually absent. Perhaps the question itself is an artifact of an arbitrary definition of art, one that excludes the embodied images of worship and ritual activity. Every Christian baptism acted out Christ's death, and every celebration of the Eucharist represented it. By the second century there is testimony that making the sign of the cross had become a common gesture of Christian life. In other words, the most widespread and powerful images of the cross would be those embodied in the sacraments and acted out by other Christians. They were not absent from the visual horizon at all.

There is a scrap of "art" from the first centuries that does explicitly present the crucifixion. It is a presumed piece of anti-Christian graffiti discovered in Rome, in which a person kneels beside a cross on which hangs a human figure with the head of an ass. Beneath is scrawled "Alexamenos worships his god."[4] The derision is directed at the absurdity of worshiping an executed criminal and siding with such an outcast. The ass's head, the dehumanization of the victim, is the only touch that really marks this as an *anti*-Christian expression. Leaving that element aside, it would be impossible to reconstruct whether this was ridicule or simple Christian profession (since Christians did in fact preach the "foolishness" of identifying with the persecuted one as the divine savior).

That ambiguity, even at this distance, tells us something about the situation Christians faced. To present the cross as a positive sign of their faith ran many risks, from seeming to endorse Jesus' death (and that Christians would practice human sacrifice, or desire such an end for themselves) to being taken as incitement to violence (i.e., Jesus' death was wrong and the fate of the victim is displayed as a call to retaliation against those who opposed him, then or now).[5] The frequent appearance of anchors, ship masts, and the Chi-Rho sign in early Christian art as discreet representations of the cross avoided these risks. It may not be coincidental that we have no images of Christ on the cross until after Constantine

---

4. See Rodolfo Amedeo Lanciani, *Ancient Rome in the Light of Recent Discoveries* (Boston and New York: Houghton Mifflin, 1888), 122.

5. The well-known contemporary "mystery religion" of Mithraism had as its central image a picture of the god Mithra sacrificing a bull. The rites practiced among its members were strictly secret, but were assumed to replicate this sacrificial action in some way. Observers could have been ready to form a parallel assumption about Christians and the cross.

outlawed crucifixion as an actual mode of execution. So long as such a death was a regular occurrence, a Christian display of the picture could readily be misunderstood by outsiders as a threat from authorities or as a pattern Christians sought to repeat.

The church had to struggle with the tension in the revelation, and that tension is embodied in the sign itself. As we have seen, the passion story paralleled a mythic pattern. It was crucial to the truth of the gospel that both the similarity and the difference be understood. But it was no simple matter to balance the realistic picture of persecution and execution (an unveiling of the real face of sacrifice) with thanksgiving for the way God had used this sinful human event as the occasion to defeat its violence (a saving act).

We must also say that the church's understanding of the cross was aided by spending those earliest centuries as a vulnerable and intermittently persecuted minority. The Gospel accounts of the passion and the early Christian preaching about it came home to the actual contexts in which Christian communities lived. That fusion has left an indelible watermark on Christianity. Even though believers came from various social locations, many were of low estate, and all, by virtue of belonging, put themselves in the way of experiencing what it was like to be scapegoated or liable to it. That context of Christian life made it easier to grasp the antisacrificial dimension of the gospel, and to preserve it, even though it carried the coordinate danger that this sensitivity to the persecuted as such could narrow only to a concern for a suffering church.

The Sign of Jonah

The great continuity in interpretation of the cross that carries across artistic and textual forms comes from the liberal use of figures from the Hebrew scriptures as models to parallel the passion. It is of great importance for our topic to note the specific scriptural types that early Christians used to interpret Jesus and his death.

As a focus for our discussion, we can turn to the fullest early Christian artistic representation of the passion. This is found in a small carved ivory box, the Brescia Casket, dating from some three and a half centuries after Christ. The casket and its images have been the subject of an extraordinary work of scholarship by Catherine Tkacz.[6] The top of the casket has

6. Catherine Brown Tkacz, *The Key to the Brescia Casket: Typology and the Early Christian Imagination*, Collection des Études Augustiniennes. Série Antiquité, 165 (Notre Dame, Ind.: University of Notre Dame Press; Paris: Institut d'Études Augustiniennes, 2002).

five large panels, clearly the thematic focus of the work. They are scenes from the passion narrative: Christ in the Garden of Gethsemane, the arrest of Christ, the denial of Peter, Christ before the high priest, and Christ before Pilate. The scenes chosen highlight elements of the victim's story that are left out in myth. The crucifixion is not depicted directly (the first known example emanates from thirty or so years later). On the back and the front of the casket, these incidents from the passion are interpreted and their meaning underlined through the use of certain Old Testament types. The casket is unusual as a work of art that explicitly draws these parallels, but the choices are not at all idiosyncratic to the artist, since these types are extensively used by Christian writers in discussing the cross and the images themselves are found widely in early Christian art. What is of particular interest is the way the juxtaposition emphasizes the antiscapegoating theme we have been exploring.

One scriptural type used to parallel the passion is Jonah. Jonah is one of the most popular figures in early Christian art. On the front of the Brescia Casket, two sections are taken from his story: the great fish swallowing him and the fish spewing him out on dry land. These clearly represent the death and resurrection of Jesus, two events in the passion story not depicted on the cover. A second set of types is taken from the biblical book of Daniel and the apocryphal books of Susanna and Bel and the Dragon.[7] The casket has an image of Daniel in the lions' den (as well as an image of the three young Hebrew men thrown into the fiery furnace), likewise serving as a reference to Christ's death and resurrection.

To grasp the full significance of the images we must recall the scriptural stories involved. Jonah is called by God to travel to the city of Nineveh, capital of the Assyrians (great enemies of Israel), to call them to repent, lest God should destroy them. Jonah rejects this mission and boards a ship sailing to the most distant port he can find. At sea the vessel is beset by a storm and in danger of sinking. At this point something very interesting happens. The story of the prophet Jonah becomes also a scapegoat story. The sailors on the ship "said to one another, 'Come, let us cast lots, so that we may know on whose account this calamity has come upon

---

7. The book of Susanna (the thirteenth chapter of the Greek book of Daniel) and the book Bel and the Dragon are two apocryphal books relevant to the Brescia Casket. The Greek version of the book of Daniel contains portions not found in the traditional Hebrew text. Three such passages are included as three "books" in the Apocrypha, a collection accepted as canonical scripture in the Roman Catholic and Eastern Orthodox churches but not generally among Protestants. These texts were cited and treated as scripture through most of the church's history.

us.' So they cast lots, and the lot fell on Jonah" (Jon. 1:7). In the face of this accusation, Jonah admits that he is the cause and volunteers for sacrifice: "Pick me up and throw me into the sea; then the sea will quiet down for you; for I know it is because of me that this great storm has come upon you" (1:12). The sailors resist this suggestion and try to row to land. But the storm gets worse. And they cry out to Jonah's God, "Please, O LORD, we pray, do not let us perish on account of this man's life. Do not make us guilty of innocent blood; for you, O LORD, have done as it pleased you" (1:14). They throw Jonah overboard and the sea calms. "Then the men feared the LORD even more, and they offered a sacrifice to the LORD and made vows" (1:16).

A fish comes and swallows Jonah, and he stays three days and nights in the belly of the fish. At the end of this time he offers up a psalm, the prayer of a delivered scapegoat who has been rescued by God. It concludes this way:

> But I with the voice of thanksgiving
>   will sacrifice to you;
> what I have vowed I will pay.
>   Deliverance belongs to the LORD! (2:9)

Jonah is then thrown onto the land and takes up his task of announcing God's call to the city of Nineveh.[8] Against all expectation the people repent most dramatically. The king proclaims fasting and decrees that "All shall turn from their evil ways and from the violence that is in their hands" (3:8). At this, God pardons the city, much to the distress of Jonah, who complains that this was why he had fled in the first place. "For I knew that you are a gracious God and merciful, slow to anger, and abounding in steadfast love, and ready to relent from punishing" (4:2). Jonah asks God to kill him and goes out of the city to sulk. God has a plant grow up over him to shade him, for which Jonah is grateful. But the next day God withers the vine, to Jonah's great anger. And the book ends with God asking Jonah that if he is concerned about the bush, should not God be concerned about the lives of so many people in Nineveh?

Jonah's story is that of a scapegoat sacrifice turned upside down. His sojourn in the fish is an obvious image for death and resurrection, but the attachment to the story is so strong that it must go further than that. The

---

8. On this aspect of Jonah's story I have benefited from James Alison, "Spluttering Up to the Beach to Ninevah," *Contagion: Journal of Violence, Mimesis and Culture* 7 (2000).

artistic representations of Jonah usually include a cycle of three or four scenes: Jonah being thrown overboard, Jonah swallowed by the fish, Jonah thrown out again, and finally Jonah under his vine.

The shipboard event is a familiar sacrificial scenario. Crisis threatens the vessel. The community immediately turns toward inward conflict, asking whose fault this is and who should be punished. They identify the guilty party (who is helpfully compliant) and, as a last resort, carry out the killing. It produces its expected effect, and the little community busily sets up its sacrificial rituals to carry on from there. As it stands, this is a good mythical pattern, and if the story stopped here and we read it with suspicion, we might conclude that Jonah was framed and hadn't defied God at all. But the story goes on. God has appeared so far as complicit in the scapegoaters' action, backing up the charge against Jonah. But God acts now to save the sacrificed one. Jonah is swallowed by a great fish and vomited up on shore. He undertakes God's original commission to call the city of Nineveh to repentance. From being himself a classical mythical scapegoat, Jonah is saved to go on an antiscapegoating mission. Nineveh is not called to find the guilty ones in its midst, to offer them as a sacrifice in collective violence to avert judgment. Instead the city is called to collective repentance. Jonah himself is dismayed to see punishment turned aside and is reproached by God for this lack of mercy. Rather than an imaginary crime (of the one endangering the many) and a real execution (of the one by the many) on the mythical model, here we have a real crime (Jonah's disobedience to God) and averted violence (in Jonah's rescue), with the "raised" Jonah becoming the instrument of repentance and mercy for the people of Nineveh. Yet Jonah also expresses very directly the resistance to the antisacrificial message. He has it just backward, jumping at the opportunity to be a victim himself but clinging to his own hatred for the Ninevites and his desire to see them destroyed. In terms of his motives and desires, Jonah at this point in the story is an antitype of Christ. But Jonah is a clear structural type of Christ, as one rescued from scapegoating in order to overcome it.

Clearly, Christians connected the resurrection of Jesus with the return of Jonah from the belly of the whale, and also saw baptismal imagery in his being thrown into the sea and emerging a new man who now obeys God's call. But the popularity of the story suggests that Christians saw a deep resonance between the entire Jonah tale and the meaning of Jesus' death. In some parts of the Western Church, the entire book of Jonah was read on the eve of Good Friday as a preparation for the passion.[9]

9. In the lectionary readings collated from the surviving sermons of Ambrose of Milan,

That the early Christian imagination should seize upon this prophet's story in correlation with the work of the Savior tells us a great deal. God takes a scapegoating incident and uses it quite against the expectations of those who carry it out, in the service of a wider mission of grace and averted punishment. The mission of Jonah to a nation outside Israel would of course be a striking point for Gentile Christians. But the central dynamics of the story itself — the sacrificial scenario that casts Jonah into the sea and the nonsacrificial way God deals with the Ninevites — must have struck Christians as integrally connected with the work of Christ. Of course, they had good authority for this, since in Luke and Matthew when Jesus is asked for a sign, he answers that no sign will be given to them but the sign of Jonah. As Jonah was three days in the belly of the sea monster, so the Son of Man will be three days in the heart of the earth. And the people of Nineveh will rise up at the judgment to condemn this genera-tion, as they repented at the preaching of Jonah, and "something greater than Jonah is here" (Matt. 12:41).

Christ and the Vindication of Susanna

The type of Susanna is even more fascinating. Before turning to the pan-els on the casket that depict her, we will briefly review her story. Susanna is a beautiful Jewish woman highly trained in the law and married to a prominent leader in the Jewish community of Babylon. Two elders in that community are consumed with lust for her and hide in the garden of her house when she comes to bathe there. When she is alone, they demand that she have sexual relations with them. If she doesn't, they will raise an alarm and claim that they have caught her in adultery. Susanna resists them and cries out for help: "I choose not to do it; I will fall into your hands, rather than sin in the sight of the Lord" (Sus. 23).

She is then brought to court, and the two elders offer their false testi-mony against her. She is convicted and led away for the collective execu-tion. Susanna cries out, "O eternal God, you know what is secret and are aware of all things before they come to be; you know that these men have given false evidence against me. And now I am to die, though I have done none of the wicked things that they have charged against me!" (vv. 42-43).

The text says God heard her cry, and "God stirred up the holy spirit of

---

the book of Jonah was appointed to be read in its entirety on the Thursday before Easter (Maundy Thursday, the eve of the passion).

a young lad named Daniel, and he shouted with a loud voice, 'I want no part in shedding this woman's blood!'" (vv. 45-46). Daniel then interrogates the two elders separately and exposes their lie (since they cannot agree on which kind of tree they caught Susanna and her supposed lover under), resulting in Susanna's vindication, a judgment against the elders, and the text's conclusion: "Thus innocent blood was spared that day."

In many ways this story parallels the incident of the woman taken in adultery in the Gospel of John, except that Susanna (like Job) is unequivocally innocent. Daniel, whose "holy spirit" or advocate is stirred up by God, disrupts the unanimity of the crowd about to stone her. The community was on the verge of asserting its identity and unity in the act of killing one who had broken its laws, polluted its integrity. But Daniel exposes this collective sacrificial act as nothing but a cover for the private sins of the two religious leaders.

To return to the Brescia Casket, on its front there are two sections on Susanna. One shows her in the garden, confronted with the terrible dilemma posed by the demands of the two elders. The other shows her being judged before the court. A third section shows Daniel in the lions' den. The Susanna scenes are clearly parallel to the scenes on the cover, where in the top panel Christ is seen in the garden facing arrest and in the bottom panel Christ is seen first standing before the high priest and then standing before Pilate. Susanna in the garden corresponds to Jesus in the garden. Susanna before the court corresponds to Jesus before the court. The image of Daniel in the lions' den corresponds to the death of Jesus, which is not represented on the cover. Daniel being cast among the lions and then returning unharmed was a common representation of Jesus' death and resurrection.

Susanna serves as a primary type of Christ. By taking her story to exemplify the meaning of Jesus' passion, the artist is emphasizing her innocence, wrongful condemnation, and divine vindication. She is saved from scapegoating, from dying for others' sins. This point is reinforced on the back of the casket. Here there is a scene of "Susanna triumphant," standing alone with arms raised, an image of the risen Christ. Next to it is a picture of Jonah resting beneath his bush, the scapegoat converted from scapegoating. And next to this is an image of Daniel, poisoning the dragon.[10] The underlying story behind this last image, little known today,

---

10. This story comes from the apocryphal book Bel and the Dragon, which ostensibly is a fourteenth chapter to be added to the canonical book of Daniel, as the apocryphal book Susanna is a thirteenth chapter.

comes in an account of the way Daniel exposed the Babylonian gods and their sacrificial practices. The Babylonians are said to worship a great serpent or dragon as a living god, and the king requires Daniel to worship it. Instead, Daniel asks for permission to kill the dragon "without sword or club." Believing the dragon is invulnerable, the king agrees. "Then Daniel took pitch, fat, and hair, and boiled them together and made cakes, which he fed to the dragon. The dragon ate them, and burst open. Then Daniel said, 'See what you have been worshiping!'" (Bel and Dragon 27). Subsequently a crowd of Babylonians gather in anger at the death of the dragon, and threaten to kill the king and all his household unless Daniel is handed over. When he is, he is thrown into a lions' den, from which he is miraculously delivered. This scene is clearly also meant as a typological representation of Christ's victory in the passion. Daniel has taken the usual sacrificial practice of offering cakes to the dragon and turned it into a means to destroy the dragon. The typology compares Daniel's poisoning the dragon to Jesus' tricking and overthrowing Satan through the crucifixion.

These three failed scapegoats — Jonah, Susanna, and Daniel — are the chosen examples to illuminate the meaning of Christ's passion. Yet none of the examples treats Jesus' death in what we might consider traditional sacrificial terms. Each one has its own antisacrificial plot. Each story contains players who advocate collective killing as a divine imperative, but those players are never the heroes and always the villains. Each story is about *averting* such a death. If the point of Jesus' death is the need for blood to be shed in order to satisfy God's justice, then none of these illustrations gets the point. Taken together, their commentary on the cross points in one consistent direction: Jesus' death is about saving victims, disrupting collective violence, "poisoning" the whole mechanism of scapegoating sacrifice.

In fact, one link that the artist may have had in mind in assembling these parallels (the story of Jonah and the Susanna and Daniel stories) was a verbal one. As Tkacz puts it, "How striking it is that the designer of the casket has portrayed Christ before Pilate on the lid of the casket and then, on the front, both of the only two Old Testament types of Christ — Jonah and Susanna — whose histories also refer to innocent blood, and in words formulaically like Pilate's."[11] Pilate says, "I am innocent of this man's blood; see to it yourselves." The sailors who throw Jonah into the sea cry, "Do not make us guilty of innocent blood." Daniel, moved by the

11. Tkacz, *Brescia Casket*, 81.

Holy Spirit, cries out, "I want no part in the shedding of this woman's blood," and the text concludes, "Thus innocent blood was spared that day."

These connections are not limited to the imagination of one artist. I noted that Jonah may be the single most common visual image in early Christian art. Daniel was not so popular, but still well represented. As for Susanna, it may be surprising to some that a married woman accused of adultery should be presented as a type of Christ, but this tradition is long and deep. It was present in writings by Ambrose, Augustine, and Jerome. We have seen how important it is in this earliest and fullest artistic representation of the passion. It is reflected in the *commendatio animae,* a very old prayer for the dying that in some form may even antedate the Brescia Casket.[12] One of the petitions asks for deliverance, "as Susanna was delivered from her false accusers." This traditional emphasis on Susanna remained prominent for at least another thousand years, through the time of the Reformation.[13] Even more striking, for much of the liturgical history of the Western Church the story of Susanna was read on the third Sunday of Lent (leading toward Christ's passion), alongside the story of Jesus and the woman taken in adultery (which we

---

12. The "commendation of souls" is a set of prayers for/by the dying that asks for deliverance in the manner of a whole string of biblical figures. See Tkacz, *Brescia Casket,* 116-17. So, for instance, "Deliver, Lord, his/her soul, just as you delivered Noah from the deluge." Included among the eleven or twelve prayers in the set are these:

Deliver . . . just as you delivered Job from his sufferings.
Deliver . . . just as you delivered Isaac from sacrifice and from the hand of his father Abraham.
Deliver . . . just as you delivered Lot from Sodom and from the flame of fire.
Deliver . . . just as you delivered Moses from the hand of the Pharaoh, King of Egypt.
Deliver . . . just as you delivered Daniel from the den of lions.
Deliver . . . just as you delivered the three boys from the furnace of burning fire and from the hand of the wicked king.
Deliver . . . just as you delivered Jonah from the belly of the whale.
Deliver . . . just as you delivered Susanna from the false charge.
Deliver . . . just as you delivered Peter and Paul from prison and torments.

13. Catherine Tkacz has in recent years explored Susanna's history in literature and art, and documented her prominence in the Christian tradition and imagination up through the Reformation. She discovered at least 800 primary texts dealing significantly with Susanna and over 1,700 artistic images of her, many more than scholars had previously assumed. The prominence extended into general culture. Tkacz found that one of the most popular songs of the sixteenth century was a song about Susanna, translated a dozen times into the vernaculars of Europe and set to music by some forty different composers.

discussed in chapter 4).[14] These two explicit antiscapegoating texts set a frame for approach to the cross. Christians seized upon Susanna as a type of Christ because they saw these points of connection. She is a victim, vindicated by God and the Holy Spirit. Clearly the elements of false accusation and the "mob psychology" of collective persecution were central to their understanding of the passion story. They identified Christian faith in the risen One with the grace to resist this process.

In the Brescia Casket the actual death of Jesus as a sacrifice is interpreted with primary reference to the stories of these three figures, none of whom actually dies and all three of whom in various ways resist or overthrow collective acts of sacred persecution. In Christian typology more widely, these three figures are prominent, and they are joined by others that underline the same points. Job also figures as a type of Christ, for instance, and texts from Job were also read in Lent. All this emphasis on averted sacrifice and rescued victims as the pattern of Christ's work clearly reflects that the cross is about ending scapegoating as usual.

We Can Put Away Our Knives

Early Christians understood the cross as a sacrifice to end sacrifice. The power of that event changed their individual lives and their practice of community. It resulted in a complete withdrawal from participation in the ritual *pharmakos* scapegoating or its cultic relations. Many aspects of the transforming power that marked the early churches clearly reflect liberation from the dynamics of sacrifice. This is true of the new community of Jews and Gentiles who had before been divided by cult and purity. It is seen in the fact that the church attracted and offered special care toward those who stood in the prime location for victims: slaves, widows, orphans, the socially and morally ostracized. It shows up in widespread disavowals of violence, new roles for women, the rejection of infanticide. And perhaps most strikingly it was reflected in the radical practice of mutual care and reconciliation in the Christ community. In other words, many distinctive features of the church — the way its membership mingled people from conflicting groups, the way it showed special interest in those li-

14. Catherine Brown Tkacz, "Susanna as a Type of Christ," *Studies in Iconography* 20 (1999). In Milan, Susanna's story was read on Maundy Thursday along with the entire book of Jonah. See p. 133 n. 85 for references to various lectionary and missal sources. See also Valerie J. J. Flint, "Susanna and the Lothar Crystal: A Liturgical Perspective," *Early Medieval Europe* 4 (1995).

able to scapegoating, and the way it built unity without sacrifice — can be referred to the understanding of the cross as an end to sacrifice. These implications of Jesus' death were often associated with eschatological fulfillment. Such changes in human life heralded the nearness of the final reign of God.

As Christianity spread, this core dimension sometimes stood out with special clarity. In writing of Saint Patrick and the conversion of the Irish, Thomas Cahill views sacrifice as the decisive point. Commenting on a victim of Celtic ritual sacrifice found preserved in a bog, he observes:

> Here is the ancient victim of sacrifice, the offering made out of deep human need. Unblemished, raised to die, possibly firstborn, set aside, gift to the god, food of the god, balm for the people, purification, reparation for all — for sins known and unknown, intended and inadvertent. Behold god's lamb, behold him who takes away the sins of all.
>
> Patrick declared that such sacrifices were no longer needed. Christ had died once for all. . . .
>
> Yes, the Irish would have said, here is a story that answers our deepest needs — and answers them in a way so good that we could never even have dared dream of it. We can put away our knives and abandon our altars. These are no longer required. The god of the Three Faces has given us his own Son, and we are washed clean in the blood of this lamb. . . . From now on, we are all sacrifices — but without the shedding of blood. It is our lives, not our deaths, that this God wants.[15]

The language of sacrifice is used to proclaim the end of sacrifice. The fervor that had previously revolved around factional warfare and ritual killing flows with undiminished power into exertions of piety, monasticism, and reconciliation.

We can say that the more explicit the tradition of ritual human sacrifice in a culture and the more peacefully Christianity enters it, the more dramatically people grasp this core element. The very sacrificial terms in which the Bible describes the plot made the meaning and relevance of the passion unmistakable clear. What Cahill says of Celtic Christianity was to

---

15. Thomas Cahill, *How the Irish Saved Civilization: The Untold Story of Ireland's Heroic Role from the Fall of Rome to the Rise of Medieval Europe*, 1st ed. (New York: Doubleday, Nan A. Talese, 1995), 140-42.

be repeated in other times and locations. In places as different as some Pacific islands, northeast India, and parts of Latin America, Christian mission encountered societies at periods of intense sacrificial crisis. The result was a swift acceptance of the gospel in which the indigenous people themselves quickly provided an interpretation and application of the antisacrificial meaning of the passion.[16] In many cases, when the cross encountered the explicit, ritual reality of the scapegoating it was to overcome, the connection was made almost immediately.

But precisely because this vision is carried in tandem with the sacrificial tradition that it means to illumine and reverse, it is itself subject to confusion and misappropriation. I am not suggesting that early Christians grasped and implemented the meaning of the cross in all its aspects. There was no originating point of perfection, but an uneven and continuing process of realization, whether we are thinking of knowledge or practice. Christianity certainly could and did produce sacrificial readings of its own revelation.

It is not long after Christianity's rise to official power that an explicit iconography of the cross begins to flourish, more in the manner we have come to know. Some take this as evidence that atonement theology is associated with Christianity's endorsement of state power, and that the visible images of the cross go hand in hand with a new acceptance of violence. When the emperors became Christian, Christian theology became imperial, and — so the argument goes — exaltation of the cross somehow corresponds to this change. It is certainly true that the transition to wielding power rather than being subject to it posed a challenge for the faith we have described. The primary test in this new context was whether Christians could see the connection between the victims of their own power and the victim on the cross. They often failed that test.

Tensions around the Cross

But the contrast of an early nonviolent Christianity without a cross and a later, imperialist Christianity with a cross is far too simple. For one thing, seven hundred years would elapse before a fully developed substitutionary

---

16. See, for instance, Bailie's discussion of Polynesia in Bailie, *Violence Unveiled: Humanity at the Crossroads* (New York: Crossroad, 1995). This may be a significant factor in the dramatic success of Christian mission among traditional peoples as compared with its reception by some of the other world religions.

theology of the atonement would appear. The supposed effects seem to flourish long before their cause.[17] Insofar as Constantine, the first Christian emperor, had a "theology" of the cross, it was not focused on substitutionary bloodshed, but on victory over opposing powers, precisely the themes that contemporary opponents of atonement theology and the "fall" of the church often want to reclaim as the liberating meaning of the cross. Second, if emphasis on the cross is supposed to be the preferred theology in the marriage of church and state, it is an inconvenient fact that in the eastern half of the church, where an actual Christian empire was maintained for a millennium, an emphatic theology of atonement did not develop at all.

Historical Christianity does struggle with the cross at the heart of its gospel. The nature of that struggle has to do with how the meaning of Jesus' death is translated through time and practice. Under the same broad outline of the gospel story, and even under a similar emphasis on the cross, quite contrasting implications can be drawn. The centrality of the cross meant one thing in the conversion of the Irish and in Celtic Christianity. It meant something subtly but importantly different in the conversion of the northern Germanic peoples under the relentless military pressure of Charlemagne's armies. A window on the difference is opened by the ninth-century epic poem that renders the gospel story into Old Saxon, the *Heliand*.

The work was composed by a Saxon Christian at a time when the forced evangelization of his people still met resistance. Its genius was to build on the insight that "the very military defeat which alienated the audience from *Christianity* serves to establish their closest identity with *Christ*."[18] Herod and the Romans are described in terms that identify them with Charlemagne's conquering Franks, while Jesus becomes the great chieftain of a Germanic clan and his disciples become pledged liege men. The passion story becomes their last stand in the face of an overwhelming enemy. The poem carefully follows a traditional harmony of the Gospels, but into the form of that fidelity its author breathes the spirit of his own Saxon warrior culture. Every detail open to martial embellishment receives it, so that when Peter defends Jesus in the Garden of Gethsemane he cuts off not only a soldier's ear but the whole side of a face, and holds a

---

17. See Hans Boersma, *Violence, Hospitality, and the Cross: Reappropriating the Atonement Tradition* (Grand Rapids: Baker Academic, 2004), 156.

18. G. Ronald Murphy, *The Saxon Savior: The Germanic Transformation of the Gospel in the Ninth-Century "Heliand"* (New York: Oxford University Press, 1989), 96.

small army at bay with his flashing sword. Jesus bears his execution with noble submission, as a good Nordic warrior would. Although he is defeated, his death and resurrection are presented, respectively, as an escape from his tormenters and a return to resume command of his own band.

The power of this approach should not be minimized. Those forced to become Christians discovered an identification with the victimized Jesus as an ally and support against their new Christian rulers. They saw in the cross a connection to their own experience and need, which allowed them to make the faith their own. Yet the violent terms under which the gospel came to them, combined with their own warrior traditions, made it all too easy to translate the meaning of the cross itself in those terms. The passion turns into a battle between parties. The interpretive framework from Hebrew scripture and the Old Testament types we have examined falls away, and so too does any ready sense of a universal dynamic of sin and sacrifice from which we need redemption. The *Heliand* is one of the fertile fields out of which grow the ideas of the "Christian knight," a feudal warrior pledged to fight for Christ as he would fight for his local lord.[19] And from here it is not hard to draw a line to the military orders and the Crusades.

If one thing is clear in the New Testament account of the risen Christ, it is that he does not take or command any revenge against his persecutors. But we have seen an example of a path by which that absent note is projected back into the story, through the fidelity of faithful warriors who would defend their lord's honor. This note would play its role in the background of Anselm's atonement theology. His own age and culture were immersed in this emphasis. A twelfth-century poem, entitled "The Vengeance of Our Lord," describes the destruction of Jerusalem by the Romans in the year 70 as a punishment for Jesus' death.[20] Concern for the crucified one is transmuted into a war against his enemies.

Another poem similarly provides a radical revision of the gospel. It has Christ on the cross promising not forgiveness, but eventual retribution in the form of crusaders:

> . . . the people are not yet born
> Who will come to avenge me with their steel lances . . .
> A thousand years from today they will be baptized and raised

---

19. For a more extensive discussion of the *Heliand* in this connection, see Bartlett, *Cross Purposes: The Violent Grammar of Christian Atonement* (Harrisburg, Pa.: Trinity, 2001), chap. 3.

20. Bartlett, *Cross Purposes,* 102.

And will cause the Holy Sepulchre to be regained and adored . . .
Know certainly
That from over the seas will come a new race
Which will take revenge on the death of its father.[21]

Crusaders might lift the cross in this spirit, treating it as an atrocity that cried for retribution. But Saint Francis was no less a devotee of the cross, and for him it dictated that he must approach Muslims without weapons. On the one hand, the exercise of political authority and the contextualization of the gospel in its propagation and reception in cultures like the Saxon culture had their role in blunting the antisacrificial impact of Jesus' death. On the other hand, from the time Christianity began to attain positions of power, a strong countermovement arose within it. The extraordinary growth of monasticism and its constantly reforming and renewing offshoots was, at the most basic level, a social experiment rooted in the cross. It was an attempt to live a new form of community, centered on the crucified one. Through prayer and worship, these new societies sought to disarm the processes (material possessiveness, sexual rivalry, desires for power and status) that ordinarily lead to crises of division, and to live without sacrifice as an antidote to such crisis. It is no accident, I think, that the full cycle of Psalms from the beginning held such a central place in the prayer of monastic communities. Those who live in intense proximity, seeking to overcome divisions and maintain unity without recourse to violence and sacrifice, find in the Psalms a road map of the emotions and dangers that must be overcome.

One of the great early Cistercian abbots, Ailred of Rievaulx, allowed only one image on the monastic altar, a crucifix.[22] More and more emphasis was placed on a tender empathy with Jesus' human suffering, as a way of fostering compassion toward others and softening pride. This was reflected in new forms of the crucifix itself, which graphically represented a sagging, suffering, and wounded Jesus. The empathetic response evoked by that image was understood as part of the profound inner transformation of Christian conversion. Women mystics like Julian of Norwich and Margery Kempe gave eloquent expression to this sense of bodily intimacy with the broken Christ, an intimacy that transcended social and gender lines.[23] Such an ap-

21. Quoted in Bartlett, *Cross Purposes,* 102.
22. See the citations in Bartlett, *Cross Purposes,* 119.
23. See Caroline Walker Bynum, *Jesus as Mother: Studies in the Spirituality of the High Middle Ages* (Berkeley: University of California Press, 1982); Ellen M. Ross, *The Grief of God: Images of the Suffering Jesus in Late Medieval England* (New York: Oxford University Press, 1997).

proach to the cross had obvious, concrete application for life in community as well. For this intimacy with the crucified Christ not only opened up a closer relation with God, it also fostered a compassionate empathy with others that could overcome conflict and maintain the unity of a monastic society. It is not surprising that Ailred's most famous work was a discussion of friendship and the conditions that nurtured it. At the extreme, we may tend to regard monastic spirituality as ascetic athleticism or even masochism. Members of such orders are likely to see it as simple practical realism. For a closely bound group to maintain peace, sustain order, and avoid scapegoating is a work for which near miraculous means are needed.

Anthony Bartlett has pointed out that contrasting appropriations of the cross could come together in a single person. The example he gives is Bernard of Clairvaux, a great teacher of mystical love and an ardent preacher of crusade. "The coexistence in Bernard of this crusade ideology and an intense Christ-centered mysticism would be incomprehensible, except perhaps there is the possibility of ambivalence in the very image of the Crucified itself."[24] Our analysis to this point accounts for just such an ambivalence, the tension between the antiscapegoating work of the cross and the sacrificial script that it is working to overcome. We can glance briefly at two examples of this ambivalence in historical Christianity, cases where Christianity and its theology were agents of evil but where the cross was also a key to overcome the evil.

How Can She Ever Escape?

One is the much discussed example of witchcraft. The social phenomena of witchcraft and sorcery in human society provide textbook illustrations of scapegoating violence. Though we tend to focus on the witch crazes of early modern Europe, the underlying reality is widespread and far from extinct.[25] We might say it is one recurring way that the sacrificial process appears. Very often, violence against supposed witches has a collective and spontaneous character that very closely mirrors the nature of prototypical sacrifice. When I lived in India, local newspapers often carried small

24. Bartlett, *Cross Purposes*, 118. I do not agree with all of Bartlett's conclusions, but his book is one of the most stimulating recent works in the whole area of atonement, and notable for connections that he draws to a wide range of sources.

25. I mean to refer here to the cross-cultural social phenomenon of witchcraft as sociologists and anthropologists would consider it, and not to contemporary neo-pagan communities or traditions.

matter-of-fact items that in a particular village or neighborhood a crowd had attacked and killed someone accused of harming others by an occult act. The state of Bihar officially counted 483 killings in witch hunts in the 1990s.[26] Similar accounts turn up regularly as brief paragraphs in our international news sections. One such was a brief wire service note that in a region of Indonesia over three months 140 people had been brutally killed as supposed sorcerers.[27] The Enlightenment supposition that witchcraft consisted in only a mistake about causality is similar to the supposition that ritual sacrifice itself was based on only the same mistake. In fact, the two are closely related, as collective action against witchcraft typically has a kind of ritual, sacrificial quality and is more likely to take place in conditions of social crisis. Outbreaks of witch persecution are anything but unparalleled in global perspective. What is unusual is their systematic elimination.

Early modern Europe saw repeated, dramatic outbreaks of this violence, so intense in places as to claim hundreds of victims in only a few years. Popular hysteria was supported and incited with a detailed theological rationale. A work like the *Malleus maleficarum,* a kind of witch-hunter's handbook, provided the blueprint for an unrestrained program of Christian persecution, specially targeted at women. In those places where the witch craze peaked, a form of legal process remained. But it was a process totally captive to the dynamics of victimization, riddled with catch-22s for those accused. Trials became a way of spreading and inflaming the violence, not a curb on it. If the faith of the church contained a gospel against scapegoating, this is an episode that would seem to prove it had been totally lost.

It had been lost, to the point of supporting an outbreak of witch persecution extreme even by global standards. Some would suggest that within Christianity the cross was the major source of this evil. I would suggest that in fact it had a key effect in ending the witch trials, and on the fact that where they were ended, virtually no more would follow. This is manifest in the fact that, directly contrary to common impressions, the tide against witch persecution in Europe was turned decisively in the church courts.[28] The first and most significant objections to the witch

26. See Janaki Bahadur Kremmer, "In India Villages, Cries of 'Witch,'" *Boston Globe,* August 6, 2000. This is certainly a conservative count, for this one state.

27. See Reuters, "Indonesia President Seeks End to Killing Spree," *Boston Globe,* November 1, 1998.

28. See a review of evidence in Rodney Stark, *For the Glory of God: How Monotheism Led to Reformations, Science, Witch-Hunts, and the End of Slavery* (Princeton: Princeton University

crazes, and even to the reality of satanic witchcraft, came from church-men in the Inquisition, not from early scientists.[29] Convictions were fewer, punishment lighter, and execution rare when charges were brought in the ecclesial judiciary, as opposed to secular courts.[30] The rules of evidence developed by the Inquisition were notable for their recognition that accusations were both likely to be based on scapegoating motives and could inflate and misstate others' intentions. The most important application of this last point was to reject the inference that practice of some form of unofficial (nonchurch) magic necessarily implied an intention to work harm or to conspire with Satan.

These developments preceded semiscientific attacks on the reality of spiritual causality, which did not appear until long after the witch persecutions had subsided. During the critical period, major figures in early science (like Robert Boyle) supported witch hunts and none opposed them. One of the most bitter enemies of the church (and indeed a secret atheist), Jean Bodin, believed nonetheless in demonic forces, and wrote one of the books that did the most to incite the witch hunts.[31] This realization prompted Girard to note that the burning of witches did not stop because of the rise of modern science, but that modern science arose because the burning of witches was stopped.[32] It is more the case that growing suspicions that accused witches were innocent (that they were scapegoats) led people to the conclusion that witch-hunting should stop, rather than that the argument that witchcraft was causally impossible led people to conclude that those accused of it must be innocent.

Press, 2003), chap. 3. Stark also points out that recent scholarship puts the total number executed over more than three centuries in the range of 60,000 to 100,000, with women accounting for at least three-quarters of the victims.

29. This sentence paraphrases one in Stark, *For the Glory,* 221.

30. My comments about the Inquisition are not meant as any general rehabilitation of the institution. The record on witchcraft is different from the record on heresy, where the practices and results reflected much more persecutory zeal. There were several separate inquisitions. In the Spanish Inquisition, over the century and a half at the peak of the witch craze, 50 percent of all charges were for heresy and only 8 percent for witchcraft. The overall execution rate for those brought to trial on any charge was just under 2 percent. The evidence suggests that executions for witchcraft followed the same pattern, coming to well less than 100 over this period. Most of those tried were reconciled with the church and freed. See Stark, *For the Glory,* 256-58.

31. Stark, *For the Glory,* 220.

32. "We teach children that we stopped hunting witches because science arose. But it is the contrary: science arose because, for moral and religious reasons, we stopped hunting witches." René Girard and Michel Treguer, *Quand Ces Choses Commenceront* (Paris: Arlea, 1994), 86.

Rodney Stark observed that a very high proportion of the witch persecutions took place in a few specific regions of Europe (along the Rhine and in what is now Switzerland).[33] These overlap in large part with the regions that had seen the major outbreaks of violence against Jews around the time of the Crusades. This leads him to ask what made these areas different. He presumes that throughout most of Europe at this time there was local practice of folk magic, and there were groups of people with religiously unorthodox views. There also were large numbers of church and political leaders who advocated punishment for witchcraft. None of these was sufficient to prompt significant persecution, except when another factor was added: a strong credible threat to the existing religious/political authorities. Such a threat was posed by Islam prior to and during the Crusades. In the early modern period it was posed by the continuing military challenge of Islam, and by the fierce wars of religion between Protestants and Catholics, in which heresy became the rallying charge for catastrophic destruction. Still, these influences were felt all over Europe, and yet witch crazes erupted in certain places and not others. The further necessary factor, Stark argued, was the absence or breakdown of effective centralized control by the church or secular government in these areas. The regions in question were notoriously troubled or devastated ones. The presence of effective church control (Protestant or Catholic) elsewhere was usually enough to prevent or quickly stifle the violence.

We can readily translate the conditions Stark describes into the elements of sacrificial crisis that we have been describing. There are existing persons within a given community who can be readily isolated as candidates for sacrifice. An external threat brings crisis to the community and sets off the search for an internal offender to scapegoat. The result is a spontaneous convergence toward unanimous violence, a convergence that readily sweeps up political and religious forces with it. But in early modern Europe it is the organized religious authority that finally effectively resists this tide. It is not where the church and its doctrine of the cross are most powerful that violence follows most inevitably, but just the reverse.

Those who brought the witch hunts to an end did not rule out the reality of witchcraft. But they were deeply concerned that innocents not be scapegoated and were highly sensitive to the mimetic contagion of accusation and violence. One Spanish inquisitor, after conducting an extensive investigation, said he could find no evidence that even a single act of witchcraft had occurred. He suggested that public discussion and preach-

33. Stark, *For the Glory,* chap. 3.

ing on the subject be discouraged, as "there were neither witches nor be-witched until they were talked and written about."[34]

Perhaps the most influential single work in ending the witch trials was written by Father Friedrich von Spee, a professor of theology at Würzburg. He lived at ground zero in an affected region where the devas-tations of war and plague created the classic conditions of sacrificial crisis for the ravaged communities. He had served as confessor to a number of those about to be executed, and he quickly became convinced that he was seeing a process in which those in charge of the trials were unknowingly manufacturing false witness by torture. He did not cease to believe in the possibility of witchcraft, but he insisted that the greater imperative was to avoid becoming the crucifiers of the innocent. Not incidentally, Spee has a second, literary claim to fame. He was a poet and the author of many hymns that remain in the German Catholic hymnbook to this day. Promi-nent among his works are many meditations on Christ's suffering on the cross.[35]

In his book on the witch trials, Spee identifies clearly the sacrificial dy-namic he sees at work: "[S]hould some plague infect cattle . . . , should a doctor not know the cause of some new disease . . . , then some sort of shallowness, superstition, or ignorance immediately leads us to turn our thoughts to sorcery and conclude that witches are the cause. Then we ex-claim that we hold the source of the evil in our hands."[36] Among the chief inciters of persecution are lawyers, who do so for gain, and crowds of jeal-ous and malicious people who, he says, "everywhere avenge their feuds through defamation" (50).

He directly demystifies the inner logic of this scapegoating practice, focusing on women as the primary victims. If the woman accused has a bad reputation, this proves her guilt. If she has a good reputation, it does the same, for witches notoriously put up this appearance. "If there are any people who ever wanted to do her harm, they now have a wonderful op-portunity to hurt her. They can allege whatever they want, they will easily find things. So they shout from all sides that she is incriminated" (216).

---

34. Quoted in Henry Kamen, *The Spanish Inquisition: A Historical Revision* (New Haven: Yale University Press, 1998), 274.

35. See Friedrich von Spee, *Trutz-Nachtigall* (Trier: Verlag der Akademischen Buch-handlung Interbook, 1985); Friedrich von Spee and Theo G. M. Van Oorschot, *Güldenes Tugend-Buch* (Munich: Kösel, 1968).

36. Friedrich von Spee and Marcus Hellyer, *Cautio Criminalis; or, A Book on Witch Trials,* Studies in Early Modern German History (Charlottesville: University of Virginia Press, 2003). Page references to this work have been placed in the text.

"Since she dies whether she confesses or not, I would like to know, may God love me, how can she ever escape, no matter how innocent she may be?" (219). Either the trials must be stopped, or the judges "must in the end burn their own families, themselves and everyone else" (220).

The bulk of the book is devoted to a detailed examination of the ways the trials fabricate guilt. But its larger framework draws plainly on the biblical elements we have highlighted. Spee calls forth the examples of Daniel and Susanna to demonstrate that Christ's law requires a special concern to avoid shedding innocent blood (see 18, 36). He devotes a special appendix to the Christian martyrs under Nero, who were crucified like Christ, falsely accused as the cause of the terrible fire that had devastated Rome. Some of those innocent Christians too had named other innocents under the pains of torture. This did not make them lesser martyrs, nor break their likeness to Jesus. Spee takes his argument to the point of identifying accused witches with Christian martyrs and their deaths with that of Christ himself, with the unequivocal moral that what is happening to them is wrong and must be resisted. As I said above, Spee is not an obscure and ineffectual voice, but one that (along with others) finally prevailed against the persecutions at the time they burned most fiercely. To read his work is to grasp only more vividly the horrors of this Christian violence, and to see what elements within Christian tradition were crucial in overcoming it. We should not lose touch with either.

Where You Going to Get Witnesses?

There were areas — rejecting ritual scapegoating; sharing property; resisting retaliation; including the marginal in community — where Christians early on appropriated the antisacrificial effects of the cross. No area is more notable for failure on this account than slavery. Much could be said on the long failure to confront the systematic reality of slavery, and on the real, if subsidiary, currents of resistance marked by the acceptance of slaves as full members of the church, belief in eschatological equality, and commendation for acts of manumission. I want to focus simply on the Atlantic African slave trade carried out by Christian nations. For this provides one of the prime examples to support the charge that the theology of the cross functioned as an opiate for the oppressed. Abundant evidence shows that white Christian slave masters deployed the Bible in just the ways the critics deplore, and hoped for exactly the results that they suggest: servile acceptance of injustice. At first, North American slaveholders sought to keep Christianity from their slaves. Laws against African American literacy were animated in part by a concern to keep them from the Bible. There was a presumption in some quarters that slaves who became Christians should not be kept in bondage, and laws were enacted to rule out any legal ground for such a conclusion. This hesitancy did not bespeak firm confidence that the gospel oiled the works of victimization.

But Christian faith was eventually prescribed (or its spread among African Americans accepted) as enhancing the quality and docility of slave labor. Slave catechisms taught acceptance of white superiority. They emphasized New Testament passages that counseled slaves to serve their masters faithfully and bear injustice quietly. Christ's suffering was presented as an example of submission whose emulation would win heavenly reward. It was presented as a sacrificial pattern, whose violent victimization was to be ceaselessly repeated. All this accurately describes Christianity as seen on the "sending" side of the transmission sent by slaveholders.

On the receiving end, and in their own transmission process, African American Christians saw plainly what could hardly be hidden. Jesus was like them: unjustly punished, crushed by power, crying out to God in pain. They saw a God who identified with their plight and whose power finally vindicated the crucified one. They unerringly lifted out from the Bible all the threads lying in open sight — the voice of the psalmist hemmed in by violent crowds, the innocence of the victimized Christ, God's vindication of the scapegoat. Attempts to make this brutal oppression invisible, as simply part of some natural order, or to justify it as some kind of divine punishment were made and theologically defended by slave owners. These attempts foundered on the simple prominence of the image of the suffering Jesus and on the deep streams of biblical tradition that lay behind it. The oppressors pointed to the Gospels to insist that Jesus' suffering was divine. The slaves saw what the Gospels also proclaimed. It was wrong.

James Cone writes, "it was the cross of Jesus that attracted the most attention of black people." They were moved by the passion story because in it they saw themselves: "through the crucifixion, Jesus makes an unqualified identification with the poor and the helpless and takes their pain upon himself. Jesus was not alone in his suffering; blacks were not alone in their oppression in the United States. Jesus was with them. He was God's Black Slave who has come to put an end to oppression."[37] As

---

37. James Cone, "An African-American Perspective on the Cross and Suffering," in *The Scandal of a Crucified World*, ed. Yacob Tesfai (Maryknoll, N.Y.: Orbis, 1994), 52.

JoAnne Marie Terrell writes, in the cross "very many African Americans in and since slavery found the power they needed to survive, to be free and to express themselves. In the process they affirmed their innocence, refuted the claims of white supremacists, sanctified their own suffering and situated themselves within the cosmic drama as victims-becoming-victors."[38]

Abolitionists likened the suffering of slavery to the pains of the cross, not to endorse it but to condemn it. Harriet Beecher Stowe's *Uncle Tom's Cabin* is now best known for the reproach associated with its title character. Uncle Tom, whose selfless love toward those who own him, whether they are sympathetic or sadistic, is a figure of Christian devotion who may today set even the most devout teeth on edge.[39] Uncle Tom has come to stand for spineless servility toward white oppression and head-bobbing dependence on supposed white goodwill. The stereotype names a reality in black experience, and its association with Stowe rightly points out the limits of her own ideas of equality. For many, that summary wards off any further consideration of the book.

Stowe's work was addressed to white Americans, and its single aim was to make them face their own sacrificial behavior. It deserves to be criticized for trading in racial stereotypes and lacking realistic images of African American identity and empowerment. Yet no contemporary text had more actual effect in ending slavery in the United States. The reason for this is disarmingly simple. She presented African Americans as Jesus on the cross, and white Americans as the crowd that crucifies him. She did this by painting Uncle Tom as Christ, and his death as a passion. He is brutally flogged and beaten. Stowe leaves no doubt of the identity:

> [O]h, my country! these things are done under the shadow of thy laws! O, Christ! thy church sees them, almost in silence!
>
> But, of old, there was One, whose suffering changed an instrument of torture, degradation and shame, into a symbol of glory, honor and immortal life; and where his spirit is, neither degrading stripes, nor blood, nor insults, can make the Christian's last struggle less than glorious.[40]

---

38. JoAnne Marie Terrell, *Power in the Blood? The Cross in the African American Experience,* Bishop Henry McNeal Turner/Sojourner Truth Series in Black Religion, vol. 15 (Maryknoll, N.Y.: Orbis, 1998), 34.

39. On this count (quality of the writing aside), one can readily find heroes and heroines of similar ilk in Dickens, let alone other literature of the period.

40. Harriet Beecher Stowe, *Uncle Tom's Cabin* (New York: Signet, 1966), 446-47. Page references to this work have been placed in the text.

One of the slaves who had flogged him takes the role of the soldier at the cross, and testifies that what has been done is "a dreffel wicked thing!"

Tom's passion is not, on examination, an Anselmian one. Often lost in the (correct) observation that he dies full of forgiveness and concern for Simon Legree, his depraved killer, is the fact that his death itself is an act of resistance and defiance precisely toward Legree. He is whipped for refusing to reveal the whereabouts of two women slaves who are fleeing to freedom. He literally gives his life to save theirs. As Christ stands by him on one side, says Stowe, "the tempter stood by him too, — blinded by furious, despotic will, — every moment pressing him to shun that agony by the betrayal of the innocent." He does not suffer for the edification of his persecutor. Tom is carrying out an actual rescue, but the mythology of the book often treats his death as an abstract satisfaction offered to atone for his owner's sin.

In good Victorian fashion, Tom lingers on his deathbed long enough for a devoted young friend (the son of a former owner) to appear. It is left to him to draw the moral of this passion, which he does in confronting Legree. "[T]his innocent blood shall have justice. I will proclaim this murder." But Legree's response stops him in his tracks:

> "Do!" said Legree, snapping his fingers, scornful. "I'd like to see you doing it. Where you going to get witnesses? — how you going to prove it? — Come, now!"
>
> George saw, at once, the force of this defiance. There was not a white person on the place; and, in all southern courts, the testimony of colored blood is nothing. He felt, at that moment, as if he could have rent the heavens with his heart's indignant cry for justice; but in vain. (447)

So at Tom's grave George calls on God to witness his vow. "Oh, witness that, from this hour, I will do *what one man can* to drive out this curse of slavery from my land!" (455).

From a distance the limits of Stowe's vision are clear to us. But distance cannot obscure the conclusion she drew from the crucifixion. Tom dies in the midst of an act to free others, here and now. He dies without retaliation. He testifies to life after death. His innocence and the injustice of his persecution are not forgotten; they are proclaimed by witnesses. And the distinctive meaning of his death is that the structure of sacrificial violence that killed him has been unmasked. It has been shaken, and must be ended. That will be the work of those that love him. Stowe did not invent this pattern. She simply transferred it from the Gospels.

African Americans appropriated the same pattern, in a manner more authentically representative of their experience, and they would fashion much better images of their own struggle than those in this novel. They would need them when slavery gave way to other forms of oppression. Stowe displayed the pattern in a form that flattered the sensibilities of her white readers in most ways, but not the critical one. That was the point where the face of the crucified Jesus became the face of their enslaved victim. Countless tracts and petitions had left abolitionism but a small movement. This image made it a tide.

There is nothing idiosyncratic in Stowe's example. The Atlantic slave trade and Western slavery were carried out and condoned by Christians. The Western movement to abolish the slave trade and then slavery was an evangelical Christian movement. When we ask what made one form of Christianity so different from the other, the cross must be at the heart of the answer.

These two brief glimpses focus on cases of undeniable evil in Christian history. I do this in part to make clear that my approach does not deflect us from acknowledging those evils, and the manner in which appeals to the cross are implicated in them. I do it also to draw attention to the less commonly recognized way in which the cross figured in the successful resistance to those same evils. The danger is never far away that Christianity may fall into a sacrificial reading of its own revelation, and take on a persecutory character as a result. This happens when we lose an appreciation that the sacrificial dynamic at work in the cross involves us all, and/or when we relocate responsibility for the violence of the cross from us to others (including God). The next chapter will talk about the nature of this danger in more detail.

CHAPTER SEVEN

God's Wisdom and Two Mistakes

The Struggle of Historical Christianity

> But we proclaim Christ crucified, a stumbling block to Jews and foolishness to Gentiles, but to those who are the called, both Jews and Greeks, Christ the power of God and the wisdom of God.
>
> 1 Corinthians 1:23-24

> [T]he history of Christianity is a history of crisis, provoked by its own internal struggle and frequent failure before the figure of the Crucified.
>
> Anthony Bartlett[1]

We began this section by noting a paradox seeded through the passion story: the cross saves, and it ought not to happen. This tension is closely linked with the Gospels' insistence that it was decisively important that Jesus died in the specific way he did. We have seen that the paradox is not there by mistake. It is at the heart of the Gospel story itself. The challenge for a theology of atonement is to stay faithful to that paradox. When it disappears, historical Christianity is ever prone to remythologize its tradition. In this chapter we will first summarize where we have come so far, and then look at two paradigmatic ways of going astray.

---

1. Anthony W. Bartlett, *Cross Purposes: The Violent Grammar of Christian Atonement* (Harrisburg, Pa.: Trinity, 2001), 129.

Nothing but the Blood of Jesus

The passion accounts are stereoscopic. They tell two stories, superimposed on each other, the same story from two different perspectives. The complicating factor is that the first story already has its own paradox. A frank description of scapegoating sacrifice reveals a good/bad tension at the basic level. Its violence can in fact save a community from more violence. But it persecutes unjustly. The recurring social need for sacrifice is a chronic evil, an addiction whose effect is undeniably real but never lasting. In the biblical tradition generally and in the passion specifically, explicit description of blood and violence (with all its dangers) is there to tell this truth. To purge these elements (as in the imagined substitute for the passion narratives we discussed at the beginning of this section) would reflect a naive confidence that we are in greater danger of being corrupted by the language than of falling prey to the sin it describes.

To see this clearly into the nature of sacrifice is already a revelation, an unveiling of the hidden reality of sacred violence. We might call this revelation the first side of the cross. While keeping one eye on the true character of this reality, the Gospels add a perspective from a second side of the cross. The peace that depends on sacrifice (the "reconciliation" Herod and Pilate aim for in Christ's death) now also registers as something that ought not to happen. The old good/bad paradox of sacrifice is overlaid with another. In the Gospel tension it is the entire complex of sacrificial violence (including the "good" violence that drives out bad violence) that is treated as a bad thing, its ephemeral stability along with its arbitrary bloodshed. The cross decisively demonstrates God's opposition to this way of solving human division. God's willingness to bear the worst that this system visits on its victims, in order to deliver us from it, is the good thing. The paradox of good and evil in the ordinary business of sacrifice is topped with another, the paradox of God turning it inside out.

It is in this context that Jesus' willingness to face death, specifically death on a cross, takes on the quality of the "wisdom of God" that the New Testament so surprisingly discovers in it. If God's plan for salvation somehow required Jesus to come and die, then he could have died of illness or old age or a fall. Any of these would have sufficed for Jesus to share the human condition, to set the stage for resurrection and the promise of eternal life. Is there any point in Jesus dying this specific kind of death? Yes. The cross includes death in all those generic aspects. But we might say God takes advantage of the occasion of death in general to directly address a universal feature of human sin. God is willing to die for us, to bear our sin in this way, because we desperately need deliverance from the particular sin this death exemplifies. Death and resurrection are located where they can make an irreversible impact on this horizontal evil in human life. God breaks the grip of scapegoating by stepping into the place of a victim, becoming a victim who cannot be hidden or mythologized. God acts not to affirm the suffering of the innocent one as the price of peace, but to reverse it.

This revelatory quality of the New Testament is thoroughly continuous with Hebrew scripture, where an awareness and rejection of the sacrificial mechanism are already set forth. The averted sacrifice of Isaac goes with the reversed sacrifice of Jesus. The story of Joseph; the prophets' condemnation of scapegoating the widow, the weak, or the foreigner; the story of Job; the Psalms' obsession with the innocent victim of collective violence — all go hand in hand with the transparent account of Jesus' death in the passion narratives and with the biblical interpretations of a new community that grew up in solidarity around the risen crucified victim. A common thread links all of these. They reveal the victimage mechanisms at the joint root of religion and society and reject them. Jesus is the victim who will not stay sacrificed, whose memory is not erased and who forces us to confront this reality.

He is wounded for our transgressions. We can hardly deny that Jesus bears the sin of scapegoating, nor that we are implicated in that sin, since it is a ubiquitous feature of our human communities. Christ died for us. He did so first in the mythic, sacrificial sense that all scapegoated victims do, discharging the community's conflicts in collective violence. Jesus also dies in our place, because it is literally true that any one of us, in the right circumstances, can be the scapegoat. That we know these things is already a sign that he died for us in a second sense, to save us from that very sin. As the letter to the Hebrews argues, Christ is a sacrifice to end sacrifice, who has died once for all. By mapping the crucifixion against the yearly sacrificial ritual of atonement for sin at the temple, Hebrews makes the stereoscopic view as plain as possible. With the parallel in view, it emphasizes what is different about Jesus' death. It is not to take place year after year. It is not to conform to the pattern of suffering "from the foundation of the world." The writer underlines the fact that the former reconciling ritual was always performed by one with "blood that is not his own." But Jesus has offered his own, so that there should be no more of others'.

Is Christ's death unique? Its uniqueness depends completely on its sameness, its identity with the death of other victims. It is the commonality of the passion story with theirs that allows the stereoscopic vision we have been describing. The cross is unique because it is the one death that has been happening since the foundation of the world that in the reversing light of the resurrection reveals the sin in which we are everywhere enmeshed and offers us a different way.

Christians are often urged to get over their exclusivism about Christ's death. There have been numberless crucifixions, numberless religious sacrifices. It happens all the time. Yet Christians talk about this death as "once for all." They sing:

For my pardon, this I see,
Nothing but the blood of Jesus;
For my cleansing this my plea,
Nothing but the blood of Jesus.[2]

Christians are fixated on Jesus' death and will accept no other like it. The accusation is perfectly correct. To believe in the crucified one is to want no other victims. To depend on the blood of Jesus is to refuse to depend on the sacrificial blood of anyone else. It is to swear off scapegoats. Sacred violence promises to save us from retaliatory catastrophe. But what will save us from sacred violence? Only some event that may achieve once for all what sacred violence attempts by endless repetition.

Jesus, like Herod and Pilate, does not seek a spiral of reciprocal violence. The sacrificial mechanism is the way the powers of this world contain their own violence. Jesus and the Gospel writers do not intend to endorse or comply with that mechanism. Seen from this perspective, the somewhat enigmatic actions of Christ make complete sense. To resist victimization by means of counterviolence would be to reinforce the very evil sacrifice seeks to contain. And it would only feed the demand for sacrifice. On the other hand, to submit passively to the sacrificial mechanism would do nothing to change it. That only smoothes the way for future victims and condemns them to invisibility. Such is the dilemma, the malignant wisdom of an evil we seem doomed to serve whichever way we turn. Humanity is caught in this bondage, caught without even being able to name it directly. We know not what we do.

This is presented dramatically in the person of Peter in the Gospels, who successively occupies all of these fruitless positions. At Jesus' first an-

---

2. "Nothing but the Blood of Jesus" is a gospel hymn by Robert Lowry. See William Doane and Robert Lowry, *Gospel Music* (New York: Biglow & Main, 1876).

nouncement of the passion, Peter objects. This fate must never happen to Jesus. It is incompatible with the role of a victorious Messiah, who presumably must defeat the opposing powers by a direct battle. Later he reverses course and tells Jesus that he is ready to go and die with him. At Jesus' arrest in the garden, he draws his sword and attempts to violently defend Jesus against the cross. In the first and third cases he is rebuked by Jesus, and in the second Jesus predicts that far from dying with him, Peter will deny he even knows Jesus.

The incomprehension of the disciples is not hard to understand, for we have been reproducing it ever since. How to hold together these apparent contradictions? What is happening to Jesus is wrong, but Jesus must not avoid it. It is shameful that not even one of the disciples will stand up for Jesus. But their abandonment is one of the things that makes the revelation even more complete. God would never build a world on innocent sacrifice, but since humanity did, God will find a way, once, to turn to good what we have founded in evil. We who still find it so hard to make sense of the cross, can hardly patronize the stupidity of the disciples.

God steps into this double bind and overcomes it. No other could. Jesus does not encourage his disciples to think they might do what he is doing. This task is appointed to him alone. No ordinary victim can change this process, can uncover what is obscured in the constant practice of scapegoating. Redemptive violence — violence that claims to be for the good of many, to be sacred, to be the mysterious ground of human life itself — always purports to be the means of overcoming sin (removing pollution, punishing the transgressor who has brought disaster on the community). The sin it characteristically claims to overcome is the offense of the scapegoat, the crime the victim has committed. But in the passion account the sin in view is that of the persecutors. It is not the sin of the one that jeopardizes the many, but the sin of the many against the one. In the passion narratives redemptive violence stands forth plainly and unequivocally as itself the sin that needs to be overcome.

Any human being can be plausibly scapegoated (we are all sinners), and no human can prevail when the collective community turns against her. Nor is it sufficient to simply instruct us about our situation, for we are all too fully enclosed in the scapegoating process to be able to break the spell. It is historically hard to come to see this process for what it is. And it is much more difficult for us to recognize our own actions as scapegoating. It is an extraordinary step even to arrive at the awareness of our own susceptibility to that dynamic, as is expressed by the disciples at the Last Supper. When Jesus predicts his own betrayal, they piteously ask him, "Is it I, Lord?" A hardheaded reader would object that at this late date they ought to know if they are going to do it or not. But they have understood enough to know that they can't be sure. They are not exempt. When the cock crows the third time for Peter, it crows for us, to state the truth that when we become part of a mob, we too will likely be the last to know.

Only one whose innocence can be undeniably vindicated may, by suffering this sacrifice, reverse it. Here we gain an interesting additional perspective on the church's commitment to a high Christology. The work of the cross is the work of a transcendent God, breaking into a cycle we could not change alone. It is a saving act of God, a victory over the powers of this world, a defeat of death. If we limit Jesus' work to that of a human exemplar, the crucifixion becomes more of a prescription for suffering than if we grasp it as the work of the incarnate one, once for all. The place of the ritual victim is open to all, and refilled perpetually. Jesus' role cannot be replaced and therefore should not be.

The human situation is not just one of ignorance about the mythic process, though even at this level it is hard to see how people can "think their way out." From inside the process, the misrecognition of what is happening, the invisibility of victims, is difficult to overcome because, though the process operates on lies, no one is consciously telling any. Everyone acts in good faith in the sacrificial system, and no clues are left to stir up trouble. But the problem is a good deal more serious than this. Even were people to grasp the situation, there would still be no way out of it. The testimony of the Gospel is that only God has had the power to solve this dilemma of human bondage, the no-win choice between using violence to stem violence (which is only more of the sacrificial prescription) and simply joining the line of victims. It is God alone who can reveal the entire reality of the sacrificial process, reverse through resurrection its obliteration of victims, and structure an alternative option for human solidarity. This is why Christ is explicated in the New Testament as the truth, the life, and the way. Each of these tasks requires an act of transcendent power and wisdom. It is a complete misunderstanding to suppose that what we have been discussing might be reduced to some sociological or anthropological insights, clothed in symbolic, religious terms. Anomalous as such knowledge might be, it would hardly be sufficient to save and reconcile humans in the midst of such conflicts.

Deeper Magic from Before the Dawn of Time

True teachings are dangerous, the Buddha is supposed to have said. And the best teachings are the most dangerous. The theology of the cross can be the best or the worst. The two are poised close together. We have seen that the cross is a kind of intersection, where different atonements meet.

The Romans are at odds with the Judean Jews. Jewish factions are at odds with each other. The Romans are afraid of rebellion. The religious leaders are afraid of repression. Pilate is ready to make Jesus a politically redemptive sacrifice, to keep his contagious preaching from stirring social crisis. Some of the chief priests are ready to make Jesus a religiously redemptive sacrifice, to keep his blasphemy and sin from contaminating the community. They all expect Jesus' death to have a reconciling effect on this situation. That seems to be precisely what Caiaphas and Pilate have in mind. It makes enemies like Pilate and Herod friends before it even happens. There's nothing like a little redemptive violence to bring us all together. This is atonement, of a sort, but the New Testament was not written to commend it.

Mel Gibson's movie *The Passion of the Christ* missed a momentous opportunity to illuminate many aspects of the passion accounts we have been considering. There are scenes where the occasion to do so lies painfully close at hand. One key point comes when Jesus is brought back before Pilate and the crowd, after having been whipped and brutalized. The plot goes to and fro, with Barabbas being released and Pilate temporizing. As things draw on, the throng grows more restive. Pushing and shoving break out in the front ranks, between the Roman soldiers and members of the crowd. Conflict is rapidly escalating. This moment of crisis is the catalyst. Things snap. Crucify him, Pilate says.

Satan is a visible figure in Gibson's film. With that convention, this is the one moment Satan certainly should have appeared (but doesn't) . . . moving in the crowd and whispering, "We've got to get rid of Jesus or he's going to bring the Romans down on us." And moving among the Roman soldiers, saying, "We've got to get rid of Jesus or there will be rebellion and blood on the streets." And nudging up to Peter and John and Mary, advising, "Don't say anything — do you want to get killed like that too?" And standing behind Pilate: "It's for everyone's good. We have to stop the violence." Satan is the advocate for reconciling persecution, orchestrating it from all sides in an age-old snare that closes around Jesus in a fit of unanimity.

So is this the way God works? Is God really just another member of the crowd, full of wrath at the whole human race and in need of a victim to vent that anger, a victim around whom God and his former enemies can gather in peace? Is this God's plan, on a cosmic scale, to avoid killing us all? We have gone astray if we think God endorses the mechanism of scapegoating sacrifice and that the crucifixion is just the largest and most powerful example. Such a view leaves the mechanism unquestioned and focuses instead on the special qualities of the victim. God feeds a bigger and better victim into this machinery to get a bigger payoff. But that is not the truth. Jesus' accusers intend his death to be sacrificial business as usual. But God means it to be the opposite.

I have perhaps made this sound more complicated than it needs to be. It is not as though it has not been expressed often enough, and in a way children can understand. C. S. Lewis did so in his Christian allegory, Chronicles of Narnia. In the land of Narnia the evil powers have imprisoned creatures by turning them to stone, one by one. These powers have been aided by a human traitor, Edmund, who has gone over to their side, but whom they now intend to sacrificially slaughter. He is rescued at the last minute, and returns to fight on the side of the Christ-lion Aslan. But the evil powers under a flag of truce insist that Edmund must be handed over to them, that there must be retribution for every treachery, death for death. The Christ-lion Aslan agrees to be handed over and killed in Edmund's place, on the condition that the evil powers renounce their claim on his life. This law of retribution and the sacrificial process of exchange based on it (in which an innocent one may die on behalf of others and so protect them) are known to all from the earliest times. It is called "Deep Magic from the Dawn of Time." This has been going on for ages. There is an ancient stone altar on which Edmund was to be killed, and upon which Aslan is actually sacrificed. The act has a mysterious, sacred aura and an air of inevitability. The evil powers love this arrangement and, incidentally, have no intention of keeping their bargain. Once Aslan is dead, they intend to kill also those he meant to save. This treachery is a key point, because it tips off the reader that this exchange itself cannot be the final word, nor the substance of the divine plan. It is a decidedly lower magic.

The resurrection comes into this story as an unexpected development, from what the book calls "Deeper Magic from Before the Dawn of Time," something about which the evil powers know nothing. The violent mystery of sacrifice goes back to the dawn of our human time. But it has no purchase in the original blessing of creation that stands even further back still. And when Aslan rises from the dead, the ancient stone altar on which the sacrifice was offered cracks and crumbles in pieces, never to be used again. The substitution of Aslan for Edmund cannot save if it is simply a variation on the same sacrificial theme rather than an act to overthrow that process altogether. The stained stone may have been the centerpiece of religion and sacred awe in human history. But it was not God's altar. The gospel is not ultimately about exchange of victims, but about ending the bloodshed.

What Is There to Be Sad About?

The terms and structure of scapegoating sacrifice are laid bare in the Bible. This is the first side of the cross. In the Bible, particularly in the passion narratives, these terms are actively turned against themselves. That is the second side of the cross. In the traditional practice of sacrifice, the divine powers typically stood on the side of the crowd and endorsed its violence. But we saw how the God of Israel becomes a God who sides with Job and with the persecuted victims of the Psalms, the God of the prophets. And in the New Testament God becomes the scapegoat. The afflicted one was always assumed to be punished by divine wrath as well as by unanimous human judgment. In this case, it is God who is condemned by consensus, God who is punished as an enemy of God. It is God who undergoes the sacrificial process in order to turn it inside out. Sacrifice is turned against sacrifice.

This combination of factors is at the heart of the truth and power the passion narratives convey. It makes these texts quite distinctive in religious history, whether one regards them as divinely inspired or not. This dimension of Jesus' death can be grasped only through its setting in the Hebrew scriptures. That setting includes texts that cover the full range of the sacrificial landscape, from the Leviticus passage that endorses scapegoat violence to Job and the Psalms and the prophets who reject it. This variety, like the range of interpretation in the New Testament texts, allows scripture to provide a stunning bird's-eye view of the whole sacrificial reality, of each of the layers we have described. But this variety is also there because the biblical texts themselves reflect an internal struggle to understand God's relation to sacrifice. I have argued that the trajectory in both biblical scriptures is consistent, but it is a trajectory that emerges out of conflict. The Bible, partly because of its unusual bluntness about sacred violence, has elements that can be and have been developed into sacrificial readings and sacrificial practice. The Bible is not a perfect medium, or at least not so perfect that it is proof against the faults of Christian interpretation of it.

I have sketched the revelatory and liberating tradition I see uniting the Bible and illuminating the cross. That tradition is real and decisively important. We have given at least a few examples to show that early Christians recognized this dimension as well. But if it is hard for us to disentangle all these threads, it has also been hard from the beginning. Our well-worn habits of sacrifice are all too ready to reassert themselves. Historical Christianity has carried the paradox of the cross, a treasure in earthen vessels, but it has also at times evaded and remythologized that paradox.

I would like to stress two specific examples, two ways to remythologize Jesus' death, two ditches on either side of the narrow way of the cross. One is a very old way, to which Christianity is tempted to return. And one is a new way, which Christianity, to its shame, invented. Despite their differences, both ways are hostile to the Jewish scriptures and to Judaism, a telling indicator. There are other ways to betray the gospel than anti-Semitism.[3] But it seems there are few ways of betraying the gospel that don't eventually incorporate it.

Our first example is the alternative offered to early Christians by a Gnostic view of Jesus. Gnostics denied the goodness of the material, bodily world. They rejected the creator God who was responsible for it and the Hebrew scriptures revealed by that God. The God of Genesis is a kind of Satan to the Gnostics, and the serpent is an enlightened hero. For our purposes, two things are particularly important. First, in rejecting Israel's God and the Hebrew scriptures, Christian Gnostics cut themselves off from the critique of scapegoating outlined there. While that constitutes the fundamental context for Christian interpretation of Jesus' death, the Gnostic savior figure is an opponent of the Jewish God and defined by a contrasting, mythic tradition. Second, the crucifixion of Jesus was one element of the Gospels that Gnostics insisted on removing altogether or altering beyond recognition.

Christ is not a real human being and therefore could not be killed. So either the crucifixion does not happen to him at all or it happens only on a plane of appearances. As one version of the Gnostic myth put it, Christ

---

3. In this book, and particularly in referring to the second path of remythologization in this chapter, I use the word "anti-Semitism" because what I have primarily in view is the specific historically Christian animosity that has gone by that name. I realize that there are a host of questions that surround this term (especially its supposed racial and ethnic assumptions) and its alternatives, like "anti-Judaism." Those questions are for the most part outside the scope of this discussion.

appeared on earth as a man, and he performed deeds of power. Hence he did not suffer. Rather, a certain Simon of Cyrene was forced to bear his cross for him, and it was he who was ignorantly and erroneously crucified, being transformed by the other, so that he was taken for Jesus; while Jesus, for his part, assumed the form of Simon and stood by, laughing at them. For because he was an incorporeal power and was the intellect of the unengendered parent, he was transformed however he willed. And thus he ascended to the one who had sent him, mocking them.

The author of this text emphatically rejects any connection with the executed one: "Anyone who confesses the man who was crucified is still a slave and is still under the authority of the beings that created bodies; while anyone who denies him both is freed from them and has acquaintance with the unengendered parent's providential arrangement of events."[4]

The Gnostic Christ is not a victim. The Gnostic myth has no passion narrative account of scapegoating. The killing of an arbitrary substitute (the very essence of sacred violence) is approved. This Gnostic Jesus finds it quite humorous. Simon's killing belongs to the "providential arrangement of events." Only unspiritual and unenlightened persons concern themselves with such bodily matters, or would believe in a savior who was literally crucified. In other words, already in the first generations Gnosticism offers a coherent opportunity to draw the entire Jesus story safely back within a mythic framework. The revelation of and the challenges to scapegoating that stand out in the Gospel accounts are all smoothed away. An alternative to atonement theology was ready at hand, an alternative in which a Jesus who could not suffer mockingly organized the execution of a man who could. Not regarding this as an improvement, the church of the crucified one chose to canonize the passion texts, keep the Hebrew Bible, and remember the cross.

What the Gnostics rejected in the incarnational faith of their Christian opponents were those elements that diverged from myth. They objected to the literalness of the insistence on Jesus' real humanity and his real death, as well as the interest in the historical grounding of the passion narratives and the resurrection. In their view, orthodox Christians are caught up in bodily and material concerns, obsessed with the sordid

---

4. From "Basilide's Myth," in Bentley Layton, *The Gnostic Scriptures: A New Translation with Annotations and Introductions,* 1st ed. (Garden City, N.Y.: Doubleday, 1987), 423.

details of condemnation and execution, moralizing about considerations of guilt and innocence, and somehow connecting Jesus' death with their own sin. The God-with-a-body Christians appalled their Gnostic cousins, who thought they had taken a perfectly good myth and spoiled it with the introduction of a flesh-and-blood victim.

As we have seen, Gnostic Christians did not necessarily deny that the event of the crucifixion or something that looked like it took place. The more fundamental convictions were that whatever happened was not wrong and had no effect on the spiritually enlightened. For the same reasons that the Christ of our Gnostic text above could laugh at the suffering of a nonspiritual person in his place, a Gnostic Christ could equally well laugh off his own crucifixion. From this perspective, it is not hard to be impervious to pains that exist only at the level of illusion, and the escape from the life of the body is a glorious truth to be celebrated.

These views fit well with the mythic heritage, and they are very much alive today. We can take an example again from Joseph Campbell. Campbell and Bill Moyers are discussing the dying and rising god myths, and the idea of sacrifice. Campbell observes that these express a fundamental balance between death and life as two aspects of the same thing. Is that true of all these stories, Moyers asks? Campbell answers: "All of them. I know no story in which death is rejected. The old idea of being sacrificed is not what we think at all. The Mayan Indians had a kind of basketball game in which, at the end, the captain of the winning team was sacrificed on the field by the captain of the losing team. His head was cut off. Going to your sacrifice as the winning stroke of your life is the essence of the early sacrificial idea. . . . The name of the game was to become worthy to be sacrificed as a god." And then Campbell turns to another historical example.

> There is a report by the seventeenth-century Jesuit missionaries in eastern Canada of a young Iroquois brave who has been captured by an enemy tribe. He is being brought to be tortured to death. The Northeastern Indians had a custom of systematic torture of their male captives. The ordeal was to be suffered without flinching. That was the final test of real manhood. And so this young Iroquois is being brought in to endure this horrible ordeal; but to the Jesuits' amazement, it is as though he were coming to celebrate his wedding. He is decorated and loudly singing. His captors are treating him as though they were his welcoming hosts and he their honored guest. And he is playing the game along with them, knowing all the while

to what end he is being conducted. The French priests describing the occasion are simply appalled by what they interpret as the heartless mockery of such a reception, characterizing the youth's captors as a company of savage brutes. But no! Those people were to be the young brave's sacrificial priests. This was to be a sacrifice of the altar and, by analogy, that boy was the like of Jesus. The French priests themselves, every day, were celebrating Mass, which is a replication of the brutal sacrifice of the cross.[5]

Campbell is surprised the Christians can't see the obvious: this is the same thing they act out every day. It's the same myth. The two match up perfectly. Instead of appreciation, the priests are appalled. I think we can assume that it is not because they do not see the connection Campbell suggests. It is because they draw the opposite conclusion. The passion narratives follow the plot of sacrifice to challenge it, not to celebrate it. The young man is like Jesus. But Jesus ought not to have been killed. The collective sacrifice of Jesus for the sake of reconciliation was a sinful thing that God acted to overcome. God entered that act to end it once and for all. Their daily memorial of the victim was not preparing them to be delighted when they saw another one, but almost reflexively inclining them to sympathy with the scapegoat . . . even if the scapegoat has adopted the myth as well.

If the priests had possessed more spiritual insight, apparently, they would have been thrilled by this event. That spiritual immaturity is demonstrated by the fact that they can't celebrate a little torture and murder. From a Christian point of view it is just the other way around. It is Jesus' story that allowed us to see the horror of others like it. The problem is not with these missionaries' failure to admire this torture. It is the failure of so many in the colonization and conquest of the Americas to see violence against the native peoples in the same light.

Campbell fills in what he thinks the priests may be missing by pointing to what he calls an "equivalent scene" to the one just described, found in the Gnostic Christian book the *Acts of John*. He finds it one of the most moving passages in all of Christian literature. In the New Testament Gospels we are told only that at the end of the Last Supper Jesus and the disciples sang a hymn and went out. But the *Acts of John* gives us a detailed account:

5. Joseph Campbell and Bill D. Moyers, *The Power of Myth*, 1st ed. (New York: Doubleday, 1988), 108-9.

Jesus says to the company, "Let us dance!" And they all hold hands in a circle, and as they circle around him, Jesus sings, "Glory be to thee, Father!"

To which the circling company responds, "Amen."

". . . I would eat and I would be eaten!"

"Amen."

"Thou that dancest, see what I do, for thine is this passion of the manhood, which I am about to suffer!"

"Amen."

"I would flee and I would stay!"

"Amen."

"I would be united and I would unite!"

"Amen."

"A door I am to thee that knocketh at me. . . . A way am I to thee, a wayfarer." And when the dance is ended, he walks out into the garden to be taken and crucified.

[Campbell concludes] When you go to your death that way, as a god, in the knowledge of the myth, you are going to your eternal life. So what is there in that to be sad about? Let us make it magnificent — as it is. Let us celebrate it.[6]

What Campbell sees lacking in the New Testament passion accounts but is magnificently present in this later Gnostic version is *Jesus'* enthusiastic endorsement of his own killing. The paradox of the passion narratives and Jesus' vivid human anguish are dispelled in favor of poetic affirmation. The victim agrees with the persecutors to celebrate his death, and to teach us to do the same. This what the Gnostics thought the story of Jesus' passion ought to look like, if it were to be a really good myth. After all, the Gnostic Jesus is pure spirit and none of this supposed violence affects him in the least. Only unenlightened fleshly minds stumble over such matters — the kind of minds that produce the New Testament Gospels with their bloody images.

The seesaw paradox of the Gospels, in which the cross is terribly bad and gloriously good at the same time, is gone. The problem is removed. Jesus doesn't really die or death is really unimportant. Celebrate it. There is barely a cross at all, and it has only one good side. Christians could readily have remade their faith in these terms. In many ways it represented the line of least resistance, a path that kept Christianity in line with tradi-

6. Campbell and Moyers, *The Power of Myth,* 109.

tional myth and with the conventional metaphysical dualism of the time. A significant number took that option in the first centuries. And the appeal remains.

What we have just described was literally a *re*mythologizing of the cross, a return to older models. If successful, it would have made Christianity "just another myth," one that would work as well as any other as a cover for sacrifice. The other example to consider was a genuinely new invention. If the first tried to downplay the cross, the second graphically emphasized it. If the former followed myth by erasing any evidence of a victim or victimizers, the latter clearly identified them. If gnosticism is the name of the former, Christian anti-Semitism is the name of the latter. If one is still a live option, so is the other. Both go to the very root of Christian belief.

Anti-Judaism is a bridge connecting the two, and that bridge is embodied in the work of Marcion. For the early church in the second and third centuries, Marcion could claim the title of arch-heretic. No other single person in this period commanded a similar volume of refutation (Tertullian alone wrote no fewer than five books against him). Nor was this simply a war of words: the Marcionite church was probably the most significant alternative organized church structure alongside that which eventually prevailed. Like the Gnostics, Marcion rejected the creator God of Israel as an evil power. He therefore rejected not only the Hebrew scriptures but virtually all of what would become the New Testament, save some of Paul's letters and a revised version of the Gospel of Luke. As with the Gnostics, his Christ was a spiritual visitor, without a human birth or a human body.

But Marcion had little interest in the elaborate mythology of the Gnostic teachers. He elaborated a consistent attack on the Jews as children of the devil (i.e., the creator God) and enemies of Christ. Jesus was the messenger of a God of love who was completely opposed to the Jewish God of violence. Gnostics rejected both Jesus' human birth and his actual crucifixion; Marcion too was concerned to deny the birth (bodily birth would mean that Jesus belonged to the creator), but the cross was important to him. Humans belong to the creator God and to the violent directions of that God. To redeem them God had to purchase or ransom them, and this was done with the death of Jesus. In other words, Marcion believed in the cross as a ransom from the devil, and the devil was the Jewish God, whose worshipers carried out the crime. Marcion drew the conclusion then that Jesus had died to save all of humanity *except* those who believed in the creator God. It was because of their faith in that God that

Abraham and Moses and all who followed them could never be saved.[7] Marcion championed a God of mercy and nonviolence he found in his (radically edited) New Testament, in bitter opposition to an Old Testament God of law and sacrifice. This translated into a hostility of Christians toward Jews as a unique class of offenders. He formulated a second, and more distinctively Christian, mistake.

Inventing Evil

One of the remarkable things about the earliest Christian preaching is that whoever the hearers were, a single assumption applied: Christ died for you. Christ died for our sins. We have already noted that the passion texts unsparingly paint the failings of all parties to the crucifixion, from Pilate to Peter to Caiaphas to Judas. No one takes a stand beside Jesus, no one takes the role of the advocate or *paraclete* for him. Even so, it is odd to see Christians assuring people who had been nowhere near Jerusalem and knew nothing about what happened there that Christ died for their sins. How could their sins have anything to do with it? This makes sense only if we assume a solidarity in sin. We weren't the ones to actually do that deed or agree to it, but it is just the sort of thing we have done. In particular, we are all participants in the sacrificial dynamics of our communities. This is one very concrete way in which those sins are our sins. Contrary to the many books that ask *who* killed Jesus, the real context for the passion is a conviction about *what* kills Jesus, namely, scapegoating sacrifice.

Paul, who had played no role in the death of Jesus but is engaged in the same kind of practice against Christians, encounters the risen Christ, who asks, "Why are you persecuting *me?*" It is Christ's identity with other victims that makes this universal claim — Christ died for your sins — possible. That is the basis of the good news these Christians believe they have to share, news about deliverance from the sin that killed Jesus and in which we have all participated at least passively. A key element of the revelation in the passion narratives depends on the collectivity of the violence it describes, and on the fact that each of us has been implicated in that collectivity as it is replicated in our own settings.

One of the crucial things that makes the church a new community is its constitution in unity not against some sacrificial victim, but by identi-

---

7. See Adolf von Harnack, *Marcion: The Gospel of the Alien God* (Durham, N.C.: Labyrinth Press, 1990), 86-87.

fication with the crucified one. The sign of conversion and commitment to the risen Lord was to do what the disciples had failed to do at the time of the crucifixion: to testify for the victim. After the resurrection Peter, who had denied Jesus three times, is now able to say this to a crowd in Jerusalem: "You rejected the Holy and Righteous One and asked to have a murderer given to you, and you killed the Author of life, whom God raised from the dead. To this we are witnesses. . . . And now, friends, I know that you acted in ignorance, as did also your rulers. In this way God fulfilled what he had foretold through all the prophets, that his Messiah would suffer. Repent therefore, and turn to God so that your sins may be wiped out" (Acts 3:14-15, 17-19). Peter himself is guilty and has repented. He invites the same repentance from the people and even their rulers, all of whom he says acted in ignorance.

A key example of this repentance is the vision he receives from God to regard no foods as unclean. When the Gentile Cornelius sends for Peter to come to his house, Peter says, "The Spirit told me to go with them and not to make a distinction between them and us" (Acts 11:12). Thus he enters the house that is ritually impure for him as a Jew, and eats there, sharing the gospel with Cornelius. The work of the Spirit, testifying to the risen victim, is to bring Peter across the very barrier that would otherwise mark Gentiles to him as outsiders and likely scapegoats. This is the shape of the good news of the resurrection we have seen repeated in many texts.

But some of these same texts proved highly susceptible to another use. Take Stephen's words, "You stiff-necked people, uncircumcised in heart and ears, you are forever opposing the Holy Spirit, just as your ancestors used to do. Which of the prophets did your ancestors not persecute? They killed those who foretold the coming of the Righteous One, and now you have become his betrayers and murderers" (Acts 7:51-52). This is part of Stephen's witness on behalf of the persecuted Jesus, a witness given in the midst of his own execution. It is a voice that can be heard in Job, in the Psalms, in the Prophets. When Stephen speaks of "your ancestors," he is also speaking of his ancestors. His witness rests on the bedrock conviction that Jesus died for our sins, for everyone's sins, and his death is an example of our paradigmatic shared sacrificial sin. But these words and others like them became a way to back away from that conviction. "*You* stiff-necked people . . ." became an occasion to do exactly what the Holy Spirit told Peter not to do. They became an occasion to make a distinction between them and us, and at the one most crucial point. To many Christians the words came to mean "You Jews."

Christians who had received the revelation of the resurrection and the instruction of the passion were no less liable to rivalry, envy, conflict, and violence than their neighbors. Nor had they been delivered in some magical way from sacrificial impulses. They struggled to live out the new creation promised in Christ and the Spirit. To the extent that they succeeded, they changed their own lives, created a new kind of community, and eventually affected the life of the societies that surrounded them. To the extent that they failed, they sinned as people had always sinned. Actually, this is not right. They pioneered a new way of sinning.

Prior to the time of the church, Jews were sometimes disliked and persecuted by Gentiles with reference to their religious practices and especially Jewish disinclination to acknowledge the reality of their neighbors' deities, let alone worship them. But in large measure the conflicts followed the pattern of those between other groups, based on national or ethnic tensions. Christians added a distinctive new note. It was the charge that Jews were responsible for the death of Jesus, "Christ killers."

At the very beginning, Christians were themselves Jews and could hardly escape blame for Jesus' death with this charge. The gospel that came to Gentiles was not "Jesus died only for the sins of Jews. It had nothing to do with you." Quite the opposite. But gradually the early church and the community of rabbinic Judaism parted ways, became two distinct religious paths. This divergence was hastened by the growth of Gentile Christianity, and above all by the Roman destruction of Jerusalem and its temple, with the dispersion of the Jewish population. Christians readily interpreted this as a divine judgment on a religious order now superseded by Christ and, most particularly, as a dramatic correlative to the end of sacrifice at the cross. Thus Jews and Judaism came to figure as rivals to the church. This laid a groundwork whose destructive effect was not fully realized until Christians began to attain some measure of political and cultural power. By that time, when Christian communities experienced crises of conflict, Jews outside the church or "Judaizers" inside it became prime candidates for scapegoating.

Thus the old pattern repeats. Jews now become sacrificial victims. And the charge to bring against them, horrible enough to account for any social crisis, is not far to search. The Jews have killed God, perhaps the maximal possible persecutory accusation. The passion narratives become a charter for violence. The postresurrection witness of the disciples about the evil of Jesus' death becomes testimony against an isolated guilty party. Christians exempt themselves from the collective act of crucifixion.

There is no darker fact in the church's history than this, and not because the church has not engaged in other forms of violence and domination. The darkness of anti-Semitism goes to the very heart of the revelation. It is not just wrong, but perfectly and diabolically wrong. It makes the very best into the very worst. It makes the revelation against scapegoating the excuse for scapegoating. It does to Jews what was done to Jesus. It makes of the cross an incitement to cast the first stone.

Sacrificial violence happens everywhere in history. If Christianity simply conformed to this common reality, then Christian anti-Semitism would be a rather unremarkable evil, no different in principle from any other in-group/out-group animosity. But there is a tendency inside and outside the church to regard it as something distinctively new and peculiarly destructive. This is a valid judgment, one ultimately based on a recognition of the power of the biblical unveiling of sacrifice in general and the passion narratives in particular. The evil of Christian anti-Semitism is parasitic on that very power.

The centrality of the accounts of Jesus' passion, the focus on the crucified one, has made it increasingly difficult to be unconscious of scapegoats or to mystify them in myths. To make these accounts themselves into persecutory texts requires a new move and a new kind of accusation. Myth always obscured the reality of a victim and deflected attention away from the real nature of the sacrificial process. We saw that these things are unavoidably presented in the passion narratives. So Christian persecutors have no choice but to put them in plain sight as well. Which they do. The perverse innovation is to make scapegoating itself the charge by which to scapegoat. It is a charge that never appeared among classic sacrificial accusations before. This particular kind of persecution lays out a full description of the sin, and then practices it. The Gospel account of how Jesus is made a scapegoating sacrifice is made into justification for scapegoating the Jews. This is something new under the sun. Never before had the practitioners of sacred violence described its true nature so flatly and explicitly, in the very act of enacting it.

At many points in Christian history we see preachers telling the story of a mob collectively killing the innocent Jesus, in order to incite a mob to collectively kill innocent Jews. At the time of the First Crusade, Peter the Hermit spoke on a Good Friday at the cathedral in Cologne, exhorting a congregation that then poured out into the city on a murderous rampage through the Jewish community. The scene was repeated elsewhere, leading a Jewish chronicler of the time to write: "They taunted us from every direction. They took counsel, ordering that either we turn to their abominable faith or they would destroy us 'from infant to suckling.' They —

both princes and common folk — placed an evil sign upon their garments, a cross."[8] Those who wear the cross now force others on to it.

In the Middle Ages Christians take this to a further extreme with the appearance of the blood libel. Jews are accused of kidnapping and killing Christian children to use their blood in the preparation of Passover matzoth. They are likewise charged with stealing consecrated hosts from the communion service, to inflict the same violence on Christ's eucharistic body that had been inflicted on his earthly one. One notable case became a pretext for the expulsion of Jews from Spain, the "holy child of La Guardia." Eleven Jews were executed for the supposed crime of having crucified a Christian child and then using the child's heart along with a communion host in a conjuration intended to result in the death of all Christians.[9]

These charges became the occasion for more massacres. The charges against the Jews become a virtual catalogue of the practices of scapegoating violence, ritual and otherwise, always beginning with the case of Jesus' crucifixion itself. Christian anti-Semites laid out the entire paradigm of founding murder and ritual violent sacrifice, a picture that the biblical tradition had uncovered. But it is deployed as a justification for violence, making the revelation against sacrifice a new rationale for sacrifice.

Christians in history have not scrupled to use classical scapegoat charges against Jews. Those would be accusations like the ones given in the medieval chronicle we discussed in chapter 2: bestiality, poisoning wells. According to such charges, Jews are an unhealthy minority, polluting and corrupting the social body. They are the few, responsible for the ills of the many. But alongside these claims are typically layered other different and apparently incompatible ones. According to these charges, Jews are somehow an effective "majority," in the sense that they control great power, conspire with a vast network of accomplices, and make all others their sacrificial victims. It is imperative in this perspective that Jews be cast in the role of scapegoaters, practicing the collective persecution of the weak and the few, on the model of the collective execution of Jesus. It is this latter note, or its uneasy amalgamation with the first, more traditional sacrificial script, that is the distinctive note of Christian anti-

---

8. Robert Chazan, *European Jewry and the First Crusade* (Berkeley: University of California Press, 1987), 225.

9. See B. Netanyahu, *The Origins of the Inquisition in Fifteenth Century Spain*, 1st ed. (New York: Random House, 1995), 1090.

Semitism. In this Christians can be said to have lamentably pioneered what in its more pallid forms we call political correctness, the practice of sacrificial violence against victims who are ritually charged with the practice of sacrificial violence.

This is why anti-Semitism is a test for a healthy atonement theory. The moment we point a finger at some "they" as Jesus' killers, we have enacted the sin that the cross specifically revealed and meant to overcome. We cut the branch behind ourselves. In anti-Semitism the Christian revelation becomes a grim parody of itself, an ironic mirror of mythical sacrifice. The gospel of Jesus' death reveals to us that the scapegoating solution to the crisis of violence is itself a violence that needs changing. But the anti-Semitic reading of the Gospels turns the cure back into a disease. Christians bear a special responsibility for this evil, greater than that which attaches to "ordinary" scapegoating, just as a nurse would bear a special responsibility if she used a medicine to poison instead of to heal. We who read the Gospels can scarcely claim we know not what we do. Our sacrificial violence toward Jews proclaimed the very sin it practiced.

When Christians consider their tradition's history of anti-Semitism, they incline to one of two responses. One is to regard this history as a record of accidental failings that blemish the tradition but have no roots in its core. Prejudices and hatreds common to the human condition, not unique to Christianity, have compromised a pure teaching. This is unconvincing and at least incomplete, since there is something about Christian anti-Semitism that *does* draw on elements special to the heart of Christianity. The other tendency is to view pogroms and contempt as the necessary results of the passion narratives and Christian core beliefs themselves. Anti-Semitism is intrinsic to Christianity virtually from the beginning. The cross made us do it. But there is something inadequate in this too. It underestimates just how directly the message of the cross tells against this use of it.[10] Without that element, ironically, it is hard for

10. This is illustrated in Marc Chagall's painting *White Crucifixion,* which depicts a Jewish figure with a prayer shawl as a loin cloth, hanging on a cross. If the cross is the sign under which Christians have persecuted Jews (and undoubtedly it is), then such an image might naturally appear as an incitement to exactly that behavior. But I think it would be a rare person who would not read Chagall's painting as an obvious reproach to Christian anti-Semitism. Why? Because such an image identifies the persecution of Jews with the situation of Jesus, and to do that is to delegitimate that persecution. The persecution of Jews tries to identify them with the crucifiers of Jesus, not with Jesus; with the perpetrators of the cross, not the one who suffered it.

those who maintain that anti-Semitism is built into the essentials of Christianity to give a convincing account of what is specially Christian about it.

I call anti-Semitism a test for atonement theory because if we have not gotten the paradox of the cross right, this is one way our error will quickly show up. The incoherence of that theological approach is not hard to spot. It requires us to put together two contradictory things. The first is the contention that "the Jews are the ones responsible for killing Jesus and for practicing scapegoating sacrifice. We Christians aren't." And the second is the root theological principle of the cross: Jesus died for our sins. Christians applied the words from Isaiah to Jesus:

> All we like sheep have gone astray;
> > we have all turned to our own way,
> and the LORD has laid on him
> > the iniquity of us all. (Isa. 53:6)

The two don't fit. The first breaks the very link the second affirms. If Jesus dies because of our sin and his dying somehow makes it possible for us to be saved from that same sin, then it would seem that were his death the fault of only some people, they are the only ones who would get the benefit.

If you want to hold these two things together, you have to take a decisive step in another direction. You have to say that the sins of ours that Christ bears in his death are unrelated to the sins that actually bring about that death. You say, for example, it is the sins of the Jews that kill Jesus, that cause the event. But on another level, Jesus is dying to offer satisfaction or restitution for all the sins humans have committed (lying, stealing, adultery — the entire list). God does not kill Jesus, for that would be an evil thing for God to do. We don't kill Jesus, because that would add guilt instead of subtracting it. But Jesus needs to die to balance out our sin. The Jews then become the "sacred executioners" whose providential role is to do the killing and bear the guilt for it.[11] They are the middlemen needed for this transaction. At the extreme, the redemption of the rest of the world depends on their sin and punishment. Jesus may die to save us, but Jews will be damned to save us.

There are theologies of the cross in Christian history that give essen-

---

11. The term "sacred executioner" is from Hyam Maccoby, *The Sacred Executioner: Human Sacrifice and the Legacy of Guilt* (New York: Thames and Hudson, 1982).

tially this answer. They are wrong.[12] And it is important to see the first step that takes them astray: making the paradox of the cross relate to two different groups of people and to two different sets of sins. This theology begins with the paradox that Jesus' death is wrong but saves the world, bad but good. However, it dissolves the tension, with the bad part apportioned as the Jews' responsibility and the good part reserved for others. This theology retains in part the critique of sacrifice that is part of the paradox. Those who made Jesus a scapegoat (the Jews) are punished, while those who did not (who are not "Christ killers") are rewarded, with the benefits that come from the death of the scapegoat! The antisacrificial revelation has become a rationale for retribution against the Jews, who become the entire crowd, while Christians are subtracted from it. In other words, this theology picks up some authentic elements (the paradox, the antisacrificial message, the fact that God has a saving purpose counter to that of the persecutors) and mismatches them.

This example highlights one reason I think the theme of this book is so important. Scapegoating sacrifice is not the only human sin, nor even the only dimension of Jesus' death. But it is an absolutely crucial link in the logic of the theology of the cross, because it is the fundamental sin that causes Jesus' death and it is a concretely universal sin. It specifies a manner in which we are all involved in Jesus' death, the sense in which Jesus died for *our* sins. So long as we grasp that, we forestall the first step of separating the sins of those who killed Jesus from another kind of sin belonging to those who were saved by his death, the first step of dividing humanity into the bad ones responsible for the cross and the bad ones who benefit from it.

Summing Up

Part 2 has tried to outline why it makes sense to speak of the "good news" of the cross. In this chapter I summarized the substance of that news, and then considered two specific alternative paths that have appeared within historical Christianity. The Gnostic approach attempted to stamp out the truth of the scapegoat, and anti-Semitic formulations turned that truth

---

12. Anselm himself — regarded as the very fountainhead of substitutionary atonement theology — explicitly formulated the principle that God would never make any creature's salvation depend on the damnation of another. See further comment about this below in chapter 10.

into a rationale for persecutory violence. Despite the official rejection of the Gnostic and Marcionite options, the church has often effectively taken one of these paths, especially the second.

In the first chapter I said we were looking for an insight into the cross and atonement theology that would allow us to understand the full range of their effects. How could the same thing be experienced as liberating and transforming on one hand and as destructive and perverse on the other? Some see it as a precious truth, at times misunderstood and misused. Some see it as an intrinsically abusive framework whose evil influence at times was overbalanced by decent people who refused to take its meaning to heart. Neither general assumption tells us why the doctrine should go wrong in the specific ways that it does or why it should be associated with the peculiar types of good that it is.

The perspective we have offered does both of these things. In fact, a dangerous theology of the cross is much closer at hand than aggressive Christian apologists may want to acknowledge. The Gospel narrative follows the outline of an ancient pattern of sin (in the course of revealing and opposing it) that can be read as a prescription rather than a diagnosis. And even when the truth it offers is received, it can be twisted into a novel rationale for sacrifice. These liabilities are not merely accidental, for they are in a sense built into the heart of the gospel. They can't be completely subtracted without eliminating what is essential. Their negative power is parasitic on a distinctive good in the story of the cross. At the same time, the saving and transforming power that so many testify they have found in the cross is also not an accident. It flows from a special clarity about sacrifice and victims, from a light that breaks on the scapegoat and the crowd and a power that speaks with grace to both. The message of the cross unveils and rejects this sacrificial process and the myth that accompanies it. The result is a new awareness of victims and a call for us to be converted from the crowd of persecutors into a new community that vindicates scapegoats and seeks to live without them. That is the theme of the next section.

PART THREE

In Remembrance of Me

The Cross That Faith Keeps Empty

Perhaps the *anthropological* role of the Christian church in human history might be simplified as follows: To undermine the structures of sacred violence by making it impossible to forget how Jesus *died* and to show the world how to live without such structures by making it impossible to forget how Jesus *lived*.

Gil Bailie[1]

1. Gil Bailie, *Violence Unveiled: Humanity at the Crossroads* (New York: Crossroad, 1995), 274.

CHAPTER EIGHT

Substitute for Sacrifice

Living with an Empty Cross

> Peace I leave with you; my peace I give to you. I do not give to
> you as the world gives.
>
> John 14:27

In part 1 we considered the cross against the background of sacred violence, arguing that the realism of biblical texts lays bare the character of
sacrifice that myth typically obscures. The cross stands in a tradition of
witness, exposing the reality of victims. In part 2 we considered the passion
accounts as explicit antisacrificial testimony. They explicate the process of
scapegoating and our complicity in it. Christ's passion follows the sacrificial script that human sin has sanctified. But having made that once invisible script evident to us, it turns it inside out, witnessing to God's vindication of the victim and a hope for the end of redemptive violence. At each
turn of the passion narratives, God reverses the role of the divine in the
script of sacred mythic sacrifice. But these steps are incomplete, their revelatory or saving power limited, without yet a third dimension. It may require an act of divine power, in the resurrection, to truly overturn our assumptions about sacrifice. But however dramatic that saving effect of the
cross may be, there is more involved than simply showing forth the truth.
Because we have seen the very real danger that sacrifice exists to avert, we
understand that it is not enough simply to "see through" the myths of sacrifice or to identify with victims rather than with the unanimity of the
crowd. Though God may call us to both steps, by themselves they are
hardly comprehensive good news. Taken alone, they might simply point us

on an apocalyptic path where sacrifice grows at once bloodier and less effective.[2] This truth alone cannot save us unless there is an alternative, peaceful way of overcoming the rivalry and reciprocal violence that sacrifice exists to contain.

The problem sacrifice addresses is real and its solution has been effective. If we realize that the solution itself is wrong, how will we live without it? How can we live with an empty cross? Scapegoating is deployed to overcome a crisis created by the human contagion of escalating conflict. And the cure it applies uses the same dynamic. It incites an infectious hatred toward the victim that sweeps through the fractured community and brings it unity. The threat of fractious dissolution is met with a solidarity in communal violence.

The revelation in the passion narratives hobbles this sacrificial process, by placing the story of the unjust killing of an innocent scapegoat at the center stage of culture. The existence of a community that sides with the crucified one and witnesses constantly to God's repudiation of sacrifice will make traditional sacrificial consensus more difficult to maintain, even if it may develop its own persecuting practice (as we discussed in the last chapter). The gospel of the cross is a disruptive element that makes it more difficult to assemble a unanimous mob on the old terms. But does it have anything to put in the place of sacrifice? An alternative would need its own means to prevent and/or dispel crises of conflict. It would need its own positive form of contagion. And this is just what the New Testament presents to us in its description of Christian faith and the life of the church. It proposes a substitute for sacrifice, made possible by God's new creation in Christ. It is at this point that we can clearly see the connection linking Jesus' death with his life and teaching.

One consistent strand of this new life or new creation is a remaking of the grounds of human community. This sounds grandiose when we think of the fragile institutions we know as churches. Yet the implausible experiment that is the Christian church today constitutes the largest single voluntary human community of shared identity, seeded across virtually all geographical and cultural sectors. Christianity does not claim to possess a complete revealed constitution that specifies in permanent detail all of society's structures, from families and law to banking systems and military practice. Instead it puts a major focus on changing certain root dynamics, including the dynamics of sacrifice and social unity we have taken as our topic. This dimension is a characteristic, essential feature of Christianity. Christian faith could not flow forward in history unless individuals found it transforming

2. We will pick up this point in the next chapter.

for their personal lives here and now, without waiting for a wholesale re-creation of human social life itself. But new persons cannot be completely separated from pilot communities. The two go together, and transformation in the Christian life works through a web of relationships, a web that begins in the church but extends to the greater human community.

Change from the Inside

In the last section we mentioned the double bind that seems to trap opponents of sacrifice. The only models we have are to imitate the persecutors or imitate their victims. Passive acceptance merely reinforces the violent process. Direct resistance fosters more conflict and violence, which in turn heightens the appetite for sacrifice. We are like bound hostages whose every struggle pulls the knots tighter around us. Christ opens a way out of this dilemma. His path to the cross eschews all violence, yet it exposes the evil of scapegoating at every step. The resurrection vindicates the victim and condemns the persecutors, but without turning to vengeance.

The community of faith in Christ faces this same dilemma. Should the resurrection vindication of Jesus rally them in a campaign of revenge against whatever persons and powers they identify as persecutors? Or should it enlist them as an army of ready victims, lining up to seek the death he accepted? The bind still remains, so long as the question is limited to which role one will choose in the standard plot. What is needed is to change the plot, to build community in a new way and to resolve its crises in a new way. This is the work of the crucified one that only the Spirit can complete.

Some years ago a friend, Leander Harding, who is an Episcopal priest, was in the midst of doctoral studies in psychology, focusing specifically on family systems theory. He would often read texts related to this topic in the evening. During the same period he continued his common practice of reading regularly from the writings of early Christian authors. He reported that late at night he would sometimes nod off over his book, and when he came awake he found it more and more difficult to remember which of the two he had been reading, family systems theory or early Christian theology. He became convinced that this was not a confusion born of fatigue but the reflection of a profound structural similarity between the two at the particular point of the atoning work of Christ.

He offered the example of a family entering therapy because of the son's increasingly bizarre and psychotic behavior. The mother is deeply involved in attempts to improve the son's condition and severely dis-

turbed and consumed by the effort. The father has been somewhat with-
drawn, and silently at odds with some of the decisions taken so far regarding the son's treatment. After some months of therapy, the father
takes a sudden new course, actively engaging with the problem, breaking
some of the past patterns in the family, committing himself to a new
course of behavior in the future. His wife bitterly attacks him for a lack
of love and want of appreciation for all she has invested in past arrange-
ments. In the next few weeks the family is consumed by crisis. The son
has a severe psychotic episode, and the friction between the parents becomes intense.

By the time the family next reports for therapy, however, "the mother
and father have found a renewed intimacy. . . . The mother talks movingly
about how much of her life has been lived vicariously through her son, acknowledging that this has been destructive for both of them. She talks
about her well-thought out plans to pursue some life goals that she set
aside years ago. The son has surprised personnel at the treatment center
with a rapid recovery and a new interest in completing his education."[3] In
some cases, though one person may be the most visibly disturbed, there is
a wider problem, a disease-supporting network of relations. In such a situation, healing change often cannot be initiated by those who are most
wounded or incapacitated. Instead, what is required is for one of the
strongest and most willing members of the family to become the focus for
change.

This is done not mainly by words but by adopting a new pattern of
individual behavior. Everyone in the family system has relations with
this actor, and those established relations are affected by this change,
whether the other family members wish it or not. This typically results
in enormous resistance and even in coordinated attacks against the initiating member, efforts to maintain the existing patterns that, however
difficult, are the well-worn "solutions" into which the family constella-
tion has settled. The one changing is charged with causing new and
worse problems, demonstrating his or her lack of concern for the family,
and so on. The person in such a position is isolated and suffers a good
deal. If the course is wise and well founded, and he or she can persist on
it without being caught up in retaliation, a breakthrough point can

3. Leander S. Harding, Jr., "A Unique and Final Work: The Atonement as a Saving Act of
Transformative Obedience," *Journal of Ecumenical Studies* 24, no. 1 (1987): 87. Harding does
not intend this as a complete analogy for the atonement. It is an example that can help us
understand the shared, organic character of our human nature in distinction from an
atomistic individualism, and thus to see how the actions of one can change us all.

come at which all the members of the family network flip into a new configuration of relations. It is impossible to maintain the old pattern because of the firm alteration in one person, and a new, healthier equilibrium can emerge.

Harding realized that this was essentially the story he had been reading in the church fathers, the story of Jesus who had resolutely lived a new way of life and had attracted the resistance of all the powerful networks of which he was a part, resistance that culminated in his death. The one who has changed suffers at the very hands of those for whose sake he has made the change. And through that death and resurrection new realities for personal existence were opened. It also helped to explain why these early Christian writers saw no conflict between the idea of Jesus' death as an objective, real change in the structure of things and the idea of Jesus' death as an inspiring example of obedience and faithfulness. It is both. When one party in a network of relations truly and definitively changes, the whole has been objectively changed. And each other party is under real pressure to change as well. The other actors have been offered the inspiration of a new possibility. But even before they respond to it, their world has already actually been transformed.

For the early Christian writers, the "family" was the whole of humanity. Its pattern of relations had become destructive and fallen. As Harding puts it,

> Life that was faithful to the intention of God would provoke the most intense resistance and would have to endure the most intense suffering. It is hard to imagine an ordinary human being who would be able to persist in the face of such resistance. Just as it is usually an act of creative suffering by the healthiest member in a pathogenic system that purchases a new and life-giving reality for all others in the system, we can imagine the paradigmatic act of creative suffering that would be necessary to remove the barrier of sin that stands between humankind and God. . . . Here are all the traditional themes: of a price which must be paid that we can not pay ourselves, and of Christ as a ransom — a putting away of sin, and as an overcoming of an ontological barrier.[4]

To change the system in this way, you must belong to its web of relations. A change in the pattern can begin only with one who is part of the net-

4. Harding, "Unique and Final Work," 91-92.

work. Christ had to be human. To persevere to the point of new life, a power was needed that no human has. In fact, what was needed was a perseverance that could go even beyond death, so that the new relations Christ had established with others would continue, and so maintain their transforming effect on the human family. Christ had to share the divine nature. This is why incarnation was the path of divine wisdom.

Harding's analogy fits perfectly with the very specific instance we have been following, the practice of scapegoating sacrifice. Sacred violence attributes the crisis and afflictions in the whole community to the failings of only one or a few, and collectively persecutes them. But the problem that is thought to be isolated in the one guilty party is in fact distributed through the whole community, and the problem continually reappears, along with the need for more victims. The system itself can be changed only from some new pattern that arises within it, maintained with enough strength that all the elements must respond to it. And his analogy is particularly helpful at this point in our discussion, because it underlines the integral connection between the specific event of Jesus' death and a new order of life for human communities. That is precisely the element we want to explore in this section.

Now We're Going to Play Something Else

Let me give another example. The following comes from a letter from a friend, who has long struggled with the sacrificial death of Christ.

> [Our conversation] suddenly shed light on something in my life that goes back 15 years ago, when we first moved here. To get to know people in N., I tried getting involved in things in the church community — the choir and a neighborhood Bible study group. The latter was led by former missionaries, very evangelical, and as soon as Easter came around I was embroiled in this same argument with them: if God is love, why does he demand a blood price? There was no resolution, and it became emotionally exhausting for all parties.
>
> I think it must have been the next winter. I was still in the group, but our conflict was smoldering at a low level by then. I was down in the laundry room here in our building, surrounded by hanging sheets, towels, and kids' jeans. Somehow I began having a daydream of nearly 40 years earlier, when I was eight years old. My parents were then missionaries in S., and I attended an American school for

224

English-speaking children of many nations, quite like the international school here. Our third grade class was probably pretty much like others, though, with the usual tensions. And we had a scapegoat. There was one kid who was just too pretty to be an eight-year-old boy. Probably he didn't smell like the others. Anyway, he had big limpid blue eyes and that kind of sensitive skin that blushed if you just looked at him. And we reduced him to tears daily with our torments. Just the way we said his name at him, putting in all the lewdness we could with our crummy kid-sized half-awareness of sexuality. . . .

I was right there in the pack, destroying a human being, and it was perfectly clear to me why. If I didn't, I could easily be the next victim. I was too skinny for my skirt to stay up, and my mother made me wear suspenders! That would have been enough. So every day, at age eight, I looked upon the face of evil, and it was our collective face — "we have met the enemy, and they are us." But we were little kids, and we were afraid: afraid of our scapegoat's weakness and of our own weakness.

But in my daydream, suddenly there was somebody who never was in our class. He looked just like H., our scapegoat, but he was totally different because he wasn't afraid. An eight-year-old-sized kid, the same as the rest of us, absolutely without fear. He stood there on the playground beside H., protecting him, and everything stopped, the whole miserable scene. We were flummoxed. We couldn't have stopped by ourselves. This new boy had done it. Nobody knew where he came from, he was just suddenly there. Then he said, "Now we're going to play something else." And we all followed him, and we played. I can't remember what we played, just the huge feeling of relief in my chest, and moving around giddily with the other girls, bumping into each other and giggling. We were set free.

The daydream ended, and I was still standing there in the laundry cubicle, surrounded by my sheets. Later of course my mind kept going back to it, to what happened to him. And I remember a brief flash of him hanging on a fence. In S. a common kind of fence was made of bamboo woven on the diagonal, with the top ends sticking up jaggedly this way and that, ten or twelve feet off the ground. Sometimes painted black. How those sixth and seventh grade bastards could get him up there, don't ask me.

After telling me this, she said, "The trouble was, I could never find out whether this scene says something theologically valid about who Jesus was. . . . The only story in the Gospels anything like it is the woman taken in adultery."

My friend's vision says something profoundly valid indeed about Jesus. It is more a criticism of our atonement theology than of her faithful imagination that it was so hard for her to find any connection between the two. Her vision points us plainly to the link. It is no accident, I think, that it centers on the experience of collective scapegoating, and that Jesus appears in it (looking "just like" the victim) to end that sacrificial activity. The image of this same Jesus, crucified, hanging on a fence, comes to her later, almost separate. It is as if to say that the earthly Jesus or the risen Christ would surely behave as the new child in the vision does, but that this behavior has nothing to do with his own death, which floats apart, a disconnected fact. From this perspective the cross is puzzlingly irrelevant to this task of reconciliation and nonpersecution, or even contradictory to it.

Yet her vision also makes the connection. It suggests what might happen to one who disrupts the sacrificial process. When wondering "what happened to him," she sees him made a scapegoat as well. And it is that identification that drives toward a new life without sacrifice. The missing key is in plain sight, but lost because of the insistence that it is God who demands a blood price. The one who lived without scapegoating is made a scapegoat. But resurrection and divine vindication make that witness permanent and inescapable. The Jesus who was a victim protects the victim. The Jesus who looks just like our scapegoats has infected us with the knowledge that our scapegoats look like Jesus. The Jesus whose persecution and passion followed the well-worn script of divinely sanctioned unanimity was raised to reverse that script and to make possible the insight around which my friend's vision revolves: we have met the enemy and they are us. We can't stop by ourselves. Only the crucified one can teach us to play something different.

Holy Spirit and New Community

When early Christians speak of new life in Christ, one major element they have in mind is precisely an alternative to sacrifice. The New Testament writers affirm that a new foundation for reconciliation has been established through the death and resurrection of the crucified one. At many levels — individual, social, ecclesial, mystical, liturgical — a new way has been established. This emphasis shows up in the basic elements of Christian faith and practice, though we may not be used to viewing them in this light.[5]

We can take the Holy Spirit as an example. In the last section we talked of the Holy Spirit in its role as the *paraclete,* the advocate and defender of scapegoats. The Spirit sides with sacrificial victims and inspires others to do the same. But it is not enough to expose and oppose the sacrificial solution to community harmony. There is a positive task on the other side of this negative one. The Holy Spirit's other characteristic work is the inspiration and nurture of a new kind of community. A good summary, where both aspects can be seen together, is given in this passage from Acts. Peter and John have just been released after a trial, a deliverance in which accusations have been refuted and sacrifice avoided. The community receives them with a collective prayer:

> "For in this city, in fact, both Herod and Pontius Pilate, with the Gentiles and the peoples of Israel, gathered together against your holy servant Jesus, whom you anointed, to do whatever your hand and your plan had predestined to take place. And now, Lord, look at their threats, and grant to your servants to speak your word with boldness, while you stretch out your hand to heal, and signs and wonders are performed through the name of your holy servant Jesus." When they had prayed, the place in which they were gathered together was shaken; and they were all filled with the Holy Spirit and spoke the word of God with boldness. Now the whole group of those who believed were of one heart and soul, and no one claimed private ownership of any possessions, but everything they owned was held in common. With great power the apostles gave their testimony to the resurrection of the Lord Jesus, and great grace was upon them all. (Acts 4:27-33)

The passage begins with a pointed recollection of the collective violence against Jesus, a violence in which all were involved — Gentiles, the peoples of Israel, Pilate, and Herod, all acting together. It contrasts this with the disciples, who now are empowered by the Spirit to speak up boldly in the name of the victim, and are formed in a very different kind of unity, in which believers share their possessions rather than a mur-

---

5. For a searching exploration of the positive personal and social contagion of this alternative to the violent version of the sacred, see James Alison, *On Being Liked* (New York: Crossroad, 2003).

der. Here is an alternative way for a community to be of "one heart and soul."

In the Gospel of John, Jesus tells the disciples that after he is gone "the Advocate, the Holy Spirit, whom the Father will send in my name, will teach you everything, and remind you of all that I have said to you. Peace I leave with you; my peace I give to you. I do not give to you as the world gives" (John 14:26-27). The Advocate, the representative for the accused, will come to teach them. And Jesus promises some new kind of peace, a peace different from the one the world gives, through its sacrificial practice.

The notable work of the Holy Spirit, in addition to testifying with scapegoats, is to bring unity across difference and division. It is the crisis of fragmentation that calls forth the violence of sacrifice. If the call of the gospel is to stop the sacrifice, then a new force for reconciliation is required. The account of the believers having everything in common is a picture that replaces rivalry and escalating conflict with peace and mutual care. Famine and plague were archetypal occasions for people within a group to turn against each other and fall into division and contention. In the Acts account of the church, need or difficulty within the group becomes an occasion for the parts to be bound together in mutuality.

The premier event associated with the Holy Spirit happens at Pentecost. This harvest festival took place in Jerusalem fifty days after Passover. Thus in a sense it is a parallel scene to Holy Week. Jews from many places and nations have gathered for the feast. It is a crowded religious event that, like the Passover of Jesus' death, if on a lesser scale, raises tensions and threats of conflict. On the earlier occasion, festering divisions led to a crisis that led to Jesus' crucifixion. But on this occasion the witness about Jesus brings an opposite result. Divisions are bridged and reconciled without violence. The Holy Spirit descends on the disciples, who begin to speak in many languages, so that "each one heard them speaking in the native language of each." Peter then preaches to the crowd about Jesus, his unjust execution and his resurrection. He invites them to repent and be baptized "so that your sins may be forgiven; and you will receive the gift of the Holy Spirit." The account ends by telling us that "All who believed were together and had all things in common; they would sell their possessions and goods and distribute the proceeds to all, as any had need. Day by day, as they spent much time together in the temple, they broke bread at home and ate their food with glad and generous hearts, praising God and having the goodwill of all the people" (Acts 2:44-47).

The Pentecost story ends as the earlier passage does with an emphasis on the radically new kind of community that forms around the crucified one. This text is often taken to describe the birth of the church. And the New Testament writers do not tire of emphasizing that the key mark of this new community is the way it brings together what one would ordinarily presume to be conflicting parties, and does so by peaceful means, not by sacrifice. Christ has broken down barriers, and in this body of believers there is neither Jew nor Greek, slave nor free, male nor female. The miraculous effect of the risen Christ through the spirit is reconciliation of the sharpest and strongest differences, resolution of conflicts that could and would, normally, tear a community apart. Early Christians were accused of being "antisocial" precisely because they rejected the standard-issue ritual means for cementing community order. They believed and demonstrated that there was another means than sacrifice to achieve this end.

Baptized into His Death

Baptism is another example. Paul says, "Do you not know that all of us who have been baptized into Christ Jesus were baptized into his death? Therefore we have been buried with him by baptism into death, so that, just as Christ was raised from the dead by the glory of the Father, so we too might walk in newness of life. For if we have been united with him in a death like his, we will certainly be united with him in a resurrection like his" (Rom. 6:3-5). Baptism is the ritual entry into the Christian community. This initiation is an act of identification with Christ and his death as an unjustly scapegoated victim. It was common for initiations in the ancient world to involve sacrifice and bloodshed. Baptism does not. Consistent with belief in the cross as a sacrifice to end sacrifice, and a death "once for all," each baptized person enters into what is in effect a reversed sacrifice, looking not to share in the benefits of an offered victim but to walk in the newness of life of one who overcame scapegoating. The baptized are to be united with Christ in a resurrection like his, participating in that new creation. Peter preaches in Acts that when God raised up Jesus, he sent him "to bless you by turning each of you from your wicked ways" (Acts 3:26). This bears on our peculiar individual sins, but certainly it applies with special force to our shared, collective wicked ways.

We were not actually killed with Jesus, but we associate ourselves with that death through baptism, aligning ourselves with the victim, not the persecutors. In this act we step into the place of the sacrificed one, at the same time identifying with Christ and with every other member of this new community, who has likewise been "buried with Christ." Baptistries in early churches were small separate buildings attached to the larger sanctuary. Candidates emerged naked from the font, were clothed anew and led into the larger church to be welcomed by the assembled congregation. The old self left behind in the waters is the one who identified with the crowd, the one who held the first stone. The one who emerges enters a reconciled community. This baptismal identification means that when we look at scapegoats in the future, we should see two faces looking back, the face of Jesus and our own face. This association is not merely liturgical. The New Testament gives special emphasis to solidarity with precisely the kinds of people most liable to be scapegoated, and Matthew 25:31-46 even makes this a test of our relation with Christ on the judgment day. There is a radical ordering of life with favor toward victims and potential victims.

If baptism is a dramatic identification with Jesus' death, it throws us back to the tension we have repeatedly discussed. Is this an identification with the sacrificial intent of those who persecuted Jesus or with the parallel but opposite divine purpose to end sacrifice? The description of the new life that is to follow on baptism clearly opts for the latter. Sacrificial language itself is redefined to this end. Robert Daly has argued that for early Christians sacrifice became a primarily ethical category.[6] This is nicely illustrated in the twelfth chapter of Romans, which begins, "I appeal to you therefore, brothers and sisters, by the mercies of God, to present your bodies as a living sacrifice, holy and acceptable to God, which is your spiritual worship. Do not be conformed to this world, but be transformed by the renewing of your minds, so that you may discern what is the will of God — what is good and acceptable and perfect." What follows in the chapter is a long train of exhortations having to do with harmony in diversity, including injunctions to bless rather than curse those who persecute you, and ending, "Beloved, never avenge yourselves, but leave room for the wrath; for it is written, 'Vengeance is mine, I will repay, says the Lord.' No, 'if your enemies are hungry, feed them; if they are thirsty, give them something to drink; for by doing this you will heap burning coals on their heads.' Do not be overcome by evil, but overcome evil with good" (Rom. 12:19-21).[7]

In view here is a conspiracy of goodness, in contrast to the conspiracy

6. Robert J. Daly, *The Origins of the Christian Doctrine of Sacrifice* (Philadelphia: Fortress, 1978).

7. Virtually all translations have "the wrath of God" in verse 19 as the implied meaning, but manuscripts simply say "the wrath."

of scapegoating. "Sacrifice" has become a way of living, not of killing — a way of living that seeks to avoid any participation in sacrifice of the classic kind. It is striking that contemporary critiques of Christian views of atonement emphasize the claim that Christian belief encourages excessive self-abnegation. Such attacks tacitly concede that a major influence of the cross has been to turn our notions of sacrifice away from violence against others. "Sacrifice," even in our common secular usage, has become a word that very rarely refers to our killing or persecution of another, but most often refers to self-denial or self-restraint. In the passage from Paul we just considered, the primary thing we are encouraged to deny ourselves is revenge.

A related passage is 2 Corinthians 5:16-21, which says that if anyone is in Christ there is a new creation. "All this is from God, who reconciled us to himself through Christ, and has given us the ministry of reconciliation; that is, God was in Christ reconciling the world to himself, not counting their trespasses against them, and entrusting the message of reconciliation to us." This focus on reconciliation is telling. God has acted to short-circuit the peacekeeping process of fallen humanity, the process of uniting against a scapegoat to form community by sacrifice. God exalts and vindicates the crucified one. But God does not do so through retribution and violence. Instead a new community forms, built around the memory of the victim as innocent, not the official memory of a justified sacrifice. They gather for their central act not to ritually perform another sacrifice but rather through the simplest of meals to recall the one whose death is to be final, to deliver us from further violence. And in this way they see a truly new creation taking place, a new basis for human life, closing ranks not against the victim but with the victim. Jesus' "new covenant" in his blood is an end to the justification for shedding blood. This community takes that covenant to be the end of the cycle of repeated violence as the basis for human life, a cycle that puts humans continually at odds with God. With a way out of this cycle, we can be reconciled with God and, in a new way, reconciled with each other.

Sacrifice and Eucharist

The focal point for this is the last supper Jesus shares with his disciples, which becomes the central ritual act of the church's life. Whether or not the original meal was actually a Passover meal, it was associated with Passover. At Passover lambs were offered for sacrifice in the temple and the bodies returned to those who offered them, to be eaten at their domestic celebrations. Thus the whole setting is an explicitly sacrificial one. The lambs are killed in recollection of the firstborn children who were spared in the exodus and not destroyed, as the firstborn Egyptian children were.

It is in this context that the Gospel accounts have Jesus set a new pattern. He tells his disciples that in the future they should do this — share the bread and the wine — "in remembrance of me." More specifically, he says of the bread, "This is my body, which is given for you," and of the wine, "This cup that is poured out for you is the new covenant in my blood" (Luke 22:19-20). This means that recollection of Jesus' death is all that is needed. No other death or sacrifice is necessary. Jesus' actions have concrete echoes of the temple sacrifice. Temple animal sacrifices involved both "body" (the flesh of the animal sacrificed) and "blood" from the animal. Different actions were prescribed for the priest in respect to each of these elements (and in some cases for different portions of the body). With Passover lambs the blood was sprinkled against the altar and the bodies returned to those who had offered them. In other types of sacrifices the bodies might be burned. In any event, the instructions for such ritual practices would specify the uses for the body and the blood. In this sense "body" and "blood" are technical terms.

When Jesus stood before the disciples and offered the bread and wine, his words can be taken in two ways at the same time, both important. "This is my body" means that this bread stands for my body, and reminds you of the death I will suffer. But it can also mean that this bread is my "body," that is, it serves as my ritual sacrificial element, taking the liturgical place of the dead body of a sacrificial victim.[8] In the first case the communion event points to the reality of Jesus' death as a scapegoat. In the second case, it points explicitly toward a substitution, an alternative practice to replace sacrifice.

Celebration of the Eucharist explicitly mirrors the sacrificial event. It

---

8. See Bruce Chilton, *The Temple of Jesus: His Sacrificial Program within a Cultural History of Sacrifice* (University Park: Pennsylvania State University Press, 1992), 152. I draw upon portions of Chilton's very valuable work, though our approaches are different. Chilton argues against those who would necessarily attribute even this short core of the "words of institution" to the later church. He maintains that such a substitution of common table elements for the sacrificial victims used in the temple fits well with the program of forgiveness and table fellowship that he sees in the ministry of the historical Jesus. He further speculates that information about such an innovation, conveyed by Judas, might have been the catalyst for Jesus' arrest. This book contains an extensive and fair critique of Girard's perspective, arguing that there are aspects of sacrifice not comprehended in his theory.

gathers the community as a crowd around the altar and the victim. But it gathers to remember the victim's innocence, to make peace without violence. In some communion services those who receive the elements are enjoined to "feed upon them in your hearts by faith." Just as bread and wine replace victims, so does this act become the unifying bond among the members, instead of a shared participation in killing. The spiritual practice of making Christ's own inner life the model for ours is the communion that makes us one. As one postcommunion prayer says, "Grant that we who share these gifts may be filled with the Holy Spirit and live as Christ's body in the world." The crowd does not gather around a body; it gathers to become Christ's body in the world, animated by the Holy Spirit of peace.

In the ancient world sacrifice was very commonly associated with meals at which the body or portions of it would be eaten. Purity specifications surrounded such meals, as they surrounded the act of sacrifice itself, and the communal ties established by eating together in this way were crucially important social boundaries. They constituted communities and defined who was in and who was out. Sacrifice and the meals around it were the sacred glue that held the social order together. From the perspective on sacrifice and community we have explored, we can see this connection as much more than superstition. Communities are defined by their solidarity in sacrifice. Both politicians and priests were explicit in affirming this unifying role of cultic offerings, even as the corollary unifying role of scapegoating human sacrifice remained implicit.

In his ministry Jesus often enacts his teaching in table fellowship, as he crosses social and religious purity boundaries by eating and drinking with Gentiles, Samaritans, tax collectors, supposed prostitutes. On one such occasion critics object to Jesus' disciples: "Why does your teacher eat with tax collectors and sinners?" (Matt. 9:11). Jesus himself replies, quoting an antisacrificial line from the prophet Hosea: "Go and learn what this means, 'I desire mercy, not sacrifice'" (9:13, citing Hos. 6:6: "For I desire steadfast love and not sacrifice, / the knowledge of God rather than burnt offerings"). The fencing of the dinner table was closely tied with ritual sacrificial activities, and such exclusion likewise fostered and reinforced scapegoating persecution. The Last Supper can be seen in continuity with Jesus' practice of table fellowship, giving it an explicitly liturgical tone that casts it in explicit contrast with sacrificial practice. Instead of the rite of scapegoating sacrifice that lies at the base of historical human community, and instead of the cultic rite of animal sacrifice that reproduces its logic of exclusion and violence, this new community is founded on the communion meal. The early church was continually amazed and thankful that this table brought into one circle those who otherwise would be irrevocably separated by purity boundaries, who otherwise would be scapegoating each other and shedding each other's blood.

It follows that sacrifice was the natural point of friction between Christians and the world around them. Those who withdrew from the very public nexus of altar, victims, and meal (not by ignoring any particular deity or omitting one set of rites rather than another, but by dropping the practice altogether) were viewed as enemies of the common good. "To eat meat [from the altar], to participate in sacrifice, was to participate in the great cultural project of sustaining the world *as it is*."[9] The sacrificial economy holds the world together, sustains it in the face of crisis and restores equilibrium. It was seen as a profoundly unneighborly act to fail to hold up one's end of this universal task. The world-sustaining effects of sacrifice appeared to demand universal participation, just as the harmony-restoring benefits of scapegoating violence demand unanimity in the crowd. The world around the newborn Christian community took offense at it only insofar as this community stepped decisively out of that nexus.

In their own ritual life, Christians placed the Eucharist, or Lord's Supper, in the place that sacrifice had occupied in other religions. As we have seen, this replacement was quite conscious. It led to a change in the very meaning of the word "sacrifice." One scholar who has painstakingly traced the history of the idea of sacrifice in the theology of the Eucharist put it this way:

> One might suggest that we would be well advised to forget about sacrifice and to concentrate instead on the religious reality underlying these terms and concepts. For we do not offer animals in sacrifice; still less do we believe that the forgiveness of sins is tied up with certain sacrificial blood rites. But then, *neither did the early Christians*. They were, in fact, reproached as irreligious by their pagan neighbors because they neither offered sacrifice nor worshipped in temples. But, despite their radical rejection of both pagan and Jewish sacrifice, the first Christians continued to speak not only of the sacrifice of Christ, but also of themselves as the new temple, and of their own lives as sacrificial.[10]

9. Stephen J. Patterson, *Beyond the Passion: Rethinking the Death and Life of Jesus* (Minneapolis: Fortress, 2004), 89.

10. Daly, *The Origins*, 135.

Christians pick up on the prophetic critique of sacrifice but frame it in a positive way. On the one hand, early Christian writers disparage the practice of cultic sacrifice as empty or demonic. On the other hand, they insist that sacrifice, in the sense of a true offering to God, has nothing to do with killing. Instead it can refer only to the unique act of Christ's passion or the repeated acts of Christian worship or to actions of daily life that embody the dispositions of love toward God and neighbor seen in Jesus. Justin Martyr, for instance, speaks of prayers and giving of thanks as the "only perfect and well-pleasing sacrifices."[11]

We could say that Christians rejected ritual blood sacrifice because even though it represented an advance on human sacrifice, it still embodied the logic of the sacred scapegoating that lay behind it (and continued to reproduce it, for instance in the persecution fed by the purity divisions that attended the practice of ritual sacrifice). The cultic altar still defined sacrifice in terms determined by the model of founding murders. Christians struggled to redefine "sacrifice" as it figured in their own nonviolent liturgical practice, not according to that fallen archetype but to the work of Christ to overcome it.

The quotation at the head of part 3 from Gil Bailie says the anthropological role of the church is to undermine the structure of sacred violence by keeping before our eyes the reality of the scapegoating process by which Jesus died, and then to illustrate a way to live without sacrifice, based on the way Jesus lived. The celebration of the Eucharist combines both of these emphases. In some churches this is made explicit. Before reception of the bread the participants are told, "Take and eat, and may the spirit in which Christ died be your spirit also." Before reception of the wine they are told, "Take and drink, and may the spirit in which Christ lives be your spirit also." When Christians gather at communion, they encounter an unequivocal reminder of Christ's bloody death. They are faced with the fact that victims have real flesh and blood. When we hear "Do this in remembrance of me," we should hear the implied contrast that comes with emphasis on *this*. Unlike the mythic victims who became sacred models for future sacrifices, Christ is not to be remembered with scapegoating, by taking or being new victims. "This" is a humble meal and prayer, not a new cross.

Christ has offered his very real body and blood, so that at the Last Supper he can set a new pattern and say of bread, "This will now serve for us as a sacrificial 'body,'" and of wine, "This will now serve as our sacrifi-

11. Daly, *The Origins*, 90.

cial 'blood.'" Following that example, Christians believe this meal of the new community is able to accomplish the peace that sacrificial violence could, and more. Collectively gathering in community with the victim can spread a contagious unity every bit as powerful as that spread by collective violence against the victim. That is the audacious faith of this practice. In the celebration we recall a real sacrifice and celebrate a substitutionary atonement. Here on this table, bread and wine are to be continually substituted for victims, substituted for any, and all, of us. At this table, the sacrifice stops.

Contagious Peace

In diagnosing the particular problem of sacred violence, we traced its root to an emergent and largely positive human capacity, our mimetic sensitivity. This facility for imitation does not stop at the rote behavioral level. It extends more significantly to the dynamic imaginative level in which we read and appropriate each other's inner emotions and desires. Empathetic sensitivity supercharges the possibilities for learning and cultural development, at the same time that it makes us liable to runaway cycles of rivalry and conflict. This peculiarly human problem finds an effective but unfortunate solution in scapegoating sacrifice and its mythic superstructure. That solution operates mimetically also, spreading a contagion of hatred against the isolated victims.

The gospel alternative for this collective addiction to persecution works through the same mimetic medium.[12] The human "family system" locked in the pattern of treating fragmenting violence with unifying violence cannot change unless some of its participants adopt an enduring new behavior. The passion narratives and the New Testament set out a decisive, initiating change made by Jesus' life, death, and resurrection. Real and objective as that change is, it can become fully effective only as its impact spreads through the wider web of human relations, by a contagion structurally similar to the destructive process it overcomes.

The positive potential of this dynamic is already outlined in the bibli-

---

12. This approach differs from that of Theravada Buddhism, for example. Early Buddhism has a clear antisacrificial quality, and its diagnosis of the human condition has many points in common with the one we have presented. Its response is to address the problem at the root of consciousness itself, and to attempt to still the source of desires themselves, to turn off the internal mental loops that advertise our cravings to be read by others and by which we appropriate theirs.

cal material, often alongside the diagnosis of its negative power. We see it outlined in Genesis in the serpent's insinuation to Eve that God regards humans as threats and rivals. The serpent says God's prohibition against eating of the tree of the knowledge of good and evil stems not from love but from a fear that if humans do so they will "become as God." This seeded suspicion about God's motives is also an invitation to humans to imitate that imagined attitude, to view God as a rival. Their act of defiance simply embodies that suspicion. The behavior has to be preceded by a desire, and the desire is supplied by, formed on, the perception of a prior desire in God.

Once set loose, the negative construal of each other's desires has an infectious impetus. In falling out of trust and communion with God, Adam and Eve are soon in conflict with each other. Cain and Abel appear to us in a kind of competition for God's favor that rapidly becomes a violent rivalry with each other. Our doubts that other persons have our good entirely at heart rarely have to look far to find evidence or what can readily serve as evidence. Since we are each other's models as well as rivals, wherever we turn we can find ready reinforcement and acceleration for our conflictual responses to real or perceived injuries.

To say that interpersonal conflict results from a foundational estrangement from God is a theological cliché that rarely receives further explanation. But in regard to our special focus, we can be more specific. The transcendence of God in relation to humans is usually conceived in quantities of power and knowledge that outstrip any we can imagine. This emphasis on superiority and distance can be translated negatively into ideas of God's despotic power over other beings and God's indifferent detachment from them. But the Genesis accounts of the fall as a human misreading of divine motive, a projection of jealousy, alert us to a key feature of the otherness of God. This is a feature of crucial value: God's position as a nonrival to humans. The Promethean modern insistence on seeing God as a constraint and an affront to human autonomy, as a power that — whether real or imagined — must be met with defiance in the interest of human self-respect, is virtually blind to the human value of this feature.

The capacity to turn any relation into one of conflict, of rivalry, is the virus that can escalate violence into a threat to all forms of human community. And it is the startling ability of sacrificial violence to stem this escalation that grants it a sacred aura and its foundational place in the structure of human order. There is a real original sin in the "conflictualization" of the one relation that offered special purchase against this cycle, the relation with God. The difference, the distance, between the plane of the Creator and that of creatures is in fact of great value for human life, as it allows for a model and an imitative relation that can resist rivalry. From this perspective the injunctions in the Old Testament against putting ourselves in the place of God are not animated so much by a fear that God will be diminished by these actions as by recognition that we will be harmed by them. The distance of divine transcendence has great positive value in taming our contagious conflict.[13] A God beyond rivalry is a model, a subject of devotion and communion, who can purify our desires.

Let us consider two paradigm cases of rivalry, or what Girard often calls "acquisitive mimesis." One is competition for an object or a reward. The other is a romantic triangle. In the first, two or more people pursue something that can go to only one of them, whether a job, a building, or a reputation. In the second, two people seek the exclusive love of a third. If we consider such situations as simply accidental (by circumstance some people will happen to desire the same thing) or entirely the product of scarcity (there are not enough basic necessities to go around), we are mistaken. Of course, true situations of objective conflict exist: too many people for one lifeboat, not enough food to go around. Many of our desires feel to us as natural and objective as those at issue in such situations. A teenager wants a certain kind of clothing, an adult wants a certain car or a particular job, with an intensity as unquestioned as that in a matter of life and death.

But there is another human dynamic driving such situations, a dynamic illustrated not only in the Bible but in much of the world's philosophy and imaginative literature.[14] Most of our desires, our individual and supposedly unique wants, are neither intrinsic to us nor independently generated. They are formed and shaped in us through imitation. We learn what to want by seeing what others want. This does not at all mean that everyone necessarily wants the same specific things, that everyone registers the majority desires and these then become universal and uniform.

13. Obviously, in a polytheistic environment the same conflict we have been exploring in the human realm can be readily replicated in the divine one, where a sacrificial dynamic also arises, as certain myths reflect. The two realms become mirrors of each other, and sacrifice is only intensified by being reflected between them. The path to monotheism then is a perilous and tricky one, since the claim to be the one true God in distinction from rivals can plainly foster conflict and violence, even as an acknowledged monotheism contains special resources to dampen them.

14. It is described acutely, for example, by Hobbes in *Leviathan*. Girard has explored it extensively in literature. See particularly Girard, *A Theater of Envy: William Shakespeare*, Odeon (New York: Oxford University Press, 1991); Girard, *"To Double Business Bound": Essays on Literature, Mimesis, and Anthropology* (Baltimore: Johns Hopkins University Press, 1978).

No. There is ample scope for variety in that each of us chooses and is attracted to his or her own set of models, people who become designators of desire for that person. And it is part of the distinctively human variety on this score that the range of models can include purely cultural ones, i.e., figures in stories or texts, divinities in myth or worship. In addition, each model presents many different aspects, real and imagined, for imitation. Two people with the same models may be primarily shaped by quite different features.

For our purposes, the important point is that the nature of our desires is inextricable from their relation to models. Because models form our desires by their own desiring, there is an intrinsic logic by which models also may become rivals. Learning to want what they want, we can easily become competitors. The tension in the relation between teacher and disciple fits well into this description. The favorite pupil arouses new sentiments in the teacher when she threatens to surpass the instructor. The anointed successor, handpicked by a senior to be the one to carry on her career and legacy, may provoke extraordinary hostility by diverging from that path. In a romantic triangle, two persons' desires for a third are often heightened or even generated by imitation. The desirability of the woman or man is confirmed or enhanced by the fact that a particular person finds her or him desirable. When two people are focused romantically on the same person, and the two serve as models for each other, a powerful loop of reciprocal reinforcement is created. This fact is rehearsed endlessly in literature, both as comedy and tragedy.

The problem of conflict and violence is inextricably linked with the origin and nature of our desires. New Testament writers talk of living "in the flesh" and "in the spirit." These two ways of life cannot be distinguished by two entirely different lists of the kinds of things that are wanted in each. They are distinguished by the process by which desires are developed. The members of the early church maintain that in having God in Christ as their model, they can be significantly delivered from many of the necessary conflicts that follow upon the desires that arise "according to the flesh." To have Jesus as a model in this sense does not mean to imitate Jesus' behavior and person in all particulars (thus to be at a loss when a situation arises where there is no act of Jesus to imitate). A model in Girard's sense is not primarily a person to be mechanically emulated in practice, but one whose example is implicitly decisive in shaping what we want and seek. We could, for instance, learn from a model to desire economic success and still discern that we need to pursue that desire in another field and by different means than the model did. If we have caught a desire from someone, we will be quite capable of pursuing that desire in circumstances different from any in which we ever observed our model.

The potential for conflict rises as models and their subjects occupy the same plane. Young people who take their decisive models from their immediate peer group are notoriously liable to rounds of falling-out and infighting. Desires tend to converge with uniformity. And anyone's positions or attainments are never far from being equaled or surpassed by others in much the same location. This can make for very high levels of conflict and instability, since shifts in models and desires can sweep the group in dramatically different directions.[15] This volatile environment is famously fertile ground for scapegoating. These same factors are very much at play among adults as well.

God is presented in the Bible both as the one who preeminently designates what is desirable, who teaches "what is good," and as one who is on a different plane from humanity, whose thoughts are not our thoughts and whose ways are not our ways, who does not need or desire the things we characteristically want and over which we characteristically come to blows with each other. As such, God is the ideal nonrivalrous model. God can indicate what we should long for. Yet our attainment of it is no threat to God, and God's enjoyment of it is no loss to us. The New Testament views Jesus himself in just this light.

Our mimetic capacity is basically positive, yet even in relation to those we admire and take as models it can breed competition, conflict born of our agreement in desire. We also have powerful mimetic impulses in relation to our enemies. Every mistreatment or perceived mistreatment calls forth in us an inclination to give as good as we got. In this sense our adversaries are models also, and we catch their negative desires readily and powerfully, perhaps even more than we catch their positive desires. We mirror back hate for hate, imitating the desire and reversing the object. Or, as with an abused child perhaps, we may adopt the model even more literally and develop emotions of self-loathing, valuing ourselves as we perceive how our abuser regards us. The double bind in our mimetic capacity is that relations with our enemies and relations with our positive models both have a capacity to lead into conflict.

We have seen how Jesus as the one victimized addresses the problem

15. Studies of adolescents often remark upon the difference it can make for young people in such an environment to have relationships even with one or two significant adults other than their parents. The existence of significant models outside the intense, narrow world of peers can constrain some of the effects of the volatility and runaway imitation in that world. Religious faith can play an analogous role for adults in their social world.

with enemies, breaking the chain of revenge by not exacting any punishment. But it remains to specify how Jesus likewise deals with the problem among friends.

The risen crucified one, as the model for Christians, is not only one who embodies an opposition to sacrificial violence. Christ is also one whose status is quite beyond rivalry. The insistence of Christian writers on Jesus as the only savior, as very God, as seated at the right hand of the Father, makes this point. The same negative dynamics still exist, but they must operate at least on another level. This is illustrated by the disciples who quarrel over who will sit at Jesus' right hand in the kingdom. If direct competition with the model is out of the question in this case (the disciples do not ask to replace Jesus), then competition as to who will best follow the model is not.

But here we encounter the double negative character of Jesus as a model. What he has designated as desirable is precisely nonrivalry itself. If people will contest with each other for this goal, they can attain it only by ceasing to contest with each other. When Jesus' disciples dispute over who is greatest, they are told that "the greatest among you must become like the youngest, and the leader like one who serves. For who is greater, the one who is at the table or the one who serves? Is it not the one at the table? But I am among you as one who serves" (Luke 22:26-27). Here Jesus holds himself out explicitly as a model, but as the kind of model one cannot finally turn into a rival through the attempt to displace or supersede him. Jesus has already stepped out of the place of greatest power, and become as "one who serves." If he is to be outdone in this, it will have to be through efforts to imitate his humility and his willingness to share his position with others. To compete in this way will be to compete against rivalry and conflict, as Paul exhorts his readers to do: "Love one another with mutual affection; outdo one another in showing honor" (Rom. 12:10). As such a model, Jesus shows himself paradoxically to be irreplaceable, and without rival.

What is different in this case from simply telling people "Don't be rivals" and "Don't fall into conflict and violence" is the provision of a powerful mimetic path toward this end, a path constituted by relation with Christ through prayer, action, worship, and community. The spiral of conflict and violence cannot be avoided without a special kind of model, the model that Christ as the incarnate Word of God, risen crucified victim, provides. Simply as a good and wise man, Jesus invites imitation and rivalry. As God with us, Jesus removes that focus on his person and frees us to realize the desires we nurture "in Christ" without any conflict. This lack of rivalry already exists on Christ's side, as evidenced in Christ's words in the Gospel of John: "Very truly, I tell you, the one who believes in me will also do the works that I do and, in fact, will do greater works than these, because I am going to the Father" (John 14:12).

In fact, Jesus' discourses in the Gospel of John often follow this pattern, making it clear that Jesus has come to incite in others the relation to God that he has, so that through faith in him they may share in the desires and relations he has, and have them fulfilled. This is the idea summarized in the patristic motto "God became as we are so that we might become as He is." Everything Jesus has and is, including above all his relationship with the Father, he offers to his disciples. It is a vision of shared fulfillment that quite transcends any rivalry or conflict, and yet proceeds by the thoroughly human process of awakening desires through a model. In Christ God has not only become fully human, a person. God has worked with us in a thoroughly human way, through the very structures of human relation out of which our sin emerges and through which now redemption can arise. Any model we might replace invites conflict. But Christ's distinction from us is secure enough to invite our participation in his desires. What is special about Jesus is that he can neither be displaced nor incensed by our attempts to share his relation with God. The more deeply those efforts are fulfilled, the more unique Christ's role becomes.

Even in its corruption, our relationship with models has many positive features. The formation of our inner lives through interaction with others is a fundamental expression of the interpersonal character of our own humanity. It is the stamp of the image of God. We are not and cannot become persons alone. Our relation with God through Christ reclaims the fundamental goodness of human desire. The availability of God as a human model around whom we can order our desires, to whom we can be attached passionately without generating conflict, frees us to interact with all our other human models in a much less polarized way. The members of Christ's body refer their conflicts and rivalries to this common relationship they share, to their life "in Christ." This is not just a simple reminder, via the image of the crucified Savior, to refrain from victimizing each other. It is a very concrete way of life that provides the means to do so.

This is the difference, for example, between a group of urban young people who hear a social worker tell them that their gang membership is jeopardizing their lives and who understand the truth of her statement, and the same group undergoing a conversion to affirm that "Jesus is our gang leader now." One might argue that the cash value of these two conclusions works out to be pretty much the same, the second one just a "metaphor" to express the first. But the difference, in terms of capacity for change, may be decidedly different. The first is information, even insight. But it offers no alternative, no way to reform the desires that could lead away from the current situation. What the second provides is a relationship and a model through whom the human dynamics we have discussed can work to produce dramatically different results: reconciliation, peace, nonrivalry.[16] All the legitimate and unavoidable human dynamics that form and express our desires are engaged by the model of Jesus.

Our human models — key individuals and the primary communities that have patterned our desires — can set us on a steady course in our own inner lives that can be maintained even when those particular models are no longer immediately present to us. But under some circumstances the pressure and inclination to adopt new models is extraordinarily powerful. The dissenter, the prisoner cast into solitary confinement or subjected to the manipulation of our mimetic nature which is brainwashing, can ultimately preserve an alternative commitment only through access to some model that transcends those contexts. Such access may come from memory. According to faith, it can also come "in the Spirit," through the living presence of the crucified one. This is the testimony of countless such people who have found the direct role religious faith (even a previously ignored one) plays in such a situation.

This theological truth is not without analogies in other areas of human experience. Some aspects of what we have been discussing can be seen in the role of literary models. That is, some people find models in fictional characters or in the lives of historical figures. Such models have certain benefits that flow from their "transcendent" status. They are not actually present to "turn" on their disciples, to emerge as rivals or to offer resistance to their imitators. They mute conflict in this way, and they can be very significant in helping to mitigate the influence of powerful and destructive actual models in one's immediate environment. But though they may do this, they cannot make up for a complete lack of real human models. A model who is a real human being, and with whom one is actually in relationship, is by far the most transformative reality. And this is who the risen Christ is in the lives of Christians. The availability of this model is a divine act of grace. Its presence does not violate the character of natural human life, but it also cannot be explained or expected as an ex-

---

16. It is quite true that any caring person who worked with such a group could serve as a model, and this could have significant effect for change. But this alone will rarely have as much power as the *combination* of that personal model with a religious model.

trapolation of that life alone. The death of Jesus cuts to the heart of what has gone wrong with our mimetic nature, and the living presence of Jesus is a model for healing it.

The Way of the Cross

When we grasp the mystery of the cross, we see its three sides as part of the whole. We see first the hidden, mythic practice of scapegoating that it reveals. The passion narratives (relying on the light given by the Hebrew scriptures) show us a process constantly repeated in history, but never fully described. Second (again in continuity with Hebrew scriptures), we see that God opposes scapegoating sacrifice and has acted to vindicate its victims. Most particularly, God has taken the place of the scapegoat, has lived the violence from the side of the persecuted, has endured sacrifice in order to end sacrifice. Third, we see the cross and resurrection as a charter for a new way of life. Once we clearly understand the first two, it is plain that they point to a way without sacrifice. The life that corresponds to the cross is a way of life without victimization.

This way of life has its own paradox, parallel to that of the Gospels themselves. Behind much discussion of the theology of the cross lies a very simple question. Is the way of the Christian the way of the cross? Are Jesus' followers called, commanded even, to suffer? If Christ is truly our model, then it seems we should each take up our own cross to follow him. But if Christ died to reverse scapegoating, a sacrifice to end sacrifice, then it seems we should resist such a fate to the utmost, for others or ourselves. If Christ's endurance of the cross is a supreme act of love, how can we rule out the expression of such love? If the cross is an act of pervasive evil, how could it possibly be faithful to accept it?

Jesus decides to go to the cross and will not be deflected from the path that leads there. That is clear. Yet at the same time nothing could be plainer in the passion narratives than that Jesus does not want to be crucified. "If it be possible, let this cup pass from me," he prays. His sweat falls like drops of blood in the anguish of his anticipation. "Why have you abandoned me?" he cries to God from the cross. "I thirst," he says in pain. All this is important, to keep us in touch with the second half of the general theme of the Gospels: this death saves the world, but it ought not to happen. Jesus' actions, and even his words, may be paradoxical. But his desire is not. Jesus seeks to end sacrifice. He seeks to end it first and foremost without any suffering, including his own. We see that clearly in his ministry, whether in the woman taken in adultery or where Jesus himself escapes stoning and violence. Even for Jesus, the step to make his own death on the cross a means to overcome sacrifice is one that can come only with difficulty and a kind of terror.

His purpose is to do the will of a God who vindicates victims, forgives without vengeance, stops the crowd's first stone. This is the model Jesus provides. It is the desire that unifies the condemnation of the cross and the conviction that God has used it. And, as we have seen, it is also the desire around which the early church built its idea of a new life. To be baptized into his death was to rise from the water as someone who should live without scapegoating. To gather at the communion table to remember his death was to practice a substitution for sacrifice, a reconciliation of conflict that needed no blood. To belong to the body of Christ was to practice, however imperfectly, community without crosses.

The simple idea that if we wish to follow Jesus we should aim to be crucified makes no more sense than the idea that if we should seek to be like God we should try to create a universe in six days. The whole point of theological teaching about God's transcendence and Jesus' divinity and the "once for all" quality of the atonement is quite the opposite. Redemptive violence is what we are to be saved from, not what we are to copy, either as perpetrators or victims. Jesus' own saying, "If any want to become my followers, let them deny themselves and take up their cross daily and follow me" (Luke 9:23),[17] points toward the redefinition of sacrifice we have seen in the early church. The cross of execution is an evil Jesus bears as part of a unique redemptive act. He speaks to his disciples of taking up their cross daily, uprooting it from a fixed site as an instrument of execution and making it the sign of an ongoing way of life, a "living sacrifice."

The paradox remains. To follow the crucified one is to live a life without sacrifice, where "sacrifice" is redefined to be an offering of praise, and rivalry is transformed into outdoing each other in love. The necessary path away from scapegoating, both cognitively and practically, is identification with the victims. Yet with such identification comes also the risk of sharing their fate. Christians, in all honesty, cannot rule out ending up on a cross. But it is the last thing they should intend.

We began this book by noting that one of the most serious criticisms of the theology of the cross is that it encourages, even mandates, a de-

---

17. Luke's version of this saying is notable in comparison with Matthew and Mark for including the word "daily."

structive masochism. It holds up the ideal of suffering like Jesus, an ideal that fosters dysfunction in healthy people and rationalizes the pain of the oppressed. There is merit to this criticism, and there have been Christians who, ostensibly under the example of the cross, sought suffering for its own sake. Asceticism has been commended on the assumption that there is an intrinsic value in pain itself. This is an error, even if hardly a widely popular one in our culture in comparative historical perspective. On the other hand, much that our cultural conventions regard as asceticism (a standard Benedictine monastic regime, for instance) has nothing in common with such masochism. The Christian life is about the formation, or reformation, of our desires. That process may involve disciplines that are not acquired without effort and pain, but their whole purpose is to form a life of joy. It is important then to recognize the difference between voluntary steps of formation in the Christian life and the rationalization of existing conditions of suffering or injustice.

The first thing that is crucial is to distinguish Christ's suffering on the cross from all suffering per se. As we have already argued, God did not become human for the purpose of general suffering, nor did God mandate a maximal intensity of suffering as the condition for human redemption. If that were so, then Jesus' entire life should have been one of utter pain, rather than having the intense suffering limited to a brutal day at the end. Jesus' life of public ministry may have been one of great simplicity and empathy for others' distress, but it was also marked by what many of his critics took as unseemly laxity and celebration. Jesus' suffering is undeniably central in the Gospels, but central for a particular reason. There are many forms of sin and estrangement, addressed in various ways by Christ. And many of those forms express the human estrangement from joy and delight in God's creation. They too are the subject of Christ's redemptive work, work that goes on in the winemaking at the wedding in Cana as well as on Good Friday. The specific event of the cross was the path needed to address the specific and profound problem of our scapegoating violence. It was the saving way God acted to overcome that evil. The suffering of Christ was not desired by God or by Jesus himself. It was needed for a very specific and narrow redemptive purpose, and in that respect it is no more a universal pattern for us than it was for Jesus' own life.

Nor does the event of the cross somehow endow all suffering with intrinsic positive meaning . . . since the suffering of Jesus had no such intrinsic meaning. In intrinsic terms his suffering was innocent and unjust, like that of so many other victims. The redemptive purpose superimposed on it came from the unique divine power to turn it against itself as a lever against the entire process. The positive meaning to this suffering comes only from the divine desire to end suffering. To put it plainly, to know that there would be even one additional cross after Jesus' could only make the suffering of Jesus that much worse, since its purpose was that there need be and should be no more. Every additional scapegoat is only added weight on that side of the passion accounts that treats the cross as what ought not to happen. Every resisted persecution and every avoided violence that flow from awareness of victims are added weight on that side of the passion accounts that claims that the cross saves the world.

So the tension continues. The Christian life lived under the sign of the cross seeks to live without a cross. It seeks a way without redemptive violence or suffering, a way that the church attempts to mirror in its sacramental life and in its actual community. Early in this book we gave an account of a prison in Latin America where the condition and rehabilitation of prisoners had been dramatically improved. The cell blocks formerly used for isolation and abuse were emptied, their inmates replaced with a single, life-sized crucifix. This is a concrete parable of the cross, and the life intended to flow from it.

To follow this same illustration, one may observe that even in such a prison suffering is hardly abolished — the loneliness of incarceration and separation, the hardships of privation, the pangs of conscience and regret, the pain of the struggle toward new habits and opportunities. All of these also pose a challenge for faith. The cross may figure among the resources that help to heal these varied wounds, but it is not necessarily the primary one. The special dimension of the cross is particularly its relevance to collective scapegoating, the social purpose of "redemptive violence." There is a legitimate, nonscapegoating purpose in restraining evil and protecting the vulnerable that may require incarceration. There are legitimate rationales for confinement as a response to crime, having to do with deterrence, rehabilitation, and even punishment. But the actual practice of correction can readily cross a line into another realm, where the pain, suffering, and condemnation of a certain class of offenders begin to serve other ends than their rehabilitation or the protection of their neighbors. They become larger than life, held responsible for society's inner conflicts, and they become the objects of a unifying collective passion that makes them convenient sacrificial victims. The punishment visited upon them takes on a quality distinct from their actual cases and serves the unifying role of sacred violence. It is here that the cross speaks directly.

Christian language about the cross is extravagant, rightly so. But this can mislead us if we take it to mean that the cross is the solution (and an unvarying one) to every possible problem that presents itself. It would be such a misreading to suppose that the Christian response to any challenge should be to find the course of action that may be helpful to others and that will bring one the greatest possible intensity of personal suffering, since in that way one will be most like Jesus. This, of course, was not *Jesus'* response in every instance, or any, with the central exception of the cross.

There are passages in Paul that certainly sound as though the Christian vocation is to imitate Jesus' suffering. In Philippians he says, "I want to know Christ and the power of his resurrection and the sharing of his sufferings by becoming like him in his death, if somehow I may attain the resurrection from the dead" (Phil. 3:10-11). These verses are preceded by a number in which Paul catalogues the advantages and benefits he has cast aside to follow Jesus. In such texts Paul comes close to making conformity to Christ's suffering a kind of commandment, an achievement on which heavenly reward is conditioned. This was a point of half-conversion, where Paul gives up the idea of justification by fulfillment of the moral and cultic law in favor of an idea of justification by matching the sacrifices of Christ. We can become acceptable to God only if we give up everything, just as Jesus did on the cross.

But there is an obvious problem here. If Jesus' death really shouldn't happen, if it is a manifestation of sin and our captivity to sin, then any mandate to keep taking Jesus' place is a commandment to keep repeating evil. The deeper breakthrough is the realization that suffering is not God's requirement for reconciliation. To put this in personal terms, Paul can't earn his own salvation by imitating every misery that was inflicted on Jesus. Walter Wink points out that this idea of salvation by trial may have been at one time the implicit shape of Paul's faith, before he realized that Christ had died to save him also from the requirement to imitate that death.[18]

This throws a special light on justification by faith as put forward in Paul's letter to the Romans. We are used to reading this teaching as a contrast between obedience to the law of Moses and faith in Christ, but it applies also to what we might call a "law of the cross," which would be the expectation that we attain righteousness only when we pass the test of suffering as much as Christ did. Now Paul drops the idea that there might

---

18. See his reference to the work of Robert Fortna in Wink, *Engaging the Powers: Discernment and Resistance in a World of Domination* (Minneapolis: Fortress, 1992), 366 n. 40.

be something lacking in Christ's suffering that we have to supply, or that we cannot receive the gift of salvation unless we die as he did. Instead, he throws all the weight on Christ's work as an accomplished fact, one that does not have to be repeated, one that has made us acceptable to God apart from sacrifice, including self-sacrifice. As he says elsewhere, "If I give away all my possessions, and if I hand over my body to be burned [some translations say 'so that I may boast'], but do not have love, I gain nothing" (1 Cor. 13:3). Instead of modeling a standard of suffering we have to match to be saved, Christ's death was an instrumental act to free us to live as he did, not to die as he did. "For if while we were enemies, we were reconciled to God through the death of his Son, much more surely, having been reconciled, will we be saved by his life" (Rom. 5:10).

Famously, after making the case that we are already justified, and need only accept that justification by faith, Paul addresses the obvious question. If God is wiping out all our sins by grace, shall we just go on multiplying our sins so that grace can abound all the more? No, precisely because the dominion of sin has been broken, we can and should live new lives. The way Paul expresses this is notable. Whereas in Philippians he said he wanted to share Christ's sufferings by becoming like him in his death, Paul now says we all have been united with Jesus in a death like his, by baptism. "Therefore we have been buried with him by baptism into death, so that, just as Christ was raised from the dead by the glory of the Father, so we too might walk in newness of life" (Rom. 6:4). There is no need to earn salvation by literally conforming ourselves to Christ's suffering.

Paul says the news that we have been objectively accepted by God, without a price that has to be paid in our blood, won't lead any who truly believe that news to multiply their sins out of a sense of immunity. There is a parallel idea hidden under this one. If we were required to suffer like Jesus in order to be righteous before God, that would in fact necessarily mean that sin must abound. For the multiplication of suffering like that of Jesus can mean only the multiplication of sin. Paul has looked far enough down that path to see that it cannot be the right one.

I have been trying to clarify the simple point that suffering as Jesus did plays no necessary part in the Christian life. Yet at times those who follow the Christian life may end by being forced onto a cross. We cannot deny that for many faithful Christians their baptism in water was matched by a baptism in blood. This was famously the fate of Peter and Paul and other apostles. To give continuing witness to Christ's death and resurrection, and to imitate Christ's love, can place people in the path of persecution.

Paul is ready to follow Christ into that danger, but he realizes he is not obligated to seek it.

The early church at times had to restrain an enthusiasm for martyrdom. The restraint is important, since it emphasized just the point we have been making. There is no value in gratuitous suffering, and it should not be a Christian ideal. The enthusiasm for martyrdom was fueled by many factors, some of which were not peculiar to Christians (such as the idea that a noble death would get you a through ticket to heaven). Even here, however, there is an interesting touch. An admiration for suicide (something Christians were forbidden) was common in the ancient world, and a stoic attitude toward suffering was also a virtue in some philosophies. Christian martyrdom was not distinguished simply by the acceptance of death or the presence of suffering. It required the peculiar additional condition of dying as an explicit victim of unjust persecution, a confessor bearing witness for Jesus, the innocent scapegoat. This distinctive element is *location,* we might say, location on the side of the scapegoats. The church's argument with those who were avid for martyrdom did not dispute their conclusion about the location faith pointed them to, but objected that no one should seek to occupy it.

If we could take an example much closer at hand, we can think of Martin Luther King, Jr. King can hardly be regarded as a man who sought death or idealized suffering. His program of nonviolent resistance was a way of life and struggle, a desire neither to inflict nor to suffer evil. It called African Americans both to refuse to be victims any longer and to refuse to victimize. King's encounter with Mahatma Gandhi's thought and work sparked what was at first only a personal realization. Shortly afterward, when King was thrust into the leadership of the Montgomery bus boycott, that realization would become the seed of a transformative social movement. The realization was that nonresistance to evil, which many Christian pacifists took as Jesus' example on the cross, was not the same thing as nonviolence. Nonviolence could be a strategy, a powerful force, for active resistance and transformation. Innocent suffering was not an intrinsic good, important as a mark of one's own moral purity. Abstaining from violence could be a way of changing the world, not a way of standing aside from it. Here was a way of understanding the cross as a way of life, not as a call to become a victim, but as a mandate to refuse to be a victim. The reason this became the basis for a social movement rather than simply the idiosyncratic idea of an individual, rests in the fact that it could be grounded in the existing faith of the African American church and of wider Christian circles, the faith in the crucified one.

David Garrow's fine study of King is titled *Bearing the Cross*.[19] The title is wonderfully ambiguous. It can be taken to refer to the suffering that King and others in the movement endured as a result of their stand. It can be taken to refer to an outward sign, in the sense that the civil rights advocates marched, spoke, and sang with the explicit images of the Christian gospel and of the passion. And it can be taken in yet a further way that combines both: King and his movement held up before the eyes of a nation, side by side, the evident oppression of African Americans and the central symbol of the Christian faith. In that sense King uncovered, bared, the cross and set it before us in a way that made its relevance inescapable. The voice that had spoken to Paul — "I am Jesus, whom you are persecuting" — could not be stilled. King was killed as a result of his work. But his driving desire was not to imitate Christ's crucifixion. It was to imitate Christ's desire to end sacrifice. His model was not the cross, but the way of life the cross inspired. His public life was a profound struggle to lead a nation to realize its unity without scapegoats. It was a life completely shaped by a hope for the new community the cross makes possible, what King called "the beloved community."

When we consider the KKK and their burning crosses, there is a sense in which the civil rights struggle can rightly be seen as a battle over the cross. What side was it on? Who spoke for it? Crucifixion, or in this case assassination, was not needed to make Martin Luther King's ministry more fully Christian or King's "imitation" of Jesus any deeper. The effect of that assassination on others, however, is telling. King's death was like Jesus' death, a fact so obvious and compelling that it needed no commentary and effectively ended any battle over the cross in the civil rights era. It could not credibly be claimed for the service of racism when it had been demonstrated so dramatically where Jesus' place would have been in this struggle.

To summarize, in the practice of sacrifice a victim's suffering and death are required, false accusation is believed, divine justification for persecution is affirmed, collective agreement is enforced, and the victim's voice is silenced. When suffering comes in the course of the Christian life, its character should be the opposite of this. It should arise only by virtue of resistance to all of these sacrificial elements, not because of their acceptance.

---

19. David J. Garrow, *Bearing the Cross: Martin Luther King, Jr., and the Southern Christian Leadership Conference,* 1st ed. (New York: Morrow, 1986).

The Scope of Sacrifice

If the first criticism of the theology of the cross was that it invited suffering, the second has been that it underwrites domination and violence. The supposition that God demands an innocent sacrifice to balance out the guilt of humanity has been attacked as a charter for earthly powers to practice sacrificial violence in God's name. The idea that Christ's death provided an infinite satisfaction to offset humanity's infinite offense is taken to empower those who regard themselves as the custodians of that merit with the right to conquer and condemn others. The apparent contradiction in these two criticisms — the cross makes Christians abase themselves and it makes them exalt themselves — does not mean they don't have substance. Christianity can in fact go wrong in both these ways. That reflects the paradox of the Gospel narrative itself. If both sides are not in order, then either one or both will go astray.

The way of life that follows on the cross depends on recognition that the death of Jesus ought not to happen. It is not God's recipe that innocent suffering is the way to restore peace: God's purpose (to end such a pattern) is superimposed on that event of humanly sanctified violence. Sacrificial scapegoating is not something invented by those under the spell of the passion narratives, but something revealed and opposed there. Just as it is an error to think that it is somehow a Christian requirement to be a victim of redemptive violence, so it is an error to think there is a Christian responsibility to administer it. Christian parenting that goes far astray in this sense will claim some need to apply violent coercion or inflict pain for general redemptive purposes (to break an ungodly spirit or teach submission) rather than any proportionate specific ones.

Rather than insist on being victims, the Christian way of life calls us to do without victims. Faithfulness in that effort is however no guarantee that one will not encounter suffering. In a parallel way, rather than employ the structures of sacrificial violence, the Christian way of life calls us to find alternative forms to build community. Faithfulness in that effort, however, does not mean that valid human order is emptied of all elements of coercion.

Some critical reconstructions (or rejections) of the theology of the cross conclude that the only authentic Christian life is one of absolute pacifism or total nonviolence.[20] This conclusion may be correct, but if so

---

20. An example we have already noted would be Weaver, *The Nonviolent Atonement* (Grand Rapids: Eerdmans, 2001). Another would be Wink, *Engaging the Powers*.

it needs more than an analysis of the cross to establish it. I have stressed that the cross does not in principle address all suffering, nor does it address all conceivable violence. Its direct relevance to those must be traced from its primary focus on scapegoating sacrifice and on the tributary forms of mimetic conflict that lead to it. In confronting this kind of collectively sanctioned violence from the place of the suffering victim, God neither sanctified all suffering nor condemned all collective sanction.[21]

"Scapegoating" and "sacrifice" are terms we have applied to cases other than ritual and cultic ones. Indeed, following Girard, I have argued that the ritual and cultic practices in fact stem from (or are assimilated to) a prior kind of social violence. Such supposed "founding murders" or recurrent social dynamics have a very particular profile. Not all violence or coercion falls within that profile. It is a measure of the impact of the biblical tradition that in Western thought particularly there are strong tendencies to collapse the two.

Christian theology throughout its history has had to make assessments. Where does the pattern of sacrificial violence apply, though we may not have realized it? And where is that not the appropriate category? There are "private" forms of sin, like dishonesty or theft or one person's physical assault on another. Christian life and faith certainly address these wrongs. But they are not the same wrong as sacred violence, even if these personal sins feed in various ways into the social dynamics that support that violence. And there are dimensions of collective coercion, even violence, that are not sacrificial in the sense in which I've been speaking. They may or may not be consistent with a Christian way of life, but that cannot be decided simply by reference to the distinctive meaning of the cross we have explored.

The leveling of taxes is a coercive collective act, and the enforcement of that act may involve imprisonment and even bodily violence against those who resist it. But a tax code does not in principle constitute sacrificial violence. Nor does an economic structure in which some people succeed more than others. Nor does a legal system in which after due process people can be deprived of property and liberty. Nor does abortion. Nor does a police force that at the extreme exercises deadly force. Nor does war.

Christians can argue theologically for or against participation in any of these structures or activities, without necessarily making reference to

---

21. For a rare and thoughtful contemporary defense of violence as a part of the divine salvific activity, see Boersma, *Violence, Hospitality, and the Cross: Reappropriating the Atonement Tradition* (Grand Rapids: Baker Academic, 2004).

the cross. Any of these can exhibit features of scapegoating or become captive to sacrificial violence. And an absolute Christian prohibition against participation in one of them might well include an argument that by its nature it must necessarily devolve into sacrificial uses. None of them figure in the final Christian hope for the redeemed life. But the understanding of the cross we have set out does not settle our Christian questions about these matters. The one clear, special standard it offers us is an understanding of sacrifice and an invitation to live without scapegoating. Therefore at the very least Christians must challenge any of these systems or practices, or others, when and insofar as they become instruments for that sacrificial violence.

The discussion over the last few pages may have disappointed people who are sympathetic to the antisacrificial reading of the passion on the assumption that it requires an ethic of absolute nonviolence. I sharpen the issue because I do not think the passion narratives by themselves resolve that question. The full dimensions of the Christian life cannot be constructed from the cross alone. There is also a good practical reason to frame the question more modestly. Those on the various theological sides of the long-standing arguments touched on above are unlikely to come to sudden resolution of those differences. But it would represent a significant step forward if those on different sides could agree that unveiling and overturning scapegoating violence is a major dimension of Christ's saving work, and perhaps the distinctive one associated with the specific plot of Jesus' death.

We could agree that this is included in what we mean when we confess that Christ died for us, even though it is not the sum total of what we mean. While other differences of interpretation remain, this agreement would go a long way to heal our theologies of the cross. If this conviction were solidly established at the heart of our faith, we would be less liable to fall into the destructive readings that have fostered masochism, destructive surrogacy, passive suffering, and sanctified violence. That common ground would clarify the true connection and continuity between the meaning of the cross and the way of life Christians are called to follow. It would resolve much of the contradiction so many see or feel between the example of Jesus and the New Testament prescriptions for the Christian life on one hand, and the supposed violent mechanism of God's saving purpose in the crucifixion on the other.

Toward Abolition of the Cross

The perspective set out in this book has great promise for fruitful interaction with other strands of theology. This is certainly true of liberation theology, broadly conceived. C. S. Song has written that the task of Christian mission is "to work toward the abolition of the cross," the cross understood as "the height of human cruelty and the depth of God's suffering with humanity."[22] For many such thinkers, the church's existing theology is an obstacle in the attempt to confront the scandal of a crucified world. The reverence for the cross in the church appears unrelated, or even counter, to the struggle to end the suffering of the oppressed. But this need not be so.

Distinctive theological approaches such as the feminist, womanist, Latino/a or African American each contain much more than the issue of sacrifice. It is not that these approaches could somehow be subsumed in this theology of the cross. Instead, that theology provides a clear, specific link that connects them all and an added biblical root that supports each one. Each of these theological approaches encompasses unique features and interpretations that go beyond the dynamic of scapegoating sacrifice. But that dynamic does figure powerfully in all the contexts those theologies address. There are other kinds of oppression than scapegoating, but few fail to generate their own version of it. An analysis of the sacrificial process in light of the cross is something that all these varied approaches can share, even while each particular theology of liberation retains a unique perspective.

The anthropology of the cross sets out God's concrete solidarity with victims, and a sharp critique of the collective mechanisms of violence turned against them. It is a supple instrument, for its critique goes to root dynamics of division, contagion, violence, and unity. Its application is not limited to one social setting or a single set of issues. Various liberation movements prioritize different factors in their analysis: economic, racial, sex and gender, religious, cultural. As the movements come into mutual critique and cooperation, it becomes clear that no one of these elements can claim to account for all the others. Nor does the anthropology of the cross do so. But it identifies a dimension that cuts across them all, a thread of insight that unites them without replacing them.

An example of what I have in mind was given by a 1990 consultation of

---

22. Chaon Seng Song, "Christian Mission toward Abolition of the Cross," in *The Scandal of a Crucified World*, ed. Yacob Tesfai (Maryknoll, N.Y.: Orbis, 1994), 148.

liberation theologians in Brazil, organized to explore the thought of René Girard.[23] The timing of the event, following on the collapse of communism in Europe and the Soviet Union, was telling. Liberation thinkers were particularly interested in ways that Girard's social analysis overlapped with their own concerns. But that analysis rooted itself directly in the gospel, and thus bypassed many problems surrounding Marxist thought and communist practice and their integration with theology.

These discussions focused primarily on economic issues and on the violence exercised in the name of national security. Girard had hitherto given little attention to economic issues, and liberation theologians had given little to sacrifice. Together they explored both sides of this question. They explored on the one hand the ways a purely economic analysis had obscured understanding of patterns of oppression in actual communist states, patterns illuminated by mimetic theory and the nature of scapegoating sacrifice. And they explored on the other hand the way unjust economic structures could be seen to parallel a ritualistic sacrificial system. As Elsa Tamez puts it, "An economic system that demands the sacrifice of innocent people in order to be able to function well is intolerable . . . it acquires the characteristics of an idol that demands sacrifices of human lives."[24] Economic oppression can take on the character of ritualized sacrifice, in which outbreaks of violent repression represent a reversion to collective scapegoating in the face of threats to the unity of the system.

This is a genuine, two-way conversation. One of the notes emphasized in the discussion is that division and crisis in a community (the assumed evils that sacrifice is to solve) may rightly be prompted by opposition to injustice. In Girard's terms, social division is presented essentially as an evil for which sacrifice is an evil remedy. But his conversation partners underline the fact that Jesus himself creates division by opposing settled features of the social and religious order. Social conflict is not an unequivocally bad thing, even if sacrificial responses to it are. The return of the crucified one is a witness that this crisis cannot be abolished by sacrifice, but only by a resolution of the injustice.

The liberation thinkers recognized that in moving the basis of analysis

23. This appreciative conversation was organized by some leading Latin American figures, and involved direct interaction with Girard. See Hugo Assmann and René Girard, *René Girard com Teologos da Libertacao: Um Dialogo sobre Idolos e Sacrificios* (Petrópolis: Editora Vozes; Piracicaba: Editora UMIMEP, 1991).

24. Elsa Tamez, *The Amnesty of Grace: Justification by Faith from a Latin American Perspective* (Nashville: Abingdon, 1993), 159.

back to the Bible, Girard's approach promised to significantly enhance their project. This is particularly true since in the Latin American context one of the crucial concerns is a critique and transformation of sacrificial forms of Christianity. This is a process that can proceed most powerfully when the point of departure is itself at the very heart of the tradition.

The intersection of the theology of liberation and a renewed theology of the cross also offers a basis of connection with the faith of the poor themselves. The victimized and the afflicted have always found a special affinity with the crucified Christ, despite the counsel of critics that this attraction is not in their best interests. The perspective we have outlined indicates good reasons why that is so. But it also articulates clearly from the inside of that commitment to the cross why God's presence there is not meant simply to provide companionship in misery or to signal passive acceptance of evil. It was a transcendent, and transforming, act of resistance.

In Central America it is not unusual to see representations of the cross in which Christ appears explicitly as a peasant farmer. One well-known artistic representation, called *Cristo campesino*, depicts such a peasant crucified on a shovel whose crossbeam is the typical peasant's machete. The context for these images usually makes clear that they do not manifest a passive acceptance of suffering in the lives of the poor. Quite the contrary, they express a conviction that God identifies with their condition and sides with them in the struggle for a transformed social world. The perspectives on Bible and tradition that we have sketched help to fill in the theological framework that supports this conviction and roots it firmly in the sources.

The Model of Jesus' Desire

The trajectory of the cross in history is such that images like the one I just described increasingly strike us as protest. But taken alone, in conjunction with certain kinds of theologies, the representations could be taken as counsels of resignation or invitations to imitate Christ's supposed docile submission to oppression. This points up the fact that concrete images of the crucifixion are liable to the same ambiguity that attaches to any images of suffering. This tension was powerfully reflected in the controversy surrounding Edwina Sandys's 1975 sculpture *Christa*, which depicted a partially nude female form in the traditional crucifix pose. Many objected to the image as a departure from tradition and an assault on the christological particularity of Christian faith. But it was also criticized variously as an objectification of women, an incitement to abuse, or an invitation to women to idealize their own suffering. When presented with a relatively novel image like this, our visceral responses testify to the way the liberating power of the cross is entangled with sacrificial and mythical tendencies. Those who objected to the sculpture because it did not represent the historical Jesus, and who wanted no explicit parallels, missed the point that part of the saving effect in that unique death was enabling us to see others in the same place. Those who dismissed the objections, and would willingly have replaced focal emphasis on the cross of Jesus with an array of representations of the oppressed, misunderstand the ambiguous nature of images of suffering in themselves.

Images of violation, suffering, and condemnation can readily become incitement or prurient stimulation. Without a tie to the particular objectivity of God's death on the cross, the sight of a suffering victim from my group can very easily arouse only a desire for retribution. It is exhibited as an atrocity that reinforces the unity of our rage against our enemies. Such images, whatever else may be said of them, are not equivalents to the cross. For an integral element of the cross is that we cannot attribute it only to others. Without a tie to the cross of Jesus, the sight of a suffering victim who is outside my own circle of identity can all too easily arouse a kind of perverse satisfaction, a sense of just condemnation, or a distanced indifference. This is no equivalent to the cross either. For another integral element is that we must identify with its victim.

There will be those who reject the cross for just the reasons noted. Some advocates of the oppressed will reject it because they believe no shadow of hesitation should fall on the white-hot anger of the aggrieved against their oppressors. And there will be those who stand in positions of advantage and power who will reject it for essentially the same reason, because no matter the legitimate case they may make for the relative justice and peace of their communities, the cross insistently requires them to ask anew, who are our victims? If when we look at the cross we see only and always the face of Jesus, its saving power has not fully reached us. If it had, we would be able to see others. But if we substitute only our preferred others, we have warded off its power as well. To be converted is to be able to see ourselves and those we love on the cross with Christ. But it is no less to be able to see our own faces in the crowd, a crowd gathered against a Christ who looks much like a stranger or an enemy.

For the Christian life generally, and particularly for understanding the cross, the crucial thing is not imitation of Jesus' actions, but the formation of our intentions and behavior through the model of Jesus' desire. A consistent desire that animates Jesus' ministerial life, his antisacrificial death, and his risen witness is the desire to overcome scapegoating as the means of social reconciliation. This is the subjectivity that unifies Jesus' resolution to go to the cross and his anguished recoil from it, that unifies the Gospels' testimony that his death saves the world and is an evil that must be reversed. This is the example that calls Christians to remember Christ's death in order to avert others, and exhibits the truth of sacrifice in order to end it. There is in Jesus no desire for death, and no desire for suffering. The reluctance, fear, anguish, and desolation that the passion narratives show us are precious testimony on this point. If we want to become "like him in his death," then the likeness we must imitate is the longing to empty the world of crosses.

The victims of sacrifice die to keep things the same — to restore communal peace in the face of conflict and to validate yet again the ancient solution to social crisis, the eternal return of the scapegoat. Christ died as such a victim, subject to that same intention on the part of his executioners, but without sharing it. His death was an act of resistance to scapegoating death, not an endorsement of it. He died to change things, most specifically to end this way of keeping the peace. He died to change the repetitive dying to maintain the world.

Those who would follow his teaching and his desire and his example, then, should have no desire to join him on the cross. If we did have such an aim, then Christ's death would be in vain. The intended reign of God is a life without crosses, peace without scapegoats. Short of the reign of God, may the faithful Christian life lead to suffering? May it bring the specific suffering of the scapegoat or of those who cross to the side of scapegoats? Yes. The only thing redemptive about such suffering is that it participates in Christ's reversal of the redemptive violence the world practices, arbitrary victimization to heal our discord. It is Christlike only if it opposes suffering. It is acceptable only if it is resistance. It is legitimate only if its desire is to end what it must endure.

CHAPTER NINE

The Bad News about Revelation

Two Kinds of Apocalypses

For if we willfully persist in sin after having received the knowledge of the truth, there no longer remains a sacrifice for sins, but a fearful prospect of judgment, and a fury of fire that will consume the adversaries.

Hebrews 10:26-27

[T]hat pseudo-humanism that calls itself Christianity intends precisely to forbid that anyone be sacrificed.

Friedrich Nietzsche[1]

C hristians claim that Christ's death changed the world. The life of the church attempts to embody the alternative that change made possible. Believers and nonbelievers will probably not be able to agree whether the history of the church and the effect of faith in countless individual lives have decisively changed the world for the better, at least to a measure that supports the claim of a decisive shift in world history. Christians and Christianity have definitely been instruments of evil as well, and what some believers would attribute to distortions of faith and the gospel, other observers might see as natural expressions of them.

---

1. René Girard and Michel Treguer, *Quand Ces Choses Commenceront* (Paris: Arlea, 1994), quoting Nietzsche, *Oeuvres complètes*, XIV, "Fragments Posthumes," 88-89 (Paris: Gallimard, 1977), 224-25.

The unresolved state of that question would tend to suggest that an exemplarist view of the cross is the correct one: the effect of Jesus' death is the response it has inspired in Christians. As the spectrum of those responses is mixed, so, we could say, is the impact of Christ's death. It is only what people make of it, and has no intrinsic impact of its own. If it actually were an event whose very occurrence objectively changed the world, then surely the world would look changed in some more obvious and consistent way.

Visible Victims

In fact, it does. With the benefit of the long view of history, we can see at least one empirical way that the world has changed in the wake of the gospel: victims have become visible.[2] No faith is required to recognize this. It is a massive change that we can miss only because it is so encompassing and because we have come to take it for granted. The fact that those in history who are victims of Christianity and those who can be construed as such are so prominent on our mental landscape is a case in point. The church is attacked (often with justice) in the name of victims by Marxists and feminists and advocates for racial justice. Why is it that Marxism and feminism and the global antislavery movement are themselves products of cultures shaped by the biblical tradition? We regularly condemn our societies for failure to do more for the poor or disadvantaged, in our own nations or around the world. And we tend to frame this not in terms of positive works of charity deferred but in terms of justice denied. Where does this concern for victims — even the recognition that they should be seen as victims — come from?

If we are outraged at the unique depredations of the West, is there something unique about our outrage? If this does not stem principally from the biblical tradition, where does it come from? Even if one were to claim (implausibly, I think) that these are all exclusively the product of an antireligious enlightenment rationalism, the question remains. Why should a rationalism with this particular character arise only in the context of the biblical witness? Even our characteristic harsh criticisms of Christianity seem in major part borrowed from it. The growing visibility

---

2. This paragraph only restates points Girard has made in many places. See especially René Girard, Jean-Michel Oughourlian, and Guy Lefort, *Things Hidden since the Foundation of the World* (Stanford, Calif.: Stanford University Press, 1987).

of victims, and the gradual and uneven recognition that more and more people count as such, is directly related to the biblical revelation. Before that leaven had worked on culture, Girard says, few would have "affirmed that a victim, even one unanimously condemned by his community and the powers that hold legitimate jurisdiction over him, could be justified over against that unanimity. This extraordinary attitude could only come from the Passion, interpreted in the perspective of the gospels."[3]

Greek or Roman functionaries would have found the idea that victims have rights incomprehensible. Defeated peoples will seek vengeance and rivals will seek to best each other — this they would understand well enough. But that the persecuted might confront their unanimous persecutors with the expectation that their innocence should be recognized and vindicated — this would be ludicrous. The very notion of persecution as we commonly understand it, like that of scapegoating, is hard to imagine apart from the sources we have reviewed. Today, when the notion of absolute truth or absolute values is frequently derided, this value appears to have become absolute, contested by no one. We can hardly defend any position effectively in our culture without claiming to side with victims. As this concern has become universalized, it has become itself at times an instrument of injustice. One can no longer victimize or sacrifice successfully except in the name of victims. Here Christian anti-Semitism has set a sad model.

To say that victims have become more visible is also to say that the mythological rationalization of sacrifice has been progressively weakened, wherever the narratives of the crucified one have spread. This process is by no means identical with Western culture. But for a period, that culture was a major theater of this transformation, for good and for ill. Movements against scapegoating and in support of persecuted groups of many descriptions rose. But so did new kinds of violence. The process is a double-edged sword. Sacrificial mechanisms did function effectively, if unjustly, to restrain reciprocal violence. As the workings of the mechanism become more obvious, and the reality of the victims less avoidable, society is thrown into a new kind of sacrificial crisis. The old mythological scapegoating solutions can be applied only with greater effort and stress (often scapegoating must use antiscapegoating language), and with more limited success. But the nonsacrificial social alternatives presented in the gospel require radical personal and social transformations that have been at best only partially realized. Sacrificial crises can become

---

3. Girard and Treguer, *Quand Ces Choses Commenceront,* 123.

more acute as the mythological solution fades and nonviolent alternatives struggle to be born.

This is the deep truth in the New Testament vision of apocalypse. Heightened stakes and dramatic choices are placed before the world wherever the nonsacrificial revelation comes into it. In this sense, Jesus brought not peace but a sword. Our societies can hardly live without the old myths of sacrifice and their updated versions, yet our awareness of their victimization of the innocent drains their capacity to reestablish peace among us. Our societies can hardly live with a nonsacrificial vision, for that requires a trust in transcendence, an openness to "religion" and conversion, which we pride ourselves on having outgrown. The paradox of the passion has become our cultural paradox. There is no way back to untroubled mythical sacrifice, and there seems no way forward to a new creation.

Apocalyptic

A recurrent theme in our discussion of the cross has been the ambiguity of its revelation. Old-fashioned sacrifice is a bad thing with real results in curbing violence. The passion narratives unmask the injustice of scapegoating and show God's vindication of the victim. But this liberating message can be turned into a new pattern for persecution, as in Christian anti-Semitism. Now I am suggesting that the presence of the biblical message in the world truly has had the transforming effect of making us aware of victims, and our own complicity in collective violence. But this is not unalloyed good news, because this awareness can accelerate violence as well as end it.

One genre of violence in the Bible that we have not yet discussed is found in apocalyptic texts, like the book of Revelation. These texts look toward future cataclysms of conflict, end-of-the-world catastrophes, battles between armies of light and darkness. Here God seems to be fully recruited into a frenzy of cosmic destruction. Such texts are frequently read as predictive timetables, psychological fantasies, obscure allegories, or veiled references to conflicts long past. It rarely occurs to anyone to read them as empirical, if symbolic, analysis.

Apocalyptic confronts us with judgment. Its primary focus is not the judgment and division of individuals, but the final resolution of world history and the fate of human community. It is about collective judgment. In apocalyptic texts an old world is disintegrating and dying. A new world is being born in fire. These texts often contrast two alternatives, the reign of God and the reign of the antichrist. The texts indicate that those two alternatives, so totally opposite in their import, may appear to have a strange and dangerously misleading similarity. The antichrist may appear as an angel of light, and, as Jesus says in the Gospel of John, "an hour is coming when those who kill you will think that by doing so they are offering worship to God" (John 16:2).

In the passion narratives, but also in the Old Testament, we find a descriptively honest depiction of the nature of the long train of sacrificial violence that lies behind us in history. In apocalyptic we have an equally honest description of *future* violence that can follow upon that revelation. Apocalypse happens, we may say, when the old reconciling power of sacred violence withers and the new way to peace fails. In fact, there are two distinct paths to an apocalyptic future, and for each of them the cross has a catalytic role. On one path the unveiling of sacrifice and its victims objectively changes the world by undermining the mechanism of sacred violence, leaving no effective substitute. The cross works to deconstruct, we might say, but its positive meaning has much less effect. In such a situation the sacrificial solution is applied with redoubled, even frenzied, effort, but with diminishing success. Redemptive violence is assimilated to the contagious conflict it is supposed to calm. The social world implodes of its own weight.

On the other path the divine vindication of victims objectively changes the world by calling forth attempts at completely new forms of solidarity. The cross inspires attempts to abolish existing human communities and replace them with a totally new construction, organized in the name of victims. The need for a positive alternative to sacrifice is grasped, but it is grasped in a violent way. Injustice against scapegoats becomes a charter for an unrestrained tide of righteous wrath against their oppressors. A new world can arise only from the eradication of the sacrificial system. So wide and deep do the roots of that system go that there are literally no limits to the reach of the violence that will be employed to displace it.

The inevitability expressed in these texts is not that of absolute predestination or divine approval, but the reflection of the historical arrow of time. From the New Testament's point of view, the cross has changed the world. It has ended sacrifice, not in the sense that it can no longer happen, but in the sense that its viability is doomed. From the moment of Christ's death and resurrection, the future of a world that does not convert like Paul to the side of the scapegoat, that does not learn to live reconciliation without crosses, has been set. And that future is given in the apocalyptic passages.

Just as It Was in the Days of Noah

The description or prediction of an explosion of violence is not the same thing as a claim that God is the one who requires it. This is an important distinction to keep in mind. A second distinction is the one between violence that is a disintegration of human factionalism and violence that is a war of cosmic revenge. And a third distinction is the difference between defining God's wrath as anger against violence and defining it as the righteous exercise of violence. Biblical apocalyptic texts combine these features in different proportions, sometimes inclining to combine the first elements in each of our set of distinctions, sometimes the second elements. The first combination we might call the more evangelical setting, because the apocalyptic texts in the three Synoptic Gospels lean strongly in that direction, while major parts of the book of Revelation, for example, lean strongly in the other.

The apocalyptic scenario can be seen on the one hand as dissipative chaos, the collapse of human communities into unrestrained factional strife, and on the other hand as a final cosmic battle between great spiritual superpowers, armies of light and darkness. In the twentieth century, history threatened to overtake apocalyptic, with its own concrete analogies for these alternatives. The Cold War held out the possibility of an organized Armageddon that could wipe out human society, a final war that lived up to the most lurid hyperbole of the book of Revelation. The collapse of that global dualism only uncovered atavistic forms of violence in the Balkans, Africa, and elsewhere, particularistic hatreds that sprang up each on its own ground, and threatened to spread more widely.

The apocalyptic passages in the Synoptic Gospels picture a world self-destructing. There is no direct claim that God will rain disaster on the earth, but a simple description of human society tearing itself to pieces. Jesus says, "For nation will rise up against nation, and kingdom against kingdom, and there will be famines and earthquakes in various places: all this is but the beginning of the birth pangs. Then they will hand you over to be tortured and will put you to death, and you will be hated by all nations because of my name. Then many will fall away, and they will betray one another and hate one another. And many false prophets will arise and lead many astray. And because of the increase of lawlessness, the love of many will grow cold" (Matt. 24:7-12). In those days it will be "just as it was in the days of Noah" (Luke 17:26). That is, people will be caught up in their own spiral of conflict and violence. But whereas in the days of Noah God destroyed the world because of its violence, these Gospel passages predict no such thing. God's promise not to repeat that act will apparently hold. God and God's angels appear only to rescue and deliver those who belong to the kingdom of God (Matt. 24:30-31). There is no cosmic battle of evil forces and good forces. The conflict is entirely between human protagonists, generated by hatred and rivalry. God's wrath plays no role in the account, except in the criticism of those who lead people into this cataclysm.

The description I have just given applies well to the "little apocalypses" in Luke 17 and Mark 13. It applies also to the parallel passages in Matthew 24. In Matthew these are followed by some portions in which God does figure (first in parable and then in an explicit description) as a judge who actively divides the sheep from the goats, with the latter being told to depart into eternal fire. This is the famous text in Matthew 25, where final judgment proceeds on the assumption that whoever has shown mercy to the "least of these" has done so to Jesus. It is Jesus' identification with victims and with those most likely to be scapegoated that is the key criterion for judgment. In the Gospels, then, the apocalyptic scenario is predominantly one of a world in dissolution from which God rescues the faithful, and when the note of an active divine judgment appears, it comes in a form that makes the practice of mercy and the avoidance of sacrifice the norm.

The Wrath of the Lamb

The picture in the book of Revelation is different in a number of ways, not least because its language of symbol and image contrasts with the comparatively straightforward statements in the Gospels. But in rough terms we may say it reverses the proportions in the picture we just described. In one passage the lamb who has been slain opens seven sealed scrolls. At the opening of the fifth seal, the writer sees under an altar the "souls of those who had been slaughtered for the word of God and for the testimony they had given" (Rev. 6:9). They cry out to God for vengeance: "How long will it be before you judge and avenge our blood on the inhabitants of the earth?" Then, the passage goes on, "the kings of the earth and the magnates and the generals and the rich and the powerful, and everyone, slave and free, hid in the caves and among the rocks of the mountains, calling to the mountains and rocks, 'Fall on us and hide us from the face of the one seated on the throne and from the wrath of the Lamb; for the great day of their wrath has come, and who is able to stand?'"

The visions of Revelation are very much about the wrath of God. That wrath is focused in a very particular way. The lamb who has been slain is the risen Christ, who appears now as the vindicator of all those who have been put on the sacrificial altar. The martyrs and the slain speak up and claim justice against their collective persecutors. Armies rise to support them. Considering all the innocent blood shed "from the foundation of the world," how awful must be the wrath of the Lamb if it actually were to be executed. The book of Job posed a challenge to God's righteousness because God allowed victims to go undefended. The book of Revelation raises the unsettling vision of what must happen if Job's cry is answered. Once all scapegoats are visible, their rights acknowledged, their cause defended, and revenge taken in their name, apocalypse is at hand.

In this text God enlists in a full-scale battle on behalf of the victims against all the powers and persecutors. The Lamb goes to war, and Michael and the angels cast down the great dragon with his angels or demons. Given our earlier discussion of the way the New Testament characterizes Satan (as the instigator of mimetic conflict and the master of sacrificial violence), the finale is striking. "The great dragon was thrown down, that ancient serpent, who is called the Devil and Satan, the deceiver of the whole world — he was thrown down to the earth, and his angels were thrown down with him" (Rev. 12:9). A loud voice from heaven proclaims that the kingdom of God and Christ has come,

> for the accuser of our comrades has been thrown down,
>   who accuses them day and night before our God.
> But they have conquered him by the blood of the Lamb
>   and by the word of their testimony. (12:10-11)

Satan, who in Job had tempted even God toward violent rivalry, who is the sower of conflict and the lord of sacrifice, is violently cast down. Even in the midst of this battle, the text says the true liberating forces are the blood of the cross and the word of testimony in favor of victims. The revenge of the sacrificed is directed preeminently at the "beast," the powers that enlist humans in violence and blaspheme against God. And yet this revenge falls also on those humans who serve or are captive to these powers. Vivid and fervid, the violence of divine rectification in this text seems a mirror image of the sacrificial forces whose destruction it describes.

Although we think of apocalyptic as coming at the end — it describes the end of the world and its most famous text is at the end of the Bible — these texts are by no means the final or most developed expressions of the

Christian revelation. They need to be interpreted from the center of the passion narratives and the Gospels rather than the other way around. Nevertheless, they add an important element to the whole story. The New Testament makes a very uncomfortable presumption. The revelation of the sacrifice at the foundation of our cultural order will not necessarily lead to peace. Quite the contrary. The real, if transitory and unjust, peace that stems from sacrifice will increasingly weaken if sacrifice itself can no longer be carried out in mythic confidence, if it is increasingly tainted with bad conscience and impeded by dissenters. The result will be intensified scapegoating and/or unrestrained war against sacrifice: intensification of all sorts. Things may well get worse, not better, as in the parable of the house from which one demon was cast out and into which seven others then came to dwell, and the last state is worse than the first (Luke 11:26).

Looking Like Jesus

Through the cross, something very unsettling has been introduced into the world, a kind of crisis. The whole creation has been groaning in labor pains, Paul writes. As with childbirth, things cannot stay as they are. The only way is forward. The old sacrificial path — the way of the powers and principalities of this world — is failing, and may call forth greater violence as it fails. The revelation that makes victims visible, by its very nature undermines the mythic order, eliciting intense efforts to shore it up. And the more vivid that visibility, the more it heightens the urge for retribution, the stronger it makes the longing for another social foundation. This tends to unleash utopian absolutism. But Christ did not die to make mythic sacrifice more costly still or to drown it in a final cataclysm of counterviolence. These apocalyptic scenarios are, we might say, default options. They are the ways history will respond to the effects of the cross if it cannot be converted by them. They are forms of false labor, painful but unproductive.

In scriptural apocalyptic the true last thing is neither the self-destruction of the world nor a climactic battle. It is a new creation into which people are adopted, a new Jerusalem that comes down from heaven. Here is another possibility that grows up alongside the apocalyptic ones. It is the one we examined in the last chapter, the development of a new contagion of reconciliation and peace to substitute for the unanimity of sacrifice. This new possibility lies open also, but it requires a transformation of the most daunting depth. The violent sacred as a dam against reciprocal destruction is eroding, and people must repent and seek a nonsacrificial basis for reconciliation. Otherwise, the future is a catastrophic one. The biblical writers in these millennial texts posed an ultimate boundary question. If the future does become apocalyptic, does that mean that the possibility of the reign of God will be truly defeated? Their answer was no. Even out of apocalyptic fire God can rescue the design for creation. But that is no endorsement of apocalyptic ends. They stand at the end of the Bible's history as the first sins or stand at its beginning, showing how God's purpose in creation can be opposed but not defeated.

The sober wisdom of apocalyptic is the recognition that a heightened sensitivity to victims is compatible with the unleashing of new depths of violence. In fact, the two are related. Christianity has traveled through history in many versions. So long as the basic structure of the Gospels remains, even corruptions of church and doctrine seem unable to block one cultural effect. That effect is a corrosion of the mythical foundations of sacrifice, the contagion of a disruptive empathy with victims.

If sacrifice is the use of "good" violence to drive out bad violence, its effectiveness depends on people being able to keep that distinction straight. In the fully mythic situation, this is accomplished because "good" violence does not even register as violence at all when it is recorded or remembered. The influence of the biblical tradition is to make the nature of sacrifice more evident and victims more visible. As a result, the cathartic unanimity of scapegoating violence becomes harder to keep in place. Once the question "why is this killing different from the killing it is meant to stop?" is asked, it becomes more and more difficult to answer unequivocally. The bright line maintained by ritual and myth between sacred violence and the violence it restrains begins to blur.

Gil Bailie illustrates this by noting Charles Dickens's lonely repugnance at happening upon a London crowd gathered in near festival mood for a public execution, an event in which they all were enthusiastic participants. He contrasts that with our current uneasiness about execution. Some opponents of capital punishment have actively campaigned to require that executions be public, on the assumption that this would turn opinion irrevocably against the practice. It is hard to understand that confidence apart from a biblical background. Why would we be sure such a public display would not inflame people's desire for killing instead, a dynamic for which we have ample evidence?

One may rightly observe that legal executions are hardly true cases of scapegoating. The guilt of the condemned may be beyond question, and elaborate steps are taken in the judicial process to remove the elements of mob rule, to defend the rights of the accused, to disassociate their specific case from larger social passions. All this is true, but at a profound level it counts for less than a simple fact: in their structural position, these people look too much like Jesus.

"Eventually," says Bailie, "the objective wickedness of the culprit will not be enough to offset the moral misgivings aroused by that similarity."[4] "Even when proven evil doers are publicly scorned or punished by persons or institutions representing the righteous indignation of the whole community, not even their glaring moral failures and criminal behavior will be enough to entirely cancel out the empathy for victims that the gospel inspires."[5] What is true about the case of execution is true across a whole range of social realities. In Matthew's Gospel, those who have come before Jesus at the judgment ask him, "When did we see you hungry . . . naked . . . imprisoned?" In a very real sense this eschatological question has seeped into our world, present alike when Mother Teresa explicitly sees the face of Christ in the dying beggar on Calcutta's streets and when a resolutely nonreligious person agonizes over what she spontaneously calls the "crucifixion" of indigenous activists in a Latin American dictatorship. The image of Jesus has a contagion of its own. We classify more and more situations as ones of victimization and perceive more and more of our collective social actions as violence. Which means we become less and less able to wholeheartedly gather on the side of good violence against bad.

This can be told as a happy and progressive tale, which it is in part. But it can be told also as a tragic story, for it does not follow from this development that violence is diminished. Paradoxically, such sensitivity can make it more likely that violence begets violence, for people have "lost faith" in the sacrificial process. The action that is meant to stop the chain and restore peace is taken by many as an offense that incites conflict and retaliation. On the one hand we become suspicious even of what once seemed the most necessary and untroubled uses of violence or coercion. On the other hand, as the line between consensually good and bad violence blurs, the limits on endorsed violence also fall away, opening the way for its expansion. It seems nonsensical to say that in the twentieth century we attained both a new level of sensitivity to victims *and* new frenzies of quantitative violence. But that is what the apocalyptic vision foresaw. And that is what happened.

---

4. Bailie, *Violence Unveiled: Humanity at the Crossroads* (New York: Crossroad, 1995), 81.
5. Bailie, *Violence Unveiled,* 81.

Two Halves of the Secret

Bailie sums up our apocalyptic situation by suggesting that we see around us three options, all untenable.[6] Those he calls reactionaries think that somehow we can revive structures of sacred violence to successfully maintain order. Those he calls revolutionaries believe we can violently destroy the people or structures responsible for scapegoating. We can sacrifice the sacrificers. Those he calls romantics believe the world is steadily coming to its senses, and we will finally "just say no" to violence in a pure insight of enlightened self-interest.

Romanticism sees the increasing awareness of victims and infers that violence must wither in the face of such consciousness. It understands violence as circumstantial and not rooted in integral features of human community. These assumptions flourish best in pockets of safety during spells of historical good weather. The last century has not been kind to them, as it has been convulsed by upheavals of both Bailie's reactionary and revolutionary types.

Only halfway through that century, W. H. Auden saw the lay of the land. In his poem "Vespers" he recounts an evening encounter between two metaphorical walkers, Arcadian and Utopian. The first is bound for Eden, the second for the new Jerusalem, each the antitype of the other. The poem ends this way:

Was it (as it must look to any god of cross-roads) simply
a fortuitous intersection of life-paths, loyal to different fibs,
   or also a rendezvous between accomplices who, in spite of
themselves, cannot resist meeting

   to remind the other (do both, at bottom, desire truth?)
of that half of their secret which he would most like to forget,

   forcing us both, for a fraction of a second, to remember
our victim (but for him I could forget the blood, but for me he could
forget the innocence)

   on whose immolation (call him Abel, Remus, whom you
will, it is one Sin Offering) arcadias, utopias, our dear old bag
of a democracy, are alike founded:

6. Bailie, *Violence Unveiled*, 99.

For without a cement of blood (it must be human, it
must be innocent) no secular wall will safely stand.[7]

Auden recognizes the founding sacrificial dynamic we have been describing. The poem is his extraordinarily concise way of describing that secret
"we would like to forget" but seem to find more and more evident in the
history around us. Arcadian and Utopian are personal types, but they also
stand for the realities Auden saw before him in fascism and communism,
two concrete faces of apocalypse.

National Socialism as a movement made no secret of its nostalgia for
the vigor of a pre-Christian German tradition, untainted by Jewish scripture and prophecy. It deployed a combination of semiscientific and flatly
mythical accusations against its targets, who were classical marginal candidates for sacrifice like the gypsies, the mentally and physically handi-
capped, homosexuals, and, above all, the Jews. By orchestrating (with new
technological means) collective hatred against the victims, it meant to
build a unified state of unparalleled power. The Nazi leaders saw this sacrificial process as no mere political ploy. They pursued the extermination
of the Jews even when it depleted resources they needed for the very sur-
vival of their regime. The longing for a pagan sacrificial past joined hands
with Christian anti-Semitism, the deepest form of Christian sacrificial violence in which the passion itself is mythologized. They made a virulent

---

7. "Vespers," from "Horae Canonicae," in W. H. Auden, *The Shield of Achilles* (London:
Faber and Faber, 1955), 76-77. Auden's poem cycle treats the death of Jesus as a collective sacrifice, with many striking parallels to our description. To take one example, here is Auden's
description of the mythic memory in the dispersed crowd after their frenzy of violence at
the crucifixion (a description that echoes the crowd dynamic in the "horrible miracle" of
Apollonius of Tyana seen in chapter 4).

> . . . not one
> Of those who in the shade of walls and trees
>   Lie sprawled now, calmly sleeping,
> Harmless as sheep, can remember why
>   He shouted or what about
> So loudly in the sunshine this morning;
>   All if challenged would reply
> — 'It was a monster with one red eye,
>   A crowd that saw him die, not I.' —
> The hangman has gone to wash, the soldiers to eat;
>   We are left alone with our feat. ("Vespers," 70-71)

Thanks to Kate Layzer for bringing this poem to my attention.

combination. The very scale of the Nazi effort betrayed something of the apocalyptic quality we have been discussing.

Remaking the Cross

Much ink has been spilled in arguing whether the religious impulse in National Socialism was more neo-pagan or Christian. This can become an exercise in shifting or shirking responsibility. German Christians, some notable exceptions aside, supported or accepted the Nazi regime. Since they made up the vast majority of the population, Christianity bears responsibility for what happened. I want to focus on a slightly different question. For those who most unreservedly supported Hitler, what *kind* of Christianity was required as the necessary ground for that support? What about Christianity did those most committed to National Socialism think most important to eliminate? Interestingly, the theology of the most Nazi-allied party in the church advocated a Christianity shorn of the elements our study has been highlighting.[8] The targets were the same as in the earliest attempt to remythologize the gospel, the Gnostic one. The Hebrew scriptures must go, with all the uncomfortable light they shed on scapegoating. So must the Jewish Jesus, in favor of an Aryan Christ. So, according to one of the most vehement of the Christian Nazis, must "the whole scape-goat and inferiority-type theology of the Rabbi Paul."[9] The New Testament must be purified of its "*exaggerated* emphasis on the crucified Christ."[10]

Christian Nazis were not enthusiasts for the atonement. The theme of cross-centered sin and redemption was regarded as a Jewish importation into the church, a debilitating doctrine imposed by theologians and foreign to the true historical Jesus. The Protestant faculty in Breslau issued a declaration to the effect that the German people should reject a religion based on sin, since they had already suffered enough from defeat in war

---

8. In what follows I focus on the Deutsche Christen, the party in the German churches that sought most directly to support National Socialism. They were an important minority, even though their most striking views were never formally adopted by most of the churches and even though many Nazi leaders scorned the idea that Christianity could be sufficiently "reformed" to truly correspond to their aims.

9. From the sports palace address by Reinhold Krause, in Peter Matheson, *The Third Reich and the Christian Churches* (Grand Rapids: Eerdmans, 1981), 39.

10. From Krause's sports palace address, quoted in Doris L. Bergen, *Twisted Cross: The German Christian Movement in the Third Reich* (Chapel Hill: University of North Carolina Press, 1996), 158.

and from their enemies' accusations of guilt. Such a theology burdened them instead of building them up. A people already struggling for their rightful place "cannot bear it, when their sinfulness is constantly pointed out to them in an exaggerated way."[11] Association of the cross with our sin was discouraged. One commentator noted that only the "Jewish" Gospel of Matthew reported Jesus to include the words "for the forgiveness of sins" when speaking of his death at the Last Supper.[12]

When the Old Testament was largely winnowed out from religious instruction, the binding of Isaac was one of the first texts to go.[13] A new pro-Nazi institute in the church prepared a revised and expurgated synthesis of the Synoptic Gospels, which it commended as "more effective than the New Testament, with its unclear, alien expression of the message of Christ."[14] The revised text dropped much narration of Jesus' life and passion in favor of stringing together a number of his familiar sayings. It eliminated Old Testament references that helped set the scapegoat context for the crucifixion, including any references to Passover in connection with the Last Supper and the quotation from Psalm 118 on the stone that was rejected. Jesus' word from the cross, "Father, forgive them, for they know not what they do," was cut. So too were explicit passages about the resurrection, as the text closed with the death of Jesus, followed only by the giving of the Great Commission to Peter and the other disciples.

Another circle in the German Christian movement published a revised version of the Gospel of John, called the "German Gospel of John." John was a preferred Gospel for the ease with which its many statements about

---

11. Quoted in Bergen, *Twisted Cross,* 158.

12. Bergen, *Twisted Cross,* 159.

13. Bergen, *Twisted Cross,* 144.

14. Quoted in Bergen, *Twisted Cross,* 162. It was prepared by the Institut zur Erforschung und Beseitigung des jüdischen Einflüsses auf das deutsche kirchliche Leben (Institute for Research into and Elimination of Jewish Influence in German Church Life). There is some confusion about the text in question, as Bergen refers to a pamphlet-sized booklet, entitled *Die Botschaft Gottes* (The Message of God), published in 1939. It contained a ninety-six-page selection of passages from the three Synoptic Gospels. It is reported to have sold 200,000 copies in six months. There is also a book published by the institute under this same title that contains the 1939 text (perhaps with revisions) along with three further sections: selected portions from the Gospel of John, selected portions primarily from the Pauline Epistles, and selected portions primarily from the book of Acts. This published version also omits the word "elimination" in the title of the institute. See Institut zur Erforschung des jüdischen Einflüsses auf das deutsche kirchliche Leben, *Die Botschaft Gottes* (Leipzig: Otto Wigand, 1940). Cf. also Susannah Heschel, "When Jesus Was an Aryan: The Protestant Churches and Antisemitic Propaganda," in *Betrayal: German Churches and the Holocaust,* ed. Robert P. Eriksen and Susannah Heschel (Minneapolis: Fortress, 1999).

"the Jews" could be used to portray Jesus as completely opposed to Judaism. The translation went further than selection and arrangement. It "made other changes that showed a propensity to discard as Jewish reminders of human sinfulness all references to atonement."[15] So, "Behold the Lamb of God who takes away the sins of the world" changed to "Behold the chosen one of God, who through his sacrifice brings blessing to the world." The same institute referred to above produced an expurgated version of the entire New Testament. One notable example of its approach was that the fifty-two verses of Stephen's speech in Acts were reduced to six, eliminating all the scapegoat stories from Israel's history where Stephen had seen the meaning of Jesus' death prefigured.

In the theology of the German Christian party, crucifixion of Jesus by "the Jews" was taken as proof that Jesus must have opposed Judaism and was in fact not a Jew himself. Various scenarios were adduced to argue that as a Galilean Jesus came from another racial background. This theology rested its weight on the narrow point of Jesus' reconstructed individuality, contrasted with a Jewish tradition that he completely rejected, and was opposed to the dogmas of an early church that quickly refolded him in Jewish doctrines of sin and redemption alien to his spirit. The religion of Jesus had been a nobly Aryan one. The religion about Jesus had come to be (as early as Paul) dangerously infected with distortion. Thus the pro-Nazi party in the church identified with Richard Wagner's plea: "Redeem the redeemer. Liberate him from everything theologians, Jews and the church leadership have appended: preach him as he is."[16]

This extensive remaking of scripture (conducted with an ostensible mandate from critical historical scholarship) also remade the place of Jesus' death. Every element that could isolate Jews as the ones responsible for Jesus' death was stressed. Elements that pointed to the cross as a confrontation with human sin generally, or that emphasized an atoning death for *our* sins, were downplayed if not removed. As a result, the Gospels lost their character as description of a universal drama of salvation, in which the cross was a key moment. They were given a new story line, one about a racial struggle, its outcome still in the balance, in which Jesus had fallen a martyr for the Aryan side.[17]

15. Bergen, *Twisted Cross,* 162. The text is *Das Evangelium Johannes Deutsch* (Bremen: H. M. Huaschild, 1936).

16. Bergen, *Twisted Cross,* 159.

17. As a leader of the German Christian party put it, "Jesus had taken up a fight against Judaism in all sharpness and had fallen as victim to [his fight]." See Heschel, "When Jesus," 81.

This version of the New Testament obliterated the entire grammar that presents Jesus' passion as the persecution of a scapegoat and the resurrection as God's vindication of the victim. Neo-pagan enthusiasts for National Socialism derided the cross as a symbol of weakness and passivity, unworthy of a warrior. Their Christian counterparts responded by purging any aura of nonviolence or antisacrificial meaning from the passion. Jesus did not die to redeem and reconcile an entire humanity that was bound in complicity with sin, including most particularly the collective sin that killed him. He died as a soldier in a war between God's party and God's enemies. Christ's principal role was not that of a teacher or a savior, but a warrior.[18] A new confirmation exam developed among the German Christians posed the question: "Who was Jesus Christ and against whom did he fight?" The required answer was "A hero and warrior who fought against Jews and Pharisees."[19] Instead of a sacrifice to end sacrifice, the cross became a paradigm example of the manly offering of Aryan blood that continually nourishes the life of the people in their collective struggle. To draw this meaning from the crucifixion emphasized it as a model of bravery and an incitement for revenge, but eliminated its critique of scapegoating and minimized any once-for-all work.

Returning to Sacrifice

We have seen briefly something of what was required for serious efforts to reconcile National Socialism and the theology of the cross. We can ask a further, related question. Why was the neo-paganism involved in the Nazi movement of such a strained character?

Nazis intended that the destruction of their victims should be regarded as the natural activity of a healthy racial organism, the German *Volk*, something that should occasion no remorse or conflict. Yet at the same time they clearly regarded their "work" as something that required a special and almost inhuman resolve. Heinrich Himmler's private speech to SS leaders in 1943 has this famous chilling passage:

I am talking about the "Jewish evacuation": the extermination of the Jewish people. It is one of those things that is easily said. "The Jewish

18. In this point, we can hear echoes of some aspects already present in the early Germanic version of the gospel, the *Heliand*, discussed above in chapter 6.

19. Quoted in Bergen, *Twisted Cross*, 159.

people is being exterminated." Every Party member will tell you, "perfectly clear, it's part of our plans, we're eliminating the Jews, exterminating them, ha!, a small matter." And then along they all come, all the 80 million upright Germans, and each one has his decent Jew. They say: all the others are swine, but here is a first-class Jew.

And none of them has seen it, has endured it. Most of you will know what it means when 100 bodies lie together, when there are 500, or when there are 1000. And to have seen this through, and — with the exception of human weaknesses — to have remained decent, has made us hard and is a page of glory never mentioned and never to be mentioned.[20]

The violence is difficult, Himmler admits. Everyone has one or another of the victims he or she wants to exempt. The murdered keep taking on a distressingly individual reality. All the party members agree to the killing in theory, but they are not the ones who have to do it. According to Himmler, the "glory" of the SS is to have seen this gory persecution through and retained the veneer of ordinary humanity, in spite of the reservations that may assail them, in spite of the fact that the true reality of the violence is something never to be mentioned or acknowledged to the world.

Himmler's point is that this extermination must be carried out against the grain, as it were, and the killers deserve the more honor for that fact. This is a dramatic contrast to classical sacrifice, where all participate, where no one has any doubts. There the events and their unanimous rationale are completely open, and the truth effectively invisible to all. Here Himmler highlights the conscious duplicity and secrecy necessary. To the outside world the extermination of the Jews is to be called an "evacuation," and those who know the truth are never to speak of it. The number of the sacrificed has radically escalated, and the executioners must tell the world a different story than they tell themselves. Something has changed, so that the persecutors are compelled to know the secret and to consciously keep it. A true return to an "arcadian" past could have made do with many fewer victims, less conscious lies, and more convincing myth. The obstacle to such a return lies in the Jewish and Christian scriptures. It lies particularly in those elements the German Christian

20. Heinrich Himmler, "Poznan Speech to SS Officers," October 4, 1943, Holocaust History Project, available at http://www.holocaust-history.org/himmler-poznan/speech-text.shtml (visited May 10, 2005).

party was doing their best to remove. Sacrificial Christianity is a danger-ous thing. Its efforts to reconstitute mythic persecution are haunted by a lack of innocence and prone to escalation.

As regards this strain in the reappropriation of sacred violence, the philosopher Nietzsche had foreseen that a modern recovery of sacrifice would require strength of will much greater than that of those who prac-ticed it of old. And he had clearly fingered Christianity as the cause of this problem. The ancients did not have to carry out their violence in a culture tainted with biblical faith. He posed a stark opposition between Dionysus and Christ.[21] "Dionysus versus the 'Crucified': there you have the antithe-sis. It is *not* a difference in regard to their martyrdom — it is a difference in the meaning of it. Life itself, its eternal fruitfulness and recurrence, cre-ates torment, destruction, the will to annihilation. In the other case, suf-fering — the 'Crucified as the innocent one' — counts as an objection to this life, as a formula to its condemnation."[22] Nietzsche strikes to the heart of the matter and sees that the myth of Dionysus and the passion narratives are both about exactly the same event, a collective murder. In Dionysian myth the god was torn to pieces by a crowd of frenzied devo-tees, an event repeated like the round of the seasons. The difference be-tween this and the passion is the attitude to this fact of collective murder, which myth celebrates and the Gospel condemns. Even further, Nietzsche recognizes that myth celebrated the event of sacrifice without facing it squarely as what it was — the arbitrary killing of an innocent scapegoat. He sees that to exalt it with clear eyes is a new step, demanding almost su-perhuman strength. His ideal is to stare down the revelation of the nature of sacrifice and to carry it on nevertheless, without reservation or qualm.

In celebrating sacrifice he sees suffering as an affirmation of life. Pa-ganism is a noble outlook, "sufficiently strong, robust and divinizing" to affirm "even a monstrous amount of suffering." Nietzsche goes on: "The god on the cross is a curse on life, a signpost to seek redemption from life; Dionysus cut to pieces is a *promise* of life: it will be eternally reborn and re-turn again from destruction."[23] He has no time for the supposition that the Dionysian myth refers to vegetation and the cycle of seasons. Its whole

---

21. See chapter 14, "The Twofold Nietzschean Heritage," in Girard, *I See Satan Fall like Lightning* (New York: Orbis, 2001). Also see René Girard, "The Founding Murder in the Phi-losophy of Nietzsche," in Paul Dumouchel, *Violence and Truth: On the Work of René Girard* (Stanford, Calif.: Stanford University Press, 1988).

22. Friedrich Wilhelm Nietzsche, Walter Arnold Kaufmann, and R. J. Hollingdale, *The Will to Power* (New York: Random House, 1967), 542.

23. Nietzsche, Kaufmann, and Hollingdale, *The Will to Power*, 543.

point is the real killing of real people. Dionysus is superior precisely because he mandates the constant repetition of the violence. The sickness of the Gospel is that it stands in the way. Sacrifice of the weak and the innocent is the way life works, constantly bringing new life out of death, nourished in the sacrificial blood. Whoever cannot celebrate this cycle in human affairs simply hates life. Those who love life must also affirm and celebrate the killing by which we live. A healthy society needs victims, as a healthy body needs food.

Nietzsche sees clearly that the fact that a suffering victim is at the center of Christianity does not mean that it affirms sacrifice: it means just the opposite. He perceives the layers in the passion narrative we have spent so much time describing. The stories of Dionysus and Jesus are both about suffering. But that similarity is the basis for a complete opposition. The suffering of Dionysus is affirmed as a necessary part of life itself. Life "creates torment." But the suffering of Christ is presented as something to be rejected, not affirmed. The "god on the cross is a curse on life," the suffering of the crucified as the innocent one "counts as an objection to this life." The cross is an objection to social life constituted by sacrifice. And to Nietzsche, that is the only life there is or could be.

In Christianity, "The individual was taken so seriously, he was posited as such an absolute principle, that he could no longer be sacrificed: but the species only survives thanks to human sacrifice. . . . True philosophy requires sacrifice for the good of the species; such philanthropy is fierce and obliges us to master ourselves because it requires human sacrifice. And that pseudo-humanism that calls itself Christianity intends precisely to forbid that anyone be sacrificed."[24]

Many attack Christianity as a tool invented by the strong to oppress the weak. Nietzsche despises it for being exactly the opposite, a sneak attack of the weak upon the strong. It expresses the resentment of the victims against the healthy cycles of violence that uphold society. Unable to resist by open counterviolence, they seek to seduce the strong by deceit, by infecting them with doubt and pity, by mesmerizing them with a superstition about the vindication of the victim. Those who would resist the siren song of that revelation and stay firmly on the path of human sacrifice, will need to master themselves in the way Himmler commended.

This is the apocalyptic path that tries to revive classical sacrifice, based in folk-traditional myth that is part of the blood and soil of each particular

---

24. Girard and Treguer, *Quand Ces Choses Commenceront*, quoting Nietzsche, *Oeuvres complètes*, 224-25.

human community, expressed in its own language and stories. As Nietzsche clearly understood, this practice is broken by biblical tradition, and strictly speaking there is no going back. Possible dissent is seeded everywhere, even in the minds of the persecutors. Each replay of the old script yields a bit less of the old peace and unity than before, and requires the dosage to be raised. Only an enormous effort of will can carry it forward, making the rituals larger and more insistent, the victims more numerous, until the sacrificial practice itself threatens to consume the society rather than preserve it.

In the Name of Victims

The twentieth century also illustrated an alternative apocalyptic path. Communism is an example of Auden's utopian vision, alongside the Nazi example of his arcadian one. The violence of National Socialism looks more like that of the Gospel apocalypses, where the world implodes as its own sacrificial processes tear themselves apart. The violence of communism most resembles that of the final battles of Revelation. Marxism intended to be a global revolution, a class war carried out in the name of victims. National Socialism was in principle about the unity and dominance of one racial, national state in a continual life struggle against all rivals (a struggle compatible at least in principle with the existence of states of an analogous type at a safe distance, such as Japan). Communism by contrast was a movement whose aim encompassed every human community and culture, replacing them all with one new society and a new humanity itself.

In the book of Revelation, massive armies arise in the final days to fight on behalf of the persecuted and to vindicate them. Those who had been abandoned and marginalized as victims now are avenged by a host of allies. Communism looks for history to provide just such a reversal. It deploys all the classical machinery of condemnation and stigmatization against the few who are responsible for the evils afflicting the whole community. In this case the few are the class of owners of capital. But Marxist thought claims the title of victim for the many who will rise up against these few. The mob gathers against a minority with the charge that the few have ganged up against the many.[25] Those destroyed by the revolution cannot be scapegoats, because the revolution is itself the uprising of the

---

25. This fits a pattern that Christian anti-Semitism pioneered, a novel form of sacrificial violence in which scapegoats are persecuted in the name of opposition to scapegoating. The mob gathers against the few with the charge that the few have scapegoated the many.

scapegoats, the mass of the oppressed. The human reality of the enemies of the revolution is downplayed in favor of an emphasis on the system of which they are the head, an enormous beast of economic exploitation. The war is not only against the oppressors but against the principalities and powers as well, the very structures of evil.

No single movement of the twentieth century practiced lethal scapegoating on the scale of communism. Although this process frequently co-opted traditionally marginalized groups (Jews, for instance), it principally depended on freshly constructed categories (economic classes, enemies of the people) constituted by its own theories and analysis. Despite the claim that these categories were scientifically derived, their utility lay precisely in the fact that anyone could at any time be defined in such a way as to belong to one of them, including virtually any leader or faction in the revolutionary movement itself.

Nazis tended to rely on classical scapegoating accusations against the Jews (and others): they contaminate the racial purity of the nation, they commit abominable crimes, they betray the people to outside enemies. They relied also on historical Christian anti-Semitic charges that Jews were responsible for Jesus' death and therefore enemies of God. But, as we have seen, Christian Nazis veered away from the most distinctively Christian anti-Semitic charge that Jews deserved scapegoating because they were themselves scapegoaters. They preferred to avoid the whole question of scapegoating as a primordial sin. And they preferred to present Jesus as a warrior who died in open battle, rather than the victim of a process that the Hebrew scriptures had already revealed and opposed. The resemblance between their own crimes and the script of sacred violence outlined in scripture was too close, and so scripture needed to be altered.

Communism, by contrast, made the dynamic of victimization its centerpiece. It brought a universal charge that bourgeois class enemies had conspired (through a system and not a literal numerical mob) to make the mass of the people their slaves. It was crucial to the logic of communism that it spoke and fought on the side of the victim. And it was equally crucial that it claimed to reveal and explain a persecutory practice that operated without the direct knowledge of any of the parties to it, that was permeated with false consciousness. Marxist movements and governments made use of classic scapegoating excuses on an ad hoc basis as well, but these were secondary to the primary rationale that ultimately was rooted in the biblical tradition's spotlighting of the victim, and in the tradition of an apocalyptic vindication of the victim.

The parallels in Marxist thought with the biblical tradition and especially with Christian eschatology have long been noted. Whereas the Nazis looked back to an ancient racial ideal for their model, communists looked forward to a new community and a new humanity. In this new community the very structures of the old societies would be transformed. Marxism shares the tenor of apocalyptic inevitability in the book of Revelation, in its certainty that the new community comes through a final, comprehensive battle. Only the most bellicose millennial reading of Revelation can match Marxism's confident assumption that unrestrained good violence has nothing in common with the evil it opposes. Such cleansing force is the means by which oppressors will be eliminated and the conditions that created sacrificial violence will themselves be removed. Under true communism (or even under the transitional rule of the vanguard party) persecution is impossible by definition, because now the victims are the ones in control. The power of the state has become the wrath of the lamb.

It is impossible to conceive the Marxist vision without this background. It bristles with parallels — the "fall" from primitive communism into class society, the corruption of human desire, the party as the community bearing the revelation and prefiguring the new world, the prophetic anticipations of millennial scenarios, the tension between a proclamation that future "salvation" is objectively assured and an exhortation to act to bring it about. There is similarity too in the insistence that all humanity, powerful and weak alike, is captive to an evil structure that is now also internalized within the individual. This evil works according to its own logic, quite apart from the conscious perceptions and rationales of human actors. Only a new human community, formed on a new basis, can change this situation.

The key point of contact, for our purposes, is that the biblical tradition uncovers the hidden victims in sacrifice and reads history from their point of view. Marxism makes that practice the heart of its philosophy, and may be the most elaborate theory of victimization ever developed. It is not hard to see how Marxism appropriates the scapegoat revelations of scripture. The analysis of class society assumes that it is based on surrogate sacrifice. That is what oppression is — the theft of the worker's blood and product for the benefit of another class. The lives of workers are sacrificed for the harmony of the market and the stability of profit, to keep peace in the economic system. The Marxist critique of all ideological superstructure (things like philosophy, religion, law, morality, emotions) is that these are essentially myths, hiding the deeper materialistic social forces and their violence.

Such "demythologizing" seems a close cousin of the unveiling of foundational violence behind classical myth that we have discussed. Just as societies needed sacrificial victims to maintain their unity, so in Marxist terms feudal or bourgeois or late capitalist societies need their particular exploited classes to maintain their economic equilibrium. Just as it is an accomplishment for the persecuted to become visible as such (as in the book of Job, for instance), so Marxism considers it a key step to break through false consciousness, which prevents the oppressed from understanding their own condition. German Christians devoted to National Socialism stripped the biblical text of its antiscapegoating grammar. The Marxists emphatically kept that grammar, while dispensing with its text and context altogether. Christianity was itself just another form of false consciousness, though Marxist historians too saw parallels, finding in early Christianity and groups like the revolutionary Anabaptists anticipations of true social analysis, veiled in the cloud of otherworldly illusion. The scapegoat grammar, stripped of all transcendence and made thoroughly materialistic and historical, is at the heart of the communist analysis of "sin and redemption." The biblical awareness of victims, seeded into culture, produced its own independent offspring.

Stripping the biblical context from the focus on victims lowers the threshold for apocalyptic in Marxism. In the early Christian years, a sense of eschatological expectation fueled new levels of mutuality and reconciled community. For communists, apocalyptic certainty about the coming world revolution authorized new levels of conflict. Violence was seen as the necessary instrument of this transformation. Nazis sought a "final solution" in the extermination of their supreme scapegoats, the Jews. But continued struggle remained part of their ideal future, and they believed repetition of sacrificial violence against enemies external and internal was an enduring feature of a healthy German state. Marxism by contrast envisions a future of perfect peace, an abolition of the class conflict that fuels all violence. The end of history means the end of sacrifice. To that purpose, no cost can be too high. The more sacrificial theologies of the cross posit a once-for-all death of Christ in which the infinite magnitude of innocent divine suffering in one person is great enough to blot out sin. Communism posits a once-for-all revolution in which any volume of innocent suffering is acceptable so long as the old world is destroyed forever. No matter how small the remnant after the final battle, provided they are truly elect, the future is assured. Since Marxist analysis reveals a nearly unlimited scope of victimization, there are no secure constraints on the amount of violence that may be required to overcome it.

Stalin's great purges are a terrifying illustration. It was not uncommon for state security forces to receive simple quotas for executions: "You are charged with the task of exterminating 10,000 enemies of the people."[26] The charges and the individuals were to be supplied after the fact. Those carrying out the purges were regularly purged themselves. The staff of one prison was entirely wiped out four times over, and prisoners often outlasted a succession of their interrogators and torturers.[27] A primary aim in every case was to induce the accused to accuse others. Sometimes neither captive nor persecutor had any inkling of what crime might be proposed to rationalize the proceeding. Prisoners were beaten to produce confessions, but could only guess at what offenses were expected. In a Kafkaesque game, the persecutors and the persecuted would together work up the details of imaginary conspiracies to fill out the paperwork on sentences already determined.[28] Victims were enlisted in fabricating the myths for their own sacrifice. By this stage it was beside the point whether either party actually believed in the myths.

The dimensions of this process were such that by late 1938 the NKVD, the primary instrument of the terror, had files to charge virtually every leading official in the entire Soviet structure and half the urban population.[29] It had become a purely arbitrary matter who would be arrested and killed or sent to gulags. The violence on behalf of victims had made everyone a potential victim. Since anyone punished by the state was by definition guilty, and since the crimes were always against the state or "the people," the category of "victim" itself had been abolished. All that remained were condemned victimizers. The violence to end scapegoating had become scapegoating on a massive scale. When traditional sacrifice worked, it unified the community and stilled for a time its inner divisions. This frontal assault to end sacrifice ended by turning each person against the next and multiplying conflict to the point of collapse, a case study in apocalypse.

The Nazi path to apocalypse ran through attempts to maintain unity with classical scapegoats. A sacrificial system weakened by awareness of the cross escalated the number of its victims in search of the traditional effects. At the same time, those who ran that system felt compelled to consciously dissemble about its reality in a way none of the ancients

26. Robert Conquest, *The Great Terror: A Reassessment* (London: Hutchinson, 1990), 287.
27. Conquest, *The Great Terror,* 279.
28. Conquest, *The Great Terror,* 289.
29. Conquest, *The Great Terror,* 289.

Nietzsche admired could have imagined. The passion narratives mirror the sacrificial pattern in mythic religion, and draw out similarities, not to support the pattern but to expose and reverse it. The Nazis attempted to recover religion prior to that reversal. That meant to frame Christianity as a continuation and confirmation of a much older Germanic tradition. The most fervent Christian Nazis did their best to reassimilate Christianity to the mythic original and to expunge those elements that most clearly expressed the opposition. In apocalyptic terms, the church itself became a temple for the prince of this world, worshiping a false christ.

The communist path to apocalypse ran through the hope to extirpate sacrificial structures root and branch. Awareness of the cross became a cry for justice for the oppressed. The purifying wrath of God that would avenge the sacrificed at the end of days became an inexorable dialectic of violence to liberate the oppressed at the end of history. The passion narratives in the Gospels are a critique of religion, in its traditional sacrificial sense. Marxism implicitly understands the critique of victimization and also adopts a general attack on all religion (particularly Christianity) as part of that project. It makes these the basis for a final war between light and darkness. In apocalyptic terms, this is another face of an antichrist, where the worst acts of persecution are done in the name of a fight against persecution.[30]

One thing these different paths — the German fascist one and the Soviet communist one — had in common (though in different degrees) was a hostility to Jews and Judaism. This is a phenomenon we see echoed in our own time in the sometime coincidence of an anti-Semitism of the right with one of the left. Nazis attacked Jews and their religious influence as impediments to sacrifice, whose antiscapegoating tradition was a debilitating virus in the soul of German nationalism. Communists attacked them on the basis of that (secularized) antiscapegoating message itself, as chief sacrificers, priests of the global capitalist system.

The close parallels between communism and Christianity made for a particularly hostile relation. Communism read one moral from this similarity. What Christianity hoped for in a supernatural heaven, concrete revolution would make fact on earth. Jesus' death is a simple failure, emblematic of the weakness of faith before objective social forces. When communism abolished material scarcity and class division, all human conflict would disappear also, and with it any need for sacrifice or for redemption from sacrifice. Since religion has to do with only these last two,

30. See Girard and Treguer, *Quand Ces Choses Commenceront,* 65.

285

it would disappear as well. To destroy religion is to hasten the day of peace and justice.

Christians saw that the roots of human conflict go deeper than material dialectics, that apart from the needs of human subsistence desire shapes economics as much as economics shapes desire. The aggressive atheism of communism and its refusal to accept any competing experiments in new human community met with an almost equally consistent opposition from the churches. So, not entirely by choice, the church was spared a role as sponsor in communism's horrors similar to that it played in connection with Hitler's. The extensive suffering and martyrdom of Christians in communist societies readily evoked images of the cross. To make that connection, even implicitly, was to critique communism at its root by contesting its title to speak for victims.

In Budapest in 1989 I visited the Kerepesi Cemetery. I went not to see its famous sculptured tombs but to see a site that officially did not exist. Following directions friends had given me, I walked to the far northeast corner of the cemetery. There, in some remote and overgrown lots, the government had buried in mass graves many of those liquidated between 1945 and the uprising in 1956. Imre Nagy and other leaders from that uprising were buried here. On this bare, unmarked land, over time, a forest of crosses had surreptitiously arisen. Some were crude, some were exquisitely carved. Ostensibly they made no political statement. But collectively they spoke loudly indeed. The victims were not forgotten. Their deaths were wrong. The enforced silence about their fate would not hold. The collective powers that had murdered them would not endure. Their innocence would be vindicated. The authorities faced a dilemma in dealing with the people who raised those crosses. They could not charge them with saying such things explicitly, for they had not. It was the story of the cross itself that did so.

When Marxists turned Christianity's critique of religion into an attack on Christianity, they were in some measure correct. Historical Christianity has taken on sacrificial forms that merited that response. The Christian "secular theologians" of the 1960s and 1970s, and others who sought a dialogue between Marxism and Christianity, were sensitive to this.[31] They saw secularization, of which Marxism was one face, as the objective impact of the biblical tradition in history. In their view the West's turn away from religion and toward concrete betterment of the human condi-

---

31. See, for instance, Harvey Gallagher Cox, *The Secular City: Secularization and Urbanization in Theological Perspective,* rev. ed. (New York: Macmillan, 1966).

tion through technology and political change fulfilled the prophetic message in Judaism and Christianity. The transcendence of the monotheistic God had in truth desacralized the world. Where hitherto myth and divinity had permeated all of nature and precluded human investigation, now a humanity "come of age" was free to understand the contingent world by independent reason and science. Despite their complacency in identifying Christianity and Western culture, and their obvious misreading of the vitality of traditional religious communities, these writers approached some of the same issues we have raised. They did not recognize, however, that the desacralizing effect of the biblical tradition applied particularly to the mythic structures of sacrifice (structures that may be just as relevant in secular forms as in traditional religious ones).

They took to heart the Marxist critique of religion, including the criticism of Christianity as a myth. Here the antiscapegoating grammar of the Bible was turned critically against the church. It was a great virtue of these theologians to perceive that this was an appropriate move, one in fact consistent with the church's own faith. Paul Tillich put this well in his articulation of the "Protestant principle," which he saw ultimately expressed in the cross. The only adequate criterion of judgment was one that was itself subject to judgment. The only faithful religion of identification with scapegoats would be one able to acknowledge its own guilt for scapegoating. The church is not innocent of the charges that it has acted and theologized in sacrificial ways. It would lose all touch with its own revelation if it claimed it was.

However, the great failing of the secular theologians, from the perspective of our topic, was to sweep away, as part of the "religion" they critiqued, the very foundations of this grammar. They tended to relegate notions of sacrifice to an outmoded supernaturalistic, mythic mentality, thus missing their relevance to the secular world. And they were largely blind to the necessary role of conversion and positive religious practice in effective alternatives to sacrifice.

The Mark the Cross Has Left

After the fierce storms of fascism and communism (each of which lives on in important forms), democratic capitalism is now the dominant political force. Auden provided no third walker to correspond to his "dear old bag of a democracy," which stood under such peril as he wrote. But his poem suggests that democracies too may be founded on the immolation of hidden victims. Consideration of the two cautionary examples in this chapter does not imply that other societies are free from the dynamics we see there. There are democratic paths to catastrophe also, and no guarantee that we will not take one.

The rule of law and political and economic freedom are in principle protections against sacrificial practice. Legal systems are a fascinating case in point. Like animal sacrifice, legal structures represent a dramatic step away from human scapegoating. Animal sacrifice kept intact the dynamic of collective violence but replaced arbitrary human victims with arbitrary animal ones. Legal systems, as they develop with a sense of accountability to universal, impartial law, rather than simply transcribed tradition, directly address the causes of sacrificial violence. That is, they deal with the conflicts that arise among individuals and groups and try to resolve them in a way that is just and prevents the escalation that invites sacrifice. Legal systems thus attempt to fit a crime with the actual offender and to fit the punishment to the actual crime. Sacrifice does neither. Its effectiveness demands exactly the opposite. Legal structures thus have a profound antisacrificial quality. But if the scapegoating dynamic is powerful enough, it can capture and employ structures meant to curb it.

Constitutions and universal law offer a structure in which the few and the weak can be preserved from the arbitrary, reconciling violence of the many. But these rules cannot function without communities in some substantive sense committed to a vision that can maintain them. A democratic capitalist order is in one respect simply a mechanism through which political and economic competition is expressed. It is an order based on the wager that political peace can be maintained by a balance of rival interests and that parties to a system of economic exchange can on balance all come out ahead. The hope is that rivalry can contain the destructive effects of rivalry, and economic competition can yield abundance and harmony rather than festering conflict. In this sense, such a democratic order seeks to organize mimetic desire and its rivalries into channels that cancel out violent effects.

Despite the demonstrated power of both of these ideas in history, they are not easy to implement. If they are true, they are fragile truths. For either or both to hold, it seems there must be a robust diversity of desires and interests in the community in question. There can be no balancing of political interests if everyone regards the same issues as of ultimate, nonnegotiable importance but disagrees about them. Economic harmony (and growth) is much more difficult if we have uniform desires, if we all want to do the same work and (apart from necessities) we all want exactly the same goods and services. In these respects democratic capitalist orders are stabilized by diversity. Yet sharpened diversity of interests and conflict between factions are also threats to their unity, with the potential for disintegration into isolated subcommunities. Unchecked competition can lead people to each other's throats. But without the regular nonviolent negotiation of conflict, any theoretical checks and balances would soon be washed away or rusted out, leaving a tyrannical unity. Too much agreement can be fatal, as can too much division.

Democratic capitalist orders are in significant measure empty vessels. They have enormous creative potential but limited intrinsic direction. No alternatives have proved better as a framework for human flourishing in the conditions of modernity. But "free markets and honest elections" is a thin substantive creed, one that in no way guarantees the goodness of the results. Such societies can be swept in either of the apocalyptic directions we have outlined, and the viability of their economic and political structures depends ultimately on the capacity of civil society (everything from families and religious groups to advocacy organizations and schools) to foster virtue and authentic community. These sectors generate the resources needed to tame bare markets and flat majority rule.

The mechanisms of such societies are not simply neutral. Life that is ordered only by the letter of legality and the logistics of material success is liable to dissipate in a manner those standards themselves are helpless to redress. Organized around individual rights and the pursuit of individual economic benefits, democratic societies raise the human mimetic temperature to a high level. We are tied together with an unparalleled technological machinery for communication and trade, a veritable highway for the contagion of conflict and then too for the propagation of waves of sudden unanimity within one group against its victims. This is a medium that can foster real and perceived sacrificial crisis on a new scale, whether the catalytic event is a shortage of oil, the spread of disease, or the threat of terror.

The openness of democratic societies can also be a vacuum, one that stimulates recurrent attempts to fill it with thicker forms of belief and ideology.[32] This is the point at which these societies are particularly subject to the tendencies discussed in this chapter. In times of crisis or threat,

32. The restless, disruptive impact of modern democratic capitalism and its cultural "thinness" can each be read either as destructive or as creative. The difference in these valuations is a major element in the current conflict threatening to entangle the Muslim and Western worlds, alongside the obvious differences over concrete economic and political policies.

like the current struggle over terrorism, the standard sacrificial dynamic has not lost its appeal. Its logic is to look for scapegoats. They could be outside, but the tendency is strong to seek them within, because it is there that the community can most readily act out unity in condemnation. We and our community must be defended, and the infection must be removed. The cross troubles this practice of sacrifice, and so Christians who would pursue it invariably prefer to remythologize it, to downplay the antiscapegoating message of the passion. Less ancient but equally powerful is the appeal of a war against sacrifice, violence on behalf of victims. Rather than practice sacrifice, identify others as doing so and unite to battle against the evil of scapegoating. The rationale in this case is less negative (self-protection) and more positive (spreading democracy and justice for the oppressed), a defense of others. For Christians this would mean an apocalyptic form of the faith, one that aims to root out sacrifice by violence.

Where is the legacy of the cross in all this? In an empirical sense it is both a wrench in the works of sacrifice and a spotlight on the practice of scapegoating. This can have negative effects, making sacrifice more bloody when we persist in it, or turning our awareness of victims into an absolute conflict with those we identify as their persecutors. But the most basic saving social effect of the cross is to disrupt all our unanimities, sacrificial or apocalyptic. Where the witness of the cross is authentically heard, the collective agreement that makes sacrifice succeed or eschatological crusades thrive is decisively broken. The unsettling effect of the cross makes us aware of our own violence, makes visible our own victims, or those we are haunted to think may be our victims. That disruption is a form of grace, even if by itself it is not sufficient grace.

We already live in a world objectively changed by the cross. It would be comforting to think that change brings nothing but good results. It would be encouraging to say that negative effects come from only error and distortions. But the point of this chapter is that the true effect of the passion is destabilizing, dangerous as well as liberating. The work of the cross is meant to make the practice of sacrifice-as-usual more difficult, and to replace it completely. Where sacred violence weakens, or where people catch the vision of a complete end to sacrifice, that work is having its effect. But insofar as these effects are not matched with the development of new modes of community, the outcome can simply raise the stakes of violent crisis.

This is the stark message of the biblical apocalyptic vision. If the knife of revelation does not cut to heal, it cuts to wound. The world is in a race between the effects of the cross and the power of the Spirit. No one may know the day or the hour, or the specific outcome of that race. But there is no turning back what has been set in motion from Jesus' death and resurrection. In the Gospels, when Jesus speaks of the last days, he warns of wars and rumors of wars. He never calls anyone to fight in them. When Jesus warns his disciples about false prophets and false messiahs in the latter days, I think we can best take it as a warning against false eschatologies, which are dangerous precisely because they can claim a partial root in the actual revelation. The caution comes to us as well. In the crisis precipitated by the visible victim, watch and pray, lest you fall prey to renewed sacrifice or to the attraction of apocalyptic battle.

CHAPTER TEN

Saved from Sacrifice

Renewing the Theology of the Cross

Christ is not divinized as a scapegoat. Those who take him
to be God — the Christians — are the ones who do not make
him their scapegoat.

René Girard[1]

At the beginning of this book I said we sought to account for both the
good and the bad associated with theologies of the cross, for the fact
that some regarded this as the very worst of Christianity and others as the
very best. The analysis we have traced goes far toward explaining that double history. It helps us understand how theologies of the cross have done
so much harm, and why even authentic ones carry unsettling, even apocalyptic dangers. At the same time, it lets us grasp the objective and liberating power of the cross, and understand why even distorted interpretations
have inspired so much good. Nothing trivial could have such power, on either count.

We have seen that the tensions around the scene that the passion narratives present to us go very deep into human history. There are foundational religious and cultural texts that lack any explicit description of the
sacrifice of a scapegoat, when in truth that is what they are about and
what they prescribe. These are myths of sacrifice. There are texts that in
some measure directly show the reality of the scapegoating events and yet

---

1. René Girard and Michel Treguer, *Quand Ces Choses Commenceront* (Paris: Arlea, 1994),
57.

still endorse or accept their necessity (in this category we could place the most venturesome of the Greek tragedies and some Old Testament passages on sacrifice). There are texts that explicitly reveal the mechanism and oppose it (many of which we have discussed, whether Joseph, Jonah, Job, the Prophets, the Psalms, or the passion narratives). There are texts that not only describe and protest the victimage mechanism but also proclaim its reversal and replacement (some prophetic texts, servant songs, the passion narratives along with other New Testament texts we discussed).[2] Each of these represents an archaeological layer, as it were, in the interpretation of the cross.

The cross belongs at the central location it has held in Christian faith. A crossless Christianity would be a shell emptied of its unique power to confront the very evils critics deplore. But the stakes are high, for this power to confront and heal is also a power to harm, and so much hangs on *which* theology of the cross we adopt. We have described a practice of scapegoating sacrifice, "a phenomenon that unbeknownst to us generates all human cultures and still warps our human vision in favor of all sorts of exclusions."[3] The event of the cross is itself the main reason we are able to give that description, to take for granted this insight into what was hidden.

The biblical tradition and the passion narratives clearly represent this practice. That representation is itself a distinctive achievement, but its purpose is not to endorse what it represents. We have seen that a community that does not explicitly represent violent sacrifice and its victims may be the most captive to that practice, while to describe it directly is the beginning of possible resistance. However, the fact that the theme of the sacrificial victim is so (unusually) obvious in the Bible can lead interpreters in the reverse direction, can lead them to uphold as a divine mechanism what was revealed only in order to be opposed.

The Bible has three of the four types of texts just mentioned (the one virtually absent is the true myth of sacrifice), and the danger is that atonement theology will interpret the antisacrificial elements in terms of the more mythical ones. Some theologies of the cross have patterned themselves too much on the mechanism that is revealed to have killed Jesus rather than on the divine act to overcome it. The influential later

2. Though our focus is on Christian tradition, we could see a somewhat parallel case in rabbinic Judaism's treatment of the Day of Atonement, and the explicit substitution of acts of repentance and praise for the practice of sacrifice.

3. René Girard, *I See Satan Fall like Lightning* (New York: Orbis, 2001), 3.

Western doctrine of penal substitutionary atonement is an example. Insofar as it turns on God's demand for violent sacrifice, satisfaction by Christ's suffering, it adopts the sacrificial assumptions that Jesus' death discredits. It accepts too much of the logic hidden behind myth simply because it can be found openly described in the Gospels (forgetting that it is *most* openly described and affirmed in these texts by those who kill Jesus). As a result, it obscures both the true revelation of the cross and its profound continuity with Jewish tradition. It makes Jesus our supreme scapegoat rather than our savior from sacrifice.

Rejection of that theory now frequently entails rejection of any consideration of Jesus' death as a sacrifice, of Jesus' dying for us, of the cross as representing any kind of transaction or "ransom," of the passion as an event with any objective as opposed to being purely illustrative. But the theology of the cross cannot be set right by throwing out this whole complex of ideas. They are rooted in scripture and tradition for good reasons. We cannot understand Jesus' death without understanding that it was a sacrifice, since this is the basis for knowing what it was doing to end sacrifice.

The reconciliation realized by those who believe in Jesus can be grasped only in contrast with the business-as-usual dynamic of sacrificial unity that sent him to his death. We cannot simply flee to other models of Christ's work and ignore or expunge all those elements that have fed "sacrificial" doctrines of the atonement. They are decisively important. That set of terms and ideas — the stones that many contemporary theological builders reject — needs to be reassembled so that the structure we have traced in this book is evident. When we learn to put these pieces together so, the result is not a minor modification, but a dramatically different picture. We recover the way the antisacrificial dimension of Christ's work at the cross coheres with and reinforces the other strands of his ministry and teaching.

In this chapter we review this renewed theology of the cross, in direct dialogue with a classic view of Christ's death as a satisfaction for God's justice, that of Anselm. We turn back to the basic, concrete terms in which the theology of the cross figures in ordinary Christian experience, to the phrases and ideas that are a necessary part of the life of faith but that in the modern period have often been captured entirely by penal, sacrificial interpretations. The way forward is not to go around all these elements, but to go through them, integrating them in the biblical vision of God's work to overcome scapegoating sacrifice. The true alternative to distorted theologies of atonement will not be one that says less about the cross, but one that says more. The third section focuses on the call to the Christian

294

community to live a life without sacred violence. That vision is clouded until we learn to see the way it is already embedded and expressed in familiar elements of our operative piety, liturgy, and tradition themselves. So in this chapter we will review our understanding of the basic confession that Christ "died for us," and a number of the associated traditional ideas regarding guilt and substitution.

Looking for the Rescue

Christ died for us. Christ took our place. This conviction, prior to and often apart from a theory to explain it, is a powerful part of Christian faith and piety. Its tenor is clear enough: gratitude to Jesus for saving us from death, suffering, and sin by intercepting them before they could reach us. The image communicates straightforwardly because it borrows an affecting plot we already know from instances where one person dies to save someone else. Jesus tells his disciples, "No one has greater love than this, to lay down one's life for one's friends" (John 15:13). But it is not clear how the death of Jesus himself actually fits that image, and this simple question is worth some attention.

This language suggests a certain kind of picture. It is as though a train were hurtling toward us or a tree were about to fall on us, and Jesus pushes us aside and steps into our place, being struck in our stead. The description "Jesus died for us" makes clear sense in such a situation. The broad shared tradition of the church has maintained this analogy by teaching that the train bearing down on us is the effects of our sin, the mortality and corruption unleashed in our own natures by our turning away from God. It is as if we maliciously or thoughtlessly brushed away the hand of one who was leading us through a dangerous thicket and, rushing off the path, knocked the support from under a dead trunk that then came crashing down. Our guide pushes us aside and is crushed herself. Only in this case what comes crashing down upon us is the evil we visit upon each other and ourselves. And it is this that Christ suffers in our place. Christ becomes a human being upon whom death falls, falls in a particular, typical way that we inflict on each other.

To change the image, it is as if through our own unhealthy practices and mistreatment of each other we had degraded our bodies to the point where a deadly plague was sweeping through our population. In the midst of this affliction one uninfected person steps forward to help. In the course of her work she contracts the illness. Improbably, after a long struggle, her immune system successfully fights off the disease. She dies, nonetheless, ravaged by complications. But she does not die before the antibodies her body had produced could be shared to provide the basis for a cure, infused in others to heal them. In this case, to be "in our place" does not mean literally pushing us aside, but joining us, at ultimate cost and to saving effect.

This generic idea of salvation provides the backdrop for all considerations of atonement. It is not one model, but the premise of all the models. The basic idea can be expressed with many images. The danger is a deadly disease that grips us. It is permanent slavery into which we have been sold. It is a sinful will that will drive us deeper and deeper into alienation. It is a legal verdict of condemnation lodged against us, whose justice we cannot dispute and whose sentence we cannot avoid. No matter the image, Christ intervenes to protect us, and the intervention always involves either sharing our fate (in order to reverse it) or taking it in our stead (in order to spare us from it). The emotional power of this picture of God's saving act turns largely on the analogy that God, in Christ, delivers us from the threat of some third party, some external danger.

Uneasiness with the theology of the cross arises partly because it is hard to see how Jesus' death is saving in any concrete way. It would be easier if claims of some cosmic benefit from Jesus' death were tied to an obvious, "ordinary" way that it was a rescue. If the story of Jesus' death were about Jesus plainly jumping under the tree or in front of the sword to save someone else, many might find it less offensive. This would not lay to rest all concerns about idealizing self-sacrifice, but if Jesus' death literally acted out deliverance, it might appear more readily to represent God's taking just such an action universally. If someone performs a rescue in one of the concrete ways we have instanced, and suffers a great deal as a result, we are not likely to criticize that person for setting a bad example in the process.

What I have tried to say in this book is that there is a concrete rescue in the cross. There is the rescue and vindication of a victim of scapegoating sacrifice, and more broadly, there is a rescue of all of us from the thoughtless bondage to that violent way of maintaining peace and unity. This is a saving transaction, in which God is willing to be subjected to our persecution in order to deprive it of future victims and end its power. That is the simple rescue, on which the other meanings of the cross are built.

Critics of atonement theology see in the account of Jesus' death no literal redemptive example. And in a sense they are exactly right, for the Gospels themselves make this point. They dramatically emphasize that the crucifixion is wrong. The Gospel presentations stress that it is an evil act, and make no effort to soften that fact. As critics see it, the theology of the cross seems to suppose that the heavenly value of Jesus' death increases in direct proportion to its failure to do any earthly good. The cross does not present us with a parable of behavior that is admirable in some general sense. Rather than the concrete demonstration of a rescue, the passion narratives give us Jesus' predictions of his death, an assurance that it will happen according to the scriptures, and an assurance that it will be offered for us. Critics do not find here any meaningful explanation of why that death would help. It is an "empty" death, and seems to invite or require the postulation of some hidden divine transaction to give it the meaning it lacks on the face of things.

The Wrong Paradox

The classic penal substitutionary theology of atonement (we will take Anselm as its representative) constructs the terms of just such a hidden transaction. It posits a cosmic bargain that takes place on a plane quite distinct from the historical reality of the crucifixion. This mistaken move has decisive consequences. But before we explore those results in detail, we need to register the many authentic elements of the passion that Anselm incorporates in his vision. These are factors that account for the many positive effects that the teaching has had, despite its deep flaws. If the result is faulty, it is because the elements are misaligned, not because he starts with the wrong material.

In developing his theology Anselm fixes on a few details as crucial cues. Nearly all of them figure significantly also in the reading of the cross that I have been advocating. His doctrine of atonement builds around many of the key antimythical elements of the Gospels. He assumes, as scripture does, the injustice of the crucifixion, the falseness of the accusations, the innocence of the victim, and the uniqueness of the divine act that takes place in this event, separate from the intentions (explicit and implicit) of its human actors. On all these points Anselm is in line with the fundamental critique of historical sacrifice present in the Gospels. He stresses that it is not humans' offering of someone else's blood that is saving. That ancient human path is identified and condemned in the passion accounts. It is not the crowd's thirst for Jesus' blood, for a third party's death, that saves us. It is God's willingness to suffer in our place that is the unique and only transformative meaning for "sacrifice." Anselm rejects any repetitive practice that exchanges some people's suffering for others' benefit.

This shows up in his discussion of whether the number of humans to be saved is defined by the number of angels who fell, and who thus must be replaced to fill out God's original plan. Anselm rejects this logic entirely, and for a striking reason. If this were the case, then each person saved would owe his or her blessedness to the fall and misfortune of another being. As Anselm says, "if anyone says that elect men will rejoice in the loss of the angels as much as in their own exaltation (since unquestionably the latter could not have come about apart from the former) how can they be defended from this perverse joy?" Therefore the number of saved humanity must be greater than that of the fallen angels, so that there could never be "occasion for joy in another's loss."[4] He understands the dynamic of "perverse joy," and knows that the project of salvation must not trade in it.

Anselm clearly breaks with the foundational mythic scenario that assumes victims must be regularly offered to assure peace and harmony. He condemns that idea, because in his view this task can belong to only one person, the incarnate Word. All of Anselm's arguments that are aimed to point up the human need for just such an extraordinary savior serve to make this point as well. On the only point that matters, atonement for sin, human sacrifices are of no avail. They cannot redeem us. Our offering of others is sinful and in vain. Even our offering of ourselves, any self-immolation, would be equally futile. Like the writer of the Letter to the Hebrews, Anselm firmly grasps this point. Without Christ, no amount of self-sacrifice, no amount of innocent suffering offered in any way could save us. With Christ, not even the smallest increment from any others is needed.

In the wake of Christ, no innocent suffering can be propounded as required by God. Suffering may come. It may even be occasioned by obedience and faithfulness to God. But it has no role to play in "satisfying" God. That was done once for all. Insisting on the necessity of divine initiative and divine action for reconciliation, Anselm rejects the assumption that human action alone may be sufficient. One good reason to deny this assumption is that whenever it is granted it tends to lend support to the common human procedure for effective atonement — sacrifice and

---

4. Anselm, "Why God Became Man," in *A Scholastic Miscellany: Anselm to Ockham,* ed. Eugene R. Fairweather, Library of Christian Classics (Philadelphia: Westminster, 1956), 128-29.

scapegoating. In these fundamental ways Anselm recognizes and affirms the antisacrificial trajectory of the passion narratives. It is the presence of all these elements in his theology that accounts for its many liberating as well as destructive effects. So, for instance, even a very sacrificial reading of the cross that treats Jesus as a divine scapegoat, often still powerfully deflects our tendency to cast our own guilt onto a human scapegoat, allowing it to be discharged instead by Christ. Those who have opposed sacred violence from within the Anselmian perspective have done so on the basis of these resources.

But the Anselmian view of the cross is defined by two major additional steps. The first is the decision to privilege legal images to represent the basic dynamic of "death for us." Anselm senses the magnitude of God's action in the cross. It is something unexpected, gracious, and of universal vicarious effect. It has the immense dimensions that earlier Christian writers often describe in the terms of a unique and final sacrifice. Anselm sought to define the scope of grace through a legal quantification of our moral debt and Christ's merit.

The second step is to conflate this legal framework with a vision of divine justice that dictates God's purpose in suffering death. If Christ steps in to intercept a blow meant for us, where does that blow itself come from? It is occasioned by our sin (so far, a view fully in accord with the general tradition). Anselm's departure is to insist with new systematic rigor that it is actually coming from God. What we need to be rescued from is the deserved wrath and punishment of God. God wishes to be merciful, and so God becomes the one to be punished on behalf of us all. God strikes the same blow that God protects us from.

In response to the criticisms of atonement in his day, which complained that only a weak or incompetent God would be compelled to go to the unseemly lengths of incarnation, and especially death by crucifixion, to redeem a wayward creation, Anselm explained the necessity of incarnation by focusing on the magnitude of the human offense, something only the infinite merit of God's undeserved suffering could overbalance. The paradoxes of Anselm's satisfaction theory attempt to reflect the paradox in the Gospels. The scriptural presentation of the crucifixion as both a bad thing and a good thing is translated to mean that the bad (undeserved) suffering of an innocent victim is finally a good thing, when it provides the merit to allow God to remit the punishment rightly due humanity. The debt to God can be paid only with what is not already owed. Jesus' death can cover the bill because God's justice cannot demand it, because it is so purely undeserved. The cross is necessary because it is not required. It works only because it is wrong. The wrongness is part of the solution.[5]

This vision draws its power from points of genuine contact with the Gospel narratives of the cross. But it has gone badly astray, at a point where even a small difference can do great harm. The wrongful suffering Jesus is subjected to, the evil the passion is meant to end, becomes the essential good to be celebrated in it. The key error is to refer both the meaning and need of Jesus' death to its character as an offering *to God.* What Anselm rejects at the level of human community, he re-creates at the level of community between God and humanity, a community whose reconciliation depends on the offering of an innocent victim. Most important, Anselm presents God as the one who *requires* this sacrifice and also as the one *to whom* it is offered.

Scapegoating is a human practice, and Anselm is clear that such a practice cannot solve our estrangement from God. But in his view God has taken over a human scapegoating sacrifice (the execution of Jesus) and turned it into a unique scapegoating sacrifice of unimaginable magnitude. God is doing what human sacrifice does, but on a much larger scale, and one time only. God has not stepped into the process to oppose it, but to perfect it. Sacrifice to end sacrifice is an accurate and biblical way to describe Jesus' death, but it is an ambiguous and delicately poised idea. Anselm has taken it to mean that God does the same thing that human scapegoaters do, taking it to an ultimate extreme. Instead of God throwing a wrench into the gears of human sacrifice, Anselm's God has endorsed that machinery, borrowing it to perform the biggest and most effective sacrifice of all. Jesus has become our all-purpose scapegoat, whose suffering generates an infinite reservoir of merit that, like his shed blood, can be dispensed through the sacraments.

These are fatal steps. Once these points become fixed, they dramatically deform the theology of the cross. To return to our simple image about Jesus stepping in between us and an evil bearing down on us, we can say that Anselm unequivocally states that what is bearing down on us is God and God's wrath. This radically bifurcates the God of justice and the

---

5. Anselm's logic seems much attached to double negatives, as in his ontological argument for God's existence. God is that being greater than which we cannot conceive another. A God who does not exist is not the greatest being we can conceive, so the very idea of God means an existing God. The necessity of God becoming human to die in order to save us is dictated by the fact that this is something God could under no circumstances be expected to do. The death is an undeserved suffering greater than which no other can be conceived. These two unthinkables seem somehow linked for Anselm.

God of forgiveness, and it appears to require a plan of salvation that sets Christ and God against each other. In contrast, I have argued that the actual transaction at the cross is one in which God is handed over to our redemptive violence in order to liberate us from it, not the transaction between God's left hand and right hand that Anselm pictures.

Even within the logic of the satisfaction theory, it is not hard to find problems. If the undeserved suffering of Jesus is of infinite compensatory value, since it is freely offered to God apart from any obligation, has not the humanity that inflicts this wrong on the Son of God likewise contracted a new and unlimited guilt? Before this we had failed in our obligations as creatures to return the finite obedience we owed our maker. In this act we committed a gratuitous offense beyond any evil that would have been possible in our ordinary existence. We end up more guilty, not less.[6]

Anselm's mistake is to make primary what is derivative. God did not become human only to die. And Christ did not die as he did to cancel an infinity of deserved punishment for humanity with the infinitely undeserved suffering of innocent divinity. The legal apparatus around the crucifixion is not there because God has a satisfaction case to prosecute and a punishment to enforce on humanity, but because the machinery of false accusation and political and religious legitimacy are part of the way sacred violence works. The death of Jesus follows the script of human persecution because that is the ongoing evil into whose path Jesus steps, to rescue us from sacrifice, to open the way to new community.

Anselm's doctrine preserves paradox, but the wrong one. He has made the cross a celebration of the sacrifice it meant to overcome. We have seen in earlier chapters how two things are stereoscopically overlaid in the passion narrative: a bare description of scapegoating sacrifice along with the rationale of its practitioners, and then a counterscript of criticism, rejection, and reversal of that practice. The second is the distinctive meaning of the cross. At a crucial point Anselm has crossed these wires and taken over part of the sacrificial rationale that was being rejected. In his vision there is a crisis of conflict that threatens to tear creation permanently apart. It is the conflict between humanity and God. Sin has put them at irreconcilable odds. The only way peace can be restored is for God and humanity to unite together in sacrificing an innocent victim. God, Judas, Herod, Pilate, Caiaphas, Peter — all join in one unanimous crowd. This is

---

6. In such logic there is an impetus to lay the responsibility for Jesus' actual death on others, an impetus toward anti-Semitism.

straightforward sacrificial logic, borrowed from the script followed in the Gospels by those who kill Jesus. And Anselm has enlisted God on its side. But it is a logic the passion narratives subvert and the resurrection denies.

The obvious change Anselm must make when this sacrificial scenario migrates into his thought from the realm of mythical sacrifice is an inescapably Christian one. Given his commitment to scripture, the true nature of the sacrificial logic cannot remain invisible. It must be directly faced. In classical sacrifice the guilt of the scapegoat and the validity of the charges against him or her are assumed. The crowd celebrates the killing because they do not recognize any victim. Innocent suffering works to bring peace because it is invisible as such. For Anselm, since the Gospels have made the victim unavoidably visible, it is the *acknowledged* innocent suffering of the victim that becomes the hinge of the whole process. The effectiveness of Jesus' death in reconciling us with God depends on our knowing full well that it is unjustified persecution. The Gospels pulled back the veil of unanimous accusation to show the hidden truth of sacrifice, the undeserved suffering of the innocent victim. What was revealed was what was wrong, and what must be changed. But Anselm insists that what we see behind the veil is right. God has become the proprietor of redemptive violence, and by that very act made it a good thing. This injustice becomes the whole purpose of the incarnation, and not one of the prime evils Christ came to defeat. Thus, at the last minute, things are turned backward. Rather than a strategic act of resistance to overthrow sacred violence, the cross becomes a divine endorsement of it. This is the missed connection, so close to the truth and yet so fatally far, that has tangled our thinking about substitutionary atonement.

Beginning with Barabbas

If current arguments between those who would exalt substitutionary, sacrificial doctrines of atonement and others who would exclude all such language limit us to those choices, we lose either way. We have seen the error of a predominantly Anselmian view. But, shut out, the sacrifice-related material will be left to reemerge again in distorted forms. We need to weave that material into its integral place in the antisacrificial meaning of Jesus' death. That integration preserves the essential contribution these elements make, at the same time that it contains their dangers.

Let's go back over the ground again, beginning with the observation that Jesus' death is not an obvious rescue in the ordinary sense. We have the benefit of centuries of history in which to observe the effect of the cross. People in the first century had a countervailing advantage of sorts in that they readily believed that sacrifice works (both purely cultic sacrifice and ritualized scapegoating), even if the rationales they accepted for that working were mythical in nature. The conviction was implicit all around them: redemptive violence accomplishes something. Thus they could understand what it meant when Gospel writers and others set out the story of Jesus' execution in sacrifice-related terms. To have this killing of an innocent presented nakedly as an evil thing, an act against God, and yet at the same time as exemplifying the practice of sacrifice, communicated powerfully that there is something wrong with that practice. The similarity is there as a critique. If we in our time look for a more explicit "rescue motif" in the passion and object to its absence, this is one more indication of the way we have been affected by the cross. We want to see Jesus helping a scapegoat, not being one. It is a criticism that Jesus died to make possible.

I suggested that people might find atonement more intelligible if the passion account fit a rescue mold. Jesus' sacrifice to save a particular person might more readily symbolize some divine act to save all. This, however, is just the point. Suppose building blocks fell from the temple wall and Jesus was crushed while thrusting a child out of harm's way. This might readily *represent* "saving" in some generic sense. But we could hardly say that event and its reporting directly cause that reality, that they effectively bring about that wider transformation for others. The act itself does not change the conditions for future building accidents. There would be no objective, constitutive effect of that event, as Christians claim is true of Jesus' death. By contrast, we have been rehearsing in this book the way the cross and the passion narratives *can* be seen not just as a striking illustration of a known reality, but as an intervention that changes the situation we had known before. That Jesus died as he did, the isolated scapegoat unjustly sacrificed for the peace of a divided community at a flashpoint of social crisis, was a way of stepping directly into the path of an evil process that bears down on all of us — victims, possible victims, and perpetrators.

Jesus' death and resurrection are a concrete confrontation with reconciling violence. God snatches Jesus out of the silence of the scapegoat's tomb and rescues not just his life, but also his persecutors from their guilt and the need for endless repetitions of this crime. That is what happens in those events themselves, and this is what they represent theologically in a more universal sense. The events and their description actually change the status and practice of such violence among us. They rescue us from our bondage to the sacrificial process. The passion may not conform to our immediate intuitive image of rescue, but that is because our intuitions themselves are in a process of conversion by the cross. The conversion is in many respects far advanced. It shows up in the simple fact that when people (of any religious or nonreligious outlook) say someone is "being crucified," they mean to point out scapegoating persecution. When we look at the crucifixion, we don't see Jesus rescuing anyone; we see him being victimized in a specially collective way. That is the basis even for our criticisms of atonement doctrines, criticisms that themselves reflect our rescue.

The concrete antisacrificial character of the passion is the decisive starting point for our theology of the cross, and the other dimensions of that theology must flow from it. Whatever implications it has for the relation of God and humans, the distinctive first-order event that is happening in Jesus' death (as distinguished from other elements of his life and ministry) is a confrontation with scapegoating. That is the specific rescue on which wider notions of a saving death need to build.

We too-readily read the passion narratives and leap to the idea that Jesus must be dying to satisfy some cosmic debt, since he obviously isn't dying for anyone's sake in the literal sense. He's just dying for the sake of dying, it seems, or at most dying in noble fidelity to his convictions. But this is to let a mistaken theology drive us further out of touch with scripture. The contention that Jesus' death did not rescue anyone is plainly false. One detail on which all four Gospels agree is that Jesus was literally exchanged for another condemned prisoner, Barabbas. Barabbas, like the two thieves on Calvary, underlines the point that sacrifice is already going on. Victims are going to be offered this Passover week; only their identities are at issue. There is a real person whose place Jesus takes and for whose sake he dies. That person is redeemed and the price is Jesus' blood. All the traditional language is here simply, descriptively true. It has a concrete, historical application. Barabbas can say, with no theological overlay at all, that Jesus died for him. Jesus bore the punishment for Barabbas's sins.

But in the Gospels Jesus' substitution for Barabbas is not some generic parable of selflessness that could as well be replaced with Jesus dying while rescuing a child from drowning or a man from a snake. It is one crucial feature in a larger picture, which is Christ's contention with sacred violence. The Jesus-Barabbas exchange is not initiated by Jesus, because the purpose of Jesus' death is not a purely individual one. The moral of the cross is not that one victim should substitute himself for another. The act of Jesus' "sacrifice" is meant to overturn the mechanism of victimage. Its primary aim is to save, not to substitute. It is an instrumental element of the story that in this once-for-all act the saving comes by substituting. The early Christian theologians underlined this when they treated that exchange as a trick, a divine ruse, a stratagem. God turns the indiscriminate hunger for victims in the sacrificial process against itself, so that it seizes the unique one who can break its power. Switching victims is not an ideal Jesus is teaching. It is a providential tactic. In the incarnation God acts savingly by exchanging the divine power and status for our human lot, so that we may exchange our fallen state for participation in the divine nature. That is the great exchange, and it is a genuine model for the mutuality of the Christian life generally. But the specific exchange by which Jesus takes the victim's place on the cross is a means, not a model.

Pilate underlines the arbitrariness of the sacrificial process in offering the crowd a choice. In the Gospel of Matthew, even the names of the two are interchangeable. "Whom do you want me to release for you, Jesus Barabbas or Jesus who is called the Messiah?" (Matt. 27:17). Just as it could as easily be Barabbas as Jesus, it could as easily be someone else as Barabbas. It could be us. The link between Jesus' dying for this one individual and faith's perception of a universal saving effect of Christ's death is the scapegoating practice, which prescribed sacrifice in the first place. That is the practice Jesus' death and resurrection bring to light and reverse. The rescue of Barabbas is good news for him alone, but the end of the victimage mechanism would be good news for all. His ransom is a concrete event that represents a general amnesty. The substitution aims not only to save Barabbas but to end the sacrificial process itself.

As surely as Jesus came between Barabbas and the cross, Jesus' death on the cross comes between us and one specific evil to which we are collectively in thrall, scapegoating sacrifice. This is the third party, whose blow was directed at Barabbas until Jesus intercepted it. Pilate and Caiaphas may be the actors, but the Gospels make it clear that they are captive to this dynamic — they do not command it. It is a power of our own sinful construction, whose destructive force hangs over us all. It is destructive in its persecution of victims and destructive too for the members of the crowd who purchase peace with violence and thereby estrange themselves from God and poison their social relationships with each other.

Redemption from this habit of purchasing unity through persecution is not the sum total of Jesus' saving work. There are many other facets. But it *is* the distinctive focus of the saving work of the cross. God's reaching out in the incarnation involved many things. Overcoming death itself, and sharing the promise of eternal life through resurrection, was part of that mission. In that respect dying (by some means) is something Christ came to do. But layered upon that saving work, if you will, is yet another that dictates a certain mode of death. That this death should take the specific form it does in the passion, with the features that the Jesus of the Gospels predicts and highlights — *that* is for the sake of engaging this special sacrificial bondage at the deep intersection of our religion and our politics. The two saving aims are combined in one event, so that a resurrection that witnesses to the triumph over death is at the same time the vindication of the victim. It is at once a promise about a life to come and a radical transformation in life here and now.

Only with a firm grasp on this starting point will the rest of the pieces fall into place. This is the concrete rescue that theology builds on. The death of Jesus set in motion a very concrete historical effect, the unveiling and undermining of sacrifice. Christ died for us, to save us from what killed him. And what killed him was not God's justice but our redemptive violence. He stepped in between our violence and our victims, and has been a haunting presence there ever since.

Stripes That Heal

The problem with most traditional language about Christ's death is not that it is wrong, but that it balances on a knife's edge of interpretation. This book suggests a key to keep in hand as we use these concepts. We can consider a few illustrations. Perhaps the most concise example would be the confession that "Jesus died for us." As a normal, sacrificial scapegoat, Jesus died for all those in the tense community of Roman-occupied Jerusalem whose peace might be at least temporarily maintained by charging him with responsibility for their divisions. We are all part of communities that have participated in scapegoating. So by extension we can say Jesus died for us, subject to the same mechanism that exists also for us. To make this connection we have to identify Jesus with our own scapegoats. We can't say, "Jesus died for us," and mean it, unless we can locate the process that killed him in our own social history, and unless we can see other ones than Jesus who died for us in this sacrificial sense. It is Jesus' revelatory identification with the scapegoat that equips us to make this connection, that enables us to look into our own context and see those who may be in Jesus' place.

This is a descriptive statement about a violent reconciliation that goes on in human affairs. There is nothing actually divine about this unifying persecution, though the process and its effectiveness were historically framed in myth as required by religious powers. This kind of vicarious atonement is a product of human sin, and it is the problem the passion narratives describe, not the solution they prescribe. The Gospels may be said to teach, or reveal, that Jesus died for us in this way, in the sense that they display this as the dynamic that drives the crucifixion and as the operative intent of its perpetrators.

Another traditional formulation is that Christ died for our sins. This amplifies what we have just said. Scapegoats are needed because of conflict and the threat or escalation of violence within a group. Whatever sins or human failings create this division and prevent its resolution by peaceful means are thus the basic reason for sacrifice, and the victim can be said to die on account of them, to die for our sins. This is true then of Christ as well.

So far we are dealing with diagnostic statements. We have discussed the way this descriptive account is developed in the Hebrew scriptures, and the impact that follows when such accounts displace mythic ones that hide the reality of the victim. The passion narratives continue in that vein. A firm grasp on this level of meaning is necessary for formulation of the confession that Christ died for us in a second way. Christ died for us to stop us from having people die for us. Scapegoats die for us because we make peace that way. Christ became one of those scapegoats and died so that we could live without them. Jesus was put to death in our way, but he went to death to end our way. Jesus became a scapegoat for us, but Jesus is not our scapegoat.

Once we grasp that point, we realize that the theology of the cross must always be reading the first-level descriptive statements about sacrifice in light of the action God is taking to change what is described. A variation of the traditional language we noted would say that Jesus bears the punishment for our sins. This is true in the first descriptive sense we noted above: scapegoats are "expiating" the aggressions and animosities that bring communities to crisis. Instead of all the individuals in the community being held responsible in some proportional way for their particular contributions to this division, the victim receives punishment for all. Jesus receives punishment in just this way, bearing the punishment the crowd has unknowingly projected from themselves onto him. This is an accurate report of sinful human practice. But there is another truth on top of it. Since the primary aim of Jesus' death is to reverse sacrifice, there is a separate way in which Jesus may be said to bear the punishment for our sin. This time the sin is the sin of sacrifice itself. To scapegoat is wrong, and for inflicting this injustice on our victims we ourselves deserve the punishment we are giving them. So in this additional sense, Jesus can be said to bear punishment for our sins also.

Christ became a curse for us. Jesus suffered for our sins. We are washed in the blood of the Lamb, redeemed by his death. Behold, the Lamb of God who takes away the sins of the world. These and many other formulas are variations on this same dynamic. They refer both to the sacrificial practice that claimed Jesus and to the redemptive purpose that worked against it. Christ became cursed and accused as all scapegoats do, for the sake of the unity his accusers sought. That is according to the fallen wisdom of sacrifice. But it is according to the wisdom of God that Christ was willing to be treated so, to become a curse for us in order to liberate victims and sacrificers alike from this changeless cycle. What makes the first sacrifice effective is mutual animosity, false accusation, unanimous blindness, unquestioned violence. What makes the second redemptive purpose (what God is doing) effective is just the opposite.

Upon him was the punishment that made us whole, and with his stripes we are healed. This is a hard-won understanding of the down-to-earth facts about scapegoating. The sacrificial violence that the victim suffers is the very medicine that restores the operative health of the community that gathers against her or him. When we say this of Jesus, we are telling a truth that, once grasped, can be seen repeated and verified elsewhere with sad consistency. To say this *diagnostically* is one element of biblical faith. Without awareness of it, we cannot see that Jesus' death exemplifies a disease but also treats it. The same words then have a second level, with special application to Jesus. With his stripes we are healed means also that because of Christ's stripes (that is, his acceptance to be subject to the entire scapegoating treatment), we can be healed of the addiction to that treatment.

We could imagine a school where students collectively scapegoated a new arrival, an outsider. The actors justify their abuse on some political or racial basis, and the school authorities rationalize it as well and turn a blind eye. For the sake of our analogy, we could add that in this case the persecuted one and his or her family may actually have come to agree with the crowd, by having internalized and accepted a sense of unworthiness and culpability. Let us further suppose that a person in a position of greater authority and power goes undercover, occupying the position of a vulnerable outsider, and undergoes the same treatment. Then in short order this agent appears in her own name, with undeniable videotaped evidence of the violent crimes, and with a conclusive judgment from higher authorities that an injustice has been committed and will be made right.

This is a revelatory act. It uncovers the true nature of what has been happening, in a way that cuts through the participants' blindness. And it is a transformative act, for it requires at least an effort at new behavior. In such a "sting" operation it would be factually correct to say of the agent who was hazed and abused that by her stripes her classmates were healed. This would be true first in the sense that it would have been accurate to say the same of any of the prior victims. This sacrificial practice brought the participants a "healing" sense of unity. But the further, profound layer in the same statement points to the fact that the agent's suffering in this special case was predicated on ending the victimization and was uniquely effective to do so. It succeeded in healing the community of its practice of persecution. Two healings are side by side here, the one produced by violent sacrifice and the one achieved by its elimination.

The challenge for the theology of the cross is to keep the first-level description of the sacrificial exchange that is being condemned and overcome in Christ's death from bleeding, literally, back into the formulation of what God is doing through that death and what Christians celebrate in faith. One check on this can be found in the relation between God and Jesus (and in trinitarian terms between the Father and the incarnate Word) that atonement theories assume. We saw that Anselm's theology requires the two to take up opposing positions in the work of redemption, one inflicting God's wrath and the other bearing it. It is central to Anselm's doctrine that this must be a quite literal opposition, where divine mercy and divine justice settle their differences by violence. The elevation of that opposition is the sign of a mistaken theology.

The truth is that God and Jesus together submit themselves to human violence. Both suffer its results. Both reveal and overcome it. God does not require the death of the Son anymore than Jesus requires the helpless bereavement of the Father. Jesus' suffering is not required as an offering to satisfy God anymore than one member of a team undertaking a very dangerous rescue mission "requires" another, dearly loved member to be in a place of peril or pain. They are constantly and consistently on the same side. By virtue of their love and communion with each other, each suffers what the other suffers. They are not playing out a war in the heart of God. If we wish to use the language of acting, then the early Christian writers were more correct when they saw the acting as directed toward the sacrificial powers, presenting an apparent helplessness before them that was in truth part of their disarming.

Those scholars who claim that the earliest "doctrine" of the cross stressed the theme of Christ's victory are right in that Christians stressed that Jesus' death was a confrontation, a battle with the powers of sin and bondage. But it is a mistake to suppose that such a perspective should downplay the importance of the category of sacrifice, or eliminate it. Its importance rests primarily in understanding what dimension of sin is most specifically at issue at the cross, and how it is being overcome. When images of Christ on the cross began to emerge in the church, it was a raised and reigning Jesus who appeared. This is the cross seen from the side of the resurrection, the scapegoat vindicated and the death reversed.

The sacrificing of Jesus was the work of sin, but the overcoming of that scapegoating death is the work of God. Sacrifice is the game the powers of this world were playing with Jesus, and apparently winning, according to the old rules. God's victory broke the hold of this game itself, "made captivity itself a captive" (Eph. 4:8). Such images dramatically affirm that God has defeated scapegoating death and returned to claim the site of that violence, the cross, as a throne. It is out of commission for the execution business and ruled by another power. Such was also the image when a Christian church was built over a site of prior sacrifice, even human sacrifice.[7] It is as if the prison where torture took place becomes a hospital.

The Stone That the Builders Rejected

The distinctive objective work involved in the specific plot of Jesus' death is the confrontation with scapegoating sacrifice. This is central to understanding Jesus' death as a historical event, one that cannot be attributed to only Jews or Romans, to religion or politics, to weak disciples or false friends, but that results from a powerful dynamic that subsumes them all. It is also key to understanding Jesus' death as a transformative act, one that has changed our situation. Much is at stake in maintaining this in-

---

7. The struggle for the theology of the cross goes to the heart of the interpretation of an image like Christ in glory on the cross. The image itself, like the construction of a church on the site of earlier religious sacrifice, can be read in contrary ways. One could look at representations of Christ in glory on the cross and see this as a representation not of victory over sacrifice, but of the sacrifice itself. God's victory *is* the dying. The violence is the triumph. The serene Christ is untouched by any suffering, a kind of mythic cover obscuring the reality of crucifixion. Likewise one could see the church rising over a site of sacrifice as an act of continuity, not opposition. So, for instance, insistence that the image of Christ in glory on the cross should have a visual monopoly in the church (over against a crucifix or an empty cross) would be a sign of such imbalance, or would foster it.

terpretive center of gravity. Anselm's conviction that a legal exchange is the heart of the objective meaning of the cross leads him to focus above all on the forensic elements in the passion narratives and to interpret all the other data in those terms. I have indicated above how a focus on sacrifice leads us to interpret the same traditional features differently. But so far we have not adequately addressed the elements of guilt and punishment that loom so large in atonement doctrine.

Anselm begins with the universal extent and profound depth of human sinfulness. Both are realities. But this general truth is not an adequate departure point for understanding the specific import of the cross. Rather it should be the other way around. We must start with the concrete nature of the sin in Jesus' death in order to articulate its connection to our wider human condition. Treating guilt and sin as a single undifferentiated quantitative value was one of Anselm's mistakes. After all, Jesus confronted the realities of sinfulness at every step in his prepassion life. And in every case he encountered those realities in concrete shapes, like greed or envy or deceit or pride. The general truth has a particular face in the case of the crucifixion as well. Specific understanding of the cross must begin not with the question of how God can be justified in forgiving the guilty. That is a second-level question. The beginning point is provided by the biblical context for the cross, the thread that runs through Abel and Joseph and Jonah and Job and Susanna and Daniel and the Psalms and the Prophets. Its question is, how can God be justified unless God sides with the unanimous victim, unless God vindicates and redeems the scapegoat?

Only the extraordinary conviction that God does in fact redeem the victim, coupled with the Gospel revelation that God has actually shared the place of the scapegoat, can lead to a further question. If God vindicates the sacrificed, if God has even been the object of our sacred persecution, then how can God be justified in saving the guilty, i.e., the victimizers? And the guilty are all of us, because, Christ excepted, there is no one who is a scapegoat who would not or has not belonged to the crowd. *Now* the issue of guilt arises dramatically, for if God is to do justice for victims, how can God fail to do justice against their persecutors?[8]

In seeing Christ on the cross, in the light of the resurrection, believers see what has happened . . . and not just to Jesus. What is revealed is not only the enormity of such violence against God, but the evil of our long-

8. This is the problem raised in one form of apocalyptic vision, as we explored in chapter 9.

standing scapegoating against each other. We can no longer say we know not what we do. And when this abyss opens before us, the order of magnitude of this sin appears virtually unlimited. It is the dimensions of grace that bring home to us the real nature of wrong.[9] We see that Jesus does not deserve to be on the cross. That allows us to see that those we put on the cross in the same place Jesus occupied, for the same socially unifying purpose, do not deserve their scapegoating at our hands (whatever their real sins may be). And when this awareness comes to us, a third link falls into place. *We* are the ones who deserve the punishment we have readily meted out to others. We are the ones who deserve to be in Jesus' place, but he has taken ours.

Jesus tells a parable in which the landlord of a vineyard sends messengers to collect his rent, only to have the tenants beat his messengers. When he finally sends his son, the tenants kill him and throw him out of the vineyard. At the conclusion of this parable in the Gospel of Matthew, Jesus asks the crowd: When the owner of the vineyard comes, what will he do to those tenants? "They said to him, 'He will put those wretches to a miserable death, and lease the vineyard to other tenants who will give him the produce at the harvest time'" (Matt. 21:41).

This story, and Jesus' presentation, echoes the famous story of David and Bathsheba. King David arranges for Uriah, one of his soldiers, to be abandoned in battle to be killed, so that David may fulfill his adulterous desire for Bathsheba, Uriah's wife. The prophet Nathan confronts David by telling him a story of a rich man who steals a poor neighbor's only lamb, to offer it as a meal for a guest. David explodes in anger that this man deserves to be killed. "You are that man," Nathan replies, forcing the king to confront his action and pronounce his own judgment. In similar fashion, Jesus allows his listeners to draw their own conclusion about the wrath that should fall on the collective sin of the tenants. And then Jesus said to them, "Have you never read in the scriptures: 'The stone that the builders rejected / has become the cornerstone; / this was the Lord's doing, / and it is amazing in our eyes'?" (Matt. 21:42).

The rejected stone — the sacrificed one — did serve as the basis for maintaining society. The ancient practice of burying sacrificial victims (human and otherwise) in the foundations of great buildings or bridges is a literal reflection of that fact. But Jesus is referring here not only to that ancient baseline of human redemptive violence, but to something new

9. An extraordinary book that illuminates this point is James Alison, *The Joy of Being Wrong: Original Sin through Easter Eyes* (New York: Crossroad, 1997).

that is the Lord's doing. He is pointing not to the descriptive norm of scapegoating but to a new kind of community founded on recognition of the victim and reconciliation without blood. When his listeners emphatically render a sentence of death against the tenants, they are condemning their own practice, and the practice that will claim Jesus. What does it mean for Jesus to respond to their outburst by quoting this passage from a psalm of deliverance? And particularly, why does Jesus introduce it as though it contradicts the judgment of wrath they have just pronounced: "Have you never read . . . ?"

Jesus is the murdered son of the owner of the vineyard, and when he returns in the resurrection he does *not* do what the crowd who heard the parable expected and demanded. He does not put anyone to death. He brings mercy to the tenants, and intends for the management of the vineyard, the kingdom of God, to be under a new lease, one without sacrifice.[10] This rejected stone of the old sort has become a foundation of a new kind. Jesus takes a familiar text and gives it a new meaning. This is exactly parallel to the event of the cross, which takes the routine script of sacrifice and turns it against itself. Jesus' persecutors make him one of the rejected stones, according to that old plan, but the Lord's doing is to vindicate a victim who will not stay sacrificed, the keystone of a new kind of community.

Anselm is not wrong to link the scope of the wrong done to Christ with the scope of the fault among us. But he is wrong to suppose that God's whole purpose was to somehow balance these out. We have rightly understood the wrong of the cross only when we realize it is the same as the wrong done to others. Like someone writing in ever larger letters, God has met our congenital blindness to our own sacrificial practice with an extreme demonstration. If we can begin to see the truth here, then we can see it elsewhere.

I discuss this parable to illustrate that when we connect the story of Jesus' death with a practice in which we participate, the reflexive response is

10. This text is one of those that has figured most prominently in Christian anti-Semitism, and therefore stands much in need of the kind of interpretive framework we are discussing. It was often taken to imply that Jews would have the kingdom of God taken away from them because of the rejection of Jesus. But in the context of Jesus' ministry and given our reading of the passion narratives, this text cannot be read as attributing to the Jews the sole responsibility for Jesus' death. It points instead to a distinction between those who would respond by following a path of reconciliation without sacrifice and those who would not, a distinction that at this point could be seen primarily as a break within Judaism.

a sense of our own guilt. As Girard puts it, "Christianity refers back to humanity the violence that humanity has always projected onto its gods. That is why we accuse Christianity of being so judgmental about our guilt . . . because in order to defend our victims the gospels are obliged to condemn their persecutors, that is to say, us."[11] The cross reveals the evil of scapegoating sacrifice so plainly that we spontaneously condemn it. And when we then see that this practice is our practice, our own judgment falls back upon us. The acute sense of responsibility for Jesus' death is, then, one of the signs that one has been savingly affected by it. We do not clearly see our sin until we see how God has acted to save us from it.

The Grace of Facing Guilt

Guilt and punishment have been primary themes in the theology of the cross. I have suggested that when Anselm took the quantitative magnitude of human guilt as his first axiom for atonement, he went astray. We stay much closer to the truth if we begin by focusing on our shared (and universal) guilt for the specific evil directly manifest in the crucifixion: scapegoating. When we do this we reverse the assumption that God's justice needed a victim in favor of the recognition that it was our helpless social self-medication that required one. We realize that God did not crush our evil through domination by power and violence, but in a kind of divine judo move threw it down by its own weight. To change things irreversibly, God stepped into the place of the victim, and remained God. "You meant it for evil, but God meant it for good."

I have suggested that general guilt should not be the interpretive point of departure for the passion. But that is not to say that it is not an important and necessary issue. In a little-remarked passage in *Cur Deus Homo,* Anselm suggested an important dimension of the question, one that has to do not with the depth of the condemnation we deserve but with the perfection of the blessedness God wants us to enjoy. He had already presented his familiar theory of the infinite scope of human offense against God and our inability to offer any recompense to God, since we owe perfect obedience already. Then he poses to his dialogue partner precisely the question that most critical readers of his theology throughout history have by this point been longing to ask. Why doesn't God just forgive human sin and forget about any need for "satisfaction"?

11. Girard and Treguer, *Quand Ces Choses Commenceront,* 139.

Anselm. But suppose it were true that God forgives him who does not pay what he owes, just because he cannot.

B. That is what I should wish.

A. But as long as he does not repay, he either will or will not wish to re-pay. But if he wishes to do what he cannot do, he will be in want, and if he does not wish to do it, he will be unjust.

B. Nothing is clearer than this.

C. But if he is either in need or unjust, he will not be blessed.[12]

Look at it from the human side, Anselm suggests. If human sin were sim-ply written off, what would it be like for us? The person redeemed in such a way will either long to have been able to offer some recompense to God for sin, or will not. We would expect to find that longing in those who have become righteous and truly love God. Their goodness dictates their sadness. It seems their very virtue dooms them to distress. The alternative would be for the forgiven persons to care nothing for what their evil has cost others and for the suffering necessary to win their freedom. Such people could be happy, but it is hard to see how one could call them good.

Here is an argument for atonement based not on satisfying God but on satisfying the saved, on creating the conditions in which people can be both genuinely good and genuinely happy. It is not the justice or wrath of God that must be appeased here, but it is the saved persons' own sense of fairness that must be satisfied. If they lack all justice and compassion, they have not been truly redeemed. If they do not, they will always be pained by their own sin. Even to know that those we have hurt may now have their lives restored does not change the burden of our own responsibility.

Besides leaving God's justice in question, the choice to simply remit all sins would leave humans in a bind. If they were grateful, as they ought to be, they would regret painfully their failure to repay God and the suffer-ing they had occasioned God and their neighbors. If they were indifferent, they would be sinning anew. Presuming that humans remain free agents, this is a recipe for resentment, distress, and new estrangement, perhaps new conflict. Anselm's psychological and spiritual insight here is striking.

When Anselm emphasizes that the "excess merit" in Jesus' death flows from its nature as a lavish, uncoerced gift, he repeatedly emphasizes that the gift is given by a human being as well as by God. This is important to him because since sin is human, the satisfaction must be human also. It must be no lie or mere pretense that the offering has come from our side.

12. Anselm, "Why God Became Man," 143.

We have contributed something. Anselm's metaphysical assumptions, which I have already rejected, are not the issue at the moment, but rather this particular reason that he gives for validating the union of humanity and divinity in the act of redemption.

We humans are not only objects of unspeakable charity but sisters and brothers of the Redeemer. It is our nature that has offered up this gift as well. It is not only the judgment of some external court that is set aside, but also the quite legitimate reasons we might continue to refuse to let ourselves off the hook, because we had literally done nothing to put things right. This, which might look at first like conscientious virtue, could only eventually go bad. For if we maintain anything that remains unexpiated, the prescription on which we insist will eventually be additional sacrifice, ours or someone else's. Anselm says God's economy has forestalled this dilemma by seeing that the means of redemption are drawn fundamentally from humanity as well as from God.

What is important is not only that humanity be redeemed, but that it be redeemed in such a manner that the groundwork is laid for new life, for liberation from repetition of the same sinful dynamic. The helplessness of humanity must be overcome in a way that does not stimulate humiliation or resentment. These would only be occasions for renewed sin, and particularly the occasion for the kind of sacrifice that claims Jesus and that Jesus' death and resurrection is to end.

There is wisdom here, though its value is largely lost in the strong general current of Anselm's theory. One thing that skews his paradigm is the near-exclusive emphasis on the relations of humans with God. Focus falls almost entirely on sin as an offense against God, with little attention to our sin against others. Yet one effect of recognizing the suffering of God on the cross is to realize its identification with that of so many others. In the Bible, sin against God and sin against neighbor are closely linked. That is, our violence and sin against each other deeply estrange us from God as well.

Anselm's insight is to see that just as it is difficult for victims to accept vindication without revenge, it is difficult for sinners to accept forgiveness without restitution. Our pride makes it hard to accept such forgiveness from strangers or enemies, and our anguish at the hurt we have done those we love makes it hard to accept forgiveness from them. We may think anyone would readily accept "free" forgiveness, but this is less true than we assume. In any event, Anselm understands that to accept it without a second thought is likely not a good sign about our spiritual condition. The desire (or requirement) to make restitution, to repent in a tangible way, is a positive force for healing. And this positive repentance must be an aspect of reconciliation whenever it is possible.[13] If forgiveness is a divine solution for what lies beyond our power to repair or restore, its effectiveness is hampered by the fact that the better people become, the harder they may find it to accept.

In the face of God's goodness, Eve and Adam yielded to an insinuation of rivalry. Suspecting that God wanted to prevent them from becoming equal to God, they defied God. In the face of God's forgiveness and suffering for us, we can be tempted by pride to refuse charity. But we can be tempted also by love. A sincere empathy and care for the one we have harmed can lead us to judge our repentance and forgiveness as too little to offer them. It can leave us longing to be able to even the score, to make up what it has cost to save us. It is at this point that Anselm suggests it is an additional grace for God to be able to say that debt is already paid. Jesus, one of us, offered back to God everything that was needed, and more. This is not a legal transaction, but more like an emotional one, a way of easing the shock of forgiveness.

For Anselm, Jesus' death was driven by a divine dictate that human suffering must be offered to meet God's justice, and the point we have just mentioned was but a secondary argument as to why a divine-human one was needed to be the actor in this drama. I suggest instead that the true objective event in the cross is God's action to free us from scapegoating, which provides its own account as to why Jesus' death was liberating, and provides a different framework for the questions of guilt and punishment. From this perspective we can see Anselm's argument about true blessedness as part of the subjective work of the cross. As the cross works in history and culture to change our sacrificial practice and promote new forms of reconciliation, the cross works at a secondary level in our emotions and inner life to make us more capable of accepting reconciliation.

A paradigm case for simple forgiveness is given in the parable of the prodigal son. The father whose counsel has been spurned and whose legacy has been squandered in sin runs to meet the returning child with open arms. In the face of the child's profound guilt — "I am not worthy to be your son; let me eat with the pigs" — the father will hear of nothing but full restoration and celebration. And this is characteristic of the way Jesus met repentant sinners in the course of his ministry. But we must ask what would happen if the father had not waited at home but had gone out to

13. For a very thoughtful analysis of these issues from the perspectives of Judaism and Christianity, see Solomon Schimmel, *Wounds Not Healed by Time: The Power of Repentance and Forgiveness* (Oxford and New York: Oxford University Press, 2002).

find the unrepentant son, in the far country of his sin. Suppose that out of love the father made those hard conditions of his son's life his own, and endured abuse and violence from the son even in the midst of sharing his lot. And suppose that after long suffering in this manner, the son repented and changed.

Would not the son's position be even more painful than in the Gospel story? I am forgiven, but I can never be happy in this forgiveness, he might say. For it has cost my father too much, and I can do nothing to repay it. All my loving service cannot replace what is lost. And the Gospel story also reminds us that others, like the older brother, can also find this imbalance a stumbling block on the way to restoration of relations. The father could respond, yes, in justice you would pay a price for the sin. But my suffering along with you was not required by justice. It was a free act of love. Let it cancel out your debt. Why should there be more total suffering in the world than even strict legality would require? Count things even, and be free.

The Protestant reformers famously maintained that sinners make no contribution to their own salvation, save their acceptance of the fact that they are freely forgiven. As we have been noting, accepting forgiveness is actually quite an accomplishment, since both sin and love can block the way. Our amplification of the example of the prodigal son underlines the way in which this difficulty deepens in a purely binary relation. The father offers his own suffering to cancel out the debt of the son, but that suffering is exactly what the son sees *as* the debt he would wish to be able to meet.

Here we sense the importance of an intermediary figure. Nothing disposes me more to be open to receive grace than the conviction that I have also had some part in returning it, the conviction that some recompense has been made to those I have harmed from my side or on my behalf. Christ's work of reconciliation and atonement operates in just that intermediary territory. For in Christ each of us can believe that something has been offered up to God on our behalf (in face of all the unmerited grace we have received) and each of us can believe that a wondrous, unlooked-for gift has been given to us (in the face of all our sins and evils). The first can help us accept grace, and the second can help us share it. Anselm's magnificently mistaken view is at the very edge of this realization. We could rather bluntly translate his theology to be saying that God is unreasonably gracious to us because someone (Jesus) has been unreasonably gracious to God. Anselm, of course, would never put it that way, but to do so illustrates both what is wrong with his approach (God must wait upon some expiation to be gracious) and his grasp of the right logic (God's saving work is to infect us with peaceful reconciliation).

When we look around us, we can see that those who have been in the place of the victim can have unusual power for reconciliation: a Nelson Mandela, Desmond Tutu, or Václav Havel. But for peaceful reconciliation to work there must also be de Klerks and Gorbachevs. The effects of persecution can lead its victims to embittered hatred. And awareness of their responsibility can lead participants in persecution to bitterness and hatred as well. This does not change the asymmetry between the two, the injustice suffered by one in contrast to the injustice inflicted by the other, the fact that hatred is stoked by a desire for revenge on one side and by a resentment of guilt on the other. Moral clarity requires that we never blur this difference. Yet there can be no peace unless these different temptations can be overcome on both sides.

This was the profound insight of South Africa's truth and reconciliation commission. Truth is what must not be denied the victims (and in many cases, though not all, this includes a requisite legal punishment for the offenders). Reconciliation is what is not possible without some exorcism of the guilt of those who will accept it. Insofar as the legacy of the cross informed that process, it was not a theory that all sins had already been expiated, all offenders are free, and no accountability is needed. Instead, it was the legacy of the ability to recognize victims, the understanding of the false ideas of unity to which they have been sacrificed, and the profound knowledge that Christ died to oppose sacrifice and to end violence.

Many of our conflicts, both small-scale and large-scale, are hardly so simple as to have all victims clearly on one side. The influence of the cross may be a primary cause of the fact that ideological fervor in our times typically expresses itself by defining my faction to be composed only of the sacrificed and my opponents' faction as populated only by the crowd. In the normal course of most human relations, however, individuals and groups have occasion to stand on more than one side of the cross's subjective meaning.

All these considerations we have just discussed come after and rest upon the first-order work of the cross in overcoming sacrifice. They hold their shape only when oriented to that basis. Jesus died for us in all these ways, but the animating energy flows to them from the reversal of sacrifice. Some might dismiss these last points I have discussed as merely subjective or psychological glosses on that primary reality, but I believe that the process of subjective appropriation of God's objective acts is included in the redemptive economy. God does not disdain to look this far into our need, and the power of these images is itself part of the rippling effect of the one saving work.

I unequivocally advocate a reversal of polarity in our common theology of the cross. We are not reconciled with God and each other by a sacrifice of innocent suffering offered to God. We are reconciled with God because God at the cost of suffering rescued us from bondage to a practice of violent sacrifice that otherwise would keep us estranged, making us enemies of the God who stands with our victims. We are reconciled with each other because, at the cost of suffering, God offered us an alternative to our ancient machinery of unity. So long as our peace depends on scapegoats, we are never truly reconciled with each other. We only appear to be one community until the next crisis, at which point the short straw of exclusion will be drawn by some one or more of us.

All this is simply another approach to very traditional categories describing stages of Christian faith. The first is the conviction of sin, and in our presentation this comes with the realization of our participation in sacrificial scapegoating. It corresponds to Peter's tears when the cock crows the third time. The second is conversion, when we are drawn to commit ourselves to the vindicated victim. It corresponds to Paul's response to his encounter with the risen one: "I am Jesus, whom you are persecuting." The third is sanctification, the life of a new community without sacrifice. It corresponds to new life in the power of the Holy Spirit, the Spirit that both witnesses for scapegoats and overcomes our divisions.

Theology classically contrasts justification and sanctification. How can God accept us while we are still sinning against God and our neighbors? On the other hand, how can we become truly righteous friends of God, new creatures, so long as we bear the burden of God's just judgment? To state this as a crude polarity would pit an amnesty so absolute that it seems to annul all ethical urgency against a demand for righteousness so strict that it seems to cancel all mercy. Virtually all theologies bridge this gap, stressing a free obedience that follows from gratitude or the gracious assistance that makes growth in goodness possible.

Our approach provides a cross section of one aspect of Christ's work, and allows us to be much more specific about the way these two facets fit together. Christ's death and resurrection are acts that — prior to any change on our part — objectively alter our bondage to the specific sin of sacrifice and definitively declare to us God's intention to accept us despite our failures. This act reaches us in the midst of our captivity to sin, and provides us the means for a new and different life — community without scapegoats. Only as we give ourselves to that new life is it fully realized. We can rightly say on the one hand that real effects of this event are moving through history even apart from our belief or unbelief, and on the other hand that until we are authentically converted by it, true peace eludes us. In one sense we are saying nothing different from what traditional Christianity of various stripes has said. We are grounding that confession in more concrete terms, backing the general claim that in Christ God has acted to change us objectively and subjectively across many dimensions of life with our explication of the specific instance of scapegoating sacrifice.

One Sin and Many

I have emphasized that we need to view the cross in light of a very particular kind of evil, and God's project to overcome that evil. The first-order issues are about our universal participation in scapegoating and the way to a new process of reconciliation. But from an early time in the tradition there has also been a kind of transference. What about all our other sins apart from sacred violence? What about all our individual cases of false witness and violence and theft and betrayal? Many Christians take it as a given that Jesus died to atone for numberless miscellaneous sins that have no connection whatsoever to the crucifixion or its specific causes. Does Christ's death apply to sins of every conceivable description, and to my guilt for them? At the most immediate level, no. Christ practices forgiveness toward tax collectors and cowardly disciples and the woman taken in adultery without waiting for an atoning death as a condition. Jesus appears able to elevate God's mercy over wrath quite apart from any violence at all.[14]

But Christians definitely came to speak and worship in terms of Jesus dying "for the forgiveness of sins" in comprehensive terms. This makes sense in two respects. The first is that many if not all of our individual sins are tributary to sacrifice in that they sow the conflicts that flower in

14. Such forgiveness is separate from deliverance from the power of sin. It is one thing for God to refuse to press charges for some extrinsic punishment, but it is another for the intrinsic effects of our sin to continue to corrupt our persons and to shatter our relations. Forgiveness is an immense grace, but without deliverance it is almost beside the point. Today's forgiveness means little if I will always need it tomorrow for the same reason. This is why the cross is important as an event that decisively changes our practice of sacrifice, in addition to demonstrating God's willingness not to punish us for it.

social crisis and lead to redemptive violence. They are part of a single complex. Since Jesus was a victim of sacrifice, we can say that Jesus died for private sins (like envy and greed and theft) because these sins set people against each other, creating the conflicts that sacrifice is deployed to resolve. In this sense Christ objectively died for "private" sins. As our individual sins likewise contribute to sacrifice, we can say that Christ died for those sins too. When we look at conflicts and scapegoating reactions that arise in small-scale communities we belong to (families or workplaces, for instance), it is usually not hard to see individual acts of omission and commission that fueled the fire. Sacrifice is the medium by which these individual sins are integrally related to the cross.

The second respect in which we can refer all sin to the cross is a representative one. Once Christ has suffered and died to free us from the economy of scapegoating violence, it becomes possible to refer to that event in a second-level manner. The objective event by which Christ overcame this specific sin now stands as the sign and guarantor of God's general character and disposition toward us. The death on the cross does not cause God to be this way, but it is an affecting demonstration that God is that way. On this level, "Christ took away all my sins on the cross" means something like "Once I saw what Christ did on the cross, concretely rescuing humanity from sacrifice, I knew how God would deal with all my sins." This representative meaning rests on the truth that in Jesus' death God does address some of my sins directly and effectively, not only symbolically. Once we have grasped the primary distinctive work of the cross, what uniquely takes place there, we can also appreciate that it has this derivative dimension as well.

The cross is related to individual sins (to the extent these can be in principle separated from involvement with sacrifice) in a representative way, much as is presented in exemplarist views of the atonement. The depth of love and grace shown in God's willingness to suffer to concretely save us from the grips of scapegoating communicates to us God's merciful nature, but the exercise of that nature does not require blood sacrifice as a condition. An exemplarist view of the cross is sometimes advanced as the exclusive and complete view. Jesus' death is no more than an exhibition of God's care for us. That care is expressed by Jesus in other ways as well, and the cross is an especially affecting demonstration of what God is willing to bear as a result of coming to model love and teach us God's will. This is insufficient as a description of the primary objective work of Christ's death. If no other purpose is served by Jesus' suffering than to appeal to our emotions, to underline what we could see in other episodes in

Jesus' life already, then this doctrine seems to deserve as much criticism as Anselm's, and for the similar reason that it makes God an instigator of gratuitous violence. The cross is not effecting any rescue. It is simply pain exhibited for the sake of pain's effect.

I am arguing that the cross is both an objective transformation and a representative one. If the cross is actually an objective act to reverse our human sacrificial violence, then there is a valid related sense in which we are affected by contemplation of the cost Jesus endured. The suffering impresses us with Christ's love not because that is its sole purpose, and not because the suffering itself saves us, but because it accompanies a saving act we needed. The visibility of Jesus' suffering is part of the act that breaks sacrifice's hold on us. For some persons the suffering itself may have a subjective, transformative impact, even apart from any clear understanding of its larger framework. This is a positive thing. But it ultimately needs the structure we have sketched if it is not to limit the meaning of the cross exclusively to this subjective impression or to lead to a sacrificial view where the value of the cross is found only in its suffering.

To take an example from another dimension of Jesus' life, during his public ministry Jesus was effectively homeless and survived on gifts from disciples and followers. It would be a mistake, however, to conclude from these facts that his primary aim was to avoid hospitality to others, and that all who follow him should likewise be consumers of hospitality only and not providers of it. Jesus' practice of table fellowship and the vision of God's reign it expressed were the larger realities within which these elements must be understood. Fasting and lack of attachment to our possessions have particular value in connection to that vision. And in Jesus' life they served that project. Taken purely as ends in themselves, or as the whole purpose of Christ's ministry, they could lead us astray.

So too, the point of the cross is not that there is some all-purpose value to generic suffering, or that Christians should seek out suffering in order to identify with Christ as a model. Jesus' suffering was part of the very specific task of confronting a specific evil. But once given that fact, it is also true that those who suffer for reasons unrelated to scapegoating sacrifice (such as illness) know that Christ has shared the reality of their anguish and pain. He has truly, representatively, suffered with them.

We have seen that our understanding of the cross must have several levels, as the event of the cross itself has several layers. We have seen also that this can be a source of confusion and misappropriation. A dramatic positive feature of this complexity is a richness of "double effect" present in the passion. The resurrection that promises life after death is at the same time a vindication of the scapegoated victim. The suffering incident to a nonviolent victory over the powers of sacrifice is at the same time a representative assurance that God participates with us in the depths of human estrangement. The one whose death most clearly reveals the extent of our sin proclaims through that same death the scope of God's encompassing love. The paradox in the cross is only a reflection of the multiple dimensions through which God must reach us to make us whole.

We can bring this perspective to the point at the heart of Anselm's theology of atonement: the offering of unmerited suffering to pay the price of our punishment. The whole argument of this book is that we cannot agree that this is the cause of the cross, or the one necessary reason that God became human. But let us suppose for the sake of argument that there is some element of truth in Anselm's perspective, though not in the terms he framed it. (Suppose, for instance, one were to say that God's creation of a world in which the good of free will results in suffering is unjust unless the Creator is willing to be subject to the same conditions.) We might put it this way. *If* in any sense God's moral governance of the world requires some such "atoning" suffering, or if (as Anselm also suggests) *we* require an assurance that something has been offered on our behalf on this score if we are ever to be truly free, then the wonder of the passion is that whatever was needed was already included in the act of rescuing us from sacrifice. It happened in, with, and under the saving work of the cross, which already had a compelling plot for our redemption. God already had a saving reason to become one of us, and to become one of us who goes to the cross.

To use an admittedly crude analogy, suppose that one son in a family had become estranged from parents and siblings through a life of sin, through deceit and faithlessness within his own family, and through a legal but still destructively enabling role in the economic structure of the global sex trade in women and girls. Suppose further that one of his sisters, through her attempts to reach him, and her own involvement in attempts to end that trade, was herself abducted and ultimately killed. As a result her brother began a new life, taking up her work to end the system of which he had been a part. Add one other detail. The son was deeply in debt to his parents (who had in fact mortgaged their home to support him when his own misdeeds had left him and his family in desperate straits), with no means to repay them. His sister's life insurance policy made him the beneficiary and supplied what he could not. The sister's death was hardly lacking redemptive meaning apart from the satisfaction of that debt. Its saving effect was the change it brought to her brother's life and to the lives of those caught up in a sacrificial practice. The joy of the parents' reconciliation with their son was not hindered by any care on their part for the money. Yet we could reasonably wonder how the son could be freed from care for their situation and his debt, whether love would not always struggle to repair it. In the actual event, it is simply an academic question.

The issue of satisfaction is a moot question, at the very point Anselm made the center of his inquiry: Why did God become human in the first place? There is already a comprehensive meaning to the incarnation and Christ's death — a meaning based on Christ dying to save us from our sins — which does not require us to turn to satisfaction as the explanation. God would no more require innocent suffering to satisfy an offended holiness than the parents would demand their daughter's death for the life insurance money. But God, in the process of dying to rescue us from our sins, is not above (if I may put it that way) doing so in such a way that we may regard our impossible debts to God as redeemed in the process.

The message that Christ died for you has a profound individual dimension. People respond to its direct application to their personal condition of guilt, estrangement, and hopelessness. They draw a straight line from the cross to their own private brokenness. Now, as throughout Christian tradition, people may thankfully receive its grace for their own situation without any reasoning through the reversal of humanity's legacy of sacrifice or, for that matter, through the details of a traditional theology of substitutionary atonement. Christ's saving death becomes an event of life-changing intimacy, whose compassion takes on the special shape of each heart that receives it, meeting and transforming each unique profile of sin and loss.

It is not illegitimate to preach or respond to the gospel in this way, to believe that Christ has borne my sins. It is a central feature of faith. What we have been exploring is the theology that explains this conviction. It is not grounded in God's insistence on finding someone to punish instead of me. Its truth rests instead on the fact that God suffered the effects of my sin as God rescued me from it. My personal and social sins were focused in the practice of sacrifice that claimed Christ, the fire through which he passed in order to carry us out of it. The cross is this central event of rescue, and it is also a sign that stands for numberless other, bloodless, transformations in which Christ by faith transforms our individual sins and desires.

If we were to take the most powerful historical stories of conversion and new life based upon this conviction, the greatest examples of Christian life, preaching, liturgy, and writing animated by views of atonement like Anselm's, and to translate them entirely into the terms that we have been using, I am convinced they would lose none of their power for good. But they would be much less likely to produce negative effects. And they would gain a new clarity and coherence.

Three Sides of the Cross

In this final chapter I have tried to trace a renewal in the theology of the cross. The change I am suggesting touches every aspect of the theology of atonement. But it is also subtle, because its purpose is not to cast aside the language of sacrifice but to transform our perspective on it. There are Christians or might-be Christians for whom the whole debt and payment image does not readily compute. For them it will be important to approach Jesus' death on a fresh path, marked out by our addiction to socially vicarious sacrifices and by God's confrontation with the evil of scapegoating. Here they can find the point of departure to appropriate Jesus' death as part of a saving work, and to relate it to their own lives. A new theology of the cross is an invitation to faith that respects (and even enriches) the valid concerns that have held some back. That invitation leads back to most of the traditional language (if in a different light) and, perhaps, to a reconciling participation in the very elements in the church's life that before posed a barrier (the celebration of communion, the imagery of baptism, the language of Paul, the sign of the cross itself).

Those who find the familiar terms of atonement life-giving and transforming will have the different task of disentangling the source of that power from problematic formulations long associated with it. They may encounter a disquieting sense that though the basic terms of faith have changed little, nothing seems quite the same. I believe they will find that this reformed inner logic flows from the sources themselves and not from an arbitrary imposition. The vindication of the approach for them must be demonstrated by its capacity to sustain the saving power they have experienced, but with much less liability for running or luring others into the destructive paths that atonement language has sometimes encouraged.

We should decisively reject some theological formulations. But the truly important change is to recover a different orientation toward the work of the cross, one that then permeates the meaning of each of the individual traditional elements. So, for instance, we have seen the error in the way Anselm constructs a hidden transaction at the cross, a transaction between God's justice and God's mercy, expressed in quantitative equations whose variables are legal guilt and unmerited suffering. But there are transactions at the cross, and if we miss them we miss the heart of the matter. There is the repetition of a very old transaction, in which we trade in our hostilities toward each other for a shared hostility toward our common victim. This is no new fact, but the awareness of it is a new thing, one we owe to the Hebrew scriptures, without whose light the cross would not even be visible to us.

And there is another, different transaction superimposed on the first. In this one God submits to be handed over to the sacrificial process that has come to hold humanity captive to its power. When God becomes incarnate, the mission includes (as a part, not as the whole) the willingness to be offered as a kind of ransom. This ransom is not a payment made according to the law, but one demanded by crime. God's response is not dictated by recognition of the "justice" of the devil's claim to humanity, but by the need to avoid falling captive to the same evil. To defeat the sacrificial powers by violence and domination would be to participate in the same evil. Divine resistance to our sin must find another way.

So God accepts to be a victim of our original social sin, to step into the place of the scapegoat, and to do what no human being can do. Humans fitted to the role of sacrificial victim are inflated beyond their true stature. The crimes they are charged with always outgrow their actual offenses and capabilities. They are held responsible in a wildly disproportionate way. And every victim proves inadequate, in the sense that even when sacrifice works, it works only temporarily and requires repetition. If the victim were truly responsible, then eliminating the victim would truly solve the problem. Just as the sacrificial subjects are not really adequate to the condemnation they receive, so they are not adequate to overcome the powers that converge against them. They do not have the means to prove their innocence of the outsized charges. They cannot resist the judgment of a unanimous community. They cannot change the script of their own deaths that is written after them, in which any protest is erased.

In exchanging an ordinary victim for the incarnate one, all this changes. The "ransom" is like money that leaves an indelible dye on the hands of the kidnappers. Resurrection vindicates the victim, and makes him a living witness against the process that sacrificed him. Faith preserves the account of the cross, from the perspective of the crucified, and destabilizes all myth. A new community seeks peace by remembering what hitherto communities generally united by forgetting. The powers of sacrifice from now on must contend with a permanently visible victim, a fact that will steadily but irrevocably have its effect.

Our original sin was to turn away from God. Instead of forming our desires on the positive model of the divine love, and on that image of God in each other's inner lives, we fell into the conflictive contagions of rivalry and envy. These alienations went hand in hand with the emergence of scapegoating. Our divisions with each other call forth sacrifice as the solution, a practice that still further estranges us from God and each other. In acting to reverse this process, God at the same time addresses our sins against each other and our separation from God.

The unique meaning of Christ's death depends on its similarity to countless others. It reveals what it is meant to end. Christianity's focus on the cross must be seen first of all in contrast with religious outlooks where it is invisible. Scapegoating sacrifice quite assuredly takes place where it is not registered and re_membered. It cannot be reversed until it is recognized.

Christian representations of the cross have taken many forms. Three of the most common are the crucifix of the suffering Jesus, the image of Christ in glory on the cross, and the simple sign of the empty cross. Various Christian communities have tended to elevate one of these, often to the exclusion of the others. But all three have a necessary place in representing the full theology we have outlined. The crucifix corresponds to the visible victim, to the fact that at the center of sacrifice there is a real suffering person, whatever mythic stories or horrific accusations may be put in place to obscure that fact. To recognize this, to recognize those who may be cast into this place by our own communities, and to recognize that this is the place to which we consigned Christ, is one part of the meaning of the cross. The risen Christ in glory on the cross speaks to the vindication of the victim. God's identification with the suffering and weakness of the crucified one should not be taken as idealization or submission to scapegoating. Christ returns in the Holy Spirit as an advocate, a power to overcome sacrifice. The risen Christ "occupies" the cross, as one might occupy a railway track to prevent its use to transport prisoners to a concentration camp. It cannot be used for that purpose without opposition, an opposition that has infiltrated our language and our consciousness. The empty cross stands for a life without sacrifice. It is a cross left rusted and unused, by virtue of reconciliation that proceeds without violence or victims. It reminds us that a bare cross is no historical memento, but a repeated accomplishment. For a church or any human community, to surmount a moment of crisis without turning to sacrifice is one of the true, simple signs of the reign of God.

Our faith cannot do without any of these images and their meanings. The cross has three sides. The theology of the cross encompasses them all. Scapegoating sacrifice is the stumbling block we placed between God and us. It is a root sin buried in our life together. The passion is a divine act revealing, reversing, and replacing our redemptive violence, which we so long and tenaciously hid from ourselves in the very name of the sacred. When our sin had so separated us from God and built our peace on blood, God was willing to come and die for us, to bear our sin and suffer the condemnation that we visit upon our victims and so deserve ourselves. God saved us from our form of reconciliation, healed us of our dependence on that sad medicine.

Jesus died for my sins. This is concretely true, in the ways we have described. And it is therefore also representatively true in numberless additional ways. The God who gave his life to save ours in one way, who laid down his life for his friends, even while they insisted on being his enemies, is a God who will redeem us in many. The God who paid the cost of the cross was not the one who charged it. We are saved from sacrifice because God suffered it. To be reconciled with God is to recognize victims when we see them, to convert from the crowd that gathers around them, and to be reconciled with each other without them.

Bibliography

Alison, James. *The Joy of Being Wrong: Original Sin through Easter Eyes*. New York: Crossroad, 1997.

———. *On Being Liked*. New York: Crossroad, 2003.

———. *Raising Abel: The Recovery of Eschatological Imagination*. New York: Crossroad, 1996.

———. "Spluttering Up to the Beach to Ninevah." *Contagion: Journal of Violence, Mimesis and Culture* 7 (2000): 108-24.

Anselm. "Why God Became Man." In *A Scholastic Miscellany: Anselm to Ockham*, edited by Eugene R. Fairweather. Library of Christian Classics. Philadelphia: Westminster, 1956.

Assmann, Hugo, and René Girard. *René Girard com Teologos da Libertacao: Um Dialogo sobre Idolos e Sacrificios*. Petrópolis: Editora Vozes; Piracicaba: Editora UMIMEP, 1991.

Auden, W. H. *The Shield of Achilles*. London: Faber and Faber, 1955.

Aulén, Gustaf. *Christus Victor: An Historical Study of the Three Main Types of the Idea of the Atonement*. London: SPCK, 1970.

Bailie, Gil. *Violence Unveiled: Humanity at the Crossroads*. New York: Crossroad, 1995.

Barth, Markus, and Verne H. Fletcher. *Acquittal by Resurrection*. 1st ed. New York: Holt, Rinehart and Winston, 1964.

Bartlett, Anthony W. *Cross Purposes: The Violent Grammar of Christian Atonement*. Harrisburg, Pa.: Trinity, 2001.

Bergen, Doris L. *Twisted Cross: The German Christian Movement in the Third Reich*. Chapel Hill: University of North Carolina Press, 1996.

Boersma, Hans. *Violence, Hospitality, and the Cross: Reappropriating the Atonement Tradition*. Grand Rapids: Baker Academic, 2004.

Bondi, Roberta C. *Memories of God: Theological Reflections on a Life.* Nashville: Abingdon, 1995.

Brock, Rita Nakashima. "And a Little Child Will Lead Us: Christology and Child Abuse." In *Christianity, Patriarchy, and Abuse: A Feminist Critique,* edited by Joanne Carlson Brown and Carole R. Bohn, 42-61. New York: Pilgrim, 1989.

Brock, Rita Nakashima, and Rebecca Ann Parker. *Proverbs of Ashes: Violence, Redemptive Suffering, and the Search for What Saves Us.* Boston: Beacon Press, 2001.

Brown, Joanne Carlson, and Carole R. Bohn, eds. *Christianity, Patriarchy, and Abuse: A Feminist Critique.* New York: Pilgrim, 1989.

Burkert, Walter, René Girard, Jonathan Z. Smith, and Robert Hamerton-Kelly. *Violent Origins.* Stanford, Calif.: Stanford University Press, 1987.

Bynum, Caroline Walker. *Jesus as Mother: Studies in the Spirituality of the High Middle Ages.* Berkeley: University of California Press, 1982.

Cahill, Thomas. *How the Irish Saved Civilization: The Untold Story of Ireland's Heroic Role from the Fall of Rome to the Rise of Medieval Europe.* 1st ed. New York: Doubleday, Nan A. Talese, 1995.

Campbell, Joseph. *The Masks of God.* New York: Viking Press, 1970.

Campbell, Joseph, and Bill D. Moyers. *The Power of Myth.* 1st ed. New York: Doubleday, 1988.

Carroll, James. *Constantine's Sword: The Church and the Jews; A History.* Boston: Houghton Mifflin, 2001.

Carter, Jeffrey, ed. *Understanding Religious Sacrifice: A Reader.* Controversies in the Study of Religion. London and New York: Continuum, 2003.

Chazan, Robert. *European Jewry and the First Crusade.* Berkeley: University of California Press, 1987.

Chilton, Bruce. *The Temple of Jesus: His Sacrificial Program within a Cultural History of Sacrifice.* University Park: Pennsylvania State University Press, 1992.

Cone, James. "An African-American Perspective on the Cross and Suffering." In *The Scandal of a Crucified World,* edited by Yacob Tesfai, 48-60. Maryknoll, N.Y.: Orbis, 1994.

Connelly, Joan B. "Parthenon and Parthenoi: A Mythological Interpretation of the Parthenon Frieze." *American Journal of Archaeology* 100, no. 1 (1996).

Conquest, Robert. *The Great Terror: A Reassessment.* London: Hutchinson, 1990.

Cox, Harvey Gallagher. *The Secular City: Secularization and Urbanization in Theological Perspective.* Rev. ed. New York: Macmillan, 1966.

Daly, Robert J. *The Origins of the Christian Doctrine of Sacrifice.* Philadelphia: Fortress, 1978.

Doane, William, and Robert Lowry. *Gospel Music.* New York: Biglow & Main, 1876.

Dumouchel, Paul. *Violence and Truth: On the Work of René Girard.* Stanford, Calif.: Stanford University Press, 1988.

Euripides. *"The Bacchae" and Other Plays.* Translated by Philip Vellacott. Baltimore: Penguin Books, 1972.

Evangelium Johannes Deutsch, Das. Bremen: H. M. Hauschild, 1936.

Ezell, Rick. *Defining Moments: How God Shapes Our Character through Crisis.* Downers Grove, Ill.: InterVarsity, 2001.

Flint, Valerie J. J. "Susanna and the Lothar Crystal: A Liturgical Perspective." *Early Medieval Europe* 4 (1995).

Frazer, James George. *The Golden Bough: A Study in Magic and Religion.* 3rd ed. New York: Macmillan, 1935.

Freedman, Samuel G. *Upon This Rock: The Miracles of a Black Church.* 1st ed. New York: HarperCollins, 1993.

Garrow, David J. *Bearing the Cross: Martin Luther King, Jr., and the Southern Christian Leadership Conference.* 1st ed. New York: Morrow, 1986.

Girard, René. *Deceit, Desire, and the Novel: Self and Other in Literary Structure.* Johns Hopkins paperback ed. Baltimore: Johns Hopkins University Press, 1976.

———. *I See Satan Fall like Lightning.* New York: Orbis, 2001.

———. "Is There Anti-Semitism in the Gospels?" *Biblical Interpretation* 1, no. 3 (1993): 339-52.

———. *Job, the Victim of His People.* Stanford, Calif.: Stanford University Press, 1987.

———. *La Route Antique des Hommes Pervers.* Paris: Grasset, 1985.

———. *The Scapegoat.* Baltimore: Johns Hopkins University Press, 1986; paperback ed., 1989.

———. *A Theater of Envy: William Shakespeare, Odeon.* New York: Oxford University Press, 1991.

———. *"To Double Business Bound": Essays on Literature, Mimesis, and Anthropology.* Baltimore: Johns Hopkins University Press, 1978.

———. *Violence and the Sacred.* Baltimore: Johns Hopkins University Press, 1977.

Girard, René, Jean-Michel Oughourlian, and Guy Lefort. *Things Hidden since the Foundation of the World.* Stanford, Calif.: Stanford University Press, 1987.

Girard, René, and Michel Treguer. *Quand Ces Choses Commenceront.* Paris: Arlea, 1994.

Girard, René, and James G. Williams. *The Girard Reader.* New York: Crossroad, 1996.

Hallie, Philip Paul. *Lest Innocent Blood Be Shed: The Story of the Village of Le Chambon, and How Goodness Happened There.* 1st ed. New York: Harper and Row, 1979.

Hamerton-Kelly, Robert. *Sacred Violence: The Hermeneutic of the Cross in the Theology of Paul.* Minneapolis: Fortress, 1991.

———. *Sacred Violence: Paul's Hermeneutic of the Cross.* Minneapolis: Fortress, 1992.

Harding, Leander S., Jr. "A Unique and Final Work: The Atonement as a Saving Act of Transformative Obedience." *Journal of Ecumenical Studies* 24, no. 1 (1987): 80-92.

Harnack, Adolf von. *Marcion: The Gospel of the Alien God.* Durham, N.C.: Labyrinth Press, 1990.

Heim, S. Mark. "Christ Crucified: Why Does Jesus' Death Matter?" *Christian Century* 118, no. 8 (2001): 12-17.

———. "A Cross-Section of Sin: The Mimetic Character of Human Nature in Biological and Theological Perspective." In *Evolution and Ethics: Human Morality in Biological and Religious Perspective,* edited by Philip Clayton and Jeffrey Schloss, 255-72. Grand Rapids: Eerdmans, 2004.

———. "Visible Victim: Christ's Death to End Sacrifice." *Christian Century* 118, no. 9 (2001): 19-23.

Heschel, Susannah. "When Jesus Was an Aryan: The Protestant Churches and Antisemitic Propaganda." In *Betrayal: German Churches and the Holocaust,* edited by Robert P. Eriksen and Susannah Heschel, 68-89. Minneapolis: Fortress, 1999.

Heusch, Luc de. *Le Pouvoir et le Sacré.* Brussels: Université libre de Bruxelles Institut de sociologie, 1962.

Heyward, Carter. *Saving Jesus from Those Who Are Right: Rethinking What It Means to Be Christian.* Minneapolis: Fortress, 1999.

Hill, Charles E., and Frank A. James III, eds. *The Glory of the Atonement: Biblical, Historical, and Practical Perspectives; Essays in Honor of Roger Nicole.* Downers Grove, Ill.: InterVarsity, 2004.

Himmler, Heinrich. "Poznan Speech to SS Officers." October 4, 1943. Holocaust History Project. Available at http://www.holocaust-history.org/himmler-poznan/speech-text.shtml. Visited May 10, 2005.

"Indonesia President Seeks End to Killing Spree." Reuters. *Boston Globe,* November 1, 1998, A8.

Institut zur Erforschung des jüdischen Einflusses auf das deutsche kirchliche Leben. *Die Botschaft Gottes.* Leipzig: Otto Wigand, 1940.

Jensen, Robin Margaret. *Understanding Early Christian Art.* London and New York: Routledge, 2000.

Kamen, Henry. *The Spanish Inquisition: A Historical Revision.* New Haven: Yale University Press, 1998.

Keeley, Lawrence H. *War before Civilization.* New York: Oxford University Press, 1996.

Kierkegaard, Søren. *"Fear and Trembling," and "The Sickness unto Death."* Garden City, N.Y.: Doubleday, 1954.

Kremmer, Janaki Bahadur. "In India Villages, Cries of 'Witch.'" *Boston Globe,* August 6, 2000, A13.

Lanciani, Rodolfo Amedeo. *Ancient Rome in the Light of Recent Discoveries.* Boston and New York: Houghton Mifflin, 1888.

Layton, Bentley. *The Gnostic Scriptures: A New Translation with Annotations and Introductions.* 1st ed. Garden City, N.Y.: Doubleday, 1987.

LeBlanc, Steven A., and Katherine E. Register. *Constant Battles: The Myth of the Peaceful, Noble Savage.* 1st ed. New York: St. Martin's Press, 2003.

Lefebure, Leo D. *Revelation, the Religions, and Violence.* Maryknoll, N.Y.: Orbis, 2000.

Levenson, Jon Douglas. *The Death and Resurrection of the Beloved Son: The Transformation of Child Sacrifice in Judaism and Christianity.* New Haven: Yale University Press, 1993.

Lewis, C. S. *God in the Dock: Essays on Theology and Ethics.* Grand Rapids: Eerdmans, 1970.

———. *Surprised by Joy: The Shape of My Early Life.* 1st American ed. New York: Harcourt Brace, 1956.

Lungu, Stephen, with Anne Coomes. *Out of the Black Shadows: The Amazing Transformation of Stephen Lungu.* London: Monarch, 2001.

Maccoby, Hyam. *The Sacred Executioner: Human Sacrifice and the Legacy of Guilt.* New York: Thames and Hudson, 1982.

Matheson, Peter. *The Third Reich and the Christian Churches.* Grand Rapids: Eerdmans, 1981.

Milbank, John. *Being Reconciled: Ontology and Pardon.* Radical Orthodoxy Series. London and New York: Routledge, 2003.

———. "Stories of Sacrifice." *Contagion* 2 (1995): 75-102.

Moltmann, Jürgen. *The Crucified God: The Cross of Christ as the Foundation and Criticism of Christian Theology.* 1st U.S. ed. New York: Harper and Row, 1974.

Murphy, G. Ronald. *The Saxon Savior: The Germanic Transformation of the Gospel in the Ninth-Century "Heliand."* New York: Oxford University Press, 1989.

Netanyahu, B. *The Origins of the Inquisition in Fifteenth Century Spain.* 1st ed. New York: Random House, 1995.

Nietzsche, Friedrich Wilhelm, Walter Arnold Kaufmann, and R. J. Hollingdale. *The Will to Power.* New York: Random House, 1967.

"Passion Play Is Banned." Associated Press. *Boston Globe,* May 16, 1997, 2.

Patterson, Stephen J. *Beyond the Passion: Rethinking the Death and Life of Jesus.* Minneapolis: Fortress, 2004.

Philostratus and Eusebius. *The Life of Apollonius of Tyana, the Epistles of*

Apollonius and the Treatise of Eusebius. Translated by F. C. Conybeare. Loeb Classical Library. New York: Macmillan, 1912.

Ross, Ellen M. *The Grief of God: Images of the Suffering Jesus in Late Medieval England.* New York: Oxford University Press, 1997.

Rylaarsdam, J. C. "Atonement, Day Of." In *The Interpreter's Dictionary of the Bible,* edited by George Arthur Buttrick, 1:313-16. Nashville: Abingdon, 1962.

Sayers, Dorothy. *Gaudy Night.* London: Hodder and Stoughton, 1970.

Schaff, Philip, and Henry Wace. *A Select Library of Nicene and Post-Nicene Fathers of the Christian Church.* 2nd ser. New York: Christian Literature Company . . . , 1890.

Schimmel, Solomon. *Wounds Not Healed by Time: The Power of Repentance and Forgiveness.* Oxford and New York: Oxford University Press, 2002.

Schwager, Raymund. "Christ's Death and the Prophetic Critique of Sacrifice." *Semeia,* no. 33 (1985): 109-23.

———. *Must There Be Scapegoats? Violence and Redemption in the Bible.* 1st ed. San Francisco: Harper and Row, 1987.

Schwartz, Regina M. *The Curse of Cain: The Violent Legacy of Monotheism.* Chicago: University of Chicago Press, 1997.

Sherman, Robert. *King, Priest, and Prophet: A Trinitarian Theology of Atonement.* Edited by Wallace M. Alston, Robert Jenson, and Don S. Browning. Theology for the Twenty-first Century. New York: T. & T. Clark, 2004.

Song, Chaon Seng. "Christian Mission toward Abolition of the Cross." In *The Scandal of a Crucified World,* edited by Yacob Tesfai, 130-48. Maryknoll, N.Y.: Orbis, 1994.

Spee, Friedrich von. *Trutz-Nachtigall.* Trier: Verlag der Akademischen Buchhandlung Interbook, 1985.

Spee, Friedrich von, and Marcus Hellyer. *Cautio Criminalis; or, A Book on Witch Trials.* Studies in Early Modern German History. Charlottesville: University of Virginia Press, 2003.

Spee, Friedrich von, and Theo G. M. Van Oorschot. *Güldenes Tugend-Buch.* Munich: Kösel, 1968.

Stark, Rodney. *For the Glory of God: How Monotheism Led to Reformations, Science, Witch-Hunts, and the End of Slavery.* Princeton: Princeton University Press, 2003.

———. *One True God: Historical Consequences of Monotheism.* Princeton: Princeton University Press, 2001.

Stowe, Harriet Beecher. *Uncle Tom's Cabin.* New York: Signet, 1966.

Tamez, Elsa. *The Amnesty of Grace: Justification by Faith from a Latin American Perspective.* Nashville: Abingdon, 1993.

Terrell, JoAnne Marie. *Power in the Blood? The Cross in the African American Expe-*

rience. Bishop Henry McNeal Turner/Sojourner Truth Series in Black Religion, vol. 15. Maryknoll, N.Y.: Orbis, 1998.

Thornton, Sharon G. *Broken yet Beloved: A Pastoral Theology of the Cross.* St. Louis: Chalice, 2002.

Tkacz, Catherine Brown. *The Key to the Brescia Casket: Typology and the Early Christian Imagination.* Collection des Études Augustiniennes. Série Antiquité, 165. Notre Dame, Ind.: University of Notre Dame Press; Paris: Institut d'Études Augustiniennes, 2002.

————. "Susanna as a Type of Christ." *Studies in Iconography* 20 (1999): 101-53.

Vanhoozer, Kevin J. "The Atonement in Postmodernity: Guilt, Goats and Gifts." In *The Glory of the Atonement: Biblical, Historical, and Practical Perspectives,* edited by Charles E. Hill and Frank A. James, 367-404. Downers Grove, Ill.: InterVarsity, 2004.

Weaver, J. Denny. *The Nonviolent Atonement.* Grand Rapids: Eerdmans, 2001.

Williams, Delores S. *Sisters in the Wilderness: The Challenge of Womanist God-Talk.* Maryknoll, N.Y.: Orbis, 1993.

Williams, James G. *The Bible, Violence, and the Sacred: Liberation from the Myth of Sanctioned Violence.* 1st ed. San Francisco: HarperSanFrancisco, 1991.

Wink, Walter. *Engaging the Powers: Discernment and Resistance in a World of Domination.* Minneapolis: Fortress, 1992.

————. *Naming the Powers: The Language of Power in the New Testament.* Philadelphia: Fortress, 1984.

————. *Unmasking the Powers: The Invisible Forces That Determine Human Existence.* Philadelphia: Fortress, 1986.

Index

Abraham: argument with God about Sodom and Gomorrah, 74; and sacrifice of Isaac, 67-68, 71-72, 79-80, 92n.25, 152n.12; as type prefiguring Jesus, 136, 138

Acquittal by Resurrection (Barth), 145

Acts, book of, 105; on the Holy Spirit, 154-55; and Nazi treatment of scriptures, 275; and Philip's reading from the prophet Isaiah, 104; presentation of the early Church, 135-40; sermon of Stephen, 135-38, 208, 275; story of Paul's conversion, 138-40

Acts of John, 204-5

Adam and Eve, 8, 71, 91

Aeschylus: *Agamemnon,* 46; *Eumenides,* 37, 45-46, 45n.10

African American theology, 255

Agamemnon (Aeschylus), 46

Ailred of Rievaulx, 181-82

Ambrose, 175

Amos, 94, 136-37

Animal sacrifice: and Passover meal, 232; as replacement for human, 71-72, 79-80, 80n.17; and sacrifice of Isaac, 71-72, 79-80, 80nn.17-18; and story of Cain and Abel, 71

Anselm's atonement theology, 4, 180, 214n.12, 297-302, 309, 311, 324;

antisacrificial message, 297-99; and deformed theology of the cross, 300-302; guilt and punishment, 313, 314-17; human sinfulness, 311; legal framework with and divine justice, 299-300; legal quantification, 299, 311; and ontological argument for God's existence, 300n.5

Anthropology of the cross, 9-14

Antiscapegoating interpretations of the cross in Christian tradition, 165-91; and African slave trade, 187-91; and ambivalence about the cross and evil, 182-91; artistic images of the cross, 166-72, 173-76; and Christian missions, 177-78, 178n.16; early Christian interpretations, 176-78; and failed-scapegoat figures from the Hebrew scriptures, 168-76; and monasticism, 181-82; ninth-century poem, the *Heliand,* 179-80; Saint Patrick and conversion of the Irish, 177-78; and tensions around the meaning of the cross, 178-91; transition to imperialist Christianity, 178-79; warrior interpretations of the cross, 179-80; witchcraft and scapegoating violence, 182-87

Anti-Semitism: and charges of respon-